RELIGION IN SOCIETY _____

A Sociology of Religion

Fourth Edition

Ronald L. Johnstone

Central Michigan University

PRENTICE HALL, Englewood Cliffs, New Jersey 07632

Library of Congress Cataloging-in-Publication Data

Johnstone, Ronald L.
    Religion in society : a sociology of religion / Ronald L.
Johnstone. -- 4th ed.
        p.   cm.
    Includes bibliographical references and index.
    ISBN 0-13-772385-7
    1. Religion and sociology. 2. United States--Religion.
I. Title.
BL60.J63 1992
306.6--dc20   91-32863
                                                  CIP

In loving memory
of my father, Ross (1905–1990)

Editorial/production supervision: Alison D. Gnerre
Cover design: Patricia Kelly
Prepress buyer: Kelly Behr
Manufacturing buyer: Mary Ann Gloriande

 © 1992, 1988, 1983, 1975 by Prentice-Hall, Inc.
A Division of Simon & Schuster
Englewood Cliffs, New Jersey 07632

Printed in the United States of America

10 9 8 7 6 5 4 3 2 1

ISBN 0-13-772385-7

Prentice-Hall International (UK) Limited, *London*
Prentice-Hall of Australia Pty. Limited, *Sydney*
Prentice-Hall Canada Inc., *Toronto*
Prentice-Hall Hispanoamericana, S.A., *Mexico*
Prentice-Hall of India Private Limited, *New Delhi*
Prentice-Hall of Japan, Inc., *Tokyo*
Simon & Schuster Asia Pte. Ltd., *Singapore*
Editora Prentice-Hall do Brasil, Ltda., *Rio de Janeiro*

Contents

Preface

This introduction to the sociology of religion in the fourth edition follows an outline that with continuing modifications has worked successfully in over three decades of teaching courses variously titled Religion and Society, Sociology of Religion, and Religion in Contemporary Society. The book is intended primarily for a first college-level course in the sociology of religion, taken preferably by students who have had at least an introductory course in sociology.

The book consists of four parts. Part I is an introduction to the sociological perspective on religion. It grapples with the problem of defining religion and considers the fascinating but ultimately frustrating question of the origins of religion. Part II focuses on the distinctive perspective that sociology has on religion as a social phenomenon. That is, how do general laws and principles of social and group life impinge on religion as it organizes itself into groups and carries on its activities? Also we look closely at the classic church-sect continuum of religious organization and evolution and consider how conflict figures so commonly in the life of religious organizations. In Part III we look at the relationship of religion to major social institutions and structural features of society: religion and politics, religion and the economy, religion and social class, and finally religion and the role and perception of women in society. In Part IV we look specifically at some of the major features of religion in the United States—the social environment and experience of a majority of the readers of this text. After exploring several highly important socio-historical developments within American religion, particular attention is paid to American socio-religious developments, namely the black church, Native American religion, and the phenomenon of denominationalism. The section concludes by focusing on primary sociological factors that will significantly affect the future of religion.

In this progression the reader will experience firsthand some of the problems inherent in the enterprise we call the sociology of religion and will become involved and somewhat expert in the process of applying the sociological perspective. The reader also will develop insight into the place of religion in society that will supplement her or his prior understanding, whether gained from the inside as a believer or from the outside as an observer of the religious scene.

While the fundamental thrust and outline of this fourth edition follows that of the third, the reader will note several major changes: (1) a major new section on Native American religion to parallel the section on black religion in the United States; (2) an expanded treatment of New Religious Movements (cults) with particular emphasis on deconversion and deprogramming; (3) updated discussion of the condition and impact of fundamentalism and the New Christian Right; (4) a reintroduction and revision of material from the second edition on the measurement of religiosity; (5) expanded discussion of social change within Roman Catholicism in the United States; (6) additional discussion of women in the clergy role; and (7) brief consideration of non-Western religions and New Age Religion in the United States.

In reflecting on the contributions of others to this edition, I want to identify and thank in particular Alison Gnerre, whose suggestions and help brought many improvements throughout the text.

1

The Sociological Perspective

Religion is a social phenomenon and is in an interactive relationship with the other social units that constitute a society. This seemingly obvious assertion, which lies at the very foundation of the sociology of religion, is actually not nearly as simple as it may seem. Nor is it so readily accepted as one might expect.

Many people, particularly the religiously committed, think of religion in an entirely different way. Some prefer to see religion as the context of people's communion with the supernatural, and religious experience as something outside of ordinary experience, while others see religion as an expression of an instinctual reaction to cosmic forces. Still others see religion as an explicit set of messages from a deity. These viewpoints certainly de-emphasize, ignore, or even reject the sociological dimensions of religion. Nevertheless, whether we are talking about religion in general, or a particular religious family such as Christianity or Buddhism, or a specific religious group such as the First Baptist, religion will be seen to interact with other social institutions and forces in society and will follow and illustrate sociological principles and laws.

In other words, whatever else it is (or is not), religion is a social phenomenon and as such is in a continual reciprocal, interactive relationship with other social phenomena. That, in brief, is what the sociology of religion

1

is all about; and this book is concerned with the specification and elaboration of this point in a variety of dimensions and on a number of levels.

CHARACTERISTICS OF THE SOCIOLOGY OF RELIGION

Asserting that religion is a social phenomenon suggests several things. In the first place the statement has a *nonevaluative intent*. Thus we are not going to be able to, or even want to, speak about the truth or falsity of religion. Speaking of religion in terms of the good, the true, and the beautiful may be worthwhile and even stimulating for philosophers and theologians—or anyone, for that matter (even sociologists); but such considerations have nothing to do with sociology. Sociology that claims to describe reality accurately demands that its practitioners approach their subjects—religion no less than any other (and perhaps more than most)—with all the neutrality and objectivity they can muster.

Of course, no sociologist can always (if ever) be perfectly neutral and objective with regard to his or her subject, let alone one so value laden and emotionally charged as religion. Recent studies in the sociology of knowledge, as well as honest discussions that have punctured the myth of a "value-free" sociology, have been sufficient to discourage any such pretensions. Nonetheless, a conscious, deliberate striving for neutrality and objectivity must be present—indeed, it should be evident—in any sociological investigation.

The sociology of religion is also *empirical*—it can only study and reach conclusions about phenomena that are observable. In order to confirm or refute any particular theory, the sociologist must test that theory with relevant empirical observations, or *data*. And since data are by their nature limited to the observable, the measurable, the quantifiable, whatever elements of religion are spiritual or supernatural, in the sense that they cannot be seen with the eye or otherwise measured or recorded, are by definition beyond the purview of sociology.

Our characterization of the sociology of religion so far, as objective and empirical, can be summed up by stating that the sociology of religion is conducted according to the *scientific method.* By the scientific method we mean (1) the systematic search for verifiable data ("facts") firmly rooted in prior knowledge and theoretical formulations; (2) the production of evidence as opposed to hearsay, opinion, intuition, or common sense; and (3) the following of procedures that others can verify and replicate (reproduce under essentially identical conditions).

It is at this point that the sociologist of religion encounters probably the most strenuous objection from the religiously committed, which usually runs something like this: Since religion relates primarily to the supernatural—that is, to forces that are usually unseen—and involves matters of the heart as well, anything the sociologist can say about religion, limited as he or she is to describing the observable, will be at best superficial and unimportant, at worst false and misleading. J. Milton Yinger has supplied some useful imagery in speaking to this issue. He frames the objection to the empirical study of religion with the question, "How is it possible to see a stained-glass window from the outside?"[1] That is, the beauty and the message or picture of a church's stained-glass window is visible only when one is *inside* and can see the sunlight shining through. Professor Yinger goes on to note, however, that the view from the inside constitutes only part of what can be learned about the window. Only from the outside, for example, can the viewer appreciate the exterior framework or context within which that window exists. Furthermore, there are, as Yinger suggests, pieces of information potentially important to understanding the significance of the window that have nothing to do with viewing it from the inside (or from the outside, for that matter): who built it, who installed it, who provides for its repair, who goes in to view it from the inside. We can also consider the reason it was installed, what "outsiders" think of it, how it resembles or differs from other windows, whether the style of newer windows is the same or is changing, and so on.

Rather than belabor the obvious parallel that we are suggesting between this situation and the study of religion, it is enough to note that questions like these can be answered empirically, that they are important questions, and that the answers to them amplify our understanding. Granted, empirical data do not constitute the only information of any importance about religion. Nor can we claim that empirical or observable measures of religion reveal its "essence." Studying religion empirically places a certain restriction on our enterprise, but no more severe a restriction than is placed on the position of those who claim religion to be strictly concerned with spiritual matters and therefore off-limits to empirical investigation. Each "side" of this issue can contribute to an understanding of the total phenomenon.

CENTRAL SOCIOLOGICAL ASSUMPTIONS

Having established that the scientific study of religion is a legitimate endeavor, it remains for us to indicate why, for the sociologist, it is an important one—that is, how it furthers sociology's task of understanding the dynamics of people living in groups. For this purpose it will be helpful to identify some of the central assumptions of sociology, whether applied to

---

[1] J. Milton Yinger, *The Scientific Study of Religion* (New York: Macmillan, 1970), p. 2.

the study of religion, the family, the class system, or any other social phenomenon.

The Sociological Perspective

In the first place, what exactly *is* sociology? Very briefly stated, sociology is the study of the interaction of people in groups and of the influence of those groups on human behavior generally and on society's other institutions and groups. Thus sociology has a twofold goal: (1) understanding the dynamics of group life—what groups are, how they function, how they change, how they differ from one another; and (2) understanding the influence of groups on individual and collective behavior. One fundamental assumption of sociology implied by this is that all human activity is influenced by groups. Throughout a person's lifetime groups impinge on her or his biological "raw material," shaping it, modifying it, influencing it—*socializing* it, to use the sociologists' term. This process begins with the family and proceeds through the hundreds of educational, associational, peer, and work groups that a person participates in and has contact with throughout his or her lifetime.

In both fundamental senses of the sociological enterprise—explaining group dynamics and explaining group influence—religion qualifies perfectly as a field of sociological study and analysis. Leaving aside for now the question of whether religion is also (or even primarily) an individual phenomenon, it is obviously at least a group phenomenon. Thus to the extent that religions organize themselves into groups—congregations, denominations, dioceses, cells, fellowships, and so on—an important task for sociology is the study of the structure and functioning of these groups simply *as groups*. In other words, we want to determine how and to what extent religious groups follow sociological laws governing group life in general. In what ways does a congregation, for example, operate like any other voluntary association—like, say, the League of Women Voters? Or how and to what degree do major religious denominations function like other large bureaucracies—like, say, General Motors or the United States Army?

Insofar as religion is organized into groups, it exerts influence not only on its members, but also on nonmembers and on other groups and institutions. The second dimension of our preliminary definition of sociology—as a study of group influence—thus suggests that religious groups have at least the potential for influencing people just as do groups that center around one's family, peers, or workplace. The question is not so much *whether* such influence exists but *to what degree, in what ways,* and *how it can be measured.*

Human Nature

A number of assumptions in sociology center around the definition of human nature. Here we shall emphasize three of these assumptions.

First, and perhaps most obviously, a human being is a *biological organism*—a creature with physiological drives, needs, potentials, and limitations. The socializing influence of groups is thus both directed at and limited by biological factors. Religion is of course among those socializing agents that attempt to influence or modify biological nature. For example, different religious groups have different approaches to, and provide or allow different outlets for, sexual drives. And insofar as people in fact internalize these different emphases—whether they be permissive, compensatory, restrictive, or whatever—to that extent people will have different personalities and evidence different values and attitudes. In short, although the sociological perspective rejects notions of biological determinism, it recognizes as openly as possible that the human being has potentialities and limitations that are biologically provided.

Another sociological assumption regarding human nature that is worth mentioning is the apparently unique *ability of people to symbol.* By this we mean the ability arbitrarily to attach specific meanings to things, sounds, words, acts—meanings that are not intrinsic to the items themselves but that people have created. By establishing consensus on these meanings, groups are able to communicate and to accumulate knowledge. Using language as the prime symbolic mechanism, people can deal with abstract concepts and emotions, such as love, justice, and equality as easily as they can ask someone to pass the potatoes at the dinner table.

The ability to express meanings symbolically is primarily responsible for the variety of groups, cultures, ideologies, and technologies throughout history. There is no activity in which people are engaged that does not involve acts of symbolizing—whether lecturing, voting, making love, or "being religious." Religion in fact consists entirely of symbols and of activities that are interpreted and mediated by symbols. This is true whether the symbols have empirical referents or not. God, hell, salvation, Star of David, nirvana, guru, mana—all have meaning to those initiated into a particular symbolic system. The meaning of each of these is not inherent in the word itself or in the combination of sounds, but is supplied by the believer. Even if divine truths have been revealed to people by a supernatural being, those truths have been expressed in human language, or are immediately translated into human language—otherwise the message would have no meaning for people.

Yet another primary sociological assumption about human nature is that *people become human only in groups*—admittedly, a dramatic way of stating that the influence of groups on the human organism through socialization is crucial and far-reaching. We do not propose to debate the academic question of whether the newborn baby is in fact human. The point is simply that the newborn infant is not yet very much of what it is going to become, and that what it does become will be largely attributable to socializing influences. One of those socializing influences is religion, which in fact affects everyone, whether or not they are born into a "religious" family or attend Sunday school or are married by a member of the clergy, and so on. For religion also exerts an indirect influence on people, if only in an inverse way as a negative reference group or through its influence on secular institutions.

Human Action Is Directed Toward Problem Solving

A fundamental assumption of sociology is that *every human action is in some form and to some degree a problem-solving act or mechanism.* Whether working at a job, getting married, planning a party, or genuflecting, the human being is engaged in the process of solving or resolving some existing (present) or anticipated (future) problem. The problem may be how to satisfy a biological need for nourishment, how to achieve victory on the athletic field, or how to get God to help you pass an exam this afternoon. In any case, the person perceives a problem that she or he must solve, either now or, if he or she fails to take appropriate action, in the future.

Religious behavior is problem-solving like any other social activity. Praying, attending church services, observing religious laws, and having and talking about "mountaintop experiences," for example, are all religious activities that contribute in some way (at least from the perspective of the religious participant) toward solving a problem, either existing or anticipated. Note that we are not suggesting (or denying) that religion in fact either solves problems or creates them. Rather, our point is that people often engage in religious activities *in the belief* that such behavior can solve problems. Lest there be any misunderstanding, once again we will emphasize that throughout this book no attempt is made to determine or question the truth or falsity, the efficacy or inefficacy, of religion in general, of any specific religion in particular, or of anyone's personal religious beliefs. Engaged as we are in sociological investigation, we are concerned solely with what can be observed, including what people *believe* exists and happens.

All Social Phenomena Are Interrelated

The final sociological assumption that we need to clarify before delving in detail into the sociology of religion is that *all social phenomena within a given group or society are interrelated.* That is, all social phenomena are continually interacting, and every part becomes linked with every other in at least an indirect way. More specifically, part A may not be influenced directly by part F, but F may be having some indirect influence through a chain of other factors or social phenomena called B, C, D, and E. Most important for our purposes, religion interacts with—is in a dynamic reciprocal relationship with—every other social phenomenon and process. Religion both influences them and is influenced by them; religion both acts and reacts, is both an independent variable and dependent variable, both cause and effect. This principle of the continual dialectic involving religion and other social phenomena is a central theme of this book, for determining the nature and extent of these mutual influences are key tasks in the sociology of religion.

We have now identified in at least an introductory way what sociology is. Now, what is *religion*—the second term in our subject, the sociology of religion?

A SOCIOLOGICAL DEFINITION OF RELIGION

Everyone of course "knows" what religion is. For our purposes, however, such knowledge needs to be systematized. We need to achieve some consensus on the boundaries of our subject matter, which we all recognize as having great diversity, before we can proceed to analyze it. Without denying the validity of any individual's private definition, we need to establish some ground rules that we can follow throughout this text. Clearly there is nothing absolute about a definition—no definition, of any phenomenon, religion included, is inherent in the phenomenon itself. What we require, then, is a *working definition* of religion—specifically, a definition that we can be fairly sure includes the major ideas of this concept, a definition that is moreover flexible and responsive to changing conditions and new evidence—so that we can communicate fairly sensibly not only among ourselves but with others as well. Although we will not include everything that anyone has ever thought religion might be, we will try to isolate the core or essential elements.

THE CHARACTERISTICS OF RELIGION

The English word *religion* has a Latin root; that much is certain. But there is disagreement over whether the Latin root word is *religare*, meaning "to bind together" (suggesting possibly the concept of a group or fellowship) or *relegere*, meaning "to rehearse, to execute painstakingly," referring probably to the repetitious nature of liturgy. Either word makes sense as a root, and each taps a dimension of religion that we will include in our definition. Yet it is clear that etymology by itself will not provide us with an ultimate answer to our problem of definition.

Religion Is a Group Phenomenon

Let us start with the concept suggested by the Latin word *religare*—the concept of the group or fellowship. The assertion that religion is a group phenomenon is significant both for what it says and for what it fails to say, for what it excludes. What it excludes is of course the individual aspect. Certainly religion is an individual matter in any number of ways: in that it involves personal emotions and thoughts; or insofar as one's religion is a matter of personal beliefs; or insofar as individuals are free to commit themselves to whichever religious system they prefer. Still, it would not make sense to expect that one could somehow systematically study every individual's personal religious beliefs. Sociology, being committed to systematic study of group behavior, has no such problem in that it concentrates on the group dimension of religion.[2]

Throughout history and in every corner of the world, people have engaged in religious behavior. Congregations, ceremonial gatherings, denominations, prayer meetings, family pilgrimages, ecumenical councils—all are examples of religious activity. Even when a lone figure is acknowledged to have experienced visions or received supernatural dispensations, she or he frequently attracts others—that is, he or she becomes a leader (perhaps even a prophet) with a following, often whether the person seeks it or not. True, we also see occasional isolated mystics and religious hermits in mountaintop seclusion. Even most of these, however, belong to some subgroup of a major religion (such as Catholicism or Buddhism), which may encourage or even structure and coordinate such activity.

Elaborating our admittedly arbitrary division of religion into its personal and group dimensions, J. Paul Williams suggests that there are at least four types or levels of religiousness: (1) the *secret* level, which a person keeps to himself or herself and does not divulge or discuss; (2) the *private*, which she or he divulges or discusses with only a few carefully chosen intimates; (3) the *denominational*, which the individual shares with many others in a large group; and (4) the *societal*, which the person shares with the members of society at large.[3] Williams's first two categories will occupy very little of our time—not because they fail to involve religion (they obviously do), but simply because of the reasons already mentioned for narrowing our range of coverage, and also, to some extent, because solid sociological research into individual aspects of religion has only recently begun. For example, Chapter 4, while it does not deal with precisely what Williams means by "secret" religiousness, focuses on what we might call the social-psychological dimension of religion—the process of individual internalization of religion. Our primary attention, however, will be on what Williams identifies as de-

---

[2]This is not to ignore the fact that sociologists, particularly social psychologists, also study the behavior of individuals. For example, the current considerable sociological interest in the nature of religious commitment and in the process of religious socialization and internalization of religious concepts and values obviously necessitates careful attention to individual behavior. Nevertheless, the purpose of such research with individuals is primarily to be able to generalize to larger groups and categories of people.

[3]J. Paul Williams, "The Nature of Religion," *Journal for the Scientific Study of Religion 2*, no. 1 (1962), 8.

nominational and societal religion, with particular emphasis on the former, again reflecting the fact that most research in the sociology of religion has been in this area.

So much for what is excluded by our characterization of religion as a group phenomenon. Now we may ask, What is *included* in this aspect of our definition? Answering this question requires that we specify exactly what a group is; in this regard, fortunately, sociologists are very explicit.

According to one definition that most sociologists would accept, a group has six major features. The first and most basic is that *a group is composed of two or more people (members) who have established certain patterns of interaction* (including communication) with one another. Such interaction does not necessarily take place continually, or even daily. Nor does every member of a group interact with every other member. Nor is this interaction necessarily face to face. The point is simply that the people who constitute a group—group members—are aware of one another (perhaps even know one another) and have established patterns of interaction characteristic of their group.

The second major feature of a group, according to our definition, is that *group members share certain common goals*—in fact, this is the reason they came together in the first place (although they may not have known it then). The process of forming a group thus involves the fundamental sociological concept, introduced earlier in this chapter, that all human behavior consists of some sort of problem-solving activity. Saying that a group has common goals implies that individuals who are confronted with common problems have made contact and have agreed to work together toward the goal of solving those problems. Imagine, for example, five individuals, each deeply concerned about industrial-waste pollution in a certain trout stream, who through casual conversation (perhaps while trying to fish the stream) "discover" one another and subsequently form a group called STEP (Save Trout from Environmental Pollution), whose primary goal is reducing pollution in this and other trout streams. Thus what was originally the separate concern of five individuals has become a group concern, which in turn implies a certain common goal or set of goals that they share with one another.

Third, as a result of the above, *a group is guided by shared norms*. For once a group defines its goals, it then determines how to reach them; that is, the group specifies that such and such is what its members will do, as well as when, where, and how. All such specifications are norms—more or less formal expectations concerning appropriate behavior by one or all members of the group.

Fourth, *every group member has a role*, or set of functions, to fulfill. As such, a role consists of a set of specific norms the group wants carried out. The development of different roles within the group gives rise to what is known as *the division of labor*. Thus, whenever a member leaves the group or adopts a new role, the group may need to keep the division of labor in balance by recruiting someone else—either another member or an outsider—for that particular role.

Fifth, *a group functions collectively in accordance with a status system*, a hierarchy in which different amounts of power, authority, and prestige are accorded to different roles and to the individuals in them. Different groups, of course, have different criteria for establishing status rankings. Roles involving group coordination, decision making, and interpretation, for example, which inherently carry the greatest authority and prestige, are often assigned to those individuals who are believed to perform these tasks most ably, although such other factors as seniority, wealth, and kinship can also be influential.

Sixth, *group members feel and express a sense of identification with the group*: "I belong," "This is my group," "Yes, I'm an active member of STEP." The degree of group commitment, dedication, and identification varies from member to member, and most groups are able to tolerate some such variability. But without a certain minimum amount of identification and commitment on the part of its members, a group will soon disintegrate.

These six characteristic features of a group obviously apply to religious groups no less than to any other kind. Thus in studying religion as a group phenomenon, we already know many things to expect and even some questions to ask: How does a given religious group differ from all others in terms of these six aspects? What, for example, are the religious group's goals, its norms, its roles, its status criteria?

Religion Is Concerned with the Sacred and Supernatural

A second characteristic that we wish to include in our definition of *religion* is its involvement with what Durkheim identified as the "sacred," with what Rudolf Otto termed the "holy" or the "wholly other,"[4] and essentially what Mircea Eliade refers to as "sacred space" that is qualitatively different from all other "homogenous" space in which regular, everyday occurrences and activities take place.[5] There is a universal tendency for religion to express awe, reverence, and fear with regard to certain things, beings, or situations and to distinguish them from the ordinary, the mundane—or, as Durkheim defines it, the "profane." Old Testament Jews removed their sandals upon entering the temple, many Christians make the sign of the cross when praying to God, Hindus give cows the right of way, Muslims undertake pilgrimages to Mecca, American Indians avoided disturbing holy plots of ground. All such behavior expresses the recognition of a sacred

---

[4]Emile Durkheim, *The Elementary Forms of the Religious Life*, trans. Joseph Ward Swain (New York: Collier, 1961), p. 52; Rudolf Otto, *The Idea of the Holy*, trans. John W. Harvey (London: Oxford University Press, 1936), pp. 8–41.

[5]Mircea Eliade, *The Sacred and the Profane*, trans. Willard R. Trask (New York: Harcourt Brace Jovanovich, 1959), p. 20.

place or situation. In each instance people acknowledge being in the presence of something special—something above and beyond them that demands adopting special attitudes, performing certain actions, and perhaps articulating special words as well.

For many people—for whole religious systems, for that matter—that "something special," the *sacred,* in fact involves the *supernatural,* a power or being not subject to the laws of the observable universe. Such a power may be personified by Jesus, by Vishnu, by Allah, or by any number of gods, devils, goblins, or spirits. Or perhaps it is simply a vague and diffuse power, such as that identified by the Polynesian term *mana* (which we shall discuss shortly).

In these beliefs a dichotomy of reality is being expressed. On the one hand there are the "profane" (ordinary) events and the visible environment of the routine workaday world. On the other hand there is the invisible, largely uncontrollable, out of the ordinary realm. To a greater or lesser degree, people can control and predict familiar everyday situations—the choice of daily tasks, conversations with others, the acts of eating and copulating, the seeking of nightly rest, and so on. But most people seem to believe that there is more to life than such ordinary situations and events. What about the big bang in the sky last week and the twisting dagger of light that preceded it? What about my friend who dropped dead while running beside me? What about that place in the swamp where a whole hunting party was swallowed up in the mud? Such things are out of the ordinary; they cannot be taken for granted; they elicit fear, awe, respect. We are here in the presence of Otto's "wholly other"—an entirely different order of existence.

It should be emphasized that the experiences that people define as sacred vary considerably and the objects of their awe and reverence are infinitely diverse. Yet every society has its list of such awesome and mysterious things and events. Religion deals with them. Religion provides explanations and answers; religion prescribes methods of placation and of expressing appropriate reverence. The sacred, the holy, the supernatural, together with people's relationship to them, thus constitute the prime subject matter of religion.

Although the term *sacred* may occasionally connote little more than "deserving or demanding respect," with no necessary thought of a supernatural power being involved, it is usual for the two concepts to go together. That which is considered sacred is so precisely because some supernatural force or activity arouses the feeling of awe that surrounds the sacred object, person, place, or situation. While they are not strictly synonymous concepts, the sacred and the supernatural are in most societies so intimately related that most of the time we shall regard them as almost inseparable for the purposes of our definition of religion.

However, in the interests of precision and clarity of the concepts *sacred* and *supernatural,* we shall regard only the sacred as essential to religion.

This allows us to include several thought systems that most people would almost intuitively think of as religious systems, yet upon close examination are found to express no concept of the supernatural at all. We would mention as examples Jainism, Ethical Culture, early Buddhism, and early Confucianism.

Religion Involves a Body of Beliefs

A third characteristic of religion, one that is much more straightforward and easy to describe, is that it invariably includes or implies a body of beliefs. This characteristic proceeds directly from the foregoing considerations of the sacred and the supernatural. For in the act of endeavoring to deal with or justify these phenomena and experiences, religious groups develop explanations, work out rationales, and discover "facts" that are eventually systematized into a body of beliefs.

Every major religion has its sacred book or books that spell out or at least provide the basis for determining the beliefs the group holds. Some examples are the Bible, the Koran, the Book of Mormon, and the Bhagavad-Gita. Furthermore, every major religion has beliefs *in addition* to those contained in such "official" or basic writings—the interpretations and extensions of lesser prophets and of other successors to the founder(s) of the religion, for example. Then, too, there is in every religion (and not just in those of preliterate societies) the oral tradition—unwritten explanations, in the form of myths, sagas, and proverbs, handed down to each new generation by word of mouth.

Borhek and Curtis describe seven features of most belief systems: First, there are *values*—definitions of what is good or valuable; second, *criteria of validity* by which to judge new observations and messages; third, a *"logic"* that relates one substantive element in the belief system to others; fourth, a *perspective* that identifies how the group stands in relation to other groups and world views; fifth, *substantive beliefs* such as "Jesus will come again to reign a thousand years" or "Vishnu is an avatar of the Buddha," sixth, *prescriptions and proscriptions* so far as behavior is concerned; seventh, a *technology* that consists of means and techniques for obtaining valued goals.[6]

It should be pointed out that we are dealing here with a characteristic that is not unique to religious groups, for groups of all kinds have belief systems. Although we can view beliefs as attitudes or opinions so far as the individual is concerned, group beliefs properly fall under the heading of the norms established or accepted by the group. Norms, in other words, specify not only how a group's members are expected to behave but also

[6]James Borhek and Richard F. Curtis, *A Sociology of Belief* (New York: John Wiley, 1975), pp. 9–15.

what they are expected to believe, how they are to interpret and relate to things and events. The distinctiveness of religious groups so far as beliefs and norms are concerned rests simply with the subject matter of those beliefs. The beliefs of religious groups specifically concern the sacred and very likely also the supernatural.

Religion Involves a Set of Practices

A fourth characteristic of religion is that it universally involves specific practices, which consist of acting out certain normative expectations. One of the most obvious features of any religion—obvious because it consists of behavior rather than beliefs or attitudes or perspectives—is the performance of ritual and the host of other activities generated by its beliefs. The gathering to worship, the rain dance, the sacrifice of animal or person, the ceremonial foot washing, the immersing in water at baptism, the vigil—all these are examples of what we are referring to.

It is important to understand that there is nothing intrinsically religious in a given act—an act or practice becomes religious only when the group defines it as such. Thus the act of eating a meal may be no more than "filling one's belly;" or it may be an *agape* ("love feast") of the first-century Christians, or a ceremonial enactment of the Last Supper. One may wear a robe solely to fend off the cold, or (in medieval Europe) to indicate one's academic rank; or one may wear it to indicate that he or she is a holy person or messenger of God. Journeying to a distant town may be for the purpose of conducting business or shopping; it may be for fulfilling the religious obligation of making a pilgrimage to a holy city at least once during one's lifetime.

Religion Involves Moral Prescriptions

Another feature of religion that, although certainly not unique to religious groups, is emphasized in all of them, is the moral dimension. This refers to the judgment a religious group or system makes that certain thoughts, certain ideas are good and worthwhile and to be encouraged and positively reinforced, while other actions, thoughts, and ideas are bad, harmful, and to be rejected by the faithful. Another way of saying this is that a religion advocates certain behaviors with the intention of encouraging its adherents to choose such behaviors in everyday situations. Of particular significance here is that religion is unique in claiming a "higher" source or basis for its morality: You should do something or refrain from doing it because God wills it or because it is in tune with cosmic forces, not simply because our group says so or because I your leader say so. In other words, religion ultimately invokes the sacred or the supernatural in order to influence the behavior of individuals not only in extraordinary situations or situations defined as "religious," but in all the ordinary, routine ones as well.

A FORMAL DEFINITION OF RELIGION

In attempting to define religion formally we shall go no further than to gather together the ingredients we have discussed. Our definition is thus perhaps less elegant than some, yet more inclusive than many. Sociologically viewed, then, and in terms of what will come under review in this book, *religion* can be defined as *a system of beliefs and practices by which a group of people interprets and responds to what they feel is sacred, and, usually, supernatural as well.*

Let it be clearly understood that by employing this definition we are, for purposes of sociological investigation at least, adopting the position of the hard-nosed relativist and agnostic. That is, we are neither affirming nor denying the existence of the supernatural; nor are we stating whether what a group defines as sacred is or is not in fact sacred. We *are* asserting, however, that people in groups often do in fact believe in the supernatural and identify certain beings, events, and so on as sacred. These beliefs and the attitudes and behavior stemming from them thus become the subject matter of the sociology of religion.

It should also be clear by now that the above definition is to be understood as neither the final nor the best definition of religion; rather, it is a pragmatic one—one, moreover, that is reasonably in tune with what the majority of people consider religion to be. This latter point is particularly important, for it is unnecessary, and would even be unwise, deliberately to define religion in a manner too different from the way most people understand it.[7]

APPLICATION OF THE DEFINITION

Before ending our formal treatment of the definition of *religion* (in a real sense, the remainder of this book represents an elaboration and explication of our definition), two serious questions require discussion. One concerns the application of our definition, particularly with regard to whether we should include or exclude certain ways of life and thought when speaking

---

[7]It might be noted that the above definition is an example of what most sociologists would call a "functional" definition in contrast with a "substantive" one. A functional definition emphasizes more what the phenomenon *does*, whereas a substantive definition places its emphasis on what a phenomenon *is*. Cf. Peter Berger, "Second Thoughts on Defining Religion," *Journal for the Scientific Study of Religion* 13, no. 2 (1974), 125–33; Richard Machalek, "Definitional Strategies in the Study of Religion," *Journal for the Scientific Study of Religion* 16, no. 4 (1977), 395–401.

of religion. The other involves the issue of whether there is a distinction to be made between religion and magic (not stage magic, of course, but magic in the original sense of using charms and spells to control supernatural forces)—and if there is, where to draw the line—or whether the two are really a single concept.

Should the Various "Isms" Be Called Religions?

With respect to the former question, there has been much discussion about whether the various "isms," such as communism, fascism, scientism, and humanism, should be included under the heading of religion.

Proponents of this viewpoint are particularly fond of citing the characteristics of communism to support their argument, pointing out its "religious" elements—its prophets, its emphasis on orthodox beliefs, its rituals, its sacred shrines, the missionary zeal and unquestioning commitment of its adherents. And those who argue that scientism qualifies as a religion find similar patterns: a system of beliefs about the utility of scientific endeavors, a set of practices (the scientific method), prophets of old (the founding fathers of modern science), sacred places (the laboratory, the computer room), supreme loyalty and commitment of its adherents, the missionary zeal, if you will, with which proponents try to win others to share their faith in science.

Although we do not take such analogies with total seriousness, no one can deny the existence of certain striking parallels between such ideologies and thought systems, on the one hand, and religion as we have defined it, on the other. If we want to be precise, however, our characterization of religion as involving the sacred and the supernatural quite clearly places these ideologies and thought systems outside the realm of religion. Before leaving the subject, however, it is only fair to make the observation—and the point can hardly be overstressed—that certain pronounced elements in ideologies like communism are unlike anything else *outside* religion. Certainly the tenets of communism or socialism, for example, are held "religiously," and its adherents frequently exhibit "religious" zeal in pursuing group goals. The importance of this observation is that it helps us understand the behavior of such systems' organizations and adherents. We see commitment and zeal in such systems of thought and practice even if we don't happen to agree with what they espouse or do. Nevertheless, sticking by our definition, we shall not include such thought systems in our discussion of religions in the following chapters.

It should be emphasized that more than a technicality is involved here. If we made our definition of religion progressively broader and our criteria more inclusive, we would soon reach the point where *everything* could be defined as religion. Then *nothing* would be religion, inasmuch as there would be no alternative categories. Subsuming all (or even nearly all) human behavior in a definition of religion would be much like saying that all human behavior is sexual or that all human behavior is economic. In a certain sense, such assertions say something important—they draw attention to the profound fact that sexuality, economics, and religion are pervasive phenomena which touch almost every form of human activity to at least some degree. However, to reduce all human activity to any one of the categories requires stretching that category to absurd dimensions and is ultimately counterproductive. A more reasonable solution (at least this is the consensus within sociology) is to draw somewhat narrower boundaries around one's subject matter by identifying specific characteristics such as we have done above, thereby facilitating more intensive study and analysis of a more manageable body of data.

The Relationship of Religion and Magic

Resolving the issue of the relationship between religion and magic is in some ways more difficult. By way of introduction, let us consider the concept of *mana* (a Polynesian term), which is common in "primitive" religions, and vestiges of which appear in the religious systems of industrial societies as well. Purnell Benson notes, for example, that mana appears in numerous religions under various names—in Hinduism it is *darshan*; in Christianity it is *divine grace*; among American Indians it was called *manito* by the Algonquins, *wakanda* by the Sioux, *orenda* by the Iroquois, and *maxpe* by the Crow.[8]

Mana is a prime ingredient in magic. To those who believe in it there exists in the world, everywhere, and in everything, an elemental force, a primary energy—mana. Mana even exists—it floats, so to speak—in the very air we breathe. Often it is just *there*, not directly attached to anything, simply waiting to be grasped, harnessed, used. Though mana is in people, in things, in animals, in plants, and in the atmosphere, it is impotent until someone or something, or a spirit perhaps, activates it by discovering the secret key that unlocks its energies.

Enter magic, which attempts to exercise power over people and things by controlling the ubiquitous mana. The practice of magic is thus not an expression of ignorance, as is commonly supposed, but a conscious, deliberate attempt to circumvent what might normally be expected to occur. That is, magic is typically used to undercut the predictable by marshaling sufficient mana—elemental force—to change what otherwise would be inevitable.

[8]Purnell H. Benson, *Religion in Contemporary Culture* (New York: Harper & Brothers, 1960), p. 136.

In those societies where magic is most likely to be practiced and condoned (the more "primitive" societies), people make little if any distinction between magic and religion—or for that matter among scientific knowledge, religious knowledge, common-sense knowledge, and magic. Knowledge is knowledge, be it scientific, religious, or whatever. This lack of categories of course makes the task of distinguishing between magic and religion a bit more difficult.

We may begin, however, by noting the similarities and the differences or contrasts that have been suggested in the long debate over the relationship of religion and magic. First some similarities: (1) both are serious attempts to deal with and solve the basic problems people face; (2) both are based on faith in the existence and efficacy of powers that cannot be seen and can only be inferred by results; (3) both involve ritual activity, traditionally prescribed patterns of behavior; and (4) both are bona fide elements of the group's larger culture.

Some differences or contrasts follow: (1) religion more often centers on such overarching issues as salvation and the meaning of life and death, whereas magic is more likely to be employed in grappling with current, concrete problems (counteracting a viper's bite, bringing rain, defeating the enemy, for example); (2) religion is more often future oriented, while magic is primarily concerned with the here-and-now (or at least the very near future); (3) religion's orientation toward supernatural powers tends to be one of obeisance and supplication, involving sacrifice and prayer (such as asking the appropriate deity or spirit to act on one's behalf), whereas magic is more manipulative, more often suggestive of pride than of humility (the magician seeks direct control over things and events, even at times seeking to trick the deity or defeat the deity in a contest if she or he can control enough mana); and (4) religion is characteristically a group activity, with groups of people collectively engaged in rituals and worship, while magic is typically an individual affair—the magician against the world, so to speak. Of course it is important to recognize that the magician conducts his or her work within a group (the society), and that in a real sense it is the group that *allows* the magician to work. Thus even though the magician works alone, her or his work is group sanctioned.

Are religion and magic, then, different phenomena, or two aspects of the same phenomenon? Or is one a subpart of the other? The last alternative is probably the most helpful way to see their relationship. Recalling our definition of religion, we find that magic fulfills each of our criteria—magic consists of beliefs and practices; it very clearly is concerned with the sacred and the supernatural; and it is practiced within a group (in a sense it is "possessed" by a group, although practiced by an individual). In fact, the relationship of magic to religion is virtually a classic example of specialization, for magic is typically practiced where the religious system considers it a legitimate and useful activity and encourages or at least allows its use. Thus magic is probably best seen neither as a competitor with religion nor as an alternative to it, but as a specialized subunit of religion. In fact, rarely is religion without at least some magical elements, just as magic is seldom practiced entirely apart from a larger religious system that legitimates it.

FINAL REFLECTION ON THE DEFINITION OF RELIGION

As the readers reflect a moment on our attention in this chapter to the task of defining religion, they might sense some ambivalence. If so, we have achieved one of our purposes in this chapter. Frankly, as we write this text, we face a dilemma which cannot be resolved to the satisfaction of all. The dilemma resides in the recognition that (1) our definition of religion (the six characteristics) is not inclusive of all phenomena that may in some sense be "religious," and it tends to be "conservative" in the sense that the focus is inevitably upon what has been traditionally recognized as religious—the religious institution in society; and (2) that such traditional institutional forms of religion do happen to be a prominent feature of societies and as such merit analysis and understanding.

Thus we have opted in this introductory text to concentrate on what is commonly regarded as religion and seems to fall fairly cleanly within our definition (a fantastically broad array of data and developments as it is). But we recognize and draw attention to the fact that there is likely more that can legitimately be called religion than this. Thus, in one sense we conclude this chapter deliberately leaving the issue of defining religion somewhat open-ended. Yet we also proceed from a close-ended approach as we pragmatically attempt to cover a manageable subject. That is, we will spend most of our time in this text discussing religion as included in our definition. But we strongly assert that when the discussion is ended, we will only have begun to talk about what could have been included from other perspectives or definitions.

A CONCLUDING HISTORICAL NOTE: THE DEVELOPMENT OF THE SOCIOLOGY OF RELIGION

A clearly identifiable interest in a formalized sociological study of religion goes back barely a hundred years, roughly coincident with the beginning of formalized sociology in general near the midpoint of the last century. The stimulus for sociological interest in religion seems to have been the reports of anthropologists during the early and middle nineteenth century who encountered and studied "primitive" societies in Africa and Oceania. Two significant observations made by these social scientists were (1) the existence everywhere of some form of religion, and (2) the fascinatingly wide variety of religious forms and behaviors.[9] In other words, religion was observed to be as diverse as it was widespread.

Such had always been true, of course. But as long as societies remained relatively isolated, the diversity and universality of religion was not fully appreciated. The advent of European colonialism and the consequent increase in world trade and commercial interaction after the Middle Ages raised the frequency and intensity of intersocietal contacts and eventually led to ethnographical investigations by social scientists. As a result more and more people began taking an interest in understanding and explaining the worldwide diversity of religion.

Following the initial flurry of social scientists' interest in religion (initiated by early anthropologists), sociological interest in and research on religion, with a few notable exceptions, lay somewhat dormant until fairly recently. David Moberg has suggested several reasons for this: (1) some sociologists, discouraged by the close historical association of religion with philosophy and metaphysics, decided that religion could not be fruitfully studied empirically; (2) other sincerely interested sociologists yielded to the opposition against sociological research on religion that came from many religious groups; (3) those teaching in state universities were fearful of jeopardizing their positions if they should somehow overstep the boundary separating church and state; (4) others, convinced that religion was definitely on its way to extinction anyway, preferred not to waste their time; (5) still others who had personally rejected religion were reluctant to maintain any contact with it—even if only of a research nature.[10]

The notable exceptions included some of the early sociological giants, such as Emile Durkheim, Georg Simmel, and Max Weber, who devoted a significant portion of their scholarly energies to analyzing the role of religion in society. After Weber's publication of his *Sociology of Religion* in 1921, however, little research or theoretical development occurred in the sociology of religion until after World War II, when there was a dramatic upsurge in religious activity, particularly in the United States. Significant increases in church membership and attendance at religious services, extensive building programs, and the establishment of hundreds of new congregations each year engendered serious talk of a religious revival.

Sociologists became interested. Here was a social phenomenon to explore and explain, a development that was particularly intriguing in that many social scientists had long been predicting the eventual and even pre-

---

[9]This pair of observations is suggested by J. Milton Yinger in *Sociology Looks at Religion* (New York: Macmillan, 1961), pp. 11–12.

[10]David O. Moberg, *The Church as a Social Institution* (Englewood Cliffs, NJ: Prentice-Hall, 1962), p. 13.

cipitous demise of religion, particularly in its institutional form. The sociologists' new research interest in religion, which began in the late 1940s and early 1950s, has continued essentially unabated to the present. One reason for this is that these new developments in religion, which clamor for investigation and explanation, have continued at a rapid pace. Furthermore, the persistence of religion in its various forms has finally forced sociologists to renew the effort, initiated by early fathers of sociology like Durkheim and Weber, of attempting to understand the nature and function of religion. For both these reasons this book concentrates on systematizing sociological research and theoretical efforts that have appeared during the past twenty years or so—not because the newest efforts are necessarily the best ones, but simply because most of the empirical work in the field is of relatively recent vintage. Indeed, it appears that social scientists are beginning to fulfill in part the prophecy of the anthropologist James Frazer, who predicted a half-century ago that the time would come when the religions of the world would no longer be regarded in terms of their truth or falsehood, but simply as phenomena to be studied like any other expression of humanity.[11]

[11]James Frazer, *The Gorgon's Head* (London: Macmillan, 1927), pp. 281–282.

2

The Sources of Religion

We now approach what is admittedly a speculative, but at the same time a fascinating, issue in the sociology of religion—the question of the origins and sources of religion. When we realize that the question is phrased, not so often "Where does religion come from?" but instead "Why are people religious?" we see that the question of origins and sources is a relatively common one—one that has intrigued philosophers throughout the centuries and scientists more recently. When people observe what we have come to think of as religious behavior and become curious about why people are doing or saying what they are, they are raising a question that by implication goes far beyond the immediate event and the persons involved in it. Ultimately the question is: from where did these ideas and practices come? Or, to be more ultimate yet, how did the idea of a God, or supernatural and sacred forces and entities, originate in the first place? The answers to such questions, whether immediate or ultimate, have been many and varied, although we will soon discover that they can be organized fairly conveniently into relatively few categories.

The question of religion's origin per se is no longer pursued by social science, for any evidence of an origin or origins has been lost in prehistory. Attempts to reconstruct origins by examining contemporary preliterate societies have in fact served only to delay slightly the admission that such evidence, if it ever existed, is lost in antiquity. It is important to recognize that the scientific method is limited in this regard; in fact, it is incapable of establishing absolutely verifiable conclusions about past events on the basis of present or even past realities. Thus even when substantial evidence appears to support an attractive theory, any hypothesis regarding religion's origins is doomed to remain forever tentative. There will be more on this problem later in the chapter.

Yet despite such limitations in the pursuit of religion's origins, we propose to explore the question briefly. We do this because of the historical value and intellectual stimulation such a look at the past provides; but more important, such an exploration will serve to introduce us to several relevant contemporary issues in the sociology of religion that we will discuss more fully later. These are such issues as the functional view of religion, the nature and extent of social influences upon religion, and to some extent the conflict between theology and sociology regarding an analysis of religion.

With regard to prehistoric people, it seems reasonable to assume on the basis of available evidence that they seldom had questions about the sources of their religious beliefs and practices. Their religious elements were such integral parts of their culture and normative system that they most likely saw them simply as "in the nature of things." Things were that way and always had been. Therefore, there was little likelihood that questions of religious origins as such would occur to these people. There were often myths and tales of the origins of human beings or of one's society in particular, but seeing religion as something distinct from the rest of one's beliefs and practices in society was not likely.

REVELATION AS ORIGIN

With the beginning of Christianity and, before that, Judaism, part of the answer was extremely simple—God was the originator of religions. God created the world and the people in it; in the Garden of Eden he already established some general principles and laws; he later spoke through selected prophets, and they recorded God's words and their own God-inspired commentary. God himself was directly at work instructing his people, and in the process was creating religion through the process of revelation.

This hypothesis or explanation of a divine origin of religion is not unique to Judaism and Christianity. Even Gautama Buddha, the founder of Buddhism, reports having experienced heavenly inspiration of a sort as he sat under the bo tree, practically at the end of his rope in his quest for truth. The insight around which he developed his religious system hit him out of the blue, so to speak; he had a "revelation." The revelation that inspired Mormonism was in the form of golden plates buried in the hill called Cumorah in New York State. Muhammad reported receiving visions (the revelation) from the angel Gabriel in a cave near Mecca.

All such cases report the belief that either God himself or some other cosmic, supernatural force intervened in history, altered the normal course of events, and deliberately added to what had been previously known. Whether by personal contact with the divine power, an experience with an intermediary, sudden inspired insight, discovery of secret written messages, or whatever, it is the direct intrusion of a supernatural power with new knowledge and insight for humanity.

In turn, of course, such religious leaders, as they speak and write for the followers that gather around them, are themselves sources of revelation for the religious system that has begun to develop. As they become defined as gods or, at the very least, spokespersons for divinity, what they utter is revelation.

It is important to realize, of course, that such revelational explanations for the origins of religion concern what believers consider to be the only "true" religion—that is, their own. Proponents of the revelation hypothesis usually refer only to their religion as the one revealed by God. Other religions exist, of course, but their source is something else, an inferior source, although it is likely that other religions are hard at work trying to find the very truth that God has given only to "us."

THE "NATURAL-KNOWLEDGE-OF-GOD" EXPLANATION

Christian theologians, claiming direct revelation from God for their gift of "true" religion, have always been intrigued by the existence of other religions. If God revealed himself directly only to the Chosen People of Israel, they asked themselves, how did the religions of other peoples arise? The answer they settled on, based on scattered verses from the Bible, was the "natural-knowledge-of-God" concept: All human beings are born with a fundamental awareness of the divine, a rudimentary knowledge that God or some power is ultimately responsible for what they see around them. All other religions, then, are the result of peoples' striving to build on this fundamental awareness and make some sense out of it. The great diversity of religious systems is then relatively easy to explain. Because the initial awareness of God is so vague and diffuse, people are forced to call upon their imagination and experience in developing these systems. And since the imaginations and experiences of people are so diverse, the religious systems they evolve consequently differ.

Associated with the natural-knowledge-of-God idea is the "witness-of-nature" concept: The wonder and complexity of nature reinforces people's innate knowledge of the divine and motivates them to seek explanations. What I see around me—the cycle of seasons, the wonder of the flora and fauna, the majesty of the mountains, the splendor of the sun by day and the moon and stars at night—must have been brought into existence by someone or some power, some god or gods. And perhaps that god has helpers for specific spheres and activities, such as the oceans, farming, lovemaking, and war. Eventually a complex system evolves from an original "seed of divine awareness."

Sociologists can obviously neither confirm nor refute such a hypothesis. Note, however, that except for the idea of inherent initial awareness, this attempt to explain the origins of religion is basically in harmony with modern sociological concepts. That is, there is a recognition that people themselves create their norms and beliefs and thought systems in response to their experiences and surroundings, and that a fundamental factor in such experiences is their contact with the physical environment. But more on such sociological views later in this chapter.

ANTHROPOLOGICAL EXPLANATIONS

We now turn from explanations of theologians to those of social scientists, who have attempted to explain the sources or origins of religion on the basis of empirical observations. We first focus on the anthropologists, particularly those of the nineteenth century who were so instrumental in stimulating investigation of religion from the perspective of social science. They all believed that religion somehow arose in response to the experiences of people in the world in which they lived. As preliterate people encountered awesome, mysterious, even terrifying events—thunder and lightning, earthquakes, tidal waves and floods, illness, birth and death—they felt the need to understand their causes. Religious systems thus gradually evolved out of people's need to assign causes for so-called natural phenomena and other recurrent experiences.

Some differences in emphasis and focus among early anthropologists are worth noting. Max Müller, for example, is a representative of the "naturistic" school, which emphasized the role of physical acts of nature—natural events like storms, sunrises, tides.[1] Prehistoric people were fearful and almost completely defenseless and at the mercy of these events: Why do they happen and why to me in particular? Müller suggests that since prehistoric people saw other people cause events—push rocks, throw stones, shoot arrows, fell trees, and so on—they reasoned that *everything* that happens must be caused either by other human beings or humanlike agents. What evolved then was the belief in spirits—invisible beings much like people in the sense that they possessed wills and abilities to bring about effects by their actions. It is these spirits who *cause* natural events. Thus prehistoric people

[1]See F. Max Müller, *Anthropological Religion* (London: Longmans Green, 1892); idem, *Lectures on the Origin and Growth of Religion* (London: Longmans, 1878).

might suggest that a spirit crashes giant cymbals and produces thunder; that a fire-breathing spirit spits out lightning; that a spirit heaves itself out of the bowels of the earth and causes an earthquake; that a spirit takes the sun out of its basket and puts it on a shelf in the sky each morning; and so on.

Early anthropologists discovered among the "primitive" peoples they studied an apparently universal belief in such spirits, a phenomenon termed *animism*—the belief that all sorts of inanimate objects as well as living, growing things and moving creatures possess a life principle or soul of some kind. Rocks, trees, animals, and people have spirits in them, whereas some spirits are freewheeling and unattached to things. All spirits, however, are conceived of in a thoroughgoing anthropomorphic fashion—that is, they have shapes, minds, feelings, and wills, though they are invisible beings. They are much like people in that they can be amenable to sound arguments or placating gifts, particularly when they are in a good mood. They can also be quarrelsome, nasty, and dangerous when upset or angry. They like flattery, loyalty, and deference. Therefore, one must be continually vigilant to stay on their right side.

Thus when a coconut fell nearby, the prehistoric person is less likely to have said, "The coconuts are ripe; it's coconut season again," and more likely to have asked, "Who threw it? What did I do now to make a spirit angry?" Or tripping over a root in the path, they were less likely to curse their clumsiness and more likely to ask why the root's spirit reached out and grabbed them: "Was it only a playful jest, or a warning that worse may happen if I don't shape up in some way?"

Whereas Müller emphasized the external events of nature, Edward Tylor, who represents the "animistic" school, focused on such personal experiences as dreams and seeing one's reflection in the water.[2] When I dream of sexual conquest, or felling the enemy on the field of battle, or running from a tiger, what is happening is that the spirit that resides in me (my soul) is out for the night—having a ball, displaying his or her valor, or running into a bit of trouble. My image in the stream? Why it is none other than my spirit looking up at me. See, when I smile, it smiles; when I frown, it frowns.

Another representative anthropologist, Robert Lowie, focused on those experiences that generate a sense of "mystery and weirdness" in people. For Lowie, religion is not simply a matter of identifying spirits or distinguishing body and soul. Rather, religion only arose when people's emotions became involved and a sense of mystery pervaded people's observations of the activities that spirits engage in.[3]

Many more hypotheses developed by anthropologists could be cited, but the above examples are enough to make the point that what we are calling anthropological explanations for the origin of religion focus primar-

[2]See Edward B. Tylor, *Primitive Culture* (London: Murray, 1871).
[3]Robert Lowie, *Primitive Religion* (New York: Boni & Liveright, 1924), p. xvi.

ily on people's belief in spirits and in what these spirits do. Such beliefs arise essentially from needs of prehistoric people to explain natural events in the physical environment as well as their own experiences. In a real sense this is a need for rationality of a sort, for a means of making coherent the many things people have no control over.

This is what social scientists call the "cognitive need" explanation for religion. That is, people want to know and understand the "what" and the "why" of the goings on around them. Explanations evolve that place the source of mysterious events at the hands of supernatural beings and forces.

PSYCHOLOGICAL EXPLANATIONS

Another broad area of explanation, the psychological perspective, in general treats the origins of religion in terms of people's emotional needs—in other words, not so much like Müller and Tylor, who emphasized people's cognitive needs to explain the mysterious, but more in terms of their need to resolve and adjust emotionally to the mysterious and the disastrous, more like Lowie's emphasis. In this view, people seek to maintain emotional stability in the face of danger, insecurity, and disruption, particularly as they encounter illness, accident, and death: How can I keep going as my world (health, personal relationships, and so on) crumbles about me? Why do disasters happen to me and to those I love? Can I make any sense out of it all? How can I find strength to go on?

E. Goodenough expresses this perspective clearly when he describes religion as the response of human beings to constant threats to their safety, security, and future existence. In particular, people face great insecurity and anxiety related to the knowledge not only that they shall ultimately perish but that it could happen at any moment. He calls this the "tremendum"—a Latin word referring to "that which must be feared" or the "source of terror."[4]

As an extension of this, a common psychological explanation suggests that people seek solutions and answers for such frustration, anxiety, and fear by trying to fit their experience into the larger framework of a divine plan with a long-range perspective: All things work out for those who love God; things will be better in the by and by; he died because God needed him more than we did; God is testing me to see if I am worthy; my sins have caught up with me, and I am being punished.

Psychologist Walter Huston Clark has borrowed W. I. Thomas's idea that people basically have four "wishes" or drives—for security, response, recognition, and new experience—and contends that these are reasonably

---

[4]Erwin R. Goodenough, *The Psychology of Religious Experiences* (New York: Basic Books, 1965), p. 6.

comprehensive for understanding the psychological need and appeal of religion.[5] This leads us beyond the idea of emotional adjustment just expressed, although we are still dealing quite specifically with emotional needs that the individual strives to fulfill—specifically, according to Clark's approach, through religion.

Another psychologist, George S. Spinks, agrees with Clark by speaking of religion as actively fulfilling fundamental human needs, but takes this idea a step further by emphasizing the uncertainties and terrors that continually threaten to overwhelm the individual.[6] As such, he and Goodenough say the same thing.

Sigmund Freud, the "father of psychoanalysis," sees religion stemming primarily from a sense of guilt derived at least partly from the Oedipus complex and the attempts by the male to reconstruct a father image after his "love affair" with his mother and his ritual "killing" of his father. Thus, for Freud, religion is a mechanism that allows people to sublimate many primitive instincts that society represses.[7]

Another perception that Freud uses extensively is the concept of projection. In projection, the god characters are really representations (projections) of wishes and conflicts within the person. God the Father, Christ, the stories of the original paradise and the "fall into sin," the ideas of the devil and immortality—these are all projections from the unconscious mind. Freud believed that gradually psychology would fathom the relationships.

Freud adds that a basic desire of people is to control some of the terrifying forces that surround them. A model for such control appears early in the lives of many persons—that model is the child's father. Thus, the family setting and role functions within the family (the patriarchal father role in particular) become the basis for projection of "fatherly" qualities both of authority and of problem solving and answer giving to the gods and supernatural powers that make up religious systems. We might add here, although getting ahead of the story just a little, that Freud is really quite sociological in his perspective at this point. The group setting and the role structure of that group play significant parts in Freud's analysis.

In general, then, from the psychological point of view, religion serves an adjustment function. That is, it helps people survive frustration in trying to fulfill or serve drives and needs, and in trying to adapt to the frightening experiences that threaten their emotional integrity.

While we earlier credited, so to speak, anthropologists, with the cognitive need explanation as an important component in understanding reasons for the development of religion, particularly its supernatural elements, this is an emphasis within psychology as well. A prominent contemporary psy-

---

[5]Walter Huston Clark, *The Psychology of Religion* (New York: Macmillan, 1958), p. 67; William I. Thomas, *The Unadjusted Girl* (Boston: Little, Brown, 1923), pp. 4ff.

[6]George S. Spinks, *Psychology and Religion* (Boston, MA: Beacon Press, 1963), pp. 46–47.

[7]Sigmund Freud, *The Future of an Illusion* (New York: Liveright, 1928).

chologist, Abraham Maslow, says that a person has a "cognitive need to understand." Life needs to have a meaningful framework for the person to survive. Thus, a person "needs a religion or religious surrogate to live by, in about the same sense that he needs sunlight, calcium, or love."[8]

SOCIOLOGICAL VIEWS

We now turn to the sociological treatment of the issue of religion's sources or origins. Actually, to continue using the term *origins* would be misleading. Certainly contemporary sociologists no longer use the term; nor did the early representatives of sociology that we shall soon cite. A more appropriate term is *social correlates* (or simply *correlates*) of religion—that is, associations between various events and features on the one hand and religious forms and expressions on the other. As shall be evident throughout this text, one of the central concerns of contemporary sociology of religion is tracing the interaction of social factors and religion, not pretending or even hoping to discover "origins," but only influences on and modifiers of religion. In an important sense it makes little difference to the social scientist whence religion came anyway. The fact that it exists is more than sufficient to merit our attention and analysis.

As we might expect, sociologists who seek to discover the "influences" on and "correlations" of religion focus on the various processes involved in social interaction and group life. Theirs is not so much the anthropologists' emphasis on personal experiences with the physical environment, or the psychologists' emphasis on personal emotional adjustment, but theirs is an emphasis on models of what transpires in group interaction processes. These models are in a sense copied and reiterated in the religious system.

In elaborating the sociological position we shall first consider the contribution of the pioneering social theorist Georg Simmel. Patterns of social interaction that are themselves nonreligious, Simmel asserted, exert a prime influence on religion. Many feelings and patterns of expressions commonly termed "religious" are also found in other areas of life and in fact are basic ingredients of social interaction in general—exaltation, commitment, fervor, love, and so on are common to all forms of human experience and relationships. Faith, for example, is a common ingredient in relationships between individuals. Most of our interactions with people are founded on faith—faith that an approaching stranger will not shoot me as he passes; faith that the pilot of the plane knows how to fly, is not on a suicide mission, and is sober; faith that the cook at the drive-in has not laced the hamburger relish with arsenic; and so on. *Religious* faith, then (to con-

---

[8]Abraham Maslow, *Toward a Psychology of Being* (Princeton, NJ: D. Van Nostrand, 1963), pp. 57–64.

tinue the example), is a supreme form of a prime factor in everyday interaction. "In faith in a deity," Simmel writes, "the highest development of faith has become incorporate, so to speak; has been relieved of its connection with its social counterpart."[9]

Implicit in what Simmel says here is a crucial sociological assumption concerning religious "origins"—namely, that the models for many if not all religious sentiments, expressions, and beliefs reside originally in society at large, in its patterns of interaction. In other words, society precedes religion. Before religion can develop, there must first exist general patterns of social interaction—that is, a society—that can serve as a model.

Another pioneer, and Simmel's contemporary, Emile Durkheim, devoted much of his scholarly energies to studying religion and was particularly intrigued by the question of religion's origins and social correlates. Durkheim emphasized religion's role in influencing and reinforcing societal integration—in legitimating society's values and norms by providing divine sanctions for behavior that society defines as normative and by periodically bringing people together for ritual activities that strengthen their feeling of unity. Like Simmel, Durkheim believed that general patterns of social interaction provide models for religion. But Durkheim goes further in asserting (quite dramatically) that society's norms, roles, and social relationships are so closely reflected by religion that the latter is nothing more than these characteristics expressed in somewhat different form. The extreme of this position is Durkheim's contention that the real object of veneration in any religion is society itself—that which is venerated may be *called* "God," but it is really society.

In talking about god and the society, Durkheim makes much use of the concepts of "totem" and "totemic principle." A totem is an object or a living thing, such as a bird or animal or plant, that a group regards with special awe, reverence, and respect. It is what has often been mistaken by outside observers of so-called primitive people as an object of worship—a false god or idol—in Christian terms. Durkheim says the object is not worshipped per se. What is important is what the totem *represents*; what it represents is worshipped. The totem is only a symbol of something more fundamental. Durkheim himself says

> Thus the totem is before all a symbol, a material expression of something else. But of what?
>
> From the analysis to which we have been giving our attention, it is evident that it expresses and symbolizes two different sorts of things. In the first place, it is the outward and visible form of what we have called the totemic principle or god. But it is also the symbol of the determined society called the clan. It is its flag; it is the sign by which each clan distinguishes itself from the others, the visible mark of its personality, a mark borne by everything which is a part of

[9]Georg Simmel, "A Contribution to the Sociology of Religion," *American Journal of Sociology* 11, no. 3 (1905), 336–367.

the clan under any title whatsoever, men, beasts or things. So if it is at once the symbol of the god and of the society, is that not because the god and the society are only one? . . . The god of the clan, the totemic principle, can therefore be nothing else than the clan itself, personified and represented to the imagination under the visible form of the animal or vegetable which serves as totem.[10]

Undergirding Durkheim's view that society personifies itself in the form of totems or gods to revere and worship (that is, society itself is the real object of worship), is his perception of the need of society to reaffirm itself, that is, affirm its legitimacy and worth. This involves for Durkheim the creation of an "ideal" society. That ideal society is very literally the *idea* it has of itself—what it is like, what it stands for, where it has been, where it is going, and so on. This is more than the strictly *material* side of society that would include the people themselves, the ground on which they stand, the things they use, and the gestures they make. Integral to this process of maintaining the ideal aspect of society (its essence, so to speak) is religion that personifies the social ideal and is the primary mechanism for its maintenance.

As a further extension of this idea of the essential identity of god and society is Durkheim's view of the idea of a person's soul. John Wilson points out that Durkheim saw in the belief in the soul "a symbolic representation of the relation between the individual and society."[11] The moral authority of the society is the reality that stands behind the concept of the soul. So, when people refer to their souls, they are referring (without of course being aware of it) to a social element within them. This social element will of course live long after the people themselves. One would have to think at this point of the Hindu and Buddhist concept of samsara and the traditional Greek and Christian concept of the immortality of the soul.

At this point, we can not avoid reintroducing Durkheim's concept of the sacred that was discussed briefly earlier and described as an integral part of our definition of religion. The sacred refers to those things and situations and places that are *set apart*, very special, emitting an aura of the holy, and so on. But Durkheim also says that the sacred consists of "all sorts of collective states, common traditions and emotions, (and) feelings which have a relationship to objects of general interest."[12] He contrasts profane things as those that each of us constructs from our own sense data and experiences. As purely individual impressions they do not have the same prestige and influence as the more societal and collective elements that constitute the sacred.

---

[10]Emile Durkheim, *The Elementary Forms of the Religious Life*, trans. Joseph Ward Swain (New York: Collier, 1961), p. 236.

[11]John Wilson, *Religion in American Society* (Englewood Cliffs, NJ: Prentice-Hall, 1978), p. 19.

[12]Emile Durkheim, "Concerning the Definition of Religious Phenomena," in W. S. F. Pickering, *Durkheim on Religion* (London: Routledge & Kegan Paul, 1975), p. 95.

Another way to help understand how Durkheim views religion and how intimately it is associated with the society itself is to see religion as a *functional* element in society. That is, religion performs a beneficial function within society, for all religious acts (in Durkheim's view) tend to reaffirm society's legitimacy and bind its members more closely together. Durkheim's views of the functional (integrative) role of religion are well illustrated in his discussion of the social functions of religious and ceremonial ritual, as summarized by Alpert.[13] Durkheim sees four primary social functions of such ritual: (1) It serves a disciplinary and preparatory function—that is, ritual imposes a self-discipline that is necessary for social life. Members of society need to accommodate constraints, controls, boundaries. Learning to follow religious rituals facilitates development of this ability. (2) Ceremonial ritual provides a cohesive function—that is, it brings people together, reaffirms their common bonds, and reinforces social solidarity. By doing things jointly and repetitively, the members of the group strengthen their bonds of relatedness. "The essential thing is that men are assembled, that sentiments are felt in common, and that they are expressed in common acts."[14] (3) It serves a revitalizing function—that is, it makes members of the society aware of their common social heritage. It links them to the past: What we do has a history; we ourselves have a history. Such awareness can provide motivation and inspiration to carry on. (4) It serves a euphoric function. It aids in establishing a pleasant feeling of social well-being. This function takes on special significance when a group is faced with calamities, disappointments, losses of treasured members, and other threats to its stability. It helps straighten out the sharp curves and adds some rays of light in the dark tunnels of disappointment and despair.

It is appropriate at this point to mention a more contemporary application and suggestion of functional theory by Robert Merton. He speaks about the possibility of "functional alternatives." That is, although a given action or role of a particular subunit in a social system may be seen as functional, it should not be concluded that such is the only action or performance that may be functional in that particular place and time.[15] This is of particular relevance to the identification of religious functions. The fact that religion performs certain functions and satisfies certain needs of society and its individual members does not mean that religion is either inevitable or nonexpendable. Other systems or mechanisms could conceivably satisfy these needs as well or better. Actually, this may help explain why some persons are "religious" while others are not at all religious, at least not in

---

[13]Harry Alpert, *Emile Durkheim and His Sociology* (New York: Russell & Russell, 1961), pp. 198–203.

[14]Durkheim, *Elementary Forms*, pp. 431–432.

[15]Robert K. Merton, *Social Theory and Social Structure* (Glencoe, IL: Free Press, 1956), pp. 33–34.

ways traditionally defined as such by that society. That is, while some people practice major religions, others avail themselves of nonreligious functional alternatives or of religious alternatives outside the mainstream of formalized religion.

More recently Guy E. Swanson has adopted Durkheim's basic position but modified it somewhat in conducting a monumental piece of research. Starting with the basic sociological assumption that all human ideas arise from the experience of people with their environment,[16] both physical and social, Swanson attempted to discover examples of specific human experiences giving rise to certain forms of religious belief. In *The Birth of the Gods*, his 1960 study, Swanson focused on religion's preoccupation with the supernatural in an attempt to determine the origin of this concept. Like the early anthropologists, Swanson noted the predominance of spirits and of the concept of mana in "primitive" religious systems. What are the sources of the belief in such phenomena? Swanson suggests that spirits, which he defines as "organized clusters of purposes" having a personal identity and access to mana, grow out of, and consequently stand for, social patterns already present in the society.[17] That is, as Durkheim and Simmel both maintained earlier, society serves as the model for religion.

Swanson then asks, What social relationships do the experiences with spirits correspond to? He suggests four conditions or types of social patterns or groups: (1) social relationships in which there is an evident connection between cause and effect, associated with the belief that spirits have a purpose and a will; (2) relationships regarded as persisting over the generations, which relates to the belief that spirits are immortal; (3) particular groups that are the source of particular spirits, which means that every spirit has a specific identity; and (4) groups that have distinctive purposes, associated with the fact that spirits differ in purpose and role.[18]

Using this general orientation to the source or basis of belief in spirits, Swanson analyzes data drawn from preliterate and early historical societies in order to trace the relationship between certain kinds of belief (such as monotheism, polytheism, and the beliefs in ancestral spirits, in reincarnation, in the immanence of the soul, and in the efficacy of witchcraft) and various social conditions and relationships. That is, he sought correlations between religious beliefs and practices, on the one hand, and, on the other, such social factors as the society's source of food, its amount of food production, the degree of danger of attack from alien societies, the size of the population, the degree of private-property ownership, the emphasis on communal vs. noncommunal specialties within the society, social stratification,

---

[16]Guy E. Swanson, *The Birth of the Gods* (Ann Arbor, MI: University of Michigan Press, 1960), p. 1.

[17]Ibid., p. 18.

[18]This typology is summarized from ibid., pp. 19–20.

the nature and frequency of unlegitimated contacts with members of other societies, the variety and kinds of social organizations, and so on. In some cases Swanson found a surprisingly high correlation between a set of social factors and a particular religious belief or practice—that is, a particular belief was always (or almost always) present *only if* certain social factors were also present, and always (or nearly always) absent *only when* the same factors were absent. In all cases, he found fascinating and highly suggestive correlations, whether of high magnitude or not. For example, witchcraft, Swanson discovered, tended to occur in societies where people must interact with one another on important matters with no clear norms, controls, and structures to guide them.[19] Thus people resort to witchcraft apparently as a substitute, as a compensatory device for attempting to explain and above all to control what happens to them. Or to take another example: The belief in reincarnation is more likely to appear in societies where the pattern of settlement is dominated by "small hamlets, compounds of extended families, small nomadic bands, scattered rural neighborhoods, or other units smaller than a village."[20] The apparent logic underlying this is that there is a greater probability that a person will be regarded as living on through reincarnation where there are intimate, highly interdependent, long-lasting relationships within a relatively small but fairly independent social unit—where, in other words, the social unit is thought to survive the members who constitute it at any given time. The individual and his or her idiosyncracies within such groups are of considerable interest and importance. As Swanson points out, "The particular potentialities of each member are appreciated as limiting or facilitating the lives of all the others, and those effects persist after a member dies."[21] These effects are such things as "his technological inventiveness, his habits of shirking work, his fecundity, or the qualities of his voice in the ceremonial songs [that] have shaped adaptations of his fellows . . . [and that] continue after his death."[22] In other words, "the memory lingers on." Moreover, the social relationships and structure of the group provide a "model" for the development of a belief in personal reincarnation.

While Swanson himself admits that even strong positive correlations do not conclusively establish cause-and-effect relationships between social factors and religious beliefs, his achievement lies in having shown that certain beliefs are extremely unlikely to occur and be accepted unless certain social factors, conditions, or relationships are present. For example, it is extremely unlikely that a society lacking a certain degree and type of organizational complexity will accept belief in a monotheistic "high god" (one con-

[19]Ibid., Chapter 8.
[20]Ibid., p. 113.
[21]Ibid., p. 112.
[22]Ibid.

sidered responsible for creating the world), even if the belief is suggested by a member of the group, revealed by a deity, or diffused from another society. Specifically, societies that accept such a belief have a hierarchical arrangement of three or more "sovereign groups" (groups having ultimate decision-making authority over specified areas of life).[23] Although Swanson stops short of asserting any causal relationship here and would simply affirm that this social structure is likely the model for the emergence of monotheism much of the time, the relationship is strong enough to at least tempt the reader to begin thinking of talking about necessary and sufficient conditions for the development of that particular belief.

CONCLUSION

Although the origins and ultimate sources of religion can never be known with certainty, research and speculation on these subjects have not been fruitless. The hypotheses we have summarized—the anthropological theories that emphasize people's interaction with nature; the psychological theories that stress people's fears, frustrations, and emotional needs; and the sociological theories that focus on the social context in which religion exists—at the very least contribute to our understanding of what religion is, why it has come about, and perhaps also why it persists.

In summary, then, it seems reasonable to advance the following propositions concerning the forces that sustain religion, if not give rise to it: (1) People are continually and universally threatened with failure, frustration, and injustice. (2) Religion becomes the attempt of people in groups to "relativize" such threats to their wholeness by placing them within a context of a larger system or plan and by "explaining" much that happens in terms of supernatural intervention into and control over earthly events. (3) At the same time, threats similar to those experienced by individuals also affect social relationships—and, in fact, society itself. (4) Religion arises as an attempt by society to cushion such threats (both to itself and to its members) by bringing people into a ritual fellowship of common belief. Religion is thus a response to both individual and group needs. (5) The characteristic form of religious belief and interpretation in a given society is significantly conditioned by the type and complexity of existing social patterns and relationships.

[23]Ibid., pp. 62–65.

3

Religion as a Group Phenomenon

In Chapter 1 we made the point that as a social phenomenon religion exhibits patterns of interaction and process that duplicate many, if not all, patterns that all other social groups exhibit, and we suggested quite explicitly that religion is a group phenomenon. We will now pick up on these fundamental sociological observations and expand them as we look more specifically at the social organization of religion. That is, we want to see how religious ideas, regardless of their real or supposed source, become embodied in groups and how in turn these groups proceed to function, evidence similarities among themselves and with other groups, and distinguish themselves both from one another and from other kinds of groups in society.

RELIGION AND THE CHARACTERISTICS OF A GROUP

In Chapter 1 we briefly defined *group* as two or more interacting people who (1) share common goals or aims that stem from common problems and a desire to resolve them; (2) agree upon a set of norms they hope will help them achieve their common goals; (3) combine certain norms into roles that they expect persons within the group to fill and carry out in the interests of the group; (4) agree (often only implicitly) on certain status dimensions and distinctions on the basis of which they rate one another; and (5) identify with the group and express or exhibit some degree of commitment to the group, what it proposes to do, and how it proposes to do it.

Clearly, religious organizations meet all of these criteria. Religious groups are concerned with problems and with expressing aspirations, hopes, and goals. They want to know why certain things happen (cognitive understanding of accident, death, thunder, or whatever), or they want to express their dependency relationship with a deity (proper worship and ritual activity), or they want to devise methods of gaining rewards from the deities (techniques of prayer or magic), or they want to achieve a proper existence after this present life (salvation). In each case we are observing goals and the process of establishing goals.

Intimately associated with goal establishment, of course, is agreement on norms. To agree that it is an appropriate goal to appease a jealous god is to establish a norm—namely, that there is such a god, that so and so is his or her name, and so on. Any belief or assertion about the supernatural, any explanation of what it does, any established practice or ritual directed toward it is a norm. Christianity, with its elaborate doctrines, dogmas, and theological tomes, clearly possesses an extensive normative system. Its historic emphasis on "right belief" becomes partially understandable in this context. Yet "primitive" religions that appear more to emphasize behavior—the ritual that involves proper steps and stages in the rain dance, the puberty rite, or the battle preparation—equally emphasize norms—norms of right behavior perhaps more than norms of right belief.

As immediately as norms follow goals, so do roles follow both. The group agrees on a leader (priest, shaman, rabbi, guru, prophet, pastor) and defines her or his duties. It specializes other functions into dancers, cantors, sorcerers, choirs, treasurers, acolytes, deacons, theological professors, executive secretaries of evangelism, directors of research and survey, public relations directors, news release writers, members of the commission on church literature, ushers, chairpersons of the annual spaghetti supper, and so on.

Partly, but not solely, as a result of such specialization of roles, status differences appear in religious groups. Quite naturally the leader, the coordinator, the spokesperson, and the teacher of religious truths early acquire greater status—greater prestige and respect, if nothing else—than the rank-and-file participant. The status of such persons also involves greater authority and, perhaps as a spinoff, greater power as well. Possibly greater wealth and more leisure may accrue. But there are other status distinctions, too. There are those members who appear to follow the norms of the group more closely than others. Such behavior will likely be recognized by many members, who will characterize those who are most assiduously normative as "very religious," "most sincere," "Zoroastrian of the Decade," "Methodist of the Year," and the like.

Related to such ideas of status differentiation is the factor of group identification. Identification and commitment are variables that range from low (if not zero) to high. Groups tend to tolerate variability here, though most strive for high commitment from all members. Of course, as we will point out shortly, the larger the group, the more likely that the range of commitment and identification will increase.

The major point we are making is that although the subject matter of religion may be unique and although it may claim a unique (namely, supernatural) source for its norms and roles, yet as the religious group organizes itself and sets about doing what it feels it should be doing, it exhibits all the features of any and all other groups. At the level of organization and structure, it is no different from other groups. The focus of the goals may be different, the specific set of norms may be different, the combination of norms into particular roles may be unique, the criteria for status assessment may vary. But the religious group, as any other group, will have all of these ingredients and must constantly work at resolving differences of interpretation and application of its goals, norms, and roles. It must adjust them, expand them, and so on, just as any group must. Just as nations or social clubs or political parties or nuclear families differ among themselves yet also evidence similarities in the problems they need to adjust to and the ultimate resolutions and patterns they exhibit, so too religious groups, though unique in certain ways, evidence similarities among themselves and in fact with all other social groups.

This all suggests by way of practical application that the problems and challenges that any group must deal with on a day-to-day basis will be there for a religious group to deal with also. Just as a family needs certain tasks to be performed—cooking meals, washing clothes, mowing the lawn, bringing home spendable income in the form of wages or salary—so a religious group needs someone to lead the group in worship, someone to clean up afterwards, someone to provide leadership in music, and someone to keep tabs on revenues and expenditures. Just as political parties meet in convention periodically to define and refine their platforms and address new issues facing the nation, so churches gather in convention to refine their theological positions on various issues and address new issues that are brought before them. Just as a society devises a court and penal system to provide a fair hearing for those accused of deviation from society's norms and in turn to punish and attempt to rehabilitate those who are found guilty, so religious groups establish procedures to provide a fair hearing but then punish if the person is found guilty, perhaps to the point of excommunication if the individual persists unrepentant in his or her deviance—be it called heresy, immorality, heterodoxy, or whatever.

In short, a group is a group is a group.

RELIGION AND THE FIVE FUNCTIONAL PREREQUISITES OF GROUP LIFE

Recruitment and Reproduction

By way of a more systematic and thorough treatment of what we have suggested above, we can point out that religious groups, no less than other groups, are involved with meeting the challenges of the five functional prerequisites of group life.[1] First, any group must pay attention to the prerequisite of recruitment or reproduction to replace its members who die, defect, or become incapacitated. Societies accomplish this task through natural reproduction (births), acceptance of immigrants, or annexation of neighboring territories and populations. Other groups rely primarily on natural reproduction and recruitment of new members through voluntary affiliation with the group. Religious groups have historically not been unmindful of meeting this prerequisite for group continuity. In fact, many religious groups have explicitly urged maximum natural reproduction. Prohibitions against birth control, emphasis on conception as the only valid motive for sexual relations, and social ridicule or pity for the barren woman all enter in here. Although the Old Testament injunction to be fruitful and multiply has more recently been interpreted simply as a predictive statement of what would naturally happen as men and women mated, it was historically interpreted as a divine command to reproduce as prolifically as possible. Some groups have explicitly urged their members to bear as many children as possible so as to increase the numbers of God's people. Many religious groups have also worked hard at adding to their numbers through recruitment of members from outside the group—by conversion or proselytizing. Jesus' injunction quoted in Matthew, "Go ye therefore, and teach all nations," has been followed to greater and lesser degrees throughout history. Ever since (and even before) Charlemagne "converted" the barbarians through mass baptisms in 722, Christian missionaries have been attempting to expedite conversion of nonbelievers and pagans. Actually, however, it was not until the eighteenth and nineteenth centuries, when the new worlds of the Americas, Asia, Africa, and the Pacific experienced extensive exploration and colonization, that Christian groups began subsidizing significant missionary activity.

All Christian groups continue today to support missionary work throughout the world, though such activity is somewhat curtailed because of political unrest in various nations, the development of political nationalism that is often accompanied by religious nationalism (for example, in Iran note the intimate relationship of the Islamic religion with the political revo-

---

[1]David Aberle, "The Functional Prerequisites of a Society," *Ethics* 60, no. 2 (1950), 100–111.

lution that deposed the shah), and a slightly declining financial support from parent denominations. Much of the current missionary activity is highly traditional in the sense of going out into the jungles and villages to meet the indigenous peoples where they are and establish congregations: However, increasing emphasis is being placed on work within the expanding urban centers as one after another of the underdeveloped nations begins to industrialize. Along with this ministry to the urban centers often goes increasing attention to a radio and television ministry designed to reach out to the masses.

With respect to contemporary mission work, a familiar sight to almost everyone is the pairs of young Mormon men in suits, white shirts, and ties plying the streets and neighborhoods of towns and cities in many countries trying to find receptive ears for the story and message they have to tell. They are urged by their church to devote two years before marriage to full-time mission work, some in the home country, others in a foreign one.

Or look at the cult members such as those in the Unification Church ("Moonies") who divide their time between fund raising from those they are unlikely to recruit and charming the rootless, uncommitted young people into social contact with the group and convincing them to stick around and find out more. It was few people indeed who in the 1970s did not run into or at least observe such young people at work in airports and busy city streets.

Other major religions, such as Islam and Buddhism, have also actively courted nonmembers, not infrequently using force and political means when ordinary persuasion was insufficient. In fact, in Islam the political-military and religious motivations are so mixed as to be impossible to separate (which is true throughout the history of Christianity also, of course). Early in the history of Islam, the conquering of both near and far territories for both booty and land became an absorbing goal and activity. Subjugated peoples were of course also pledged to the religion of Islam. Buddhism used religious missionaries, monks, and teachers to spread their message. In fact, as early as two centuries after Gautama Buddha's death, the Indian emperor Asoka, who came to the throne in 273 B.C., conceived of Buddhism as a world religion and sent missionaries as far as Egypt and Greece.[2] These missions left no trace, however, and these attempts to spread Buddhism were apparently quite ineffective. In Sri Lanka (Ceylon) it was a different story. Buddhist missionaries sent by Asoka's son, Mahinda, in 240 B.C. were so successful that Buddhism quickly became the state religion of Sri Lanka and remains so until this day.[3]

---

[2]John B. Noss, *Man's Religions* (New York: Macmillan, 1949), pp. 175–176.

[3]Edward Conze, *A Short History of Buddhism* (London: George Allen & Unwin, 1980), p. 42.

A classic example of a group's failure to meet the requirement of reproduction and recruitment of new members is that of the American religious group called the Shakers, founded in 1787. One of their primary tenets was strict separation of the sexes and complete sexual continence. Therefore, a prime source of new members (natural reproduction) was deliberately eliminated. Sole reliance was placed on adult conversion to the faith. Perhaps in great part because of the limited number of persons willing to observe sexual continence, the group had trouble gaining enough new members to maintain itself. Not surprisingly, the group consists today of but a very few elderly people.

Socialization

A second prerequisite any group must be concerned with is developing a process of training and educating new members—what we have been calling socialization. The norms and practices of the group must be taught to new members, whether they are children of current members, converts, or conquered subjects. Religious groups of course face this challenge continually. The doctrines and the practices of the group must be inculcated in new members. They must know and believe certain bits and bodies of doctrine and ritual first of all for their own good and also if they are to become and remain members in good standing. Further, they must know and believe certain things if they are to help in preserving the group's beliefs and practices and in handing them down to succeeding generations of followers.

Accordingly, the teaching or educative function of religion becomes a major task for religious groups. It is not by chance, for example, that the full-time religious leader in Judaism, both ancient and contemporary, has the title *rabbi*, meaning "teacher." In "primitive" religions, of course, the socialization process was largely informal and accomplished through emulation as the young watched the old and began to participate in the ritual activities and as they listened to the sagas and tales that elaborated the group's beliefs. However, religious systems that also emphasize various systematic cognitive elements of understanding and belief develop formal mechanisms for conveying such knowledge and for training in ritual performance: confirmation classes, Sunday or other church and Sabbath schools, and study groups of all kinds. Religious groups that tend to rely on generalists called ministers or priests may at some point add specialists to their staff called ministers of education. An early development among American Christian denominations, for example, was to establish a publishing house to produce aids to ritual activities (for example, hymnbooks) and educational material designed to aid the religious growth and maturation (socialization) of members.

Producing Satisfactory Levels of Goods and Services

A third prerequisite for the continued existence of all groups is the production and distribution of a level of goods and services that will satisfy at least the minimal requirements or demands of their members. In the case of a total society, this task involves satisfying at least the minimal survival needs of its citizens for such items as food, shelter, and clothing. For voluntary associations such as contemporary religious groups, it means giving members what they have come to the group to find or else running the risk of members losing interest and leaving. Presumably, members of religious groups receive certain expected benefits from their affiliation, or they will not stay or would not have joined in the first place. Perhaps they are seeking eternal salvation, or comfort and reassurance, or good fellowship, or a vehicle through which they can help those in need. A religious group therefore must either "deliver the goods," so to speak—or at least convince its members that the goods are being delivered or will be in the hereafter—or see its constituency evaporate. Although this may sound almost crass, perhaps even sacrilegious when talking about religious groups, these very religions must "deliver" something that people want, or the people will go elsewhere.

Religious groups that we will be defining as "cults" in Chapter 5, which tend to be centered around a charismatic leader, are notoriously unstable and likely to disband as quickly as they formed when the leader becomes discredited or dies or the competition promises more. Followers may decide they are not receiving what they were seeking or believe that they will more fully or more quickly receive what they seek from the competition that has appeared on the scene.

The relationship of most members to their religious group is of course not so tenuous or easily shifted as what we just described in cults. Certainly, lifelong adherents to a group must overcome apathy and inertia, if nothing else, if they wish to defect—yet defect they will (and do) if evidence accumulates and the conviction mounts that what was sought has not been found or is no longer being offered fully enough by the group.

Researchers have recently been observing declining memberships in several major denominations in the United States (and increasing membership in others). Interestingly, those with declining memberships tend to be more theologically and socially liberal; those with increasing memberships tend to be conservative on both counts. We will not at the moment evaluate the hypothesis that people are increasingly becoming disenchanted with liberal theology and the intrusion of liberal social and political views into the major Christian denominations and as a consequence are leaving such groups to join more traditional groups that emphasize personal comfort and the reassurance of absolute rather than relative truths. But we can certainly agree that most people who leave a religious group, whether or not they affiliate with another one, are expressing a dissatisfaction with the "goods and services" delivered by that group—it no longer provides them what they want, or at least not enough of what they want to maintain their allegiance.

Preserving Order

The fourth primary task that groups must perform is that of preserving order. Essentially, this task involves coordinative and supervisory roles, but above all it means motivating members to pursue group goals while employing and abiding by group norms. Within total societies, this centers in the political process and the exercising of governmental controls and sanctions—the range of rewards and punishments meted out for adherence to or deviation from the norms, as the case may be. On the positive side, it involves encouraging members to cooperate with one another and to supplement, rather than interfere with, the performance of others' roles. It involves providing a context for freedom of movement and action of individuals within limits agreed upon by the group. On the negative side, it may involve incarceration, the death penalty, or ostracism.

So far as religious groups are concerned, we think here of the three major types of church government established to reach the organization's goals. First, there is the episcopal type (for example, Episcopal and Roman Catholic churches), in which authority rests with the congregations' clergy and with higher-ranking clergy such as popes and bishops. Second, the presbyterian type, in which authority rests with representative committees of clergy and church members. Third, the congregational type, in which ultimate organizational authority resides in local church members and with their representatives meeting periodically in regional or national convention or assembly.

We also think of heresy trials and inquisitions, in which those accused of deviating from official doctrine or practice are sought out, tried, and punished. Fundamental here is the conviction that if such controls are not employed, radical changes may be introduced that would result in the alienation and loss of members to the point of ultimate dissolution and destruction of the group.

Maintaining a Sense of Purpose

The fifth primary prerequisite that groups must fulfill if they hope to survive is the maintenance of a sense of purpose among its members. This task is concerned with the sixth feature of groups mentioned in Chapter 1—namely, the identification factor. Groups must develop and maintain among members a feeling of commitment to and identification with the group. Groups that fail continually to reinforce members' commitment run the risk of takeover or collapse in the face of internal opposition or outside threat. A society, for example, needs citizens sufficiently committed to pick up arms and risk death on the battlefield in the face of enemy invasion. A religious group wants to be able to count on sufficient loyalty and commitment among its members so that they are not swayed (or possibly even converted) by every fragrant new wind of doctrine that blows by. They want members who take pride in their affiliation and who will resist the wiles of other groups or philosophies that may try to win them away. Most religious groups (except most Jews and Hindus) in addition want members who will in fact try to bring others into their fold. "We've got a great group here and would like you to share its benefits with us!" Failing to maintain a sense of purpose can bring a group to the brink of destruction just as can failure in any of the other four primary tasks already discussed.

THE EFFECTS OF INCREASING GROUP SIZE

Having examined one aspect of religion as a group phenomenon—in terms of the tasks that face all groups, not just religious ones—we now turn to a discussion of the pressures for change that religious groups (no less than other groups) experience. Of particular interest and significance is the effect on groups of increasing size. Important changes occur, and new challenges develop as groups grow. Although a group may in one sense be successful by increasing its membership, serious problems may arise as a consequence. Paul Mott has summarized well the various developments associated with a group's increasing size.[4] We include only some of them—those with particular salience to religious groups.

As groups increase in size, the degree of consensus among members concerning goals and especially norms declines. In great part, a basic problem of communication and interaction is involved here. As groups grow, a point is reached when not everyone can interact with everyone else; nor can any one person interact with all others. Levels of understanding and commitment to goals and norms cannot be maintained. Not only can people not share as fully with one another and reach truly common understandings by involving everyone in decision and policy making, but also problems of increasing diversity arise as more members come in. In fact, each new person is a potential disrupter, if not a potential revolutionary, inasmuch as the ideas he or she brings or those that she or he may develop may challenge fundamental beliefs of the group. Obviously the tightknit, integrated, pri-

---

[4]Paul E. Mott, *The Organization of Society* (Englewood Cliffs, NJ: Prentice-Hall, 1965), pp. 48–69.

mary-group-like relationship that may have existed at a group's inception and during its early development begins to submit to increasing diversity and more specialized interests as different elements enter.

An almost inevitable outcome of increased diversity and reduced consensus resulting from an increase in size is increasing deviance from group norms. Since norms influence behavior, the introduction of diverse or conflicting norms results in diverse behavior. Some members may assent to many of the group's norms (they probably would not be members otherwise) yet not share others. For example, a religious group may have explicit norms defining alcoholic beverages as the devil's tools of destruction. The member who would still like a nip or two is more likely to depart from the group norm as the group grows larger. Perhaps the norm and its importance to the group has not been explained fully to him or her or is no longer reinforced through discussion and conversation; perhaps this person does not feel as closely united with the other members as she or he did when the group was small and thus does not feel so bad about disappointing them should they find out about his or her deviance. Actually, as the group grows larger, it becomes physically and emotionally impossible to feel or express as much concern about other individual members as was possible when the group was smaller and members more intimate.

As groups increase in size, the ratio of formal norms to informal ones increases. That is, when a group is small and when the members can interact almost at will with one another and with the leader, norms and ideas can be shared with everyone in an informal way. But when the group grows to the point that not everyone can talk readily with everyone else and perhaps does not even know everyone else, the group will find it necessary to formalize its norms and principles and beliefs by writing them down. It is not coincidental that almost without exception holy books and bibles are written *after* the religion has been established awhile, has gained converts, and has moved beyond small group status. For one thing, the leader can no longer speak to everyone. So someone copies down some of his or her sayings and pronouncements and passes copies around to the membership.

A fourth development as groups grow larger is that roles tend to become more specialized and part-time roles tend to become full-time ones. Such specialization removes the nonspecialist from intimate contact with the tasks of various roles. Greater autonomy for roles develops. Members who originally were involved to some degree in almost everything the group did and decided now know less and less about what others are doing.

As groups increase in size, there is greater need for coordination. As the number of roles increases, there is greater need for coordinators to interrelate those roles and ensure that they are performed in proper sequence. Nothing is wrong with that, of course. But in the process, the coordinators gain greater knowledge about the operation of the total organization than ordinary members possess; having by definition greater authority, they become increasingly isolated from the rank and file. Obviously, the original intimacy and democracy of the group fade fast in the face of this tendency. There are also, of course, increased opportunities for abusing one's power and perpetuating oneself in office, for example.

Mott lists thirteen developments within groups related to increasing group size. The five discussed here, however, are sufficient to make the point that one measure of success that groups often use—namely, membership growth—sets them on an irreversible course involving change along a variety of dimensions. In the next chapter, we will refer back to these dimensions in our discussion of the church-sect typology. First, however, we want to look more closely at one of the developments in groups related to increasing size—the bureaucratization trend that we identified earlier as an increase in the coordinative element in groups.

THE BUREAUCRATIZATION OF RELIGION

In the preceding section, we talked about the need for increased coordination as groups grow larger. This introduced us to the concept of bureaucracy, which has as its essential feature the coordinating idea. That is, as specialized roles appear and as decisions need to be made, certain persons assume or are given coordinating roles. These people tend to be ranked in a hierarchy of authority. The whole idea is that greater efficiency should be achieved because someone is organizing the activities of others so that the whole group does not need to meet and take a lot of time reaching a democratic decision. Further, these coordinators have a broader picture of what is being done and can determine the most efficient sequence of activities.

But we also need to point out that although bureaucratization appears to be an inevitable trend in groups as they grow large and develop an increasingly complex division of labor requiring careful coordination, it may also create problems and have unintended and unwanted consequences. As Hammond and Johnson point out, a key issue in the Protestant Reformation of the fifteenth century concerned how authority was to be exercised within the church. Implicitly this was a question of what to do about the church bureaucracy.[5] Certainly the Roman Catholic Church had long been organized along rather classic bureaucratic lines. An elaborate hierarchy of authority passed down through pope, archbishops, bishops, and priests, with other levels in between. Specialized training and experience were required of those who filled various specialized roles. Explicit rules were in effect for nearly every situation and role. An air of impartiality and imper-

[5]Philip E. Hammond and Benton Johnson, *American Mosaic* (New York: Random House, 1970), p. 149.

sonality pervaded relationships among leaders and between them and members.

But the leaders of the Protestant Reformation wanted greater involvement and a stronger voice for the laity. A key theological tenet stressed within early Protestantism was that every person can have direct contact with and access to God. No intermediary such as church, pope, or priest was required. Some groups were convinced that no church authority should exist or exercise control beyond the democratic assembly of each local congregation—no level of authority above the congregation (except God himself) should require the member or the congregation to do anything. Congregationalists, Lutherans, and Baptists are among Protestant denominations that still espouse this principle, though in modified form in each case.

How successful have such religious groups been in implementing this philosophy; in avoiding the bureaucratization that sociologists have documented in other types of groups? We gain some insight into the issue when we observe what happens when an individual or a local body of believers strives to maintain its autonomy but also finds it expedient to cooperate with other individuals or congregations in various joint ventures. Perhaps several congregations discover that training future clergy members is a difficult task to accomplish alone and so they join together in establishing a theological seminary. Or they may want to send missionaries to foreign lands. A single congregation usually cannot afford to support a missionary, but several congregations can. So they establish a missionary society or board or commission to handle the details, such as collecting mission contributions from the several congregations. Or they may want to produce lessons and literature for their Sunday schools, but local ministers don't have the time or perhaps lack the specialized skill. Therefore, several congregations organize a Sunday school board and organize a commission on church literature to handle the planning, writing, editing, and publishing tasks.

The outcome of such developments is that, although no one particularly intends it, the local congregations lose some of their autonomy. The boards or agencies or commissions assume some measure of authority and independence and in turn gain influence over the congregations. It is a reciprocal relationship—while local congregations may have established the goals and even some of the policies for such administrative groups, once in existence the latter influence the congregations. They train the ministers, organize and supervise the missionary endeavors, and write the Sunday school material. Thus, they become innovators and not simply implementers of policy.

The relationship between such boards and the local congregation and its members can therefore become somewhat uncertain. Such a situation is highlighted when one or more congregations discover they do not like the theological inclinations of their seminary's ministerial graduates or feel that heretical ideas are slipping into their Sunday school material. The congregation of course has the option of severing the relationship, but then it faces the problem of carrying on all these tasks by itself or linking up with yet another organization. The common reaction is to go along with the established pattern, even though the congregation loses some of its cherished autonomy in the process.

A method observed by Paul Harrison in the American Baptist Church that bridges the gap between national boards and local independent congregations is the action of the executive who heads a board or agency. If the executive secretary or other administrator of a national board or commission has charismatic qualities, he or she can gain broad-based support among local clergy and laypeople that grants him or her greater flexibility and autonomy and ultimately substantial authority and influence over local decisions.[6] Of course, even without charisma the denominational executive will have some measure of autonomous power because much of her or his day-to-day work goes on unseen and unknown by most of the constituency. As Harrison points out, most lay members have no knowledge of the internal operation of the larger church body, never attend national, state, or even local associational meetings, and most likely do not even know the names of their officials, let alone the policies they set.[7]

In other words, a bureaucracy, once formed, tends to take on a life of its own, initiates and implements policy partly of its own making, and may begin to direct the larger group of which it is a specialized part in new directions.

Robert Michels's classic "iron law of oligarchy" can be seen operating in many religious groups. This refers to the tendency, as responsibilities and authority are transferred to leaders (a process seemingly inherent and inevitable in group life), for a number of developments in combination to lead to oligarchy. Granting responsibility to leaders, for example, concentrates both skills and informal prerogatives in their hands. Leaders become more skilled than rank-and-file members in administration, coordination, manipulation, diplomacy, and so on, and they have access to information not available to others. Along with such skills and knowledge goes power. The gratitude and allegiance of members to their leaders for doing jobs they would not care to do also strengthens the leaders' position of power and influence. Further, leaders tend to be self-perpetuating in their positions. They like their power and privilege, and they want to keep it. As a result, incumbents are hard to remove.[8]

Religious organizations are not immune to such organizational tendencies. In fact, they join on an equal footing with all other democratic organi-

---

[6]Paul M. Harrison, *Authority and Power in a Free Church Tradition: A Social Case Study of the American Baptist Convention* (Princeton, NJ: Princeton University Press, 1959), pp. 74–77.

[7]Ibid., p. 92.

[8]Robert Michels, *Political Parties*, trans. Eden and Cedar Paul (Glencoe, IL: Free Press, 1949). First published in England in 1915.

zations in this tendency. This is true regardless of how zealously a group may strive to remain a pure democracy. Even those religious groups that make a strong theological point that local and individual religious autonomy is sacred are faced with the tendency to oligarchy. Of course, other religious groups, such as the Roman Catholic Church, stress a hierarchical authority pattern in the first place and have little problem living with the oligarchic tendency. Although there has been some change recently, with laypeople demanding more input into decision and policy making, the issue in such a group has traditionally been less one of laypeople wanting to curtail the power of bureaucratic church executives than of church officials trying to keep the laypeople from becoming too independent and free-thinking. It is a struggle for power either way that is based on two characteristics of groups: (1) diversity on a number of dimensions within the group and (2) the oligarchic tendency for leaders to accumulate power. Internal diversity within a group makes effective total control next to impossible, yet oligarchic tendencies serve to override diversity in the interests of bureaucratic efficiency.

RELIGIOUS LEADERSHIP

As we discuss groups, whether religious or any other kind, we cannot conclude without talking about the leadership of those groups. Certainly all groups have leaders, that is, those within the group who are looked to by the rest for creative ideas, advice, decisions, encouragement, and interpretation of the group's norms.

While there certainly is leadership by laypersons in religious groups, we will concentrate on professional leadership, that is, leadership by those with specific, often very lengthy, training, with titles like priest, minister, rabbi, guru, pastor, parson, reverend, prophet, shaman, and so on.

While sociologists prefer to consider groups before they talk about the leaders of those groups (which is exactly our approach in this chapter), it is nonetheless true that leaders are important and fill a crucial role in groups. This is particularly obvious when we are talking about a charismatic leader—a subject we will take up shortly. But sociology tells us that most leaders are able to function legitimately—are able to lead—only as their actions and programs are firmly based in the group and its purposes and values. Note the adverb "legitimately" above. It is true that dictators and despots can rule and "lead" a group if that person has sufficient fire power to keep the people in line and can keep them uneasy and frightened enough of informers and secret police so as to acquiesce. Yet most groups carry on with legitimate leadership that the current members have either chosen or accepted and as such have granted legitimacy both to the leadership role and the person(s) occupying it.

For a group to proceed with its customary activities and make progress towards its goals, it not only needs some leaders to function as coordinators and "cheerleaders" who encourage the members to keep up their good work, but it also needs them to inspire and inform, to stretch their horizons and make relevant applications of the foundation principles to which they are committed. Thus, as James Wood points out, if leaders in churches can point to Scripture and relate what Jesus or St. Paul did or said and show how this is relevant to a current event or issue (perhaps facilitate racial integration through a busing program or voting for some specific referendum or person, etc.), then the rank-and-file members are likely to consent to their leader's exhortations and deem them legitimate even if the specific application of group principles that the leader proposes was not already in members' repertoire of actions and commitments.[9]

An important distinction among clergy leadership functions is that of prophet versus priest.[10] This distinction is made by Max Weber. He identified the religious functionary who carries out the ritual and repeats the sacred messages (the priestly function) and the religious prophet who proclaims innovation and a break with tradition not on the basis of the official literature handed down through the generations (for Christians, the authority of Scripture) but because "I, your prophet, say so; I bring a new message and new insight." To the extent that the prophetic leader can convince people to accept his or her word, we see charisma at work.

As with "prophet," we have in "charisma" an overworked word. Currently, rock musicians, politicians, baseball players, business tycoons, movie stars, and many others "have charisma." As so used, people are trying to point out that the charismatic personage has special qualities that attract devoted followers, inspire high levels of emotion, and elevate the person so gifted well above the mundane level at which most of us function. Weber, however, restricted his use of the term to religion and in his own words called charisma "a certain quality" of a person by which she or he is "set apart from ordinary men" and possesses "supernatural, superhuman, or at least specifically exceptional powers or qualities."[11] And the prophet or prophetess with charisma "preaches, creates, or demands *new* obligations."[12] In other words, charismatic authority is revolutionary. A break with tradition is called for.

---

[9] James R. Wood, *Leadership in Voluntary Organizations* (New Brunswick, NJ: Rutgers University Press, 1981), p. 88.

[10] Weber identified a third type of religious leader—the magician—who performs magic rituals and acts that are consistent with our discussion in Chapter 1 of magic as a subtype of religion.

[11] Max Weber, *The Theory of Social and Economic Organization,*, trans. A. M. Henderson and Talcott Parsons (New York: Oxford University Press, 1947), p. 358.

[12] Weber, *The Theory of Social and Economic Organization*, p. 361.

TABLE 3-1   Clergy Roles

RANSON, BRYMAN, AND HININGS	BLIZZARD	HALL AND SCHNEIDER
Administrator of church affairs	Administrator	Organizer and Administrator
Celebrant of sacraments	Priest	Priest (leader of worship services)
Leader in the local community	—	—
Preacher of the word	Preacher	Preacher (giver of sermons)
Official (representative) of the church	Organizer	—
Pastor and father of the congregation	Pastor	Pastor (counseling)
Counselor (adviser and confessor)	—	—
—	Teacher	Teacher

Sources: Stewart Ranson, Alan Bryman, and Bob Hinings, *Clergy, Ministers and Priests* (London: Routledge & Kegan Paul, 1977), p. 62ff; Samuel W. Blizzard, "The Minister's Dilemma," *Christian Century* 73 (April 25, 1956), 508–510; Douglas T. Hall and Benjamin Schneider, *Organizational Climates and Careers* (New York: Seminar Press, 1973), pp. 25–26.

In contrast, most religious leaders are "priests." That is, they are representatives of established religious systems with a body of teaching and ritual to perpetuate. They are functionaries who are prized more for their faithfulness than their innovation.

But simply to distinguish between prophets and priests is not to say enough about the social functions of religious leaders, particularly those of "priests," who are by far the most common type of religious leader. Although we have hinted that the role of priest is fairly predictable and functions in a fairly conservative social system, the role functions of these religious leaders vary. In a study of Methodist ministers and Episcopalian and Roman Catholic priests in England, three British social scientists identify seven subroles for professional religious leaders. They are identified in Table 3–1.

What for years has been the classic list of clergy functions is that of Sam Blizzard, who identified six functions or subroles of American clergy. They are listed opposite their counterparts on the English list in Table 3–1. Blizzard called them "practitioner roles of parish ministers."[13] Hall and Schneider call them professional roles and refine the list to five (cf. Table 3–1). While the reader will recognize a great deal of consistency from list to list, always at issue for ministers is the question of the relative importance of these specific functions of the clergy role. Blizzard discusses how the clergy view the relative importance of these tasks and their order of preference in fulfilling them, yet reports a different ordering in actual practice. While the roles of "preacher" and "pastor" head both lists of importance and effectiveness, the role hit hardest in terms of clergy consensus about its relative

[13]Samuel W. Blizzard, "The Minister's Dilemma," *Christian Century* 73 (April 25, 1956), 508.

importance is "administration." The ordering in terms of importance that Blizzard finds in a survey of 690 ministers puts "administration" last. And it is next to last in their self-assessment of their effectiveness in carrying out that function. Yet administration consumes a higher proportion of their time than any other function. They reported two-fifths of their time spent on administration but only one-fifth as preacher and priest combined, one-quarter as pastor, one-tenth as organizer, and one-twentieth as teacher.[14]

In the Ranson, Bryman, and Hinings study of English clergy cited earlier, the ministers in all three groups listed their role as administrator next to last in importance—only slightly more important than the role of official representative of the local and denominational church organization. But they, too, like their North American counterparts, spend a great deal of their time as administrators.

Such a discrepancy between the ranking of clergy tasks in their order of importance and the actual time devoted to them is a source of personal frustration for ministers. And such discrepancies can be precursors of conflict between how ministers want to spend their time and how the congregation wants them to spend their time. This issue has surfaced as a significant problem within the past 30 to 35 years in the United States as many clergy have taken active roles in social action by participation in the civil rights movement, the antiwar movement, the nuclear freeze movement, the sanctuary movement, and the war on poverty.

Such participation has spelled trouble at home for many of these clergy activists. Although we will consider this subject again in Chapter 6, at this point we have to note that by "trouble" we mean mostly disagreement at the local, congregational level with respect to how much time and energy should be devoted to such activities by the ministers. The activist clergy have claimed that they are simply carrying out a standard, legitimate role of a religious leader, namely, that of "prophet." We are thus immediately back at Max Weber's distinction between prophetic and priestly roles. And as such, we have come full circle. We started this chapter by talking about groups and their control over people; we end on the note of tension within the group because leaders (the clergy) want to expand on the definition of the leadership role as it has traditionally been understood by the group.[15]

---

[14]Blizzard, "The Minister's Dilemma," 510.

[15]There will be further discussion of religious leadership in Chapter 10 as we look at "Women and Religion."

4

Becoming Religious

As we look at the impact of religion on society and the people that constitute society, we shall begin at the beginning, so to speak. That is, we shall look at the process by which people become religious in the first place. We assume that newborn infants have no "religious instincts." While they may have certain needs for which religion might, among other institutions as well, provide some satisfactions—such needs as security, protection, explanation, reinforcement (cf. Chapter 2)—they are not born with a ready-made religious system inside them just waiting to bloom. That they must learn, just as they learn language, table manners, and how to drive a car. All of this, including the learning of the contents of a particular religious system, is included within the fundamental social process called socialization. Thus we continue to work with the simple but basic observation that religion is a group phenomenon and that a member of a religious group is either born into it or joins it at some later stage in the life cycle; in either case she or he is taught the norms of the group and integrated into the life of the group. In this process the group socializes (it teaches and trains), and the individual internalizes the norms (he or she learns). Throughout this chapter we shall move back and forth between these two foci of the socialization or learning process.

ELEMENTS IN RELIGIOUS SOCIALIZATION

We begin with the group and the desire to socialize new members. The group desires to bring a person (a member) into a committed, functional relationship with other members of the group so that the new member knows what the group stands for, can fill a role within the group, and can help it reach its goals. Some of this process is nonstructured and occurs through informal contacts and interactions with other members; much of it is structured and formal, channeled through educational agencies and processes.

In "primitive" societies (that is, preliterate societies usually with a hunting and gathering economy), religious socialization, as with nearly all socialization, is primarily informal. Children gradually learn the beliefs and understandings of the group through conversation and by hearing their elders recount the sagas and tales passed down through the generations. In a similar manner, children learn practices associated with and growing out of religious beliefs. But through it all religious socialization is seldom distinguishable from general socialization in primitive societies, inasmuch as their members seldom distinguish the religious from other spheres of thought or knowledge.

There is nevertheless some degree of organization and planning in the socialization of primitive religion. For example, Wallace distinguishes two forms, in addition to individual expression, in which primitive religion is manifested: the shamanic and the communal. A shaman (such as a witch doctor or medicine man) is one who is believed to possess greater access to and control over mana and who performs service rituals for people. Obviously, viewing shamanic activity is a learning experience for the neophyte. Similarly, with the communal form of religious expression, conducted both by natural subcommunities (such as nuclear families, larger kinship groups, and affinity groups such as those determined by age or sex) and by the total community acting in concert, there are rites of passage from one stage in the life cycle to another (such as puberty rites), for example, or tribal totem celebrations in which everyone gathers around the symbol or symbols of their common origin and loyalty in order to reaffirm their unity as well as their common past.[1] Certainly a great deal of socialization and learning take place at all these levels of primitive religion. Nor do these forms of socialization disappear as societies evolve. A child observes the family religious activities so common in orthodox Buddhist and Confucian religious systems, and the congregational worship activities in the Judeo-Christian heritage. And the child learns.

---

[1]Anthony F. C. Wallace, *Religion: An Anthropological View* (New York: Random House, 1966), pp. 86–91.

However, although informal socialization still exists and remains influential in both agrarian and industrial societies, with the greater specialization of roles and differentiation of activities in these societies, religious socialization becomes more formalized. Religious teachers deliberately teach neophytes specifically religious norms, and formalized religious ceremonies are conducted during which neophytes learn about religious activities and gradually begin to participate in them.

The socializing or educative intent of religious groups is summarized in a classic manner by Jesus: "Go therefore and make disciples of all nations, . . . *teaching* them to observe all things whatsoever I have commanded you."[2] This refers to socialization pure and simple—transmitting knowledge as well as training in appropriate activities. Most religious groups view this process as a lifelong one. Worship services in the Western tradition are in significant ways of a socializing nature, extending or expanding on what is already known. A sermon, for example, expounds and explains, not simply exhorts and directs. The various communal ceremonies of most religious groups, in fact, are fundamentally socializing experiences. In addition to adoring the deity through giving praise and performing rituals believed to please him or her, joint activities perform a reinforcement function, reminding participants of their beliefs and of how they are to conduct themselves before the deity.

Worship services and ceremonial gatherings may also bring about the conversion or full commitment of newcomers, another aspect of socialization. When people hear something or learn something that moves them to attach themselves to the group, socialization has begun; now formal educational processes take over. The person's commitment is also reinforced through new informal socialization contacts.

Thus several things are involved in religious socialization. First the group convinces the newcomer to make a commitment to the group and what it stands for, often with little knowledge or contact. (By newcomer we mean either a potential convert or the child of a group member.) Second, there is the core process of building on that commitment through teaching the newcomer the norms of the group—its beliefs and appropriate behaviors and rituals. (Note that these stages are interchangeable—that is, people may be involved in the process of learning norms for some time before being converted or committing themselves.) Third, the group tries to extend its influence over the person to those situations where she or he is not in direct contact with the group or its members. That is, the group tries to influence *all* the individual's values; this is essentially the morality dimension that many suggest is an integral feature of religion. Finally, there is the reinforcement and encouragement aspect of continuing socialization. One reason religious groups encourage their members to continue participating

[2]Matthew 28:19–20 (Revised Standard Version). Emphasis added.

in ceremonies, attending education classes, and listening to sermons after having learned the "basics" of the religion is to "strengthen" and reinforce the members' commitment.

METHODS OF RELIGIOUS SOCIALIZATION

Formal Methods

We have already touched on the socialization methods of religious groups. At this point we need merely to systematize them. There is first the formal mechanism that most religious groups establish—an educational system. All groups establish explicit teaching activities, which may take the form of a guru gathering a few persons around him, an evangelist on a tree stump or a soapbox, a Bar Mitzvah preparatory class, or a Sunday sermon. The teaching function has been an integral and important part of religion from the beginning of the major religious systems that exist worldwide today. Certainly the founder of any religion or religious group teaches as he or she tries to get across his or her message and vision. Once established, the religious group uses diverse methods, both formal and informal, to get across its ideas and the body of its knowledge, beliefs, and practices to the neophyte member. The effectiveness of such socialization is a major topic of this chapter and is discussed at several points in the chapters that follow.

Informal Methods

Another way in which socialization takes place is informally—through interaction with the members of a religious group. Such socialization or learning from others occurs in all kinds of groups, of course. The general socialization of children into the society that occurs through interaction with peers, for example, is of primary importance and well documented. And it is popular knowledge that what you learn from associates in a work group through casual conversation is at least as important—if not more so—than the socialization that occurs through participating in formal orientation programs or by studying job descriptions.

Those who have been introduced elsewhere to major sociological concepts and theories will recognize this as an application of "symbolic interactionism." That is a widely held theory of socialization and learning which holds that the primary and certainly most effective and long-lasting method of teaching what the group stands for and wants done is through imitation and emulation, through mimicking and role taking. That is, we observe, then we do. Children mimic the behavior of adults and other children around them. This theory objects in particular to another widely held theory called the "behavioral learning theory." It suggests that people learn what the group wants by being rewarded for "appropriate" behavior and punished for "inappropriate" behavior—positive and negative reinforcement.

Interestingly, many religious groups recognize the importance of informal socialization and consequently often deliberately encourage it. A term frequently used by religious groups in this connection is *fellowship;* members of religious groups are encouraged "to fellowship" with fellow members. Such formal mechanisms as religious youth groups, men's clubs, ladies' auxiliaries, and senior citizens' groups are organized in great part with the hope and expectation that members of the larger organization—for example, the congregation—will develop friendships and maintain ties outside formal religious contexts. What is involved here is recognition of the importance of reinforcement—through continued and frequent contact with others of your religious group, the formal norms and beliefs you have been taught and have accepted will be reinforced and, as it is often expressed, "your faith will be strengthened."

Considerable empirical evidence has been gathered that tends to support this strategy, though it is difficult to determine which is cause and which effect—whether such contact strengthens one's faith, or whether those of strong faith seek out fellowship in the first place. Thus studies have shown that the person whose close personal friends are mainly members of his or her religious group tends to be more orthodox in his or her beliefs, a more regular participant in religious organization. Glock and Stark, for example, constructed an index of "religious experience," based on whether respondents were certain of having "a feeling [of being] somehow in the presence of God," "a sense of being saved in Christ," and "a feeling of being punished by God for something you had done." Almost invariably, regardless of Christian denomination, respondents with a greater number of best friends who were also members of their congregation scored higher on this index.[3]

An intensive extension of the fellowship mechanism for religious socialization occurs through marriage. Religious groups urge endogamy—that is, marriage within the group—assuming (rightly) that a marriage between two persons from the same religious group will encourage both persons to participate and remain with the group. Intermarriage with a person of another religious group introduces the risk of losing your member to the other group, and may reduce the level of participation and commitment of your member even if he or she does not defect. There is of course the possibility of gaining a new member through intermarriage of one of your members with an outsider. Some groups in fact appear to be net gainers

---

[3]Charles Y. Glock and Rodney Stark, *Religion and Society in Tension* (Chicago: Rand McNally, 1965), p. 164.

through this process. Yet few groups wish to advocate such an approach because of the risks involved. Thus, religious groups have traditionally forbidden (or all but forbidden) interfaith marriage. Until very recently Roman Catholics, for example, could not be married by a priest in church if the non-Catholic partner refused to join the Catholic Church or would not sign a statement agreeing that any children born of the marriage would be reared as Catholics. Many Orthodox Jewish families ostracize children who marry Gentiles. In the face of high rates of interfaith marriage, most groups have been relenting on this issue, although the official stance of discouraging interfaith marriage remains.

MEASURING THE IMPACT OF RELIGIOUS SOCIALIZATION

And so religious socialization goes on in both formal and informal ways. That is simple enough. But how effective is religion in this socialization process, and how do we measure its effectiveness? Also, how do we measure religiosity in the first place?

"Religiosity" usually describes the intensity and consistency of a person's practice of his or her religion. A person strongly committed to a religious system is concerned about him or herself, first of all, but concerned about others in the group as well.

Certainly individuals who are committed to a particular religious system are concerned about whether they meet their group's criteria for being religious: Am I a true believer? Have I committed the unpardonable sin? Are there any signs and indications that tell me whether I measure up or not?

Christian theologians talk about "marks" of Christianity, and theologians of every belief pore over sacred scriptures trying to distill the essential characteristics and behavior that sets the true believer apart from all others. "Do you believe in Jesus Christ as your only Savior?" "Do you bow toward Mecca at the specified five times daily?" "Do you belong to the Catholic Church and attend mass at least the minimum prescribed number of times a year?" "Do you abstain from pork and study Torah faithfully?"

Denominational administrators seek "indicators" of religiosity for the purpose of evaluating their programs. If, for example, certain congregations in their jurisdiction participate in a "Religious Enrichment Seminar" and consequently increase their contributions to the denomination's general fund, administrators may reason that this is a program to be urged on all the other congregations. Or if people who attended the denomination's parochial schools now attend church more often, contribute higher proportions of their income, and participate in the organizational life of the congregation more extensively than those who did not attend such schools, then such schools are most likely regarded as accomplishing their religious purpose.

Researchers in the sociology of religion also continually search for valid ways of defining the concept of "being religious"—what we will be calling religiosity from now on. Sociologists are specifically interested in identifying what constitutes religiosity for the purpose of measuring it in relation to other factors: Is the religious person different from a nonreligious person in any other respects? And if so, how? Is the religious person more humanitarian or less so? Is he or she more prejudiced or less? More economically successful or less? More likely to be politically liberal? Better "adjusted"? And so on.

One place to start in our attempt to define religiosity is the definition of religion that we arrived at in Chapter 1: Religion is a set of beliefs and practices, centered around a belief in the supernatural and an orientation toward the sacred, that are shared by members of a group. Thus we could say that anyone who is a member of a religious group, who believes certain things about the supernatural and the sacred, and who engages in certain activities associated with these beliefs is a religious person, and that everyone else is not. Would that it were so simple!

Some religious groups have approximated this approach in trying to distinguish the religious from the irreligious person. Historically, the Roman Catholic Church has maintained that any member who participated in a specified minimum number of ritual activities was a saved member of Christ's church, and that all others were not. Lutherans tended toward this approach also, identifying the true church and its members wherever the Word of God was taught and preached in purity, and wherever the sacraments were correctly administered.

Such neat definitions, however, leave several questions unanswered. Should any distinction be made, for example, between those who evidence maximum participation in the group's ritual activities and those who just "get by" with minimal participation? Or are such extremes to be considered equally religious when compared with others who do not participate in these activities at all? And what about the person who occasionally participates in the ritual but has not made a membership commitment? Is he or she therefore not religious? Or what about the person who participates occasionally, and who is a member, but actually is a disbeliever or at least doubts some of the group's central beliefs? Some people are more sincere in their religious beliefs than others; some are more enthusiastic in their ritual participation than others. Some "leave their religion at the church door," while others attempt to apply it in all life situations. Are all of these people religious? And if so, are they equally religious? And what about the person who shares a group's belief but prefers to mediate and worship on his or her own?

Our definition of religion is less helpful than we might hope in determining people's religiosity because of a fundamental principle of sociology, namely, that most any characteristic that can be attributed to a given social phenomenon exists at some point on a *continuum*. That is, such characteristics typically are neither totally present nor totally absent, but exist to a greater or lesser degree along a range from high to low. For example, among business organizations classified as bureaucracies some organizations are more highly bureaucratized than others. Bureaucratic organizations may therefore be ranked from high to low along a continuum called "bureaucracy." Nations, to take another example, can be arranged along a continuum called "industrialization." Or people along continua called "authoritarianism," "prejudice," "self-motivation," and so on.

Similarly it is likely that people, if not organizations, may be located at various points on a continuum called "religiousness" or "religiosity." People intuitively assume this when they make statements and comparisons such as those that begin this chapter. Our problem here, however, is how to *operationalize* the concept of religiosity—how to translate such feelings into terms of observable characteristics that will permit us to make meaningful comparisons among people. Realize, of course, that we embark on this process, not in order to make invidious comparisons among people or to judge them, but solely in order to be able to determine the impact of the different ways in which people feel and express their religiosity.

Sociologists take two basic approaches to defining religiosity and applying it to their research. The first approach centers on people's affiliations with religious organizations or groups, according to which sociologists attempt to predict and observe differences in people's behavior and attitudes. Technically this approach focuses not so much on religiosity (which involves something going on inside the individual) as it does on the organization itself. This is appropriate because whenever we talk about the effect of religion on people's behavior we are assuming a religious group's influence somewhere along the line. The second approach to identifying religiosity deals with individuals and tends to disregard religious affiliations except as a possible control variable.

SOCIOLOGICAL DEFINITIONS OF RELIGIOSITY: GROUP AFFILIATION

First, we will look at the group affiliation approach. There are two principal variants here—really simply a matter of how specific the researcher wishes to become. The first is to categorize people according to major religious families, such as Protestant, Catholic, and Jewish (in Western societies), or Hindu, Muslim, Buddhist, and Christian (in Asian societies), or any number of other relevant sets of affiliations. Extensive research using such religious distinctions has been fruitful in showing different attitudes and behavior among such major groupings. Data from national surveys between 1972 and 1984 reveal that whereas only 11 percent of conservative Protestants, 23 percent of moderate Protestants, and 31 percent of Catholics believe homosexuality is not immoral, 64 percent of Jews and 90 percent of Unitarian-Universalists hold this tolerant view of homosexuality.[4] In the same surveys it was found that while 91 percent of Unitarian-Universalists and 76 percent of Jews believe abortion should be available to women without restriction, only 9 percent of the members of the Assemblies of God—a conservative Protestant church—agree with that view.[5] In a Gallup Poll survey 72 percent of Southern Baptists say religion is very important in their lives; only 37 percent of Episcopalians and 25 percent of Jews so assert.[6]

Gerhard Lenski's 1959 survey in Detroit revealed that only 11 percent of Jews, but 34 percent of white Protestants, 38 percent of black Protestants, and 66 percent of white Catholics, felt that divorce was always or usually wrong.[7] Questions about political party preference from the same survey revealed that the Republican party was preferred by 54 percent of white Protestants, 30 percent of white Catholics, 13 percent of black Protestants, and 3 percent of Jews.[8] These are only a few of the almost endless list of research findings documenting fairly dramatic differences in attitude, behavior, and commitment among major religious groupings.

By the early 1960s, however, many sociologists began to point out that while research showing differences among such major groupings as Protestants, Catholics, and Jews may be revealing, it also tends to hide almost as much as it reveals, for these categories are still so broad that they obscure significant internal diversity. Primary objection focused on the Protestant category, which includes fundamentalists and other extremely conservative groups as well as theologically liberal groups that reject much of traditional Christian doctrine. Similar problems were seen to exist for the Catholic and Jewish categories as well—there are both liberal and conservative Catholics, and there are Reform, Conservative, and Orthodox Jews.

Moreover, in surveys, even fairly large (and expensive) samples do not include enough members of, say, the various subcategories of Protestantism to make meaningful comparisons. For example, suppose you wanted to analyze social differences among various religious groups in the United States and at some point decided to make specific comparisons between Unitari-

[4]National Opinion Research Center data reported in Wade Clark Roof and William McKinney, *American Mainline Religion* (New Brunswick, NJ: Rutgers University Press, 1987), pp. 211–212.

[5]Ibid.

[6]George Gallup, *Religion in America 1984*, Gallup Report No. 222 (Princeton, NJ: Princeton Religion Research Center, 1984), p. 23.

[7]Gerhard E. Lenski, *The Religious Factor* (Garden City, NY: Doubleday, 1961), p. 150.

[8]Ibid., p. 125.

ans and Mennonites—two groups nearly at opposite extremes on a continuum called "Protestantism." Suppose you had been able to afford to survey a fairly large sample of one thousand persons representative of the United States population. Suppose also that your sampling techniques had worked perfectly and you had picked a truly proportionate representative sample. You would then find when you went to your sample, theoretically at least, exactly eight-tenths of one Unitarian and nine-tenths of one Mennonite. You would also get only one-and-eight-tenths Seventh Day Adventists, nine Mormons, and eleven members of the United Church of Christ—hardly a sufficient number of any of these groups (not to mention a host of other small religious groups) to reach valid conclusions about any of them.

Mainline Protestant church bodies, however, such as Presbyterians, Methodists, Lutherans, Baptists, and Episcopalians, each have many more members; consequently they can provide sufficient numbers in national or area samples of a thousand or more persons to justify making comparisons among them. Thus evolved the second stage of utilizing religious affiliation as an independent variable when major subcategories of Protestants began to be studied. The research team of Charles Glock and Rodney Stark of the University of California at Berkeley, who were among the first to use this approach extensively, found significant differences among major Protestant denominations that one might have thought existed only among smaller groups which tend to hold more extreme views. For example, Glock and Stark discovered that on such a fundamental doctrinal question as the divinity of Jesus the proportion of members of major Protestant bodies who accept without reservation the traditional view—namely, that Jesus is the Son of God—and admit to having no personal doubts about it are as follows: 40 percent of Congregationalists, 54 percent of Methodists, 59 percent of Episcopalians, 72 percent of Presbyterians, 74 percent of Disciples of Christ, 74 percent of American Lutherans, 76 percent of American Baptists, 93 percent of Missouri Synod Lutherans, and 99 percent of Southern Baptists.[9] Differences among the same Protestant groups on the question of miracles is even more dramatic. The proportion of those who believe that miracles actually happened as described in the Bible are as follows: 28 percent of Congregationalists, 37 percent of Methodists, 41 percent of Episcopalians, 58 percent of Presbyterians, 62 percent of the Disciples of Christ, 62 percent of American Baptists, 69 percent of American Lutherans, 89 percent of Missouri Synod Lutherans, and 92 percent of Southern Baptists.[10] Or consider the somewhat less dramatic but still significant differences in proportion of persons who agree with the statement, "The races would probably get along just fine in this country if Communists and other

[9]Charles Y. Glock and Rodney Stark, *Christian Beliefs and Anti-Semitism* (New York: Harper & Row, Pub., 1966), p. 7.

[10]Ibid., p. 10.

radicals didn't stir up trouble": 33 percent of Congregationalists, 36 percent of Methodists and Disciples of Christ, 45 percent of both Episcopalians and American Baptists, 46 percent of Presbyterians, 50 percent of Missouri Synod Lutherans, 56 percent of American Lutherans, and 70 percent of Southern Baptists.[11] Religious affiliation among subdenominations within Protestantism apparently makes a difference.

It is perhaps becoming obvious that we are straying from a strict definition or understanding of religiosity. We have indicated some of the major ways in which researchers have attempted to operationalize the concept of religiosity—that is identify a quantifiable measure that seems to measure or "get at" something of what religion is—in order to assess its effect or impact on people's behavior.

The two types of measurement we have already looked at are in reality subtypes of the affiliation measure, which focuses on the religious group to which a person belongs. In such cases how do we know whether a person is religious? We may simply consider a person religious if he or she professes to be a Protestant, a Catholic, a Jew, or a member of any other religious group, while the nonmember would be considered nonreligious, or at most less religious than the member. Although ultimately we may want to talk about the religiosity of individual people, we wind up focusing on the general or central tendencies of groups and differences among those groups—an important focus indeed, but hardly the whole package. At most, the focus on group differences measures the effect of formal religious differences among groups, primarily differences in belief and doctrine. What we lack are measures of differentiation in intensity or sincerity of belief and degree of religious interest. Such ideas are closer to the concept of individual religiosity, which presupposes a difference of degree of commitment and interest in religious ideas, religious answers or solutions, and religious participation.

SOCIOLOGICAL DEFINITIONS OF RELIGIOSITY: THE INDIVIDUAL APPROACH

We now focus on major attempts by sociologists to measure religiosity defined more narrowly as the degree and type of commitment to religious values and norms.

Although it has not always been recognized, there is great diversity within each group discussed in the preceding section, a fact illustrated by the historical development of the attempts to measure differences related to religious group affiliation. While research that contrasted the major catego-

[11]Ibid., p. 168.

ries of Protestants, Catholics, and Jews exposed numerous differences, such broad and inclusive categories have been recognized to be just that—inclusive of a great deal of internal diversity, as numerous studies, including those by Glock and Stark, have documented. Implicit in the data from such studies, though not always discussed, are great differences within each of the subgroups, as well. For example, although only 28 percent of Congregationalists, but 92 percent of Southern Baptists, believe in miracles, there nevertheless exists within each of these groups internal differentiation—differentiation which is even more obvious within the other Protestant groups that fall between the Congregationalists and Southern Baptists as reported earlier in this chapter. In other words, although 72 percent of Congregationalists do *not* believe in miracles, 28 percent *do* believe in them; although 42 percent of Presbyterians do not believe in miracles, 58 percent do believe in them; and so on. How do we explain such internal diversity? Why do some members of a group accept one belief, practice, or social perspective, while other members do not?

Measures of Individual Ritual Participation

Such questions have led some researchers to ignore, at least temporarily, formal group differences and regroup—or more accurately, recategorize—people on other bases, such as types of commitment, intensity of belief, and so on. An early attempt along these lines, one which has subsequently been widely used, is based on *ritual participation*, or the frequency with which people attend the formal religious services of their religious group. Thus those who report attending weekly or nearly every week might be categorized as demonstrating a "high" degree of religiosity; those attending once or twice a month would perhaps be categorized as showing a "moderate" degree; and those attending less often would be classed "low" on this scale. Refinements of this measure into a five-point scale (with the addition of "moderately high" and "moderately low" categories), and even a seven-point scale, have been used. Other factors, such as frequency of participation in other activities sponsored by the religious group, have been included by some researchers. Commonly, when Protestants and Catholics are major components in the study, frequency of attendance at the sacrament of Communion, or the Lord's Supper, is used as a measure of religiosity. Quite obviously such measures attempt to assess variations in the intensity of commitment and the importance of religion to the individual.

But many researchers have objected that such a procedure does not really measure religiosity, that attendance statistics tell us nothing about how a given individual *feels* about attendance. A person's regular attendance may be simply a result of habit, and so it may mean relatively little to him or her personally. Or, a person's regular attendance may be due to family or other group pressures—he or she may not want to disappoint grandmother, or to give an employer cause to question his or her morality. Or perhaps a person attends regularly because he or she looks forward to the opportunity to socialize with friends after services.

Other Measures of Individual Religiosity

Such objections have spurred attempts to measure religiosity by other means. One method has been to ask people about their prayer life—focusing again, however, as with church attendance, on frequency. The reasoning here is that if a person reports engaging frequently in personal, private prayer (where "frequently" is usually defined as at least daily), then religion is likely more meaningful and important to him or her than it is to one who prays only occasionally or one who never prays except in groups, as in formal religious services.

Other measures that try to probe just a little more into the subjective feelings and commitments of people rely on respondents' ability, in interviews and questionnaires, to categorize themselves in terms of their personal commitment to religion and to evaluate how important religion is to them personally. These measures, occasionally composites or indexes based on more than one question, vary from one study to another, but usually are based on questions such as, "How important would you say religion is in your life—very important, somewhat important, not very important, or not at all important?" Or, "All in all, how important would you say your church membership is to you?"

Evaluation of Individual Measures of Religiosity

All the attempts to operationalize the concept of religiosity that we have mentioned in this section have in common the fact that each relies on a single measure, or on a single set of measures—for example, combining frequency of church attendance with frequency of Communion attendance, or frequency of personal prayer with extent of involvement in the total organizational life of a congregation. Such measures of religiosity have revealed significant differences among people. For example, a 1960 survey revealed that among white southern college students those who attended church were somewhat more prejudiced against blacks than those who never attended—although there were also strong indications that among the churchgoers those who attended more frequently were less prejudiced than infrequent churchgoers.[12] Or, to cite another brief example, among

[12]R. K. Young, W. M. Benson, and W. H. Holtzman, "Changes in Attitudes toward the Negro in a Southern University," *Journal of Abnormal and Social Psychology* 60, no. 1 (1960), 131–133.

American middle-class men those who attend church more regularly tend to be more upwardly mobile.[13]

Differences of this sort, however, have not been so great or so consistent as some researchers had anticipated. The primary reason, according to recent research, seems to be that religiosity is not a one-dimensional phenomenon. That is, not all people are religious in the same way. A person may rank high in religiosity on one dimension or measure, but low on another or several others. Thus if certain behavior is correlated with a high score on one scale of religiosity but a low score on another, then entirely different conclusions could be reached concerning the impact of religion on that behavior, depending upon which measure of religiosity was used.

SOCIOLOGICAL MEASURES OF RELIGIOSITY: MULTIDIMENSIONAL MEASURES

Several researchers, taking a multidimensional view of religion, have either combined several specific measures into a composite of some kind or utilized several discrete measures. The rationale for such approaches is that religion is not a single, uniform entity that can be apprehended by any single measure; rather, people can "be religious" in various ways.

In works published in 1951 and 1954 Joseph Fichter distinguished four ways in which a person could be a Catholic.[14] Based on attendance at mass, participation in confession, sending children to parochial school, other involvement in church subgroups, and expressed religious interest, Fichter constructed the typology of *nuclear Catholic, modal Catholic, marginal Catholic,* and *dormant Catholic.* Nuclear Catholics go beyond minimal requirements of membership, are active in parish life, and attend Holy Communion at least weekly. Such "ideal" members in Fichter's second (1954) sample were found to comprise only 5.7 percent of all Catholics.[15] Modal Catholics comprised about 70 percent of the membership and were described by Fichter as follows:

> Since the modal parishioner holds a position midway between the nuclear and the marginal Catholic, he may be said to live up to his religion in a "middling sort of way." He generally observes the Friday abstinence and knows the difference between Advent and Lent. His name is likely to be on the roster of the Holy Name Society at some time during his life, but he hardly ever attends a meeting. He attends Sunday Mass most of the time but has difficulty "catching Mass" when holy days of obligation occur during the working week. His chil-

---

[13]Lenski, *The Religious Factor,* p. 103.

[14]Joseph Fichter, *Southern Parish* (Chicago: University of Chicago Press, 1951); idem. *Social Relations in the Urban Parish* (Chicago: University of Chicago Press, 1954).

[15]Ibid., p. 24.

dren fill the parochial schools, and he has a kind of aloof respect for priests and nuns.[16]

The marginal Catholic (about 20 percent of Catholics) considers her- or himself to be a member of the Catholic Church and tends to be so considered by the church itself, yet may not have attended mass during the past year, may not have received Holy Communion or participated in confession, and the children in the family do not attend Catholic parochial school.[17] The dormant Catholic is one who was born into a Catholic family, baptized as a Catholic, may have been married by a priest, and perhaps asks for a priest's services as death approaches, yet is not a formal member of a Catholic congregation.[18]

It should be fairly clear from earlier comments that Fichter's typology is a simple one in the sense that his measure of religiosity essentially involves only ritual and formal participation in a religious organization. Excluded are several dimensions we have hinted at earlier and others we will be identifying as we proceed. Yet his typology made an important contribution, particularly in that it stimulated others to expand and improve on his work.

Glock and Stark found that people can be religious in several ways and that the same person can exhibit more than one way of being religious at the same time. Glock first identified four dimensions: the *experiential*, which attempts to measure the degree of emotional attachment to the supernatural; the *ritualistic*, which counts the rate of participation in the group's activities; the *ideological*, which refers to the degree of commitment to the religious beliefs of a person's group; and the *consequential*, which refers to the impact of religious commitment and involvement on an individual's general behavior.[19] Later Glock added a fifth dimension—the *intellectual*—which measures the degree of knowledgeability about the formal beliefs of a person's religion.[20] Still later Glock, together with his colleague Rodney Stark, subdivided the ritualistic dimension into two parts: ritual and devotion. *Ritual* includes such formal religious activities as attending religious services and taking Communion—what can be called public activities. *Devotion* includes such behavior as praying and studying sacred books and religious writings.[21]

---

[16]Ibid., p. 41.

[17]Ibid., pp. 61–62.

[18]Ibid., p. 69.

[19]Charles Y. Glock, "The Religious Revival in America," in *Religion and the Face of America*, ed. Jane Zahn (Berkeley, CA: University Extension, University of California, 1959), pp. 25–42.

[20]Charles Y. Glock, "On the Study of Religious Commitment," *Religious Education* 62, no. 4 (1962), 98–110.

[21]Rodney Stark and Charles Y. Glock, *American Piety: The Nature of Religious Commitment* (Berkeley, CA: University of California Press, 1968), p. 15.

The above formulations have stimulated considerable research and elaboration by social scientists. An important outcome has been a consensus that religiosity is multidimensional. Thus a person may score high on one dimension and be termed "very religious," yet score low on one or more other measures and be identified as only "slightly religious" or even "irreligious." For example, people may know religious teachings or doctrines inside and out, yet seldom or never attend religious services, never engage in devotional activities, disbelieve what they know intellectually about their religion, and evidence no effect of religious knowledge on their behavior. The fact that a person believes in and is committed to orthodox doctrine does not necessarily mean that he or she engages in an active devotional life, possesses extensive intellectual knowledge of her or his religious system, or shows any effect of faith on his or her daily life.

It is important to be aware of the many ways in which people can be religious because by relying on only one—for example, "religious knowledge" or "participation in religious activities"—we might seriously misrepresent the level of religiosity inherent in people.

Consider these research findings. Schroeder and Obenhaus, for example, note in a study of an Iowa town that among church members with above average intellectual ability and a strong commitment to and involvement in church life, less than half were able to relate a reasonably accurate version of the story of the good Samaritan.[22]

In my study of Lutheran youth, only 8.7 percent of those sampled who attended church services regularly and also attended a parochial school could correctly identify Nathanael as one of Jesus' disciples, and only 25 percent correctly identified Enoch as the Old Testament character who is described as never experiencing physical death.[23] Similarly, in a 1970 nationwide survey of adults, only 15 percent correctly identified five prominent biblical figures (Moses, Daniel, Jonah, Peter, Paul). In fact, a greater number of respondents (17.5 percent) were unable to identify even a single figure, and less than half (46.4 percent) were able to identify three.[24]

If we relied solely on religious/biblical knowledge to measure degree of religiosity, then, few would be identified as having even a moderate level of religiosity. This applies also to using the frequency of church/synagogue attendance as a single measure of religious participation, involvement, and commitment. In one national survey, fully 34 percent of those who were members of religious groups attended religious services either never or, at best, seldom (less than once a month), and 53 percent attended less than

[22]W. W. Schroeder and Victor Obenhaus, *Religion in American Culture* (New York: Free Press, 1964), p. 147.

[23]Ronald L. Johnstone, *The Effectiveness of Lutheran Elementary and Secondary Schools as Agencies of Christian Education* (St. Louis: Concordia Seminary Research Center, 1966), p. 100.

[24]Ronald L. Johnstone (project director), national survey data gathered by the National Opinion Research Center for the Lutheran Council in the U.S.A., 1970.

once a week.[25] Gallup Poll data corroborate those percentages. In a sample representing all adults (not just members of churches/synagogues), about 60 percent of the U.S. population 18 years of age and older do not attend church or synagogue on any given weekend.[26] Yet some, and perhaps many, of those not in attendance would describe themselves as "religious people."

INTERNALIZATION OF RELIGION

We have been focusing primarily on the agents and processes of religious socialization, and in assessing the effectiveness of such socialization we have focused on the group. We now turn to the obverse of socialization—namely, internalization. What are some of the processes involved, stages of development, and differences in outcome for individuals who are being socialized?

In considering the process of the internalization of religion we are immediately required to distinguish between those who internalize the religious concepts and practices of a group from birth and those who undergo a conversion experience at some later point in life. We first look at the most common pattern—that of "growing up religious" within a particular religious context.

"Growing Up Religious"

A fundamental observation is that individuals internalize the religion of their group essentially the same way they learn the language of their culture, or their sex role, or the lifestyle of their social class. The process is intimately tied up with the development of one's personality and the evolution of one's concept of self. A person internalizes—makes a part of himself or herself—what he or she hears, sees, and both consciously and subconsciously considers applicable to himself or herself. The person hears words, is introduced to concepts, and is confronted with various phenomena at the intellectual, or cognitive, level. But he or she also—especially initially—emulates or imitates what he or she sees. In a sense the person absorbs many patterns, norms, and values through the experience of seeing them exemplified by parents, peers, and others long before he or she confronts them intellectually.

Just as children learn to talk before they are exposed to the rules of grammar and spelling, so they attain an orientation toward the supernatu-

---

[25]Ibid.

[26]Constant H. Jacquet, Jr., ed., *Yearbook of American Churches, 1989* (Nashville: Abingdon Press, 1989), p. 277.

ral (and, if they are Christian, perhaps a concept of self as a sinner) long before they confront such issues in the form of religious doctrines and propositions.

This orientation fits into the broad framework of the development of the self—a process in which religion plays a part. Early in the process of this development the child becomes aware of himself or herself not simply as an "I" or subject—the center of the universe, so to speak—but also as a "me," an object with certain characteristics that others react to and interact with. They begin to learn how others expect them to behave if they are to interact successfully as well as satisfy their personal needs. Children begin to see themselves from various perspectives and in various roles—male or female, son or daughter, friend or stranger, American or foreigner, and so on. As they are exposed to religious influences in the family and in the family's religious group, they also acquire the rudiments of a religious self. They begin to regard themselves as related not only to the so-called natural and social worlds of things and people that they see and interact with, but also as related to an unseen world of the supernatural. They begin to have an orientation toward the sacred, however, that is defined by the group. As they begin to see themselves in relation to that other world, they expand their image of self accordingly.

At this point, depending on the specific religious group context, great diversity may appear. One child begins to see herself as a worthless sinner utterly helpless in the face of the supernatural, while another sees himself as a special object of creation with great worth and potential. For most, a combination of both perspectives applies. In any case, the individual becomes aware of unseen powers in the universe. To some extent this may be comforting knowledge, a convenient way of explaining much that is incomprehensible. To some extent it may be frightening, particularly as they consider or learn the ways in which they can incur the wrath of those supernatural powers and even be punished by them.

In short, then, what children learn about themselves from religious group sources supplements what they are learning about themselves from interaction with playmates, television, siblings, and so on. Initially this learning is almost exclusively through informal observing and intuiting, only later to be supplemented by more formal cognitive learning. Most children in any society in fact derive some of their self-concept from religious sources, even if they are born into families who espouse no formal religious group affiliation. For everyone is at least indirectly influenced by religion through contact with other people and institutions.

It will be obvious to some readers that the foregoing description of the process of internalizing religion leans heavily on the symbolic interaction perspective in sociology, a basic premise of which is that people relate to things, events, and other people on the basis of the meanings they assign to them. These meanings in turn develop within the person during the process of social interaction. The religious expressions of other people and the religious institutions themselves contribute to the construct of meanings people develop. Obviously the particular set of observations and interactions that a given individual makes and experiences has a crucial influence on whatever religious meanings develop within him or her.

Gaining Religious Identity

Although religious socialization primarily aims at providing a person with an appropriate stance in relation to the supernatural and instructs her or him in the nature and function of the supernatural, another important socialization process involves teaching the child her or his religious identity. David Elkind has conducted research that indicates that even this process is complex. Children, he contends, proceed through certain stages in learning who they are religiously. Thus a child of five who says, "I am a Catholic" understands that identification differently from a child of nine or a child of twelve. Elkind found that from the age of five or six most children know their religious identity and will freely admit they are, say, Protestant, or Catholic, or Jewish. But such an identity for them is not at all what it is for older children or adults. The young child tends to confuse religious identity with nationality and racial designations. Their religious identification is a name with no clear referent. By eight or nine years of age, however, children have a more concrete conception of their religious identity. They can distinguish religious from nonreligious designations and can attach behavioral description to various religious groups. Yet, it is not till the age of ten to twelve that an abstract dimension of religious identification is added—only then do youngsters begin to speak of cognitive elements such as beliefs and try to explain why particular religious groups engage in certain activities.[27]

The Role of the Family

As mentioned earlier in this chapter, much religious socialization occurs outside the formal structure of the organization, with a significant portion taking place in family interaction. Religious groups recognize this. Some have programs that focus on trying to help parents perform this task, while others at least point out the importance of the family. However, John L. Thomas, a Jesuit sociologist, found through research that the kind of religious socialization that the Catholic Church hopes parents will conduct

[27]David Elkind, "Age Changes in the Meaning of Religious Identity," *Review of Religious Research* 6, no. 1 (1964), 36–40.

for their children is not in fact occurring on the scale expected. Thomas states that although persons professionally involved in promoting organized religion agree that an important function of the family is the inculcation of religious beliefs and practices in their children, he finds that the religious training of the Catholic preschool child at home falls far short of traditional expectations.[28] Family influences are nevertheless significant in the sense of reinforcing and filtering religious influences from elsewhere, particularly from formal agencies such as parochial schools, as noted earlier.

In a study of male college students, Gordon Allport and his associates found that family influence was extremely important regarding their present "need" for some form of religious orientation or belief system. They found that a firmly declared need continued for 82 percent of those who had what they termed an "outstanding" religious education during their childhood. Religious need was expressed by decreasing proportions of students as the quality of their childhood religious socialization declined. Thus 78 percent of those who received an "ordinary" religious education, 52 percent of those who described their religious socialization as "superficial," and only 32 percent of those who received no religious education described themselves as having a present clear need for religion.[29] Although the measure of religious socialization or "upbringing" used by Allport does not distinguish family socialization from the socialization stemming from the religious institution itself, it seems reasonable to assume, with the authors, that the prime referent is the influence and training of the family.

The family's religious influence can be important in negative ways as well. For example, John Kotre studied graduate students who had attended Catholic schools for sixteen years, some of whom were still "in" the Catholic church while others were "out," and found a strong correlation between being "out" and the existence of religious conflict in the home—conflict operationally defined as either an interfaith marriage or one parent a nonpracticing Catholic.[30]

RELIGIOUS CONVERSION

As stated at the outset of the preceding section, the process of internalizing religion and developing the religious self is, so far as can be determined,

---

[28]John L. Thomas, "Religious Training in the Roman Catholic Family," *American Journal of Sociology* 62, no. 2 (1951), 178–83.

[29]Gordon W. Allport, J. M. Gillespie, and J. Young. "The Religion of the Post-War College Student," *Journal of Psychology* 25, no. 1 (1948), 3–33.

[30]John Kotre, *The View from the Border* (Chicago: Aldine, 1971), p. 143.

essentially similar to the process of internalizing other knowledge, beliefs, and skills, and merely adds another dimension to one's initial concept of self. A more dramatic form of religious internalization is that of conversion.

We shall not delve deeply into the conversion phenomenon itself, which is strongly psychological in nature and for the most part nonempirical. We cannot, for example, determine whether a particular individual's conversion is in fact a personal experience with God Himself in which the Holy Spirit enters the person and leads him or her to certain convictions. We can, however, provide some sociological insight into the context within which conversions occur, point out that conversion is not wholly a psychological phenomenon, and note that it does not occur in a wholly religious context as distinct from a social one.

The Group Context

First we must note the somewhat obvious yet important fact that conversion as a form of behavior or process is affected by the group within which it occurs. That is, what constitutes conversion, what one can expect to experience, and even whether one should expect a conversion experience at all are matters defined by the religious group one belongs to or happens to be under the influence of at the moment (during an evangelistic service, for example).

In a study of young people in the fundamentalist Swedish Mission Covenant Church, Hans Zetterberg found a number of group influences on the conversion phenomenon, which he defined as itself a stage in the social role of membership. For one thing, every member had a clear background of being religiously influenced before entering the group and undergoing the conversion experience; in fact, eight of every ten converts came from families in which at least one parent was already a member of the group. Second, conversion does not necessarily imply a change in one's way of life—the convert already has "pious habits and right belief." Conversion is simply a signal of a more conscious acceptance of this life. Third, a clear majority of conversions occur under conditions that are created and manipulated by the group (revival meetings, church camps, and the like). Fourth, although a sudden change in lifestyle may be the stereotype of conversion, such conversions are relatively unlikely. Zetterberg found that only 16 percent of his sample had conversions of this type. Much more likely are two other, more modest, types of conversion. Most likely is "sudden role identification," in which a person who has been undergoing socialization by the group suddenly feels certain of his or her salvation (although behavior does not change noticeably because he or she had been living the role of the converted for some time). The other type of conversion is "role assimilation," in which the person gradually becomes sure of his or her saved condition over an extended period of membership.[31]

Borhek and Curtis are even less impressed with the common stereotype of conversion as a sudden reversal or change of direction and commitment on the part of an individual. They suggest that the actual conversion (such as might occur in a revivalist service) is a *rite de passage* "differing from other such rituals only in the fact that the participant may be largely unconscious of its ritual, conventional character."[32] They suggest further that conversion experiences are often "so highly conventionalized that it requires real effort not to view them as rituals *learned for the occasion.*"[33]

The Age Factor

A second major point about conversion is that—in its dramatic form, at least—it is primarily an adolescent phenomenon. It is understandably no accident that the Jewish boy has his Bar Mitzvah and the Jewish girl her confirmation in early adolescence. Similarly in most liturgical Christian churches, confirmation in early adolescence, and in nonliturgical churches baptism and/or profession of faith occur at this time. Walter H. Clark cites two early studies in the psychology of religion by E. D. Starbuck and E. T. Clark (1899 and 1929, respectively) that found the most common age for conversion of males to be about sixteen and for females about fourteen or fifteen.[34]

David Elkind makes the point that until adolescence the child "knows much more than he understands about his religious identity."[35] Gordon Allport describes adolescence as the time when the person must transform his religious attitudes from secondhand to firsthand fittings of his personality.[36]

There is some indication that sexual guilt feelings and anxieties among people who have only recently begun to struggle with their sexual development, desires, and propensities are strongly influential here. The traditional stereotyped conversion in a tent meeting or evangelistic service almost invariably includes a discourse and series of prayers and altar calls that have touched on "sexual sins" more than any others and have been de-

---

[31]Hans Zetterberg. "The Religious Conversion as a Change of Social Roles," *Sociology and Social Research* 36, no. 1 (1952), 159–166.

[32]James T. Borhek and Richard F. Curtis, *A Sociology of Belief* (New York: John Wiley, 1975), p. 98.

[33]Borhek and Curtis, *A Sociology of Belief*, p. 98. Emphasis added.

[34]Walter H. Clark, *The Psychology of Religion* (New York: Macmillan, 1958), p. 207.

[35]Elkind, "Age Changes," p. 40.

[36]Gordon W. Allport, *The Individual and His Religion* (New York: Macmillan, 1957), p. 32.

signed to produce admission of guilt for what are essentially universal feelings and urges. Thouless states: "The typical adolescent conversion may be regarded psychologically as the sudden emergence into consciousness of a previously repressed system of feelings belonging to the sex instinct, which is now admitted into consciousness because it is sublimated, purified and directed to a religious end."[37]

That conversion should frequently occur during adolescence is probably not surprising considering the hormonal changes, opportunities for new experiences, and intellectual awakening that occur at this stage in the life cycle. Religion may be one among many other new ideas and systems to embrace. Or, religion that began to be internalized many years earlier may have developed to a peaking point at this time. Although we shall not discuss them at this point (see Chapter 14), it is no mere coincidence that most "Jesus freaks" and most American devotees of Eastern religions are either adolescents or recently out of adolescence. Further, many converts to cults (to be discussed in Chapter 5) are young people.

Not all conversions occur during adolescence, of course. But something akin to the psychological and emotional dislocations that occur during adolescence happen at other times in people's lives as well. Catherine Robins, in analyzing conversion of women into the East African Revival—a large scale Protestant revival movement—notes that among Kiga women from Southwest Uganda it is common for a "life crisis" to have precipitated conversion.[38] She notes that among Hima women from the same region a common precondition for conversion appears to be a marital crisis, whether that means being forced into an unwanted "arranged" marriage or finding oneself in a marriage that is dominated by a conflict of Christian values with traditional values that allow, for example, a husband's male kin sexual access to his wife.[39]

Stages in Conversion

Our third sociological observation about conversion focuses on its socialization aspect. In describing the process of conversion into a small cult called the Divine Precepts (popularly known as the "Moonies"), John Lofland distinguishes between (a) predisposing conditions—attributes of persons prior to contact with the group—and (b) situational contingen-

[37]Robert H. Thouless, "The Psychology of Conversion," in *Conversion*, ed. Walter E. Conn (New York: Alba House, 1978), p. 143.

[38]Catherine Robins, "Conversion, Life Crises, and Stability Among Women in the East African Revival," in *The New Religions of Africa*, ed. Bennetta Jules-Rosette (Norwood, NJ: Ablex Publishing Corporation, 1979), p. 197.

[39]Catherine Robins, "Conversion, Life Crises, and Stability Among Women in the East African Revival," p. 199.

cies—social factors and influences in operation after contact with the group is made.

The first of three predisposing conditions is tension and emotional dislocation, which those who later became converts perceived themselves to have been enduring at fairly high levels for some time. Such tension could have resulted from failing grades in college, a broken love affair, career uncertainties, and the like. Second, the potential converts for various reasons did not avail themselves of more conventional mechanisms for solving problems and reducing tension. Such tension-relieving mechanisms could have been psychological counseling, immersion in political or public service activities, or pure avoidance-escape techniques, such as drug or alcohol use, as a means of temporarily blotting out or dulling the impact of unpleasant reality.[40] Third, having found no psychological or socio-political avenue for releasing their tension, they sought a religious solution in conventional religious organizations and/or in reading self-help and other religious literature—all without significant resolution of their tension and emotional discomfort.

An interesting sidelight here is that Eileen Barker has found that those who become Moonies tend to come from families for whom religion is important.[41] At a more general level, Snow and Machalek observe that people are more inclined to believe than doubt.[42] If we can then suggest that this propensity to believe is most apparent among those with a religious background, what we are seeing is people with a religious background encouraged to seek out a *religious* solution, even if it is with a group others might label a cult.

According to Lofland, after the search, four situational factors appeared. These are what Lofland stresses as factors that are for all practical purposes "outside" the individual, highly *sociological* in nature, if you will. The first he calls the "turning point"—that is, when the preconverts first encounter the Divine Precepts cult, they had reached or were about to reach a crisis in their lives, for whatever they had done before had been disrupted, was completed, or had failed. In other words, some serious change in their social environment had occurred. Second, there developed or already existed an "affective bond" between the potential recruit and one or more group members. That is, a social relationship of some meaning and signifi-

---

[40]To this list Richardson, Stewart, and Simmonds would add what they call the "conventional" responses of "muddling through," or doing other typically conventional things, such as moving, changing jobs, taking a holiday, getting married, and getting divorced, before taking the more dramatic route of affiliating with an offbeat religious cult. Cf. James T. Richardson, Mary White Stewart, Robert B. Simmonds, *Organized Miracles* (New Brunswick, NJ: Transaction Books, 1978), pp. 238–239.

[41]Eileen Barker, *The Making of a Moonie* (Oxford, England: Basil Blackwell Publisher, 1984), p. 217.

[42]David A. Snow and Richard Machalek, "Second Thoughts on the Presumed Fragility of Unconventional Beliefs," in *Of Gods and Men: New Religious Movements in the West*, ed. Eileen Barker (Macon, GA: Mercer University Press, 1983), p. 41.

cance had developed for the potential recruit (convert). In this case the relationship was with a member and committed affiliate of a particular group. Third, the preconvert's affective relationships outside the cult were either weak or ineffectual. Again, something of significance had happened to the potential convert's social relationships that had preceded involvement with the cult. In this case they did not amount to much; they did not constitute much by way of competition. Fourth, total conversion required a period of intensive interaction, often abetted by residence in the group's communal dwelling.[43] Here, of course, we are talking about social interaction pure and simple—interaction that can be intensive and thorough and probing, and can as a result be very effective in producing changes in people (conversion).

What has just been described, then, is not some sudden, instantaneous experience, but a process—what Richardson and Stewart call a conversion "career."[44] In describing conversion as "career" we would observe that conversion is progressive (that is, it involves stages and a progression from one level to another), and it has a background of predispositions within a person that are based on prior socialization experiences. Thus, when conversion occurs we can observe a blending of situational and social-environmental prerequisites, psychological needs, receptivity on the part of the individual, and, above all, active socialization efforts by members of the group to which the person is converting.

Lofland has not been without his critics.[45] Some suggest the process is more complex and has more stages. Others suggest that people progress toward conversion with certain stages missing. Lofland himself and his colleague Skonovd have suggested that not all conversions are alike, and, as such, the stages in conversion will have greater or lesser importance and visibility depending on which type (motif) of conversion is being experienced. They distinguish six motifs.[46] First there is the *intellectual* motif where people consciously investigate religious alternatives and almost "convert themselves." At least they consciously and actively put themselves into interaction with members of a particular group and essentially "ask for" group influence and socialization to take over.

Second is the *mystical conversion*, which Lofland and Skonovd say is the most familiar conversion motif, where there is a high level of emotional arousal. The person is conscious of change coming on with a rush and she or he is "taken over" by a particular religion's god. This is the "born again,"

---

[43]John Lofland, *Doomsday Cult* (Englewood Cliffs, NJ: Prentice-Hall, 1966), pp. 31–62.

[44]James T. Richardson and Mary Stewart, "Conversion Process Models and the Jesus Movement," in *Conversion Careers: In and Out of the New Religions*, ed. James T. Richardson (Beverly Hills CA: Sage Publications, 1978).

[45]David A. Snow and Cynthia Phillips, "The Lofland-Stark Model: A Critical Reassessment," *Social Problems* 27, no. 4 (1980), 430–447.

[46]John Lofland and Norman Skonovd, "Conversion Motifs," *Journal for the Scientific Study of Religion* 20, no. 4 (1981), 373–385.

"Damascus road" conversion. Third, there is the *experimental* motif, where a fairly long time of "trying out" the new religion is involved. There is a gradual learning and familiarization process. The fourth is the *affectional* motif, where positive relations with members of a particular group over a somewhat extended period (usually several weeks or more) integrate the newcomer into the group. Fifth is the *revivalist* motif, which is similar to the second motif (mystical), except that it occurs in public and dramatically as the convert in ecstasy heeds the altar call and publicly demonstrates her or his rejection of evil and acceptance of the new way. Sixth is the *coercive* motif, rather rare, yet alleged with some frequency by those opposed to particular religions. It is identified by such negative designations as "brainwashing," "programming," "mind control," and the like. The individual feels compelled sincerely to confess guilt and embrace a new ideological system.

Despite critiques and modifications, there is virtually universal agreement on at least two prerequisites to conversion, so crucial in Lofland's theory: (1) the existence of prior affective bonds between a recruit and one or more members of the group and (2) intensive interaction and involvement with the group in order to facilitate conversion.

DECONVERSION

Within the context of considering conversion, it is appropriate to look also at its opposite, deconversion. People not only affiliate with a religious group through conversion, they also dissaffiliate and repudiate their former commitment. While there are a variety of terms to describe what happens—for example, defection, disaffiliation, and apostasy—we will employ the fairly neutral term deconversion, which implies an actual decision to leave. In addition, we shall look briefly at the deprogramming movement and its success despite questionable ethics and possible illegality.

As we have learned, most conversions involve a process that extends over a period of time and proceeds through stages; it is not a sudden, spur-of-the-moment phenomenon. Likewise, research shows that deconversions follow similar patterns. The leader is the focal point in most religious groups, cults in particular, and it takes time to interact with that leader, fall under his or her "spell," and place full trust and confidence in him or her. Expectedly, then, it takes some time to disentangle oneself from the leader when going through the deconversion process.

Janet Jacobs has gathered instructive data from people who have left religious cults,[47] and has found an evolutionary quality to the process of

---

[47]In a sense we are getting ahead of ourselves. In the next chapter we will be introduced to cults and to other types of religious groups as well. At this point, however, it is important to know that cults are distinctive religious groups that usually have a powerful charismatic leader—more so than other religious groups.

deconversion for 80 percent of the people.[48] She emphasizes a "multi-phase exit" that involves two separations. First, one disengages from the social manifestations of the group—group activities and interactions and exchanges with the members. Second, one disengages from the leader and breaks the emotional attachment one has had to the leader.

Most often the dissatisfaction and disillusionment with the group itself—the first step in the ultimate deconversion process—is described as "conflict over social life." This would be conflict over intimate relations, prescribed sex roles, and personal lifestyle. In other words, restrictions on one's freedom and personal life. Often this disgruntlement involves dissatisfaction with mid-level organizers, and not the leader. People can apparently survive in this stage of partial defection for some time. Jacobs notes that "partial deconversion, then, can be understood as a state of consciousness on the part of devotees in which the leader assumes a separate and divine quality that is distinct from the mundane aspects of religious commitment associated with the regulation of group life and the social demands of affiliation."[49] Some members actually leave at this point. They never actually reject the leader, but they find the group structure too constricting and alienating. Of the subjects studied, 43 percent defected without repudiating the leader, but the remaining 57 percent rejected the group, its restrictions, and the leader. However, the rejection of the leader was emotionally wrenching and painful for these people. Jacobs notes that most followers of a cult, both male and female, express love for the leader. While the sojourn with the group might have become intolerable, the love and respect for the leader might still exist. Yet we must not lose sight of the fact that over half (57 percent) of Jacobs's sample rejected both the group *and* the leader.

There were four primary areas in which leaders were perceived as deviant. Mentioned most often (by 60 percent of respondents) was psychological abuse. Next, at 45 percent, was emotional rejection. Spiritual betrayal (33 percent) and physical abuse (31 percent) round out the list.[50]

It appears clear that there is a wide range in the amount of time required for members of these New Religious Movements to defect. While most will eventually leave (Saul Levine found that almost 90 percent of converts to cults and cultlike groups will actually leave within two years of their original commitment),[51] Jacobs found the average stay for her respondents was 4.5 years, and over half stayed more than 2 years.[52] One gets a clear picture of a lot of movement both in and out of these groups. It is clear also

[48]Janet Jacobs, "Deconversion from Religious Movements," *Journal for the Scientific Study of Religion* 26, no. 3 (1987), 294–308.

[49]Ibid., p. 299.

[50]Ibid., p. 300.

[51]Saul V. Levine, *Radical Departures: Desperate Detours to Growing Up* (New York: Harcourt Brace Jovanovich, 1986), p. 93.

[52]Jacobs, "Deconversion from Religious Movements," p. 297.

that disillusionment with and defection from one group does not discourage a majority of these people from later joining other similar groups. Wright found that 78 percent of his sample of voluntary defectors from the Unification Church, the Hare Krishna Movement, and the Children of God eventually reconverted to another group.[53] And Jacobs found that among her respondents, who were all defectors, half had moved on to another similar group.

Two points seem clear: (1) disappointment with one group does not keep people from trying others; (2) underlying needs of these peripatetic types have not been met by other activities or affiliations in the meantime.

THE DEPROGRAMMING CONTROVERSY

A second means of disaffiliating from cults and New Religious Movements is what has come to be known as deprogramming. While the end result appears to be the same as in deconversion, the method is decidedly different.

Deprogramming involves kidnapping and physical withdrawal from the confines of the religious group. It is often a result of desperation, felt particularly by parents who see a daughter or son "wasting their lives away in misguided ways." Then an intensive effort is made to convince the person to recognize the evils of the group, reject them, and come home. The rationale for strong measures centers on the belief that "brainwashing" techniques were used by the cult in the first place as the person was stripped of his or her former commitments and convictions. Therefore similar tactics to bring the person back are felt to be justified. (The brainwashing idea stems from reports by American prisoners of war captured during the Korean War. They were victims of mind control techniques designed to get the prisoners to reject former convictions and beliefs and adopt an alien one.) In the case of the Chinese Communists manipulating American prisoners of war in Korea it was of course to embrace Communism and come back to the United States as political evangelists for Communism. What bothered Americans about "brainwashing" was its deliberate denial of freedom of choice and associated tactics to break down one's defenses and insert a new ideology and commitment.

Opponents of the cults and those who became deprogrammers generally agreed on a list of physical manifestations (stigmatae) of the brainwashing mind control tactic of the religious cults. Anson Shupe and David Bromley summarize them as follows: glassy eyes and dilated pupils (the "thousand mile stare"); hyperactivity and extreme nervousness; overall

---

[53]Stuart A. Wright, "Post-Involvement Attitudes of Voluntary Defectors from Controversial New Religious Movements," *Journal for the Scientific Study of Religion* 23, no. 2 (1984), 172–182.

physical debilitation (gaunt facial appearance and hollow eyes); body odor (sometimes called "Moonie odor," purportedly due to neglect of daily hygiene); facial skin rash (sometimes called "Moonie rash," purportedly due to a vitamin A deficiency); hunched or bent posture; fixed, permanent smile ("with the mouth only"); and monotonic and inflection-free voice levels and/or higher pitch and tone.[54] Couple all this with the conscious and often successful attempts by cult groups to create a new family within the cult (the group itself as family) to replace the families out of which the recruits had come, and you have very worried and concerned parents and friends of the cult members.

Small wonder that many parents became desperate, willing to do most anything to "rescue" their children from the evil influences of the group. Such "anything goes" tactics overlook the fact that the children in the "clutches" of the cult are often adults who have found something of value in the cult and have willingly joined it. Granted, the person has probably been "lovebombed" (given a great deal of attention, open gestures of welcome, and a lot of emotional support and acceptance by group members when he or she visited the group) and subjected to intensive indoctrination as time went on. But any group that recruits new members does similar things. There is warm, welcoming interaction; there is often fairly intensive education (indoctrination); there are attempts to withdraw recruits as much as possible from former commitments seen as incompatible with the ethics and commitments of the new group. One of the principle deprogrammers, Ted Patrick, advised parents: "You're not dealing with your son at this point. You're dealing with a zombie. You have to do whatever is necessary to get him back."[55]

But deprogramming is really brainwashing also, and is a glaring infringement on religious freedom, no matter how loathsome the affiliation might seem to a parent or other loved one. An interesting observation about such unethical behavior is that even if one favors the end result (i.e., disaffiliation), the deprogramming activity itself would seldom have been necessary: Relatively few remain members of representative cults for very long. James Beckford found that 75 percent of recruits had left the Unification Church of England within two years.[56] Eileen Barker found not only that few who attended the workshops actually joined the group (only one in ten),

---

[54]Anson D. Shupe, Jr. and David G. Bromley, *The New Vigilantes: Deprogrammers Anti-Cultists, and the New Religions* (Beverly Hills, CA: Sage Publications, 1980), p. 72.

[55]Ted Patrick, *Lightning News*, August (1976), 11.

[56]James Beckford, "Conversion and Apostasy: Antithesis or Complementarity?" Paper presented at conference on "Conversion, Coercion, and Commitment in the New Religions," Berkeley, CA, June 11–14, 1981. Reported in Stuart A. Wright, *Leaving Cults: The Dynamics of Defection* (Washington, D.C.: Society for the Scientific Study of Religion Monograph Series, no. 7, 1987), p. 2.

but of those who joined, a majority left within two years.[57] Other studies all report similar results. The rate of people dropping out of the New Religious Movements unassisted is high, and the duration of membership has generally been one to two years.

But, quite apart from its work with individuals to "deprogram" them, the deprogramming movement had broader impact. Publicity of its "heroic" efforts to turn evil on its ear helped turn public opinion against the cult movement, and the Unification Church under Mr. Moon in particular. The movement was successful despite its questionable ethics and illegality.

CONCLUSION

Religious socialization, the process of becoming religious, is not a unique or unusual process. It is simply socialization by a group into a body of norms that provide a set of meanings and interpretations that individuals internalize and relate to the large body of other meanings they possess. The process and ultimate outcome of religious socialization is not unlike learning the role and meaning construct of becoming a French citizen, Cuban mother, or center for the Celtics. Certain elements common to all who participate in a social category are learned. Yet a unique pattern emerges, for each individual has a unique combination of interactions and observations that eventuate in his or her meaning construct. Powerful social influences and factors impinge on the individual and are internalized. Thus, although psychological processes are involved, what we observe is not something internal to the individual that "comes out," so to speak. Rather, we see something created and induced "from without" through socialization.

But people also disaffiliate from groups. They leave. In other words, the group no longer provides the satisfaction it promised or perhaps once did provide for an individual. Or perhaps the leader becomes discredited, or another group looks more inviting. Often, like conversion, the process leading to defection is gradual. We have made the point more than once that the conversion/deconversion activity in religious groups is not unlike the joining and leaving by members of other groups. However, we do observe a difference when talking about cults as contrasted with the mainline denominational groups. On the average, there are more (a higher percentage of) defections from cults than from other groups, and even other religious groups. The reason is simply that by definition a cult's center of existence is its charismatic leader. If the leader becomes discredited in the eyes of some, many will leave. Even if not wholly discredited, as the infatuation with the leader loses its intensity, people drift away.

[57]Eileen Barker, "Resistible Coercion: The Significance of Failure Rates in Conversion and Commitment to the Unification Church," In Dick Anthony, Jacob Needleman, and Thomas Robbins (eds.), *Conversion, Coercion and Commitment in New Religious Movements* (New York: Crossroads Press, 1983).

5

The Church-Sect Continuum of Religious Organization

Up to this point, we have explored ways in which religious groups are both similar among themselves but also similar to other groups and social organizations. We now turn to some important distinctions among religious groups—distinctions that are fundamentally matters of organization—that is, sociological, not theological, differences. We begin with the *church-sect typology*—a way of identifying differences among religious groups. This typology was given its fullest early conceptualization by the theologian Ernst Troeltsch, but was introduced into sociology by his teacher Max Weber and has been used and expanded by numerous sociologists since their time.

The dichotomy of church and sect actually only identifies two polar types of religious organization. That is, the church and the sect occupy the ends of a social continuum that has several gradation points (other types of organization) in between. We first will contrast the polar types and then discuss three other types of religious organization that investigations following those of Troeltsch and Weber have shown to be important additions to the typology.

THE SECT

Demerath and Hammond suggest that differences between churches and sects can be observed from either of two perspectives, one concerning the

internal characteristics of the organization, the other the external relationships of the group with the features of its social environment.[1] Focusing on
internal differences, we can observe the following about sects:

1. A sect sees itself as a fellowship of the elect—that is, an embodiment of true
    believers.
2. Sects encourage spontaneity of religious expression involving extensive group
    participation.
3. Sects deemphasize organization and strive to maintain maximum democratic
    participation of members within an explicitly nonbureaucratic structure.
4. A sect is usually small and deliberately so.
5. Sects utilize laypeople as leaders. Frequently part-time, such leaders likely
    have little if any formal theological training. Commitment to the principles
    avowed by the group is seen as more important than "book learning." The
    element of charisma is a common feature of leaders.
6. A sect emphasizes purity of doctrine and usually demands a return to original
    religious teaching. This involves a renunciation of the doctrinal perversions
    and aberrations that it accuses the established denominational religious
    groups of having allowed to intrude into true religion.
7. A sect emphasizes traditional ethical principles and strives to influence its
    members along a broad spectrum of behavior.
8. Sects tend to concentrate on other worldly issues (salvation, deliverance,
    heaven and hell) and discount or deprecate this world's concerns. Even their
    emphasis on ethics (point 7) is focused more on its relevance to ultimate other-
    worldly concerns and less on the relationship of person to person.
9. A sect gains new members primarily through conversion. It is initially a fellow-
    ship of adults, although eventually it must turn its attention to the religious
    socialization of children.
10. A sect draws disproportionately from the lower social classes in the society.

   Implicit in many of the characteristics just outlined is the prime characteristic of a sect, namely, protest. Usually it is protest against both (1) established traditional religious forms and groups that sect members feel have
strayed too far from pristine religion and (2) the surrounding secular society, which is viewed as embodying all kinds of evil. A sect thus reflects
schism—a breaking away from and a rejection of established patterns, both
religious and secular. At this point, we encounter most directly the external
relationships of a sect to its surrounding social environment that we mentioned earlier. The sect in its protest against the evils of the surrounding
society engages in some kind of rejection of that social structure. The form
may be withdrawal in both a figurative and literal sense from most of the
typical activities people engage in. Communal groups such as the Amish
and Hutterites would fit here and would be the most extreme form of withdrawal and rejection. They refuse to participate in the surrounding com-

___

[1]N.J. Demerath III and Philip E. Hammond, *Religion in Social Context* (New York: Random House, 1969), pp. 70–71.

munity's politics (they do not vote); they send their children to school only to learn to write, read, and do basic math, and try to keep them from going beyond the eighth grade; they subscribe to no newspapers or magazines; they own and listen to no radios or TV sets; and they engage in only occasional commerce with the surrounding community, being nearly self-sufficient on their communal farms.

We might mention here in passing that there are of course many other types of sects. Although we will not get into a description of the various types here, two typologies the reader may wish to explore are those of Elmer T. Clark and Bryan Wilson. Clark distinguishes the pessimistic-adventist sects, the perfectionist-subjectivist sects, the charismatic-pentecostal sects, the legalistic-objectivist sects, and the communistic sects.[2] Wilson distinguishes the revolutionist, introversionist, manipulationist, thaumaturgical, reformist, and utopian sects.[3]

THE CHURCH

Before presenting the corresponding characteristics of the church type, we need to make clear that the church (the sect also) is clearly what in sociology we call an ideal type. That is, the concept of church or sect or any of the other types of religious organization that we will describe later in the chapter represents a summary or distillation of social characteristics and phenomena that frequently appear together and that in combination help to distinguish one set of organizations from another. It is a kind of model that expresses in pure, complete form the central characteristics of a pattern of organization or behavior. Although we do not expect to find all the characteristics of an ideal type in pure form in a particular organization at a given moment in time, we will expect to see most of them. In a sense an ideal type is used for dramatic purposes to heighten one's awareness of salient characteristics of a social phenomenon. For example, we listed ten characteristics of the sect. Yet a religious group may accurately be identified as a sect and lack one or two of the characteristics on the list or not reproduce all ten characteristics in "pure" form. Similarly, the church type represents one "extreme" form of religious organization that may have appeared at some time in history in essentially all its characteristics but probably never in pure form on all dimensions. That is, an ideal type is more a concept and less an empirical reality, though it is based on substantial empirical observations. Its value lies in providing a clear-cut base of comparison for what we observe empirically at a given point in time. Although we may be unable to observe an empirical example of a "church" at this point in history, we can

---

[2]Elmer T. Clark, *The Small Sects in America* (Nashville, TN: Abingdon, 1949).
[3]Bryan Wilson, *Religious Sects* (New York: McGraw-Hill, 1970).

understand more clearly what we do observe because of either its similarities to or differences from the ideal type we have as a base of contrast.

But now to the major characteristics of the *church* type of religious organization. The church (1) claims universality and includes all members of the society within its ranks; there is a strong tendency for "citizen" to be equated with "member"; (2) exercises religious monopoly and tries to eliminate religious competition; (3) is very closely allied with the state and secular powers—frequently there is overlapping of responsibilities and much mutual reinforcement; (4) is extensively organized as a hierarchical bureaucratic institution with a complex division of labor; (5) employs a professional, full-time clergy who possess the appropriate credentials of education and formal ordination; (6) almost by definition gains new members through natural reproduction and the socialization of children into its ranks.

A prime example of a church is the medieval Roman Catholic Church. Another close approximation was the Russian Orthodox Church of the nineteenth century. For that matter, contemporary European state churches approximate this model, though they all now at least formally tolerate religious diversity and competition—something the pure church type does not do. Although there is no really good example of a church type of religious organization to be observed today, the concept retains considerable value as a point of reference for understanding the other types of religious organization that are in clear evidence today.[4]

THE DENOMINATION

The *denomination* is in a mediating position between the church and the sect, and as such is the most important addition to the original dichotomous church-sect typology. When the church loses its position of religious dominance and monopoly, denominationalism is the result. In fact, the moment the protesting, struggling sects that have been striving to attain autonomy are tolerated, however reluctantly, by the established church, the church is by definition dead and is immediately transformed into a denomination—that is, one religion among several. As some of the protesting sects evolve (we will discuss this evolutionary process later in the chapter), they too become denominations, and this type of religious organization—denominationalism—becomes a distinct, identifiable type.

---

[4]Although we will not review them here, the reader should be aware that refinements of the church type have been made. For example, J. Milton Yinger has distinguished the "universal church" from the "ecclesia" (Greek word for church) and has further divided both into institutionalized and diffused forms. J. Milton Yinger, *The Scientific Study of Religion* (New York: Macmillan, 1970), pp. 256–264.

A denomination can be defined as follows: (1) It is similar to the church, but unlike the sect, in being on relatively good terms with the state and secular powers. The denomination's most extreme stance in this respect would be "loyal opposition." It is at home in the halls of government and occasionally tries to exert some influence in that direction—something few sects try to do. (2) A denomination maintains at least tolerant and usually fairly friendly relationships with other denominations in a context of religious pluralism. (3) It relies primarily on birth for membership increase, though it will also accept converts; some groups even actively pursue evangelistic programs, although it is directed primarily to the unconverted, unchurched citizens, not persons who are presently members of other denominations. (4) A denomination accepts the principle of at least modestly changing doctrine and practice and tolerates some theological diversity and dispute—something a true sect will not do. (5) It follows a fairly routinized ritual and worship service that explicitly discourages spontaneous emotional expression. (6) It trains and employs a professional clergy who must meet certain formal normative requirements before certification. (7) It recognizes competing demands from other affiliations upon its members' commitment and involvement; thus, it accepts less extensive involvement from members than a sect does, but often expects more than the church (where by virtue of the citizen-church member equation it is recognized that many persons will be minimally or noninvolved members). (8) A denomination draws disproportionately from the middle and upper classes of the society.

Before proceeding to look at two other important types of religious organizations within the framework of the church-sect typology—namely, the cult and the institutionalized sect—we need to analyze a bit further the relationship between sect and denomination. First, we want to look at the point of rupture when the sect protests to the point of breaking with the denomination or church. Second, we will trace the evolutionary pattern that most sects follow that eventually leads them to denominational status.

THE FORMATION OF SECTS

We stated earlier that the fundamental theme of the religious sect is protest—protest that leads to schism and a breaking away from the parent religious group, be it church or denomination. Such action, however, is not the only method of resolving conflict within a religious group. One method historically employed by church-type religious groups—of which the Roman Catholic Church is a paramount example—is by allowing, often in fact encouraging, the formation of specialized groups within the larger body. If some persons feel they cannot worship properly in the established ritual form of ordinary local congregational groups (the reasoning goes), then allow them to form a subgroup or religious order within the larger body that emphasizes extensive contemplation and private meditation, or one that encourages active participation in social and political activities, or one that engages in spontaneous, emotional, pentecostal-type behaviors. Monastic orders within the Roman Catholic Church have served this purpose admirably. Even today, the tacit permission if not encouragement of pentecostal subgroups within such standard denominations as the Catholic, Lutheran, Presbyterian, and Episcopalian churches is an excellent example of this tactic of channeling deviant and/or specialized groups within the overarching structure of the denomination.

Probably the most familiar method of resolving dissatisfaction within a denomination is simply for individuals or families to withdraw—either to drift from organized religion altogether or to affiliate with another religious group that seems to satisfy one's wishes and concerns more fully. How many present-day denominational switches are such expressions of religious protest, we do not know. Undoubtedly, many are relatively simple transfers of convenience when a family moves and cannot find its denomination represented nearby; or when upward mobility (as opposed to ideological conflict) suggests to a person that he or she should forsake, say, his or her Baptist background and affiliate with a "higher-status" Presbyterian or Episcopalian congregation; or when an interfaith marriage leads one partner to switch to the mate's religious group as a matter of form and convenience.

Another way of resolving religious conflict is for those who are dissatisfied simply to split off and form another denomination. We will soon emphasize that a prime ingredient in sect formation is the factor of social class. But if social class is not a particularly primary factor in a given controversy and the issue is more strictly political or ideological, then a denomination may simply split into two. The division of both the Baptists and the Presbyterians into northern and southern denominations during the Civil War are good examples of this process. The split within the Presbyterian Church in the 1930s over certain doctrinal issues is another example; not a sect, but another denomination formed as a result. Similarly, in nineteenth-century Europe, Reform Judaism separated from Orthodox Judaism not as a sect but as a denomination.

The final method of resolving religious group conflict is the one we keep referring to—the process of sect formation. What happens in this process and why? Ostensibly, the issue is almost invariably doctrinal or theological. Potential sect members are likely to talk about the loss of true Christianity in the parent denomination—about how doctrine has become liberalized and people are not living their Christianity the way they should. Some members finally opt out and form their own small group in order to preserve or recapture the basics and the essence of true religion and save themselves from further theological contamination and perversion. Undoubtedly, most sectarians are sincere and truly believe that theological or doctrinal issues are the real issues. Yet one suspects there is more to it than that. The social scientist continually looks for latent factors lurking behind manifest behaviors, definitions of the situation, and rationalizations. We are thus particularly intrigued when we observe that sectarians are predominantly of lower-class social status. Aware that social status influences all manner of social behavior and attitudes, sociologists thus regard it as very likely that social status also relates in some way with the sectarian break from the denomination.

In his classic analysis of the interrelationship of religion and social structure, Liston Pope reviews several hypotheses that try to account for the phenomenon of sect formation. Most writers, he notes, pay serious attention to the status dimension or at least by implication suggest that lower social status is somehow significantly involved in the motivation for sectarian involvement.[5] For example, the "cultural shock" hypothesis of John B. Holt suggests that migrants to cities seek out or form sects as a means of preserving rural religious lifestyles and values and as a defense against the anonymity of the city and the urban denominational congregations.[6] Although such factors may be relevant for some persons, Holt's analysis does not account for the formation of sects in rural and small-town settings. Holt does point out, however, that persons attracted to sects, whether migrants experiencing cultural shock or not, are predominantly lower class.

A major explanatory perspective for many theorists, then, is to see sect formation as some form of compensation for those deficiencies epitomized by inferior social status. Pope notes that sects "substitute religious status for social status."[7] The sectarian is likely to say something like, "I may not be high society, but I'm on God's first string," or "I may not have a big house, a fancy car, and a college education, but I've got what's really important—I've got true religion." Pope observes: "They transmute poverty into a symptom of Grace."[8] Socially separated from those above them in the stratification system, they then emphasize separation from "the world" as a virtue. Although they feel excluded from fellowship with those of higher education and social and economic position, they in turn exclude from their fellowship those who dance, play cards, smoke, drink, and bet on the races. Unable to afford jewelry, they make wearing of any such adornment a sin. Pope again observes: "Excluded from secular society, they set up a religious society of their own, in which standards of membership are more rigid than those of the general culture that has ignored them."[9] Reaching heaven,

---

[5]Liston Pope, *Millhands and Preachers* (New Haven: Yale University Press, 1942), pp. 133–134.

[6]John B. Holt, "Holiness Religion: Cultural Shock and Reorganization," *American Sociological Review 5*, no. 5 (1940), 740–747.

[7]Pope, *Millhands and Preachers*, p. 137.

[8]Ibid.

[9]Ibid., p. 138.

which is the supreme, ultimate reward, becomes eminently more important than earthly success and the good life here and now, which is only temporal and not eternal.

THE IMPACT OF DEPRIVATION ON SECT DEVELOPMENT

To this point, we have been concentrating on a rather simplistic distinction between high and low socioeconomic status. Charles Y. Glock has added specification to this general hypothesis by introducing the concept of "deprivation" and making distinctions among five types of deprivation.[10] First, there is *economic deprivation*, which consists of limited income and access to the material necessities of life. It may be objectively defined and measured as well as subjectively experienced and perceived. That is, although people may technically not be categorized as living at the poverty level, they may perceive of themselves as poor. Such a perception can influence their behavior and attitude as much as or more than the objective facts of their existence.

Second, *social deprivation* refers to the relative absence of such societal rewards as prestige, power, social status, and opportunity for participation in various activities and organizations. This is frequently a concomitant of economic deprivation in the sense that low economic status likely means low prestige or respect, little power or influence over others, and exclusion from much of the social and organizational life of the community. But social deprivation is not necessarily strictly correlated with economic deprivation. A person may be socially deprived yet be economically solvent, even successful. Social deprivation is one of the main emphases of the women's liberation movement. "Although I can buy all that my heart desires, I'm considered 'just a housewife' because it's my husband's income I'm spending." "I may be receiving a very livable salary, but it's less than that of a man doing comparable work." And so on. Or social deprivation may be along age lines. Consider the very young and the very old who have relatively little power and prestige even though economically they may be facing no difficulty. Further, the minority-group member, such as a Chicano or black or American Indian, may be economically successful yet a second-class citizen on other dimensions of status.

A third type of deprivation is *organismic*. This refers to the deprived condition of some in society along the dimensions of physical and mental health and biological-physical abilities. Some suffer from neuroses or psy-

[10]Charles Y. Glock, "The Role of Deprivation in the Origin and Evolution of Religious Groups," in *Religion and Social Conflict*, eds. Robert Lee and Martin E. Marty (New York: Oxford University Press, 1964), pp. 24–36.

choses; some are deaf or blind; some are paraplegics; some are mentally retarded; others suffer from one or more of an almost infinite variety of other conditions.

Another type of deprivation is what Glock calls *ethical*. This exists when persons come to feel that the dominant values and norms of the society no longer provide them with a meaningful way of organizing their lives. Ethically deprived persons have trouble finding meaning in their lives and cannot decide where to go or how to proceed to find it. Above all, these persons seek a body of ethical prescriptions on how to organize their lives and want an alternative value system to inform and guide them.

Finally there is *psychic deprivation*, which affects the person who may enjoy the material rewards of society and may subscribe to society's norms but who nevertheless lacks an adequate share of psychic rewards—the person does not *feel* satisfied or really accepted in society. Such deprivation frequently accompanies social deprivation—for example, the black professional in American society who has superior specialized skill and education, who may be economically successful, but who still feels looked down upon because of skin color, and who in many situations is made to feel inferior or second-rate. Whereas social deprivation is more or less an objective measure or dimension, psychic deprivation is a psychological matter and thus highly subjective.

To relate these types of deprivation to the sources of sectarianism, we can first of all observe with Glock that the emergence of any protest movement or group—religious or otherwise—requires some feeling of deprivation on the part of the participants.[11] They face a problem that is either not being met by the groups they are presently affiliated with or is in some way produced by a group or groups with which they are affiliated (or both). Glock suggests, however, that while some felt deprivation is a necessary condition for protest group formation, it is not a sufficient condition—there are additional requirements. The deprivation must be shared with others, and these people need to find one another; a leader must emerge to suggest a solution; and no alternative existing institutional arrangements or processes must appear to be available.[12] When such factors combine, a protest group can get underway.

But what form will it take? For example, will it be a secular group or movement, or will it be a religious organization such as a sect breaking away from a denomination? If the deprivation is either economic or social, it is likely that a religious route will be followed (1) when the nature of the deprivation is inaccurately perceived or inadequately understood—that is, when people do not realize that a prime factor in their unhappiness and

[11]Ibid., p. 29.
[12]Ibid.

frustration is their economic or social position relative to others, or (2) when, even though the nature of the deprivation is accurately perceived, people feel powerless to work directly at eliminating its causes.[13] In either case, persons may retreat into an emotionally releasing, rationalizing, other-wordly sectarian religious group and activity as a conscious or subconscious means of escaping from the harsh realities of economic or social deprivation. On the other hand, if people accurately perceive the problem and feel capable of attacking and resolving it through social change, then they are more likely to form a secular organization or attempt some other secular resolution. In other words, religious resolutions such as the formation of sects are essentially compensatory mechanisms for alleviating feelings of deprivation, while secular resolutions try to strike directly at the causes of the deprivation.

A striking example of both of these attempts can be seen in the black community in the United States. Historically, much black religious behavior and involvement has tended to be of the sect variety, quite clearly responding to economic and social deprivation in a compensatory way. More recently, however, as more blacks have become cognizant of the real nature of their problems, have rejected doctrines of inherent inferiority, and have become convinced that the system could be effectively challenged, the civil rights movement has flowered. Young blacks in particular have increasingly turned to secular organizations, such as CORE, Operation Breadbasket, and the Black Panthers, or in some cases to groups like the Black Muslims, rather than to traditional black religious organizations. More on this phenomenon and on black religion in general appears in Chapter 12.

When social deprivation is not intimately associated with or reinforced by economic deprivation, another route may be followed that is neither sectarian nor secular—very simply, another religious denomination may result. Again we turn to the American black community for an example. The African Methodist Episcopal Church came into being not as a sect but as a denomination when freed blacks, many of them of essentially middle-class economic status, reacted to unequal participation privileges and unequal voice in the white-dominated Methodist Episcopal Church and broke away in 1796.

Although we have not discussed the cult as a specific type of religious group, we should mention at this point that either ethical or psychic deprivation is less likely to result in sectarian development and more likely, for reasons that will become evident later, to cause people to form or be attracted to a religious cult. It is of course also possible that ethical or psychic deprivation may precede secular solutions and the formation of nonreligious groups.

---

[13]Ibid.

THE EVOLUTION OF SECTS

So much for the phenomenon of sect formation. We now turn to the issue of sect evolution and an investigation of the factors involved in the nearly universal tendency of sects (if they survive at all) to change and move away from their original "pure" state—in fact, to move toward eventual denominational status and to begin manifesting the characteristics of an organization from which they originally withdrew and which they earlier repudiated. We refer to the sect in its pure state as a religious group composed of the exclusive "elect" or select few, who practice what they see as "pure," authentic religion and who avoid secular involvement and contamination; and we begin with the empirical observation that a sect cannot remain a sect.

A major causative factor in the evolution of sect to denomination is quite nonreligious and very sociological. We refer here to the laws of increasing group size that we outlined in Chapter 3. For these laws to apply, we assume, of course, that the originally small sect grows. And even if a sect does not grow enough to call into play the laws of increasing group size, other nonreligious factors apply that we will discuss later. But assuming a sect adds to its numbers—as most do, since they usually want to spread their gospel and share their discovery of true religion—then some inevitable developments come about. More people automatically means a greater diversity of background. New members will not share precisely the same experiences of the original core group, and some will have significantly different personal objectives and goals that they expect the group to fulfill. Thus, problems of unanimity and total consensus arise, even though all may sincerely believe that they subscribe to the same goals and norms as everyone else. The foundation is therefore laid for ultimate modification of the sect's central goals and values.

As a group increases in size, subgroups inevitably develop. Although this phenomenon occurs the moment any few people form a group, it intensifies in geometric proportion as the group grows. Subgroups develop their own unique combinations of goals, norms, and roles while still subscribing to the overarching ideology of the larger group and respecting its structure. Subgroups not only provide internal diversity but represent the distinct possibility that a particular subgroup may become increasingly more deviant, gain more adherents, and ultimately dominate the larger group and assume guiding control. Obviously, under such circumstances the group will change.

We just mentioned deviance. As groups increase in size, deviance increases, largely through subgroup action. But that is not all. Tolerance of deviance increases, either because the deviance is unknown or unrecognized or because the task of enforcing strict normative behavior on the membership becomes more and more difficult. Clearly, the original conformity and unanimity is breaking down.

A prime need for groups as they grow larger is greater coordination. Strictly democratic decision making in all matters becomes impractical and impossible. Responsibility for coordinating the activities of many persons and roles is centralized in specialists. A side effect will likely be a declining intensity of commitment and sense of involvement among ordinary members. Also, the distance between elite and rank-and-file members will increase. The person who sees original principles changed or lost will find it increasingly difficult to communicate his or her concern to the elites in the group. Not only will change remain unchecked, but the individual who objects to change will become increasingly dissatisfied and disenchanted (while others, of course, will applaud the change).

A result may well be a legitimacy crisis, with some concluding that they must reject the authority of the leaders and coordinators. But perhaps they are voiceless or powerless. What to do? Go along silently but unhappily, or leave and form a new group—a new sect that can once again restore purity and truth to religion.

But what if a sectarian religious group manages to avoid the problems inherent in organizational growth by simply not growing or at least by not growing to the extent where a bureaucratic structure develops and members become isolated from one another? Even with no growth or only limited growth, sources of change are present and begin to work. Almost immediately after formation a formalization of norms begins and the group loses some of its spontaneity and flexibility. Then the group must answer two questions: (1) Where does authority lie? In a book? With a leader? In a doctrinal statement? That is, who or what is the ultimate arbiter? (2) What are correct beliefs? What are we going to teach our children and the adults who knock on our door and inquire about coming in?

With each development the group is becoming more stabilized as it formalizes its norms; structurally, it is becoming just a bit more like the group from which it severed itself. There is a little less chance for innovation; it is becoming a little more difficult to substantiate that the Holy Spirit is working through you to bring new insight. It becomes increasingly more necessary to reconcile that which is newly introduced with what the group has already established as normative in answering the two questions above.

Furthermore, the group must provide for leadership succession. If the group begins with a charismatic leader, what happens if he or she dies or is incapacitated or is discredited as morally or otherwise unfit to continue as leader? Norms must therefore be established that outline the process of leader selection and succession. Perhaps it will involve a training program for potential leaders. Above all, it will require specification of the qualifications and duties of the leader. After all, if we bring in a new leader, she or he has to know what the duties are. At this point something highly significant has happened—the leader has become an officeholder. The leader's role has been routinized and formalized. And one observes the beginning of formal structure and ultimately perhaps bureaucracy itself.

Also, any expansion beyond the few initial individuals or families will require attention to financial matters. A hall for meetings must be rented or purchased; some minimal equipment and fixtures must be provided; a checking account must be opened at a local bank. And again we see the spontaneous, flexible group becoming structured and routinized. It is taking the first step toward becoming the type of organization it disdained. "That church I used to belong to paid too much attention to everyday, worldly matters like meeting budgets, fund raising, and building maintenance. It didn't pay enough attention to spiritual matters—the really important things." So says the sectarian. Yet the sect itself must soon begin to have similar concerns, though at first on a smaller scale, of course.

Another factor contributing to change in the sect is the strong tendency within any group for higher-status persons to assume positions of power and be elected to office. The sect is no exception. Low-status members of a group tend to defer to those with more education, a higher-status job, and greater prestige. The result tends to be a conservative influence on the group—conservative in the sense that such higher-status leaders are likely to want to modify and tone down extremes in the sect's stance and ideology. They have more at stake in the surrounding community and do not want their names associated with too weird a group. Thus, the sect begins to change, to accommodate itself, and it becomes more compatible with the surrounding culture.

A final important factor involved in turning the sect around and leading it back toward the denominational form is the upward status mobility of some of its members. Insofar as sect formation is primarily a lower-status phenomenon, what happens when some of these lower-status members improve their social and economic condition? They will either bring the group with them along the lines of modification and accommodation just discussed, or they will leave the group and affiliate with another group (more denominational in character) that is more compatible with their enhanced social status. If they stay, conceivably they could even more or less force those in the group who have not begun to change their status level and conditions to pull out and form a new sect; this could be done consciously or unconsciously. What is involved here is effectively and poignantly stated by John Wesley, himself a founder of a sect—a sect that has become the Methodist Church in its various denominational forms:

> Wherever riches have increased, the essence of religion has decreased in the same proportion. Therefore, I do not see how it is possible, in the nature of things, for any revival of religion to continue long. For religion must necessarily produce both industry and frugality, and these cannot but produce riches. But as riches increase, so will pride, anger, and love of the world in all its

branches. . . . Is there no way to prevent this—this continual decay of pure religion? We ought not to prevent people from being diligent and frugal; we must exhort all Christians to gain all they can, and to save all they can; that is in effect to grow rich. What way then can we take, that our money may not sink us into the nethermost hell?[14]

In other words, the sect has an inherent problem—in Marxian phraseology, a seed of self-destruction or change—that leads it out of its "pure" state and into something it rebelled against at an earlier point in time. And out of a sect grows a denomination. This is precisely what happened with Wesley's Methodists; indeed, it is a pattern that has also been followed by most of the other major Christian denominations today. Such groups as the Baptists, the Lutherans, the Presbyterians, and the Seventh-Day Adventists all began at one point as sects, but each has evolved to full-fledged denominational status today. David Harrell, who focuses on this manner of development in tracing the evolution of the Church of Christ sect, mentions that the evolution of some of these sectarian groups is directly related to the changing character of the membership of the group: "The cultured element in the movement . . . simply [begins] the search for a more sophisticated type of religion."[15]

THE INSTITUTIONALIZED SECT

Another important type of religious organization is what Yinger calls the *established sect* and what others call the *institutionalized sect*.[16] It has been necessary to develop this concept to cover a route that sects occasionally take as an alternate to the predominant sect-to-denomination pattern. There is, of course, yet a third path that many sects follow—the sect-to-oblivion route. In fact, most sects do not survive long. Internal rivalries and personality clashes, problems with leadership succession, the geographic mobility of members, urban renewal that disperses constituencies and removes facilities—all conspire to make most sects transitory. Those that survive tend to evolve into denominations. However, some become institutionalized sects. Such groups manage to retain elements of their radical protest and a strong commitment to ideology while avoiding the accommodation and modification that would turn them into a denomination. Some denominational characteristics, however, usually become incorporated into the group—the group becomes somewhat bureaucratized; its norms and procedures be-

[14]Quoted in H. Richard Niebuhr, *The Social Sources of Denominationalism* (New York: Meridian Books, 1957), pp. 70–71.

[15]David E. Harrell, Jr., *Emergence of the "Church of Christ" Denomination* (Lufkin, TX: Gospel Guardian Company, 1967), p. 28.

[16]J. Milton Yinger, *The Scientific Study of Religion*, pp. 266–273.

come formalized; some of its members gain higher social status. Yet it does not become a denomination, even though it is no longer a pure sect either. An institutionalized sect is halfway between the denomination and the sect on the church-sect continuum. What is of crucial significance, however, is that it is in a state of arrested development—the evolutionary process has been brought to a standstill.

Some examples will help clarify this type of religious organization. Religious cooperative and utopian groups such as the Amish, the Hutterites, the Dukhobors, and various Mennonite groups are excellent examples. The Quakers (Society of Friends) are a fairly well-known group that also qualifies as an institutionalized sect. These groups are like the pure sect in the sense of being relatively small in numbers, engaging in protest against both the way religion has been routinized in denominations and the society itself, and emphasizing democratic involvement of members and thereby avoiding extensive bureaucratization. In fact, most such groups do not employ full-time clergy.

Members of institutionalized sects are unlike members of ordinary sects in that their socioeconomic status is often higher. Furthermore, their religious expression in worship is less emotionally charged, and they are more concerned about education than the newly formed sect, which is primarily a fellowship of adults.

How does one account for the arrested development of the institutionalized sect? The cooperative religious groups provide one significant element in suggesting an answer to this question. Groups such as the Amish have avoided unsettling influences from the surrounding society and from other religious groups by the rather dramatic tactic of withdrawing to a considerable degree from the surrounding society. As mentioned in Chapter 3, this includes physical or geographic isolation, to the degree that such is possible in a modern society, by establishing themselves exclusively in rural environments. In the process, their members collectively become nearly self-sufficient, depending on the outside world for little except machinery, fuel, and building materials. Thus, their members engage in only minimal contact with people outside their group. Such groups further increase their isolation by forbidding television sets and radios and by limiting the education of the children to elementary school. By specifying a very simple lifestyle and adopting distinctive clothing, they deliberately set themselves apart from others and maintain a readily discernable identity, besides avoiding the interaction with the outside world involved in keeping up with new styles. By deliberately minimizing contact with the outside, by making a virtue out of their uniqueness, and by carefully socializing their children, they contribute significantly to their protracted period of "suspended animation." Some of these groups have existed for hundreds of years with very little change and show essentially no signs of accelerating their pace of change today.

The Quakers, on the other hand, have not physically isolated them selves. In fact, among their members are many high-status, highly educated professionals. Quakers, moreover, are politically and socially motivated and involved, as exemplified by their support for two social action and lobbying groups in Washington, D.C. Yet the Quaker sect, which originated in the mid-1600s, has not become a full-fledged denomination. The Methodist Church and the Society of Friends today are quite different kinds of organizations, although both started out as sectarian movements. Yinger contrasts these two groups in making a very important theoretical suggestion concerning why one group will proceed along the continuum to denominational status while another will stop short at the institutionalized-sect stage. He states that differential status improvement could not be a cause, since members of both groups have moved up the class ladder in fairly equal proportions. There does seem to be some difference, however, in intensity of persecution. Quakers were more vigorously opposed and persecuted than Methodists everywhere. Thus, conceivably the Quakers could have developed a stronger feeling of cultural isolation and thus greater internal solidarity.

But at best Yinger suggests that such could only be a proximate cause. The really important question is, Why were the Quakers more vigorously opposed than the Methodists? Answering this question requires examining the nature of the group's original protest. Yinger's suggestion is that those sects that emphasize problems of individual anxiety, sin, and salvation tend to evolve into denominations, while sects whose concern is focused on social evils and injustices will become established or institutionalized sects.[17] Radically different kinds of protest distinguished the early Methodists from the early Quakers. The Wesley brothers and other early Methodists were concerned primarily with individual morality and worked to rescue people from their sin. Quakers, however, attacked society and called for political reforms, for an end to societal injustice and discrimination, for an end to poverty. Certainly society could more easily tolerate, even encourage, the Methodists' emphasis yet feel threatened by the Quakers' beliefs, a fact that goes far in explaining why one sect was persecuted vigorously and the other not nearly so much.

The point here is not so much that as a result of societal persecution and opposition a group (such as the Quakers) may be forced back on its own resources and develop higher group identification and morale. The point is that such a group finds its feeling of estrangement from society intensified—it feels less at home in society and is less likely to evolve to full-blown denominational status, one characteristic of which is a relatively cozy, supportive relationship with the governing structure of the society. The stance the Quakers adopted placed them in a role more like that of an antagonist

---

[17]Yinger, *The Scientific Study of Religion*, pp. 266–268.

and less like that of even "loyal opposition," as we understand that term from British parliamentary politics.

In a sense, the physical isolation of the cooperative, Utopian religious groups is matched by the political and social isolation of the Quakers. Moreover, the institutionalized cooperative sects are also in opposition to much that exists in society, which is viewed as basically evil and as a source of contamination. Many of these groups do not even vote in national or local elections. Institutionalized sects such as the Quakers, on the other hand, do not express their opposition to society by withdrawing; they become activists and try to change society. In either case, however, such groups are inhibited in moving along the path to standard denominational status.

THE CULT

The final type of religious organization to consider is the religious cult. A *cult* is similar to a sect in its rejection of the religious patterns and formulations of denominations—or of whatever the society's dominant form(s) of religion happens to be. Cult members were either not attracted to dominant religious groups in the first place or, like sectarians, became disenchanted with commonly accepted religious forms. The cult differs from the sect, however, in that it does not call for a return to the original, pure religion, but rather emphasizes the new—a new revelation or insight provided by a supernatural power, say, or the rediscovery of an old revelation that had been lost and unknown these many years (and which is therefore new to this age). Cults thus tend to be out of the mainstream of the dominant religious system in a society. Although there will usually be some overlapping of ideology and terminology, cults deliberately contrast themselves with dominant traditional religious groups. As might be expected, cults frequently employ new terminology and symbols. The discourses of some groups, such as the Great I Am, are hardly intelligible to the uninitiated. The themes of cults tend to be mystical and esoteric. Furthermore, a cult is more likely than any other type of religious group to be centered around a charismatic leader—that is, a person who is believed to have been given special revelation or knowledge and the ability to open the door of truth and insight to the uninitiated. Father Divine, Daddy Grace, Mary Baker Eddy, the Reverend Jim Jones, and the Reverend Moon are such types.

Cults also have a strong individualistic emphasis, stressing peace of mind and getting the individual in tune with the supernatural while exhibiting relatively little concern with social change. Cults tend to be urban centered, in part because they have traditionally not attracted great hordes of people and therefore need a large population to draw from, but likely also in part because cults tend to attract the disenchanted, those persons looking for meaningful attachments to counterbalance their anonymity—persons who are probably more likely to be found in urban settings. Cults seldom develop much of an organizational structure, often tend to remain small and informal, and can be quite casual about membership requirements. They may not even require followers to sever their other religious affiliations.

Cults tend to be rather transitory and short-lived. Being dependent on a charismatic leader, they tend to dissolve when the leader dies, disappears, or is discredited. Occasionally, however, a cult persists, develops a structure and means of leadership succession, grows in size, and actually moves toward denominational status. In a study of cults in Alberta, Canada, W. E. Mann found the following characteristics of members: Anglo-Saxon by ethnic background, more female than male, individuals rather than family units, avid readers with above average educational attainment, highly mobile, and although of comfortable financial means, seeming to lack full middle-class acceptance.[18] Although a few writers have placed the cult beyond the extreme end of the church-sect continuum, another way of viewing it is to see it as an alternate to the sect at one end that may move onto the continuum at some point and give evidence of evolution toward denominational or quasi-denominational status. Figure 5-1 shows what we are suggesting. The dotted line associated with the cult indicates the possibility that it may change, not die, and get on the evolutionary road toward denominational status. A classic example is Christian Science, which began as a cult (with Mary Baker Eddy as its leader) but today exhibits most of the characteristics of a standard denomination. Similarly, the Nation of Islam ("Black Muslims"), which originally met all the criteria of a cult—it began as a small group with a charismatic leader (Elijah Muhammed) who preached a new doctrine of black supremacy and Islam (out of the mainstream of Christianity), emphasized individual self-help rather than societal reform, and was primarily urban—is now showing definite signs of moving toward a denominational pattern.

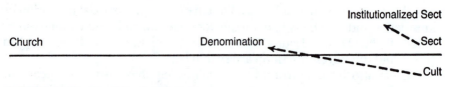

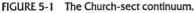

FIGURE 5-1   The Church-sect continuum.

[18]W. E. Mann, *Sect, Cult, and Church in Alberta* (Toronto: University of Toronto Press, 1955), pp. 5–8, 37–40.

It must be noted that cults are rather commonplace today. Faith-healing cults continue to abound; cults that center around Eastern religious ideas and individual gurus have gained in popularity; interest in the occult and the formation of groups around the practice of the occult have increased; and segments of the drug culture that celebrate the use of mind-expanding drugs as a religious enterprise continue to emerge. The cult phenomenon is very much alive and well, although individual cults themselves may be extremely transitory as they flower today and wither tomorrow.

JIM JONES'S PEOPLES TEMPLE AS CULT

To illustrate some of the points we have made concerning cults we will look somewhat specifically at the Reverend Jim Jones's Peoples Temple as a representative religious cult. Although Jim Jones started off traditionally enough as an ordained minister in a standard denomination that had only some slight sectarian tendencies, he gradually began sounding like a cult leader with a new message to bring.

First, that new message.[19] The date is November, 1969; the place is a bona fide Christian church—the Peoples Temple Christian Church in Ukiah, California. The Reverend Jim Jones is preaching.

> The King James Bible is full of contradictions and errors. . . . If there were a God in Heaven, do you think he would let me say these things about his Holy Word? If there is a God in Heaven, let him strike me dead![20]

Was this a "new message? If not new, it was unusual—to say the least—from a Christian pulpit. Note that Jones is not calling for a return to the original message or intent of Scripture as a sectarian would. He simply discredits the Bible and substitutes a new message. As Jones continues he sounds more and more like a cult leader.

> I have seen by divine revelation the total annihilation of this country and many other parts of the world. San Francisco will be flattened. The only survivors will be those people who are hidden in the cave that I have been shown in a vision. Those who go into this cave with me will be saved from the poisonous radioactive fallout that will follow the nuclear bomb attack. This cave is what led our church to migrate to this little valley from Indianapolis, Indiana. I

---

[19]All quotations are as attributed to the Rev. Jim Jones by Jeannie Mills. Reprinted by permission of A & W Publishers, Inc., New York, from *Six Years with God: Life Inside Rev. Jim Jones's Peoples Temple* by Jeannie Mills. Copyright © 1979 by MBR/Investments, Inc.

[20]Mills, *Six Years with God*, p. 121. Reprinted by permission of A & W Publishers, Inc.

have been shown that this cave goes deep into the earth. All the members of my church will stay in it until it is safe to come out. We have gathered in Redwood Valley for protection, and after the war is over we will be the only survivors. It will be up to our group to begin life anew on this continent.[21]

In a cult, a charismatic leader[22] not only brings a new message but is frequently deified—or something very close to it. For example, Father Divine openly called himself God and his followers regarded him as such. By way of another example, in the Unification Church it is very difficult to distinguish when references to God are to God as commonly viewed in Judeo-Christian terms or to Reverend Moon himself. Often it does indeed seem to be Moon.

We note the same pattern with Jim Jones.

Jim looked around the room again and in a loud voice called out, "Wilson." The room became silent.

"Yes?" This time it was a middle-aged black woman sitting near the front.

"You have been having a dull pain in your stomach even as you sit here today."

"Yes."

"To give you more faith I want you to know that I can see a bottle of aspirin in your bathroom medicine chest. It's sitting beside a prescription bottle that was given to you by a Dr. Edwards."

Mrs. Wilson, who had been speaking softly, suddenly shouted out, "Yes, Lord!"

"Who can know these things?" Jim asked with a sweet smile.

Tears were flowing down her cheeks as she answered, "Only God could know."

"You have a cancer in your stomach. You don't even know it is there but by the power of love I will make it pass."

Mrs. Wilson went into the restroom with one of the women that Jim indicated was a nurse and a few minutes later they returned. The nurse was holding a mass of smelly flesh covered with blood in a handful of tissues. Jim asked the nurse to take it around to show those who might be skeptical. He took his dark glasses off for a moment as he looked lovingly at the woman and said, "This is the cancer that left your body, and I tell you that it will never return. Praise God!" And praise she did, along with everyone else in the room. But the praise was not for God, it was all directed toward Jim Jones.[23]

Additional evidence of the centrality and power of the leader in a cult can be seen in the following reflections by Jeannie Mills.

[21]Mills, *Six Years with God*, p. 122. Reprinted by permission of A & W Publishers, Inc.

[22]A charismatic leader, as introduced in Chapter 3, is a person thought by his or her followers (1) to possess special qualities superior to ordinary people, sometimes to the point of seeing the leader as divine; (2) to have access to special knowledge or revelation; (3) to be directed to lead her or his followers down a new, perhaps revolutionary, path; and (4) to be able to create a special relationship with his or her followers—what amounts to a "calling" to them, of a level of trust, love, and obedience that they had not known before.

[23]Mills, *Six Years with God*, pp. 123–124. Reprinted by permission of A & W Publishers, Inc.

I was amazed at how little disagreement there was between the members of this church. Before we joined the church, Al and I couldn't even agree on whom to vote for in the presidential election. Now that we all belonged to a group, family arguments were becoming a thing of the past. There was never a question of who was right, because Jim was always right. When our large household met to discuss family problems, we didn't ask for opinions. Instead, we put the question to the children, "What would Jim do?" It took the difficulty out of life. There was a type of "manifest destiny" which said the Cause was right and would succeed. Jim was right and those who agreed with him were right. If you disagreed with Jim, you were wrong. It was as simple as that.[24]

He began to hint broadly that he was none other than "God Almighty." In a secret meeting he told us that he knew his previous incarnations. He bragged that he had been Buddha, the Bab, Jesus Christ, and, most recently, Lenin. "Of course," he warned them, "this is highly confidential and you aren't to tell anyone else. The members might not understand, especially about that last incarnation."

When he realized that his staff members were awed by this revelation, he decided that the rest of his members would probably be impressed, too. In the next Sunday service he announced that he was going to tell those who were present one of his greatest secrets. With a great deal of ceremony he announced, "I have lived on this earth before. I have come for a special mission and you who are following me are my chosen people. Most of you have been with me during some of my previous incarnations. I lived thousands of years ago as Buddha. Then I spent a short incarnation as the Bab, the person who founded the Bahai faith. I have lived on earth as Jesus the Christ, and my last incarnation was in Russia as Vladimir Lenin." He spoke with such authority and sincerity that we all believed him.

It was a wonderful secret and we felt privileged that he had shared it with us. "We are so fortunate to be able to follow him" was the sentiment expressed by most of the members. I'm sure that if Jim had known what was just around the corner he wouldn't have been so anxious to make these astounding claims. He was openly bragging that he was God Almighty by the time the San Francisco temple was ready to be used as a worship center.[25]

Sometimes the charismatic leader is viewed as having extraordinary, miracle-working power. Note Jones the miracle worker in the following scene.

There were more people than usual at the Sunday service, and for some reason the church members hadn't brought enough food to feed everyone. It became apparent that the last fifty people weren't going to get any meat. Jim announced, "Even though there isn't enough food to feed this multitude, I am blessing the food that we have and multiplying it—just as Jesus did in biblical times."

Sure enough, a few moments after he made this startling announcement, Eva Pugh came out of the kitchen beaming, carrying two platters filled with

---

[24]Mills, *Six Years with God*, p. 147. Reprinted by permission of A & W Publishers, Inc.

[25]Mills, *Six Years with God*, pp. 180–181. Reprinted by permission of A & W Publishers, Inc.

fried chicken. A big cheer came from the people assembled in the room, especially from the people who were at the end of the line.

The "blessed chicken" was extraordinarily delicious, and several of the people mentioned that Jim had produced the best-tasting chicken they had ever eaten. One of the members, Chuck Beikman, a man who had come with Jim from Indianapolis, jokingly mentioned to a few people standing near him that he had seen Eva drive up a few moments earlier with buckets from the Kentucky Fried Chicken stand. He smiled as he said, "The person that blessed that chicken was Colonel Sanders."

During the evening meeting Jim mentioned the fact that Chuck had made fun of his gift. "He lied to some of the members here, telling them that the chicken had come from a local shop," Jim stormed. "But the Spirit of Justice has prevailed. Because of his lie Chuck is in the men's restroom right now, wishing that he was dead. He is vomiting and has diarrhea so bad he can't talk!"

An hour later a pale and shaken Chuck Beikman walked out of the men's room and up to the front, being supported by one of the guards. Jim asked him, "Do you have anything you'd like to say?"

Chuck looked up weakly and answered, "Jim, I apologize for what I said. Please forgive me."

As we looked at Chuck, we vowed in our hearts that we would never question any of Jim's "miracles"—at least not out loud. Years later, we learned that Jim had put a mild poison in a piece of cake and given it to Chuck.[26]

Although the charisma of the leader is important in maintaining a cult, it is also necessary that the group have important goals and aspirations. The group needs more substance than hero worship by itself. The ostensible goals of the Peoples Temple are epitomized in Jim Jones's words, as follows:

"I have the answers to the problems of society. Someday I will be the ruler of the United States. I will eliminate racism, political oppression, ecological imbalances, and the problem of the superrich and the superpoor. I will make the whole country become like our community. I call this "Apostolic Socialism."[27]

It probably needs to be said at this point, in all fairness, that much of the time the group strenuously opposed racism, was itself highly integrated racially, and provided for the care of scores of lost, homeless, and desperate people. It hardly needs mentioning of course that some of these were among the followers who lost their lives in Jonestown.

In the following vignette, we note the introduction of the idea of mass suicide that became the ultimate test of dedication to the "Cause" as identified by Jones in the preceding quote. The year is 1973, five years before the deaths at Jonestown.

[26]Mills, *Six Years with God*, pp. 151–152. Reprinted by permission of A & W Publishers, Inc.

[27]Mills, *Six Years with God*, p. 218. Reprinted by permission of A & W Publishers, Inc.

One afternoon the P.C.[28] counsellors received an emergency message. "Come to the church immediately for a special meeting." We dropped what we were doing and left as instructed. When we arrived it was obvious that Jim was very upset.

He began, "Eight people left the church last night. They cut the telephone wires so Tom couldn't call to warn us." He was speaking in a low voice as though he were afraid the walls might hear what he was saying. "No one knows why they left, but Jim and Terry Cobb, Wayne Pietila, Micki Touchette, and four others all disappeared. Don't worry, though, I'll find them." Jim tried to sound confident, but then he shook his head in despair. "These eight people might cause our church to go down. They could say things that would discredit our group. This might be the time for all of us to make our translation together." He had mentioned the idea of a "translation" a few times before, but no one had ever taken it seriously. His idea was that all the counsellors would take poison or kill themselves at the same time, and then he promised we would all be translated to a distant planet to live with him for eternity. The few who believed this fairy tale said they'd be happy to do it anytime. Now, however, faced with death, it became obvious that there were many who didn't want to.

"What about the other church members, and our children?" Linda Amos asked.

"Oh, yes, that's the problem. Those who would be left behind." Jim was speaking slowly and deliberately now, and it seemed that he was trying to formulate his ideas as he spoke. "Perhaps we could devise a plan where the children would be sent to another country first." I relaxed as I realized that his plan wasn't as well thought out as I had feared. Since he hadn't worked out these important details, I was sure he couldn't insist that we all kill ourselves right now.

"I want to take a vote today to find out how dedicated you all are," Jim said. "Life is a bore. Surely no one here is enamored with his existence. You've seen too much reality in all the hours of counselling at the P.C. meetings. How many of you here today would be willing to take your own lives now to keep the church from being discredited? Perhaps this way we will go down in history as revolutionaries. We could leave a note saying that we were doing this as a sign that we want peace on earth, or that we couldn't exist as an apostolic socialist group, or something like that."[29]

But one begins to see, once the commitment to the group and its leader has been made and dependency upon the group has been established, most anything becomes believable. Note the following account by Mills.

Jim told us another big secret that night. "One of the things that Carolyn had been doing was negotiating the purchase of an atomic bomb for us." He was talking almost in a whisper in case the room was bugged. "We have everything but the detonator, and we are trying to get one right now. It is important for our group to have power, and any person with an atomic bomb has power."

[28]The peoples council—the inner core leaders comprising some thirty to fifty people.
[29]Mills, *Six Years with God*, pp. 230–231. Reprinted by permission of A & W Publishers, Inc.

He began to explain to us how he believed World War III would start. "I believe that someone will probably sneak up from South America and detonate an atom bomb in the United States. Then our country will assume that the bomb was sent from Russia. Our country will retaliate by sending a bomb over there, and within a short time, there will be a nuclear holocaust. Everyone will be destroyed, except the people who are living below the equator."

It was a wild theory, and most of us assumed it was another scare tactic, like the first bomb theory and his cave in Redwood Valley. The part that did impress us, though, was that we were the owners of an atomic bomb. We now felt we had enough power to make people respect and fear our group.[30]

But in the end, all Jim Jones had was potassium cyanide and the promise of an immortality that comes with dying for a cause you believe in. Yet that was enough. And a religious cult had flourished, but now is gone.

REFINEMENTS OF THE CHURCH-SECT TYPOLOGY

Although the church-sect typology that has been presented and applied in this chapter is time honored, and although we continue to see it as helpful, particularly in its descriptive capacity, the concept has had its critics. In fact a very substantial literature has emerged in the last thirty-five years on this topic.[31] Some of the critics suggest refinements; others suggest alternatives.

Actually, in a very real sense of the term, much of what we have presented in this chapter has been in the nature of refinements of the original church-sect typology. The concepts "denomination," "institutionalized sect," and "cult" are all refinements of the original typology proposed by Troeltsch and Weber.

Another approach by way of refinement has been to elaborate the list of characteristics of sects and/or churches. For example, Liston Pope makes twenty-one distinctions between the church and the sect in his classic study of the religious life of Gastonia, North Carolina.[32]

[30]Mills, *Six Years with God*, pp. 277–278. Reprinted by permission of A & W Publishers, Inc.

[31]See for example, Benton Johnson, "A Critical Appraisal of the Church-Sect Typology," *American Sociological Review 22*, no. 1 (1957), 88–92; idem, "On Church and Sect," *American Sociological Review 28*, no. 1 (1967), 64–68; idem, "Church-Sect Revisited," *Journal for the Scientific Study of Religion 10*, no. 2 (1971), 124–137; Erich Goode, "Some Critical Observations on the Church-Sect Dimension," *Journal for the Scientific Study of Religion 6*, no. 1 (1967), 69–77; idem, "Further Reflections on the Church-Sect Dimension," *Journal for the Scientific Study of Religion 6*, no. 2 (1967), 270–275; N. J. Demerath III, "In a Sow's Ear," *Journal for the Scientific Study of Religion 6*, no. 1 (1967), 77–84; Allan W. Eister, "Toward a Radical Critique of Church-Sect Typologizing," *Journal for the Scientific Study of Religion 6*, no. 1 (1967), 85–90; J. Kenneth Benson and James Dorsett, "Church-Sect Replaced," *Journal for the Scientific Study of Religion 10*, no. 2 (1971), 138–151; James A. Beckford, "Religious Organization," *Current Sociology XXI*, no. 2 (1975), 5–170, particularly 96–102.

[32]Liston Pope, *Millhands and Preachers* (New Haven, CT: Yale University Press, 1942), pp. 122–124.

Benton Johnson went in the opposite direction and suggested that there is really only one essential distinction between the church and the sect. That distinction is whether a religious group accepts or rejects its larger social environment. The sect rejects; the church or denomination accepts.[33] This distinction is of course highly compatible with all of our discussion in this chapter. Johnson is simply trying to distill everything into its essence. The sect opposes and challenges and rejects much of what it sees in the surrounding society and its culture; the church or denomination compromises, reinforces, and accepts most of that same society and culture.

Before Johnson's single-variable measure (1963), Yinger (1957) had proposed two criteria for differentiating churches from sects: degree of inclusiveness-exclusiveness of the group and degree of attention paid by the group to the task of social integration as opposed to satisfaction of personal need.[34] By 1970, Yinger added Johnson's criterion and changed his earlier second criterion to emphasize degree of bureaucratization and success in integrating a variety of subunits into one structure.[35]

Roland Robertson has suggested two criteria: the basis of legitimacy as perceived by the leaders of the religious group and the principle of membership implemented by the group.[36] The legitimacy measure contrasts views of religious leaders: (1) the view that one's group is only one among other sets of acceptable or valid religious vehicles (religious pluralism) and (2) the view that one's group is the only valid religious form (unique, true religion). The membership principle contrasts "relatively demanding standards of admission and/or religious performance" (exclusivism) with low standards of acceptance (inclusivism).[37]

Another interesting modification has been contributed by Stephen Steinberg. He has analyzed the emergence of Reform Judaism from its "parent," Orthodox Judaism, not as formation of a sect but as a "church movement." That is, Reform Judaism did not object to any "perversion of true religion" embodied in Orthodox Judaism but to the continued insistence by Orthodox Judaism on retaining the "old ways"—the Reform movement sought to "modernize" Judaism. Building on Benton Johnson's single-variable distinction between church and sect that we earlier described—in which a religious organization accepting the surrounding social environment is defined as a church and one rejecting it as a sect—Steinberg points out that the rebel group (Reform Judaism) did not follow the common

[33]Benton Johnson, "On Church and Sect," *American Sociological Review 28*, no. 4 (1963), 539–549.

[34]J. Milton Yinger, *Religion, Society, and the Individual* (New York: Macmillan, 1957), pp. 147–148.

[35]J. Milton Yinger, *The Scientific Study of Religion* (New York: Macmillan, 1970), p. 257.

[36]Roland Robertson, *The Sociological Interpretation of Religion* (New York: Schocken Books, 1970), pp. 123ff.

[37]Ibid., p. 124.

route of the sect by rejecting its social environment but accepted and accommodated to that environment.[38] Although Steinberg notes that conditions giving rise to such a "church movement" are rare, such a development is well worth noting. Furthermore, our understanding of the dynamics of such a development is enhanced by our understanding of what "normally" happens along the church-sect continuum.

[38]Stephen Steinberg, "Reform Judaism: The Origin and Evolution of a 'Church Movement,'" *Journal for the Scientific Study of Religion 5*, no. 1 (1965), 117–129.

6

Religious Conflict

CONFLICT THEORY

During their reading of the text up to now, many readers will have sensed an emphasis on what is known within the field of sociology as "structural-functional" theory. This has been the emphasis in part because much that religion is and does has purposes and functions that help people adjust to and accept the vagaries and vicissitudes of life, but also in part because to the extent that people are enabled to continue carrying out their social roles in a reasonably competent manner, the society itself is aided. Here we are thinking about such functions as providing a sense of belonging, suggesting answers to questions of deep concern, promising ultimate release and salvation, and providing a sense of life purpose.

But another major theory in sociology is in sharp contrast, namely, the conflict perspective. This perspective recognizes that there is another side of the coin. Religion not only might provide solace and comfort and explanations for complex and puzzling issues, but it can also create or at least enhance stress, anxiety, and worry, guilty consciences, and sexual "hang-ups." This perspective also emphasizes the competition and antagonisms, even outright physical conflict, that exist among both individuals and sub-groups in a society, even among religious people and their groups. Additionally, the conflict perspective features the availability within religion of considerable power and influence that can be used to control and exploit others.

As we begin our discussion of conflict theory, particularly as it applies to religion in society, we must immediately take note of the founding father of this perspective. He is Karl Marx, who over a century ago called religion the "opium of the people." As such, religion in its organized form was in direct competition with Marx's socialist political philosophy, which defined religion, although a powerful force in its own right, as an enemy of a socialistic revolutionary state. But quite apart from the sedating and misdirecting effects of religion, people and the groups of which they are a part in a capitalist society are in competition and, as such, in a conflict situation. They are continually seeking their advantage in a world of limited resources. Any cooperation and integration that might develop among these competitors is a result of expediency and self-interest and is therefore tenuous.

But in addition to identifying the competition (conflict) that exists among individuals and groups, Marx emphasized the use made of religion by the dominant and powerful in society to encourage acceptance of one's lot in life regardless of its lowly and unpleasant character, the performance of one's job as competently and energetically as possible, and a looking forward to one's ultimate reward in heaven, nirvana, or whatever. Conflict theorists speak of control and manipulation of the masses in a community or society by the powerful elite with their middle-class supporters. Marx observed that religion, with its emphasis on doing one's duty and obeying the laws of the land that are viewed in turn as the laws of God, serves as a narcotic drug administered by the elites to the less-privileged in society to keep them docile and accepting of the status quo.

In this connection, Marx asserted that despite their seeming complexity, societies can be reduced to but two social classes that are inherently in conflict with one another. These are the owners of the means of production (the bourgeoisie) and those who work for the owners and have only their muscle and energy to sell (the proletariat). The owners are out to extract as much work and product from the workers with as little expenditure in the form of wages as possible. The workers of course want more than a starvation wage and at least some share of the product of their labor. And thus you have class conflict—the eternal conflict in society—eternal, that is, according to Marx, until the workers can prevail and inaugurate worldwide socialism and over time create a perfect classless society.

We should mention somewhat parenthetically at this point that today many conflict theorists prefer to emphasize the concept of power instead of ownership. If power is defined as "the probability that one actor within a social relationship will be in a position to carry out his own will despite resistance,"[1] then having power (or having little to none) becomes crucial

---

[1]Max Weber, *Economy and Society* (New York: Oxford University Press, 1947), originally published in 1922.

and narrows human relationships to the bare essentials. It's still a contrast between the haves and the have-nots. But now management and supervisory people in the large corporations and public institutions can be included with the haves, whereas they would often have to be included as have-nots if actual ownership of the means of production were a requirement. In other words, Marx was looking at early industrial society. We are now in a postindustrial, service-oriented society in which positioning on the basis of specialized training and skills in a bureaucratic hierarchy is all important.

But, to return to the place of religion in society according to conflict theory, a major observation by conflict theorists is that while one cannot say that religion per se creates the problems faced by the proletariat—the poverty, the misery, the inequality, the shortened life expectancy, to name a few—for a great many people a religious expression or interpretation is their sole response to the injustice. That could be a response of resigned acceptance, of hope for greater reward in the life of bliss that will follow this present life, which is admittedly worse than it could be, and of bowing to the will of God, which far surpasses our own shortsighted, selfish understanding and perspective. And of course, the point made here by conflict theorists is that such a religious response is missing the real point of the issue and therefore fails its followers.

A second major point of conflict theory is that religion deflects the actions of the downtrodden from striking at the root sources of their oppression. Here we would observe the common themes of most religions that one must accept one's lot in life, carry out the duties that one is assigned, and find emotional release through acceptable channels such as participation in an expressive, emotional-release type of religious service. As such, Marx calls for the abolition of religion to eliminate the "illusory" happiness of people so that true happiness can be achieved.[2]

Those at the other end of the economic scale will thank God that they have a more favored position in life. They might carry food baskets to the poor at Christmastime but will not raise their wages, allow them into a profit-sharing plan, or give them the training or opportunity for a better job.

We should mention here that conflict theorists view religion as they would any other institution in society and as such are not particularly "picking on" religion. It is assumed that in every institution and social relationship a fundamental conflict of interest is in operation. It is assumed that one will observe exploitation, misdirected energies, false comfort, and much that sounds like "pie-in-the-sky-by-and-by" most anywhere one looks. Such a perspective from conflict theory might well elicit angry rejoinders from many believers. Yet conflict theory is at least partly right in the sense that at their core all religions try to make their members feel better and more secure as they face a future that is uncertain for everyone. Members

---

[2]Karl Marx, "Contribution to the Critique of Hegel's Philosophy of Right," in *Marx and Engels On Religion* ed., Reinhold Niebuhr (New York: Schocken Books, 1964), p. 42.

have a conviction that they know the real truth about most things, that they know what they should do (rituals) to please the supreme being(s), and that they can look forward to a better future whether in heaven or by reincarnation or by the good memories of them retained by those one leaves behind. Both proreligionists and antireligionists will grant that religion does succeed to some degree in pacifying and making hopeful many whose reward in this life is very minimal. We introduced this idea in Chapter 5 and will discuss such functions of religion further in Chapters 8 and 9. But for now we will simply grant that there is very likely truth on both sides of functional/conflict theory. And now we want to examine religion in conflict in an effort to understand that which might seem to be an inherent contradiction, namely, violence in the name and for the sake of religion. What we will look at is so-called "real-life" conflict that exists and needs to be recognized whether one subscribes to conflict theory or to structural-functional theory as the best starting point for understanding social life.

Our first observation is that the religious conflict we see today in such places as Northern Ireland, Iran, Lebanon, Israel, and India is far from new and can be observed throughout all of history. We will point to but a few examples that will lead us to an analysis of contemporary religious conflict later in this chapter.

RELIGIOUS CONFLICT IN HISTORY

If we go back to the history recounted in the Old Testament, we read about a continuous series of wars and battles. These were essentially what can be called political skirmishes of one society or tribe against another as they fought over land and resources. A fundamental reason for such warfare was the fact that the Israelites, following their escape from Egypt, were trying to occupy land that was already inhabited by others. Of course, they believed they were God's chosen people who were simply following God's instructions and proceeding with God's special blessing and assistance. In that sense, it is certainly appropriate to speak of religious conflict, particularly when the Old Testament continually speaks about doing battle not simply against Israel's political enemies but against worshipers of false gods and graven images who as such were God's enemies.

In the Middle Ages, we observe one armed religious conflict after another. They were frequently defined by the participants as "holy wars" because they often took the form of crusades marching through Europe and the Near East to Palestine to defeat the infidels (the Muslims) who had occupied God's sacred ground (Palestine) that should be in Christian hands. The conflict was then Christian against Muslim—a religious conflict.

Or think of the European wars involving the Roman Catholic Church, which often tried to suppress heresy with the sword. One might think of the well-known Inquisition or the less well-known near extermination of the

Waldensians and the Albigensians in southern France just before and after the turn of the thirteenth century. Inasmuch as these groups were branded as heretics, the church felt justified in uniting with secular authorities to annihilate them. The Third Lateran Council in 1179 even proclaimed a crusade against these French Christians, probably the first occasion when this tactic was used against people who viewed themselves as orthodox Christian believers. Pope Innocent III who ruled from 1198 to 1216 is acknowledged to have initiated the final steps in eliminating these reform groups. More crusading armies were organized. And thus, as Kenneth Scott Latourette says, "Religious zeal . . . combined with quite secular motives, sectional jealousies, and the desires of the nobles of Northern France to reduce the power of the South and to profit by its wealth."[3]

Many years of warfare ensued and a great deal of bloodshed and cruelty resulted. It has been reported that when Beziers was entered by a crusading army, the Papal Legate was asked if the faithful Catholics should be spared. He expressed fear that the heretics would feign orthodoxy to escape the sword. So he said, "Kill them all, for God knows his own." And thus the heretics were subdued through nearly total annihilation. These were people who would today have felt fairly comfortable in much of Christendom, even in some Roman Catholic Churches. They believed that laymen and women could preach and administer the sacrament of the Lord's Supper and that a liturgy in Latin made no sense because people couldn't understand it. They believed masses and prayers for the dead were of no effect and that purgatory was not really a place to which souls journeyed after death but rather consisted of the trials and tribulations that people endure in their lifetimes.

We have just been talking about the military crusades directed against the Waldensians and Albigensians. But the better-known crusades were those directed against Muslims. And although the crusades evolved out of a variety of motives, some of which were purely economic and political, several clear religious motives were articulated.

First was the goal of liberating Palestine from the control of infidel Muslims. Second was a desire to create some protection from the Muslim Turks for the beleaguered Byzantine Empire centered in Constantinople. Third was a desire of several popes in succession to heal the breach between the Western, Latin branch of Catholicism and the Eastern, Greek branch.

While Jerusalem was "rescued" for Christian occupation twice (in 1099 and 1229), in 1244 it fell to Muslim siege and was to remain in Muslim hands until the twentieth century. But crusades were not organized solely to rescue Jerusalem. They were also directed against Muslims in Spain, against "pagans" in what is now northern Europe, and against Christian groups that a given Pope might judge to be enemies of the faith.

[3]Kenneth S. Latourette, *A History of Christianity* (New York: Harper & Brothers, 1953), p. 456.

And so with the Crusades we have a nearly perfect example of religion that is not just an accessory to conflict but its initiator. Although some Christians raised voices against the cruelty, the squandering of life and property, the condoning of violence, and excess of all types, a majority of Christians accepted such eventualities as the will of God. In fact, the Latin phrase *Deus vult!* ("God wills it!") was the crusaders' battle cry.

CONTEMPORARY EXAMPLES OF RELIGIOUS CONFLICT

As we now turn to more contemporary examples of religious conflict, we find we need not look far. Almost every continent has a well-known example to display. We will identify several and then look more closely at one of them. In Europe there is the Catholic-Protestant guerrilla war in Northern Ireland. This has been going on for nearly seventy years but at a more intense level since 1970. In the Union of South Africa, as blacks struggle for freedom and equality, many whites continue to hold firm in their support of apartheid and find ultimate justification in the Bible as interpreted by the white Dutch Reformed Church of South Africa. In Lebanon, we have a classic example of religious groups waging war with one another—a situation where religious designations (e.g., Christian, Shiite, Muslim, Druze) identify who shot or bombed whom last night. Elsewhere in the eastern Mediterranean, we see both Israelis and Muslim Palestinians darting back and forth across one another's borders in guerrilla and terrorist actions. In India, a minority religious offshoot of Hinduism—the Sikh religion—garnered many headlines in the 1980s. Two Sikh bodyguards of Prime Minister Indira Ghandi assassinated her on October 31, 1984. Hindu and Muslim citizens retaliated with countless individual and mob acts of violence against Sikhs that ended in at least 2,700 killed and thousands left homeless. Sikhs retaliated against the retaliation by hiding bombs in transistor radios and killing at least eighty-five Indians in April 1985. But the Sikhs are not alone in their propensity to violence. In a country where Mahatma Ghandi's nonviolent revolution set the model for the rest of the world but a few years ago, there were 429 instances of racial or religious riots in 1984.[4]

Clearly what is old is also new and up-to-date in religious conflict. We now turn to a closer examination of the Irish case.

The Protestant-Roman Catholic Conflict in Ireland

As we turn to the Protestant-Roman Catholic conflict in Northern Ireland, we observe an escalation of conflict in recent years yet know that the

[4]William McCord, "Success Takes Its Toll: The Punjab Paradox," *New Leader* 67, no. 10 (October 29, 1984), 14.

origins and precedents for the contemporary conflict go back several generations. We also observe that the violence in Northern Ireland that resumed in 1969 and has been both continuous and at a fairly high level ever since broke a forty-year stretch of relative peace. This resumption of hostilities seemed all the more unfortunate in that activities by recent prime ministers of Ireland, Terance O'Neill and Garret FitzGerald, and the Secretary of Northern Ireland, Tom King, had been aimed at both an improvement of civil rights for Catholics in Northern Ireland and bringing about some significant rapprochement between Catholics and Protestants as they participated in ecumenical dialogue.

The situation in Ireland has been highly confusing to most outside observers and cannot be simply summarized. There are armies such as the Irish Republican Army (both Official and Provisional), the Irish Republican Brotherhood, and the Ulster Defense Association; there are political parties galore, only two of which (the Alliance Party and the Northern Ireland Labour Party) are essentially nonsectarian. The others are almost totally restricted to one religion or the other: the Catholic ones—the Republican Labour Party, the Social Democratic Labour Party, the Republican Party; and the Protestant ones—the Unionist Party, the Democratic Unionist Party, and the Vanguard Unionist Progressive Party. To top it off, there are two Irelands—one (Northern Ireland) where all the violence has been and another (the Republic of Ireland) whose creation in the first place is at the root of the modern-day problems in Northern Ireland.

The earliest evidence of conflict between Protestants and Catholics dates back to the first half of the seventeenth century, when England began to colonize Ireland by confiscating the lands of native Irish Catholics and awarding them to English Anglicans and Scottish Presbyterians. This effort was concentrated in the region of Ulster in the northern part of the island and has since been called the "Plantation of Ulster." It is this same region on the northeast coast of Ireland where the primary conflict remains after 350 years. The "planting" of Protestants in Northern Ireland was accompanied both by driving out some of the native Catholics and subduing others and restricting them to subordinate positions—a pattern that has remained to the present. In 1641, Catholics revolted and massacred numerous Protestants in retaliation for the appropriation of their land by the English and the planting on their land of thousands of English and Scottish citizens. Approximately 12,000 of these settlers were killed, some in acts of private vengeance by individual Irish citizens that were masked as acts of war.[5]

This rebellion flared for eight years until 1649, when Oliver Cromwell arrived from England with 12,000 troops, killing thousands of Catholics and confiscating still more land for distribution to the non-Irish. The last large-scale battle occurred in 1690 when James II (the last Catholic English

---

[5]John O'Beirne Ranelagh, *A Short History of Ireland* (Cambridge, England: Cambridge University Press, 1983), pp. 60–61.

ruler) was thoroughly defeated by William of Orange at the Battle of Boyne River. The anniversary of this victory is a date for a major celebration and a grand parade by Irish Protestants to this day. For Catholics, the battle cry "Remember the Boyne!" still arouses intense emotion. The displacement of Catholics from their land was so thorough that by 1703 in eight of the nine counties Catholics continued to own less than 5 percent of the land.[6]

The Battle of Boyne was followed by systematic suppression of Catholic citizens. They were excluded from the militia, civil service positions, the legal profession, and Parliament and were even denied the right to vote. They could not own land and could only lease for a period not exceeding thirty-one years. Marriages between Protestants and Catholics were forbidden.[7]

Such restrictions and prohibitions were in effect for over 100 years. Early in this period, following one of the few nonsectarian efforts, in this case of Catholics and dissident Presbyterians (a minority Protestant group in Ireland) to achieve independence from England, England disbanded the Irish Parliament and initiated direct rule from England. Midway through the period, in 1858, a Catholic paramilitary organization, the Irish Republican Brotherhood (IRB), was founded. Although the organization was roundly denounced by the Catholic leadership as being a secret and nonreligious organization and therefore on the church's list of forbidden groups, it not only survived, but it symbolized the chaffing of Irish Catholics who were a decided majority of the population when all of Ireland was considered, yet had very little control or voice in the society.

By 1916, the IRB had evolved to the IRA (the Irish Republican Army) and faced counterpart Protestant military groups, the Orange Order and the Ulster Volunteer Force, which in turn were aided by the English special force, the Black and Tans. Thus in 1916, what has come to be known as the Irish Revolution began.

The goal of the Catholics in Ireland was independence and what is called "home rule." Although bitterly opposed by Irish Protestants, the British Parliament passed a home rule resolution for Ireland in 1914. Irish Catholics were of course overjoyed. But despite the act of Parliament and its popularity among Irish Catholics both at home and abroad, the act was not implemented immediately. World War I had begun in 1914 and Britain's attention soon moved away from "the Irish Problem." Impatient and dissatisfied with British failure to follow through on its resolution, Irish nationalists (Catholics) staged an armed rebellion called the Easter Rising in the spring of 1916. They of course met armed resistance from the British garrison and the Protestant paramilitary forces.

---

[6]Richard Rose, *Governing Without Consensus: An Irish Perspective* (London: Faber and Faber, 1971, and Boston, MA: Beacon Press, 1971), p. 79.

[7]Kurt Bowen, *Protestants in a Catholic State* (Montreal: McGill-Queens University Press, 1983), pp. 8–9.

While engaged in guerrilla warfare for several years, neither side could be viewed as winning. But each side had inflicted enough damage and evidenced sufficient power that a compromise seemed in order. The compromise was that in 1920 Ireland was to be partitioned into northern and southern states. The southern part, granted independent status in 1921, constituted the majority of both land and population and was named the Republic of Ireland. This nation had a large Catholic majority and would, under a representative form of government, become a Catholic nation. The region called Ulster—a five-county area in the north—with a majority of Protestants would become Northern Ireland and be ruled directly by England.

Not all Irish Catholics were pleased with the compromise and held out for all of Ireland to be blessed with home rule as a unified Catholic nation. Actually, not until 1925 did all parties formally accept the compromise. And many Catholics continued to hope and work for the unification of North and South into a single Catholic state.

But from the time of partition until the late 1960s, Northern Ireland enjoyed relative peace internally. While Protestants retained control over land, factories, and political office, Catholics were able to make some gains, particularly in education and access to higher-paying jobs. The 1950s and 1960s became known for significant gains in civil rights for Catholics in Northern Ireland. They were attentive followers of the civil rights movement of blacks in America and even adopted its anthem, "We Shall Overcome." This movement involved a change in goals and activities by the Catholics of Northern Ireland. They were no longer talking about the unification of Northern Ireland with the Republic of Ireland and home rule. Instead they were talking about educational opportunities, elimination of discrimination in housing and jobs, and an end to gerrymandered voting districts.

But to the surprise of few who knew the situation well, the Irish civil rights movement was deliberately misinterpreted by Protestant extremists who seemed to be suffering from permanent paranoia. Although the topic had not intruded into the movement at all, some Protestants assumed that all of the talk about civil rights was just the old unification issue in a new garb. What the Catholics were really after, Protestants thought, was union with the Republic of Ireland, home rule, and Protestants losing out to Catholics on all fronts: education, housing, jobs, land ownership, political office, and civil service. As Alfred McClung Lee comments, "Unfortunately, the fact that the civil rights movement enlisted mostly—even though not exclusively—Roman Catholics made it easy for Loyalists to assume that it was an attack on their privileges."[8]

---

[8]Alfred McClung Lee, *Terrorism in Northern Ireland* (New York: General Hall, 1983), p. 72.

What happened was that right-wing Protestant extremists, led by a Presbyterian clergyman, Ian Paisley, stirred up all the old Protestant animosities and suspicions with regard to Catholics. Thus, the modern version of the Protestant-Catholic conflict in Northern Ireland began. Northern Ireland was returned to direct British rule and a contingent of the British Army was placed on Irish soil once again to try to keep the peace. Guerrilla warfare has resumed, and Protestants kill Catholics and Catholics kill Protestants, and both hate the British Army and want it off Irish soil.

Catholics are now caught up in a mind set of rising expectations. That is, it is only when a people begins to experience some of the benefits and advantages society has to offer that had previously been denied that the murmuring and dissatisfaction grow rapidly. It appears that once a certain threshold of benefits has been crossed, the demands for more become both intensive and insistent. Then conflict will be likely to ensue.

Against such a backdrop of rising expectations by Catholics, Protestants are beginning to recognize, if only subconsciously, the fundamental absurdity of the restrictions they have placed around their fellow citizens who are Catholic. Yet they fear loss of their privileged and advantaged position. So they sidestep the civil rights issue and accuse the Catholics all over again that what they are really trying to do is unify Northern Ireland with the Republic of Ireland as an independent nation in which Catholics would be an overwhelming majority nationwide (they are currently a 95-percent majority in the Republic of Ireland). And so the civil war of Protestant versus Catholic has resumed with new vigor. And vigorous and bloody it has been. O'Malley reports that in the eleven years from 1971 to 1982 there were over 28,500 shooting incidents, over 7,200 bomb explosions, and somewhat over 3,100 bombs neutralized. The total of 2,300 deaths would correspond to 345,000 deaths in the United States if the two populations were standardized. That is nearly the number of deaths in the entire Civil War in the United States.[9]

Now, how do we analyze this conflict sociologically? The first thing we need to realize is that although the situation in Northern Ireland is a classic case of down-to-earth religious conflict—conflict so real that Protestants and Catholics shoot and blow up one another at a high rate—it is at the same time much more than a simple conflict of religions. The designations Protestant and Catholic connote more than mere religious affiliation or sets of beliefs and practices. The designations Protestant and Catholic also identify ethnic groups and political groupings. As such, these religious groupings, as is the case with ethnic groups in general, are clearly stratified. Protestants in Northern Ireland are at the top, holding much more power and control of the vital institutions in the society than Catholics. Also, there is considerable

---

[9]Padraig O'Malley, *The Uncivil Wars: Ireland Today* (Boston, MA: Houghton Mifflin Company, 1983), pp. 10–11.

prejudice expressed and discrimination practiced by the dominant ethnic group against the subordinate one. Protestants tend to describe Catholics as lazy and shiftless, oversexed and with too many children, exploiters of the welfare system, ignorant, quarrelsome, and anything else that a dominant ethnic group might want to apply to a minority group in any other multiethnic Western society.[10] When such stereotypes are believed it is easy to rationalize and justify discriminating behavior toward the minority ethnic group as imparting no worse than its members deserve.

In this connection, Easthope points out that in Northern Ireland to know a person's religion is to know his or her most important characteristic. In the United States, the single most informative characteristic is a person's occupation, but not in Northern Ireland. Knowing a person's religious affiliation will in a restricted social area be highly predictive of one's residence, one's occupation and place of work, the schools one attended, one's taste in music, one's political leanings, what daily newspaper is read (Protestants read the *Belfast News Letter*, Catholics read the *Irish News*), what TV stations are watched (Protestants are more likely to watch BBC while Catholics watch Irish TV from Dublin), even what sports one likes (Protestants prefer rugby, cricket, and bowling, while Catholics like football, hurling, and boxing).[11]

Easthope also points out the indelible nature of one's religious designation. Just as one cannot deny or change one's skin color or other genetic features associated with ethnic or racial groups, so one's religious label is essentially inescapable so long as one stays in Northern Ireland. Conversions from one religious group to another are almost nonexistent, and rules requiring marriage within the faith are hardly ever violated.

Further evidence that the designations Protestant and Catholic are more than simple religious labels is observed day after day in the refusal of Catholics to abide by the law of the church and its hierarchy in the sphere of Irish nationalism. Here we refer to the fact that the Catholic Church both from Rome and at the local level has formally and consistently condemned the paramilitary organizations that were founded in the nineteenth century and continue today. Specifically, the IRA has been denounced numerous times by the Church. Catholics are actually ordered by their church to resign from the IRA; as far back as 1861, the Archbishop in Northern Ireland excommunicated all the members of the IRB, the predecessor of the IRA. Yet today, almost no one leaves either the church or the forbidden organization. O'Malley observes that "otherwise devout Catholics continue to ignore the church's denunciations—the national question transcends ques-

---

[10]Barger, *Race and Ethnic Relations*, p. 275.

[11]Gary Easthope, "Religious War in Northern Ireland," *Sociology* 10, no. 3 (September 1976), 431; Albert J. Menendez, *The Bitter Harvest* (Washington, D.C.: Robert B. Luce, 1973), p. 17.

tions of faith and morals."[12] Thus, the IRA could brusquely dismiss Pope John Paul II's impassioned plea to end the fighting made on his visit to Ireland in 1979.

Interestingly, it has often been observed that even unbelievers and those who have lost their faith are identified as Catholics or Protestants for political and social purposes. Such observations have prompted Jimmy Breslin, an Irish-American journalist, to say, "In my opinion the words 'Protestant' and 'Catholic' in Northern Ireland have virtually no religious meaning at all, they stand for the 'ins' and 'outs' of a political system."[13]

A sociological concept that can handle the shifting meanings of the designations Protestant and Catholic is that of ethnic group. Wallis, Bruce, and Taylor[14] point out that the two religious groups clearly qualify as ethnic groups as defined by Ian Robertson, who says:

> From the sociological viewpoint . . . an ethnic group is a larger number of people who, as a result of their shared cultural traits and high level of mutual interaction, come to regard themselves, and to be regarded, as a cultural unity. Unlike racial differences, ethnic differences are culturally learned and not genetically inherited.[15]

As we mentioned a little earlier in this chapter, Protestants and Catholics follow very distinct lines of activity from political party affiliation to what sports they participate in. Thus, although not different racially, culturally they proceed in their own track and rarely intersect with the other ethnic group. And as ethnic groups everywhere, they are stratified, with Protestants possessing more "ethnic honour" than Catholics.[16]

But by identifying Catholics and Protestants as distinctive ethnic groups we do not mean to suggest that the more theological or religious elements of these denominational families are unimportant. In fact, it is important to note that Protestants and Catholics in Northern Ireland are highly particularistic. That is, there is a strong sense of in-group/out-group identification and a conviction that the denominations are not only different and therefore distinguishable from one another but that there is a deep gulf between them, with one of them vastly superior to the other. It is no secret that the superior group is "my" group. The differences are so great and significant that members are likely to go so far as to assert that while our

---

[12]O'Malley, *The Uncivil Wars*, p. 5.

[13]Jimmy Breslin, statement, pp. 79–82, in House of Representatives, Committee on Foreign Affairs, Subcommittee on Europe, *Northern Ireland* (Washington, D.C.: Government Printing Office, 1972), p. 80.

[14]Roy Wallis, Steve Bruce, and David Taylor, "*No Surrender!" Paisleyism and the Politics of Ethnic Identity in Northern Ireland* (Belfast: Queen's University of Belfast, 1986).

[15]Ian Robertson, *Sociology* (New York: Worth Publishers, 1981), p. 282.

[16]Wallis et al., "*No Surrender!*," p. 3.

group will be saved for eternity, members of the other group will be damned.

While it is often true that members of highly particularistic religions are active proselytizers and try to bring others to see the light, this is not happening in Northern Ireland. In large part, this relates back to the idea of both groups being parallel civil religions. Just as a black- or brown-skinned person cannot become white, so unlikely it is that Northern Irish persons will cross over to the other denomination.

Some churchpersons both in the United Kingdom and the United States have argued insistently that the conflict in Northern Ireland is not a *religious* conflict at all. It is a civil, political, cultural, or ethnic conflict, purely and simply. What they recognize is that such a conflict is indeed an embarrassment to religion in general, to Christianity more specifically, and to Roman Catholicism and/or Protestant Presbyterianism even more specifically.

True, as Menendez points out, it is not a theological war in the sense of shooting and bombing one another in the name of "Justification by Faith" or the "Immaculate Conception" or any other fine point of religious doctrine.[17] He notes further that neither side is striving to annihilate the other religion,[18] although some Protestants use language and images that hint at genocidal goals. And there is no doubt that all the anti-Catholic slogans ever invented have been hurled repeatedly by people calling themselves Protestants in Northern Ireland. In reality, it is a religious conflict just as much as a political one. Leaders such as Ian Paisley exacerbate the suspicions and apprehensions of the people who sit before them in churches by their vitriolic preachings.

To Reverend Paisley, Roman Catholicism is a creation by the devil and is not of the Christian fellowship. As a false, demonic religion, Roman Catholicism is to be fought with every effort and strategy, fair or unfair, that one can think of. While far from all of Northern Ireland's Protestants are pleased with Paisley's rantings and many would be quick to classify him as a demogogue, as more than one writer has,[19] he does have a totally dedicated following and has almost single-handedly kept the "No Popery and No Surrender" Protestant elements stirred up and ready to sing inflammatory hymns, such as "Our Fathers Knew Thee Rome of Old and Evil Is Thy Fame," or march in an anti-Catholic demonstration.

In addition to the loss of life summarized earlier, there has been extensive damage to churches. The *Belfast Telegraph* has reported that in the five years between 1968 and 1973, sixty-eight Protestant churches were dam-

---

[17]Albert J. Menendez, *The Bitter Harvest: Church and State in Northern Ireland* (Washington, D.C.: Robert B. Luce, Inc., 1973), p. 43.

[18]Menendez, *The Bitter Harvest*, p. 44.

[19]Ibid., p. 55; Martin N. Marger, *Race and Ethnic Relations* (Belmont, CA: Wadsworth Publishing Company, 1985), p. 267.

aged and defaced, with five destroyed, while forty-five Catholic churches were damaged, and three destroyed by fire.[20]

At a less demagogic but still assertive anti-Catholic level is the Orange Order, which is dedicated to maintain the Protestant ascendency in the United Kingdom and in Northern Ireland in particular. It is estimated that 100,000 members in Ulster alone are staunch Protestants who not only oppose Roman Catholicism but strive to distance themselves from such an "evil" as much as possible. They are forbidden to marry a Roman Catholic or even cross the threshhold of a Roman Catholic church, let alone attend a church service there.

One of the reasons that the violent interaction between Protestants and Roman Catholics has continued so intensely into the present is that Irish society is imbued with very traditional sex-role patterns. That is, there continues to be a clear and wide difference in what roles boys and girls are socialized into. Particularly in the lower classes, girls are socialized into a traditional feminine role of subservient wife, nurturing mother, and household "slave." Boys learn their roles, equally traditional, to be aggressive, prepared to use weapons, and to bow down to no one, particularly someone from the other religion or the British army garrison.

While on the topic of socialization, it is important to note that most schools in Northern Ireland are self-segregated schools—some for Catholics, some for Protestants. The people and the churches want it that way because schools do more than teach the basics and prepare young people to be productive citizens. Lee notes that "the schools are preoccupied with maintaining church constituencies and inculcating middle-class respect for established authority."[21]

British and Irish Republic leaders continue to try to find political solutions. A much-heralded attempt was made in November 1985, when Prime Minister Margaret Thatcher of Great Britain and Prime Minister Garret FitzGerald of the Irish Republic signed an agreement that aimed to provide a middle ground between full control of Northern Ireland by Britain (favored by Northern Ireland's Protestants) and full absorption of Northern Ireland into the Irish Republic (favored by Northern Ireland's Catholics). The agreement allows the Irish Republic a permanent advisory seat in Northern Ireland's parliament as well as a voice in matters of security, politics, and the judiciary without taking ultimate executive authority away from Great Britain. Furthermore, for the first time the Irish Republic recognized the legitimate rights of the Protestants in Northern Ireland, and England granted that the Catholic minority in Northern Ireland still is seeking a united Catholic Ireland.

[20]Reported in Menendez, *The Bitter Harvest*, p. 43.
[21]Lee, *Terrorism in Northern Ireland*, p. 117.

The short-term effect of this agreement has not been one of complete peace, however. Over a dozen killings occurred in the one and one-half months immediately following the signing on November 15, 1985. Yet leaders remain optimistic. For example, Prime Minister FitzGerald commented: "This agreement thus involves no abandonment of nationalist aspirations, nor any threat to unionist rights; but it does offer a prospect of progress towards peace and justice for Northern nationalists, and of peace and stability for Northern unionists."[22]

When we look at religion and conflict, we are struck by an irony that is essentially endemic in group life, namely the final characteristic of groups, which we identified in Chapter 1 as the creation and maintenance of a sense of group identity among the members. On the positive or functional side, we here think of group identification, faithfulness, dedication, even sacrifice of property and life to defend the name and existence of one's group. But the obverse of the coin, as we consider this feature of the group from the conflict perspective, is fanaticism, blind allegiance, "my country (group), right or wrong," and conflict with other groups that remain unimpressed by your claims of superiority and exclusive rights.

At a relatively weak level, we encounter ethnocentrism and the almost quaint claims that "my group is just the greatest thing around." At a more problematic level, we see particularism and claims of exclusive rights and a corner on truth. Here we see some name-calling and overt attempts to convert others to one's group. But at an even more seriously problematic level, we find out-and-out conflict that reaches the level of violence. This is a level, as we have seen, that is reached by antagonistic religious groups with more frequency than most religionists would care to admit.

We should point out here that even sociologists of the functional persuasion will admit that conflict is not always bad and can even lead to beneficial results. Certainly the Civil Rights movement in the United States has involved conflict—sometimes physical conflict with firehoses, clubs, mobs, guns, injuries, and deaths. But the end result has been improvement in race relations and the opening of doors of opportunity for blacks and other members of minority groups. Also, the collective bargaining movement among American workers involved a great deal of violence, equipment and building damage, and loss of life during the last few decades of the nineteenth century and into the fourth decade of the twentieth century. Yet today, this conflict, which represented a fundamental difference of interest between the workers and the owners/managers has been normalized as both parties play by the rules of the game. People now sit around a bargaining table to settle most labor issues in a peaceful, normative manner.

[22]Quoted in the Detroit *Free Press*, November 18, 1985, p. 4A, in an editorial by Jane Eisner, "Agreement to Test the Strength of Nation's Moderates."

INTRARELIGIOUS CONFLICT

To this point we have mostly considered interreligious conflict, that is, conflict between religious groups or in some cases conflict of a religious group with the state. But another important type of religious conflict is what we call "intrareligious conflict," which is defined as conflict *within* the religious group.

At an initial and superficial level of thought, one might not expect to see much of this. People who join together in a religious group to worship God agree with one another, right? As such, they would certainly not be in conflict. Yet if we take the sociological perspective and our knowledge of social functioning at all seriously, we would actually expect less than perfect consensus from the very beginning because religious groups are in many ways just like all groups (cf. Chapter 1). They always have subgroups with special interests; local subunits (congregations) are exposed to different stimuli and influences, exist in a unique social environment, and therefore evolve somewhat differently from other subunits. This occurs despite the fact that they all formally subscribe to the same creed. Such conflict within a religious group can become extremely significant and emotionally consuming because in the minds of the participants the issues are often perceived as having life-and-death eternal significance. This is basically what the Reformation and later the Counter-Reformation were all about. If right belief and right behavior are necessary for eternal salvation, then differing interpretations of right belief and right behavior become crucial. And so doctrinal controversaries have been nearly perpetual in most religions. As we saw in the last chapter, conflict over correct interpretations of a group's sacred writings can result in sectarian withdrawal of one or more subgroups from the parent group. Such ruptures and splits can be seen in all major religions—Christianity, Islam, Hinduism, and Judaism, to name the best known. In North America, most of the major Protestant denominations have experienced splits—whether into northern and southern branches over the issue of slavery in the mid-nineteenth century or over right doctrine as in the Presbyterian, Lutheran, and Baptist denominations in this century.

We will discuss the controversy over slavery in Chapter 9. We will now look briefly only at the conflict within groups over doctrine, belief, and practice, some of which brings us up to the present day.

As we consider conflict over issues of right belief and doctrine, we immediately encounter a controversy at two levels. At one level, for groups with a Judeo-Christian heritage, is the age-old question of how to interpret the Bible (whether literally or metaphorically, whether a product of "verbal inspiration" or not). We encounter such questions as whether the birth of Christ was a real "virgin birth," whether Jonah actually lived and survived a sojourn in the belly of a "great fish," whether the miracles recorded in the

Bible really happened as described, whether the water of the Red Sea did in fact part to form two walls with a dry path between them on which the Israelites could walk and thus escape Pharaoh's pursuing army, and so on. While these are old questions and ancient battles, within some denominations they are being fought for the first time.

The second level at which doctrinal controversy occurs is in a real sense more basic and to some degree it affects all of American Christianity—and world Christianity, too, for that matter. This is a crisis of basic faith—what Hadden calls the "crisis of belief[23]—by which is implied the posing of questions about the fundamental nature and basis of the Christian religion. These are *not* the ancient, enduring questions such as the proper mode of baptism (whether to immerse, pour, or sprinkle) or whether the relationship of the bread and wine to the body and blood of Christ in the Lord's Supper (Holy Communion, Eucharist) is one of transubstantiation (Catholic), representation (Reformed), or real presence (Lutheran)—these we might call superficial issues, even though protagonists of various points of view would object to such a designation. Today, the issues seem more fundamental. That is, the kinds of questions frequently raised are whether God in fact exists (regardless of how you define the concept of the Trinity), whether baptism is valid and necessary in the first place (regardless of how much water is used), whether Christ really lived and died and rose again—not whether wine or grape juice should be used in the Lord's Supper. In other words, at this second level are questions about the reality of God as well as assumptions about the relationship of God with people that have been essentially unchallenged until now.

Returning to the first issue or level of theological dispute, we observe that even denominations that appeared to resolve the fundamentalist-modernist issue years ago by camping on the liberal side of the fence do not show the internal unanimity today that one might expect. Thus, although most Congregationalists, Methodists, and Episcopalians cannot accept without reservation that Jesus was born of a virgin or that miracles actually happened just as the Bible says they did, some of these people do. On the question of Jesus' virgin birth, for example, 21 percent of Congregationalists, 34 percent of Methodists, and 39 percent of Episcopalians accept the doctrine without reservation. Similarly, 28 percent of Congregationalists, 37 percent of Methodists, and 41 percent of Episcopalians accept the biblical account of miracles as completely true.[24] That is, although such denominations may have essentially resolved the fundamentalist-modernist controversy (if only

[23]Jeffrey K. Hadden, *The Gathering Storm in the Churches* (Garden City, NY: Doubleday, 1969), pp. 15–26.

[24]Charles Y. Glock and Rodney Stark, *Christian Beliefs and Anti-Semitism* (New York: Harper & Row, 1966), pp. 9–10.

in the sense of tolerating a diversity of views and beliefs), some of their members still hold to traditional beliefs and might even feel reasonably comfortable in another, theologically more conservative denomination.

Of even greater contemporary relevance is what is happening in religious groups that have continued to maintain an official position supporting traditional beliefs and interpretations of Scripture and whose members (according to survey data) have consistently expressed high levels of concurrence with these doctrinal formulations, but in which an erosion of doctrinal solidarity appears to have begun. Two prime examples are the Southern Baptist Convention and The Lutheran Church-Missouri Synod. Both groups have long proclaimed their adherence to a conservative version of Christianity and continue in an official way to subscribe to traditional doctrine—essentially what we have referred to earlier as fundamentalist doctrine. However, voices throughout both groups have challenged and questioned the official traditional positions by using a more open-ended approach to many historical definitions and understandings of Christian doctrine without necessarily denying them.

A controversy that had been going on for some time between the elected leadership of the Missouri Synod and the faculty at its major seminary in Concordia, St. Louis, heated up considerably after the church's 1973 convention in New Orleans (waggishly called the "Second Battle of New Orleans"). At that time, the delegates approved as binding on all clergy and seminary professors a highly specific and conservative statement of faith, approved the censure of dissident faculty members at the St. Louis seminary, and set in motion procedures for purging theological deviants. The latter process proceeded to the point that most of the seminary faculty were relieved of their positions in early 1974.

A powerful biblical inerrancy faction within the Southern Baptist Convention has been following a similar route to "clean up" the theological instruction at its seminaries and enforce its views of Scripture and traditional doctrinal understanding upon seminary trustees and faculty. The inerrancy proponents have sought to cut short the drift toward "liberalism" they sense has been occurring in this large denomination. A major goal for the 1980s was to control the election of president of the church body. At stake each year is the president's authority to appoint members to two powerful boards, which in turn select people for the boards of directors of various agencies and seminaries in the Southern Baptist Convention.

At the 1990 convention the conservative candidate, Morris Chapman, defeated Daniel Vestal, the candidate from the moderate camp (called "liberal" by the conservatives). That made twelve years in a row (1979–1990) that the conservative wing of the church body has defeated the moderates in hotly contested battles. These conventions are comprised of representative members of local congregations in numbers ranging between 30,000 and 40,000. In the past votes have been around 54–55 percent for the conservative candidate; but in 1990 58 percent voted for Chapman. Part of what renews the fervor repeatedly is that no one can serve more than two consecutive years as president.

It is of interest to note that shortly after the 1990 convention, two top editors of the Southern Baptists' news service were dismissed. Baptist Press director Al Shackleford and news editor Dan Martin have long been under fire from conservatives, who felt their reporting of the internal conflict between conservatives and moderates was not balanced. It is very unlikely that the conservative leadership of the Southern Baptist Convention will soon be voted out.

It appears that in no denomination in which such debate and conflict flourishes do the conservatives recognize the sociological realities that any large group faces, particularly as it grows. Any such group will inevitably have greater deviance and will find itself tolerating more deviance. In fact, we would suggest that the appearance of diversity and controversy in such groups is not nearly so amazing as the fact that these were forestalled or at least kept hidden for so long. The point is that unanimity does not and cannot exist and that diversity will only increase, unless one faction accumulates sufficient power essentially to split the group formally into two groups or force out the more extreme and vocal deviates.

We now return to the second level at which the doctrinal issue or crisis of belief is operating—the questioning, or perhaps more accurately, the seeming questioning, of the basic understanding of God—God's nature, reality, and activity in the world. As indicated before, various theologians within both Protestantism and Catholicism seem at least superficially to be challenging fundamental religious presuppositions, such as the reality of God and how God has chosen to relate to people. Certainly great numbers of both clergy and laypersons interpret what these theologians are saying as direct challenges to the very foundations of Christianity. Whether they are of such a significantly challenging nature is beyond the scope of this volume. However, it should be noted that all such theologians—whether demythologizers such as Rudolph Bultman, or "theology of hope" proponents such as Wolfhart Pannenburg, Jurgen Moltman, and Hans Hoekendijk, or foundational theologians, or "death of God" theologians, or popularizers such as Harvey Cox and John A. T. Robinson—all seem primarily concerned with "God-language," not just with God. For example, when former Church of England Bishop John A. T. Robinson says that our image of God must go, he is not denying the existence of God or proposing that somehow we banish God from the universe; rather, he is challenging our traditional conceptualization of God, one that he regards as inadequate for today. Whether other, related theologians are similarly inclined or whether they are going further and in fact proclaiming or even celebrating the "death" of God is a matter for theologians, not sociologists, to decide. That such suggestions have disturbed, even shocked, people in the church is, however, an understatement. That such statements and discussions have cut some people loose from "the faith" is a possibility. That such issues leave the future of Christian theology and conceptualization wide open is a certainty.

Then there is the intragroup conflict that is probably the best-kept secret of all, the conflict that occurs at the local level—within participating congregations where members find themselves on opposite sides of issues. Sometimes it's a liberal/conservative split on doctrinal questions. Sometimes it is a personality conflict between a minister and a congregation. Sometimes the rift is over social issues, epitomized in the 1960s and 1970s by many clergy and laypeople, both Jewish and Christian, actively participating in the civil rights movement and the antiwar movement. Such commitment and participation was challenged by other clergy and laypeople who were convinced that such issues as civil rights and war were social and political issues and as such of little concern to religious groups. Such issues were not to intrude into religious institutions or absorb the time of clergy who had other things to do with their time—administer comfort and counsel to their flock while leaving social activism to secular authorities and professionals.

Actually, few readers will be unaware of at least one such incident in their community. In some instances, a pastor is transferred prematurely (suggesting that representatives of the congregation have gotten to the bishop or district president); in other instances, the controversy becomes more public, with padlocks on church doors, possessions removed to the sidewalk, suits and countersuits, even deputy sheriffs restraining some among the parties to the controversy; in still other instances, congregational representatives extend a vote of "no confidence" to the minister, who then puts his or her name on a list of preachers available for a call and an opportunity to start over somewhere else.

But often the disagreements are more substantial than conflicts of personalities or style. They may represent wide discrepancies between the theology of pastor and people or disagreements on how much time and money the local church should devote to social service programs, or conflict over "gifts of the Spirit" (charismatic gifts) and speaking in tongues.

CHALLENGES TO SOCIETY FROM RELIGIOUS GROUPS

At this point we wish to introduce yet another type of religious conflict. Although this is certainly not new, it may seem new with each generation. That is the conflict that results when religious institutions or their representatives challenge one or more sociopolitical aspects of the community or society of which they are a part. Here there has been much in recent memory. Here is where many would say religion has been and can be at its finest. Here we see religious groups initiating verbal if not physical conflict with the political or economic institutions of the surrounding society. Other religious groups may be supportive, opposing, or neutral. So it is possible that conflict with other religious groups might emerge here, yet it is not necessary or inevitable.

Within recent memory in the United States some religious groups, leaders, and members have been active in the civil rights movement, the antiabortion Right-to-Life movement, and the peace movement. Not that the activism always or even most of the time was initiated by religious groups. But at an early point, they became active and significant influences in the movements overall.

Other occasions in which religion in the United States has been a challenge to the status quo and has participated in conflict with societal laws, structure, and institutions would be the Prohibition movement in the early third of this century and the "blue laws" that have pervaded American society since its founding and are not totally abolished everywhere today—laws that prohibited ball games and shopping on Sundays, restricted how close an establishment selling alcoholic beverages could be to a church or school, or legislated whether alcohol could be sold at all or whether it was legal for physicians to prescribe birth control devices to patients, let alone that people could buy condoms and spermicides over the counter (the Comstock laws). All are distinctive and well-known examples of religion wanting to have and indeed having an impact on the society that encompassed it. But in these examples, the influence was in a restrictive, conservative direction, in contrast with the more liberating approach of civil rights activists who appealed to religious precepts to reinforce social forces that would provide equal opportunity and access for those who had long been discriminated against and restricted in opportunities to follow their talents and abilities.

Another confrontation between religion and society in the United States today is known as the Sanctuary Movement. As part of this movement some 50,000 clergy and other professional church workers as well as laypeople have for some time been quietly running an underground railroad to provide sanctuary for refugees from Central American countries that are officially leagued with the United States yet engage in terrorist acts against some of their own citizens. These Guatemalan and Salvadoran emigrants have sought asylum as political refugees, but the government of the United States has defined them illegal aliens. As a consequence, those who help them have been arrested and tried. In a six-month jury trial ending with a verdict on May 1, 1986, eight Sanctuary workers were found guilty and subject to fines and imprisonment for as long as twenty-five years. Two months later, however, all were given suspended sentences and placed on probation. It hardly needs saying that those within the movement view the activities as natural outgrowths of their Christian commitment—a "fruit of faith"—while opponents view it as lawbreaking and an inappropriate application of religious convictions.

Throughout Latin America, yet another example of religion attempting to challenge and change the surrounding society and its institutions can be observed firsthand today. This is the social activism among some of the Roman Catholic leadership in these Catholic countries that flows out of what has come to be known as liberation theology. At its core, liberation theology maintains that it is inherent within Christian theology that the institutions bearing the Christian name must be dedicated to improving the conditions of society and providing for the welfare of its citizens by liberating them from economic and health deprivation. Such dedication to social reform and redemption will be in addition to standard religious responsibility for proclaiming the Gospel. The position is well summarized by a lay Catholic leader, a sociologist from Venezuela, Otto Maduro, who says:

> My own personal conviction is that to be a Catholic in Latin America today implies a radical, constant, and collective commitment to the struggle for a community of free brothers and sisters on our continent. But—likewise and in equal measure—I am aware of the fact that our church in Latin America has established such bonds with the powerful that its preaching and activity often serve to prevent persons from making the commitment the gospel seems to demand.[25]

The process of awakening and sensitizing the peasants in Central and South American countries has often started with what are called basic Christian communities in a rural village or urban barrio. These communities study biblical themes and how they relate to the people's life situation. While there is heavy lay involvement, Roman Catholic priests extend their leadership and get the theological discussions going. The earliest groups date back only to the late 1960s and have multiplied largely unnoticed by the outside world. They are part of what is essentially a grass roots movement and are built on long-established relationships of pastor and people. But the focus is not traditional Bible study or preaching or carrying out the rituals of the sacraments. Rather, it is the application of Christian tenets to the life situations of the people with clear economic goals of more equitable distribution of land and other wealth. Most would identify their vision of a better society for all as a socialist one, some going further to the left and embracing a form of Marxism.

The Second Vatican Council is almost universally credited with providing the open and tolerant religious context within which the basic Christian communities and their liberation theology could develop. Before the Council that convened in 1962 and concluded its work in 1965, the Roman Catholic Church and most of Protestantism, for that matter, believed the task of

---

[25]Otto Maduro, *Religion and Social Conflicts* (Maryknoll, NY: Orbis Books, 1979), p. XXV.

Christianity was "to get people in a state of grace and keep them there."[26] But, Berryman continues, "The Vatican Council (and the theology surrounding it) turned this view inside out: God's grace was everywhere saving humankind."[27] A view soon reached by most clergy working to apply the theology of Vatican II was that the poverty and deprivation of the rural peasants and the urban poor was not something inherent in third-world "backwardness" but was the result of systematic exploitation over a long period of time. This message and its interpretation of the source of the people's plight spread rapidly among the people.

The success of the basic Christian communities and liberation theology is measurable in part by governmental reaction to it. Berryman cites one account that enumerates over 800 priests, members of religious orders, and laypersons arrested, tortured, killed, or expelled as early as the late 1970s.[28]

In his focus on Central America, Berryman summarizes the main lines of the crisis conditions that liberation theology was attempting to address in the 1970s as follows:

1. Large groups of people, particularly small peasants and the landless rural poor, suffered real declines in their already desperate conditions (less work, declining food intake, high infant mortality).
2. These conditions had *structural causes*; increasingly, land was being used for agroexport crops and food production was growing less rapidly than population.
3. Narrow oligarchies felt no need for reform and change, particularly since they were enjoying a boom, and they thought the military and the police would be sufficient to control dissidence.
4. External factors, inflation (particularly the petroleum price rise), and natural disasters (the Guatemalan earthquake) augmented the crisis.[29]

Without belaboring any of these situations, it can be said that some ideological conflict between segments of the religious institutions in society and the industrial, governmental, and economic systems (or institutions) in the society exists even today. Some of it represents honest differences of opinion and interpretation, yet some of it appears very similar to what conflict theorists in sociology mean when they talk about inherent conflicts of interest between the powerful and the nonpowerful in society.

As an institution in society, most of the time religion is a staunch defender of the status quo and has a real fear of rocking the boat. Yet religion sometimes challenges the status quo. What is fascinating is that objections come at religion from both sides. For some, religion is not conservative

[26]Phillip Berryman, *The Religious Roots of Rebellion* (Maryknoll, NY: Orbis Books, 1984), p. 26.

[27]Ibid., p. 26.

[28]Ibid., p. 31.

[29]Ibid., p. 46.

enough and should be more of a leader aggressively fighting so-called sins in society such as abortion, legalized gambling, and the Equal Rights Amendment. At the other extreme are those who would see the church as a source of radical change in society, with confrontation leading to subsequent reform and improvement, as religion is less concerned with individual sins but rather with society-wide structural abuses and imbalances. As such, conflict is no stranger to religion; in fact, it would be difficult to argue convincingly against those who would assert that conflict is endemic to religion. Conflict will be evident because strong convictions on one side of an issue will be at odds with the other side—sometimes within a particular group and sometimes in relation to other religious groups or the surrounding society. Conflict will be evident sometimes because the powerful in society use religion as both justification for their privileged positions and the disprivileged positions of others, and as a direct means of pacification, comfort, and control of the less privileged. We will have more to say on this issue in Chapter 9.

We conclude with Daniel Levine's summary definition of liberation theology:

> Basically, liberation involves freedom from bondage of all kinds—the bondage of ignorance, alienation, poverty, and oppression. Such liberation is neither wholly spiritual nor wholly material. Rather, it is the fusion of the two which gives this perspective its unique and compelling force. Religious and political liberation go together: "Purely religious" actions, limited to the institutional Church, are rejected as a false consciousness; while "pure politics" lack meaning in the cosmic scheme of things. In this view, the key role of religious action is to join the two planes, removing traditional religious legitimization of the social order while channeling religious energies and motivations toward its transformation.[30]

CONCLUSION

While religion is a favorite rallying point and an organization that has a large number of potential recruits, and while it enables some to define their people as purveyors of truth but the other religion(s) as plotting to subvert that truth and perpetuate falsehood, thereby adding fervor to the defense of the cause, the heart of the matter in the examples we have examined is political. Although these groups in name and purpose are religious, yet they also exist as political groups and civil religions. While no one wants to suggest that the Protestant-Catholic conflict in Northern Ireland, or the Sikh-Hindu-Moslem conflict in India, or the enduring conflicts in Lebanon and

---

[30]Daniel H. Levine, "Religion and Politics, Politics and Religion: An Introduction," in Daniel H. Levine ed., *Churches and Politics in Latin America* (Beverly Hills, CA: Sage Publications, 1979), p. 30.

in Israel are not really religious conflicts at all but are political conflicts purely and simply, by the same token the conflicts should certainly not be taken at face value. That is, they are not wholly religious conflicts that are concerned only with discovering divine truth and worshiping the true god in a correct manner. They all involve religio-political groups or civil religions that transcend the purely theological character and content of those religions.

But to go further, we must observe and keep in mind that there are many people throughout the world who believe as we have seen in the last several pages that there are elements endemic to religion in general and Christianity in particular that should precipitate social involvement and reformistic activity and leadership from the ranks of both clergy and laypeople.

7

Religion and Politics

Although politics is nearly as variously defined as religion, there is consensus about at least two characteristics. First of all, politics (like its corollary, government) consists fundamentally of norms—that is, ways of reaching decisions, procedures for carrying out certain tasks, expectations about rights and privileges. Second, politics is most concerned with the societal norms that stipulate how and by whom coercive power shall be used in the pursuit of societal goals.[1] The employment of coercive power by government appears necessary primarily because the available supply of rewards that people strive for, both individually and collectively, is limited. Such rewards include money (or other means of obtaining goods and services), prestige, honor, respect, power, love, affection, and the like. Although such rewards are not necessarily in scarce supply, their supply is finite. That is to say, it is a relatively rare person who feels satiated so far as his or her share of such rewards is concerned. Most people want at least a few more dollars and a few more things than they presently possess. And universally people could use a little more love and affection and a little more respect, even if they are not specifically seeking fame or power over others.

[1]J. Milton Yinger, *The Scientific Study of Religion* (New York: Macmillan, 1970), p. 408.

The resulting discrepancy between supply and demand places people inevitably into a competitive position with respect to garnering their desired share of available rewards. At this point we encounter politics and government as the social systems or institutions in a society developed to regulate the process of reward seeking and to reduce the disruptive tendency inherent in the competition for rewards which could result in a war of all against all. Thus we understand the concept of politics to be the norms that designate the ultimate coercive power and the process by which the norms that regulate the exercise of power and authority get implemented. This accords well with Harold Lasswell's classic definition of politics as who gets what, when, and how—that is, the process of determining the distribution of society's rewards and balancing power relationships and claims.[2]

THE RELATIONSHIP OF RELIGION AND POLITICS

What, then, is the relationship of religion to politics? We should expect, considering the broad scope of our definition of politics, which implies a great diversity of processes, norms, and behavior, that there will be a variety of ways in which religion relates to the institution of politics.

This certainly has been the case. But we shall not go into all of the many types of relationships. We shall simply outline the range of possibilities and then discuss the most common pattern.

At one end of the continuum is the "pure theocracy." *Theocracy* literally means "rule by God." Thus religious leaders are seen as ruling all of society in God's name and ostensibly according to His wishes. Actually, the state as a distinct entity does not exist in a theocracy. The rule of Israel by God's prophets in the Old Testament period is an example of the pure theocracy. A prophet such as Samuel was seen as God's spokesman regarding not only religious matters but political and governmental matters as well. Interestingly, the people chafed under this arrangement—they pleaded embarrassment in the face of surrounding societies who were under the rule of kings and appealed for a similar "separation" of church and state.

Closely related is the *modified theocracy*. In this case, while the state is subordinate to the religious institution and its leaders, even in temporal affairs, the state nevertheless exists as a separate entity. The state is seen here as the enforcement agency of religion, an agency necessary because of the tendency of people to deviate from societal norms but yet to depend on religion for its authority. Most medieval European societies dominated by Roman Catholicism were of this type. Similarly, John Calvin's Geneva and the early Massachusetts Bay Colony are good examples. Further, the rela-

[2]Harold Lasswell, *Politics: Who Gets What, When, and How* (New York: Meridian Books, 1958).

tionship of Buddhism to the government of Sri Lanka (Ceylon) from the third century B.C. until the nineteenth century A.D. was that of a modified theocracy. Only a Buddhist could become king, and his chief function was to protect and promote the faith. On the other hand, the Buddhist monks not only instructed and advised the royal court and conducted the king's coronation in the temple, but they held enormous political power in their influence and control over the masses. They could incite or prevent rebellion. No king could rule without their support.

It is worth noting at this point that the inclusion of the state within the religious system, or at a minimum some kind of control over the state by religion, is not simply a quaint, antiquarian phenomenon or legacy from preindustrial times. It is an almost universal feature of the utopian and millenarian groups and movements of the nineteenth and twentieth centuries—groups that endeavored to establish models of the perfect Kingdom of God—in addition to such a recent group as Jim Jones's Peoples Temple and the Jonestown experiment in Guyana.

At the other extreme is a *totalitarian* system, in which religion is either controlled by the state as a tool or enforcement arm of the state, or is outlawed altogether. A pure form of a totalitarian system is more theoretical than real, although the goal of the Bolshevik revolution in the Soviet Union in 1917 was such. What religion they could not eradicate entirely, they intended to control and manipulate.

Midway between the extremes of theocracy on the one hand and totalitarianism on the other is the concept of *total separation*. In this arrangement the arenas in which religion and politics operate are entirely distinct with no overlap. There one must assume that religion serves the soul and the state the body—or that religion is entirely an individualized, subjective, internalized phenomenon, while politics and the state serve the group, deal with externals relative to survival, and are entirely secular. Such total separation has never been achieved, and thus remains purely a theoretical possibility.

Certainly *partial separation* is the most sociologically sound option. Inasmuch as both religion and politics are social institutions and consist of subgroups, norms, and people, they interact with one another; they sometimes overlap in their functions; they often involve the same people; they seek commitment and involvement from the same people. It is of course partial separation that describes the system with which we are most familiar in North America and Europe. But partial separation is itself a variable and tends to fluctuate toward one extreme or the other, as implied by the range outlined in Figure 7-1. Figure 7-1 presents in graphic form the options we have been discussing. That is, the middle, neutral position would be "total separation." The relationship between church and state could then go in either direction toward total religious control and domination at one end ("pure theocracy"), or total state control at the other extreme ("totalitarianism"), with various intermediate points on the way.

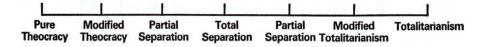

FIGURE 7-1.   A continuum of the possible relationships of church and state.

THE INFLUENCE OF RELIGION ON POLITICS

We now continue our discussion of religion and politics by looking at specific ways in which religion affects, or tries to affect, politics. That is, we shall be asking to what extent and in what ways religion can be seen to be an influence on political action and outcomes.

Religion and Voting Behavior

A widely recognized point of religious influence over politics is that of people's voting preference and behavior. The supporters of most every candidate for public office at all levels can be heard during the campaign talking about trying to get the "Catholic vote" or the "Jewish vote" or the "Baptist vote" or, most recently, the "Evangelical vote," or perhaps the support and vote of the "Moral Majority." Such interest gives very explicit recognition to the correlation that exists between religious affiliation and commitment on the one hand and voting behavior on the other. That there should be a correlation is exactly what would be expected, of course, if religious affiliation and commitment mean anything at all. What one believes with respect to that which is good, true, and desirable, as well as what God intends for people and society, could be expected to influence the choices one makes in the political arena. That is, religion should affect people's voting patterns.

As we prepare to present evidence in this area we must mention one problem that we will have in interpreting the data: Although we will see large differences by religious affiliation and commitment, the differences cannot be traced totally and simply to religion. For example, we will later see a fairly strong relationship between religion and social class. That is, certain religious groups tend to have disproportionate numbers of certain classes as members. If in a particular instance the members of a denomination tend to be predominately working class and also vote overwhelmingly for Democratic candidates, we have two correlations with political activity at work— both religious affiliation and social class. We want to be alert to such a problem of interpretation. But first some data.

If we consider party preference and voting behavior we find, as most Americans are aware, that, historically, Protestants have been more likely to

TABLE 7-1   Political Party Affiliation by Religious Membership

	PROTESTANT	CATHOLIC	JEW
Republican	29%	21%	11%
Democrat	43	48	61
Independent	28	31	28

Source: The Gallup Poll. No. 222 (March, 1984), p. 48.

be Republicans and Catholics more likely to be Democrats, with Jews even more likely to be Democrats. Recent Gallup Poll data reaffirm this relationship. In 1984, the differences by religious affiliation were as summarized in Table 7-1. The traditional pattern is reaffirmed.

In Great Britain one sees such differences as well. For example, in 1974, polling by the Gallup organization found a moderately high correspondence between membership in the Church of England and support for the Conservative political party: 67 percent of Conservatives are members of the Church of England, whereas only 58 percent of Labourites belong to the Church of England. There is a similar pattern, but reversed for Catholics: 15 percent of Labourites are Catholics, whereas only 9 percent of Conservatives are Catholics.[3]

One concludes that a modest relationship exists between religious affiliation and political party preference. But this relationship, significant in itself, is exceeded quite dramatically when actual voting patterns are viewed. The Gallup Poll data reported in Table 7-2 show some substantial differences along religious lines in voting for presidents of the United States. Protestants are clearly more likely to vote for Republican candidates and Catholics for Democratic candidates. The classic pattern is observed most dramatically in the Kennedy/Nixon vote in 1960. It was Nixon over Kennedy almost two to one among Protestants, and Kennedy over Nixon nearly four to one among Catholics. In fact, there is only one time since 1952 when a majority of Protestants have failed to vote for Republican candidates. That was in 1964 when 55 percent of Protestants voted for Lyndon B. Johnson. The contradictions for Catholics are the Nixon/McGovern contest in 1972 when a majority of Catholics voted for Nixon and the last three elections when Republicans Reagan and Bush were victors. In light of this observation, significant change may be underway. Although in two of these elections (1980 and 1988) the margin by Catholics voting for the Republicans over the Democrats was only one percentage point, the classic pattern may well be changing. If so, it could largely be explained as a concomitant of the improving socioeconomic status of Catholics in this country (cf. Chapter

[3]George H. Gallup, *The Gallup International Public Opinion Polls*, Vol. 2 (New York: Random House, 1976), p. 1306.

TABLE 7–2   Presidential Voting Since 1952, by Denominational Affiliation

		PROTESTANT	CATHOLIC
1952	Stevenson	37%	56%
	Eisenhower	63	44
1956	Stevenson	37	51
	Eisenhower	63	49
1960	Kennedy	38	78
	Nixon	62	22
1964	Johnson	55	76
	Goldwater	45	24
1968	Humphrey	35	59
	Nixon	49	33
	Wallace	16	8
1972	McGovern	30	48
	Nixon	70	52
1976	Carter	46	57
	Ford	53	41
1980	Carter	39	46
	Reagan	54	47
	Anderson	6	6
1984	Mondale	37	39
	Reagan	61	61
1988	Dukakis	32	47
	Bush	64	48

Source: The Gallup Report. No. 230 (November 1984), Princeton, N.J. Data abstracted from a table headed "Vote by Groups in Presidential Elections Since 1952," pp. 8–9, and George Gallup, Jr. and Jim Castelli, *The People's Religion* (New York: Macmillan, 1989), p. 245.

9). In general, the higher the socioeconomic status of people, the more likely they are to support Republican candidates. Perhaps in the future we will be able to say that political party preference and voting behavior correlate with socioeconomic status regardless of whether one's religious affiliation is Protestant or Catholic.

What is perhaps more important than the correlation between religious affiliation and voting tendencies, is the observation of a possible drift by Catholics toward Republican candidates. This could very well be occurring for several reasons. For one thing, Catholics are moving upward from their working-class origins and perceive things from a perspective similar to that espoused by middle-class Protestants. For another, the reform innovations by Pope John XXIII in which he not only introduced changes into the Roman Catholic Church but more importantly introduced the *possibility* of change and an openness to it may be significant. As just one of many societal arenas, politics became an area of questioning and revising of old commitments and expectations.

In the foregoing tables and discussion we have considered only the very broad categories of Protestants, Catholics, and Jews. As we'll discuss later, there is a great deal of further variation within each category. For example, Table 7-3 shows considerable variation among mainstream Protestant denominations. In fact, one group, the Baptists, actually had a higher proportion of respondents who voted for the Democratic candidate than for the Republican. Further, with their concentration in the South, they were more likely than other Protestant groups to vote for Wallace. The remaining Protestant denominations preferred Nixon over Humphrey by margins of more than two to one, with the margin for Episcopalians reaching nearly six to one (68.8 percent vs. 12.5 percent).

Although a detailed discussion of the relationship of social class to religion is reserved for a later chapter, we must point out here that an extremely important social-class factor accompanies these observed relationships between denominational affiliation and voting behavior—Episcopalians and Presbyterians, who were so extremely likely to choose Nixon over Humphrey in 1968, are also more likely than members of other Protestant groups to be of high socioeconomic status. Since higher-status persons tend to favor Republican over Democratic candidates, we find that status and religious affiliation reinforce one another and in combination yield dramatic differences in support for particular political parties and their candidates.

Legislation of Morality

Another significant area in which religion influences the political structure is in the "legislation of morality." American state and local governments have been riddled with so-called blue laws, many of which are still on

TABLE 7-3   Presidential Candidate Preference of Selected Protestant Denominations, 1968

DENOMINATION	HUMPHREY	NIXON	WALLACE	NO ANSWER	DID NOT VOTE
Baptist (N = 333)	28.2%	20.1%	9.9%	2.1%	39.6%
Episcopal (N = 32)	12.5	68.8	3.1	2.1	12.5
Lutheran (N = 120)	22.5	47.5	4.2	4.2	21.7
Methodist (N = 187)	20.9	44.4	5.3	2.1	27.3
Presbyterian (N = 67)	13.4	58.2	6.0	4.5	17.9
United Church of Christ (N = 51)	23.5	49.0	0.0	7.8	19.6
Others and No Preference (N = 185)	14.6	34.1	9.7	4.9	36.8

Source: Ronald L. Johnstone (director). National Opinion Research Center survey conducted for the Lutheran Council in the U.S.A., 1970.

the books—and most of which reflect strong religious influence. Laws restricting Sunday business activity, laws specifying how close to schools and churches bars and taverns may operate, laws restricting the sale of intoxicating beverages, laws regarding the sale and distribution of birth-control devices—all these laws evidence strong influences by religious groups. Some are carry-overs from Puritan colonization; some are related to concentrations of Catholic immigrants; some are traceable to conservative Protestantism, which has been influential throughout our history.

To be more specific in the area of the legislation of morality, we shall look at several historical relationships between religion and the political process and structure in the United States.

Prohibition and Birth Control   The struggle against "demon rum" that eventually resulted in ratification of the Eighteenth Amendment (1919), which prohibited the sale of most intoxicating beverages in the United States, is a clear example of the influence of religious groups in the political arena. The Prohibition amendment was very largely the work of a well-organized church lobby, the Anti-Saloon League. The league was organized in the Calvary Baptist Church in Washington, D.C. in 1895, and although similar temperance societies cooperated with it, churches were the primary source of its membership, support, and leadership. Leo Pfeffer reports that between 1911 and 1925 an annual average of thirty thousand local churches, predominantly Baptist, Methodist, Presbyterian, and Congregational, were affiliated with the league.[4]

Pfeffer notes that the Anti-Saloon League did not deny that it was a political organization. When confronted with that charge, a league representative replied, "The Church is a machine and the League is a machine within a machine."[5] Pfeffer goes on to say:

> Its effectiveness as a machine, as of any political machine, is measured by the fruits thereof; and the fruit of the League was the adoption of the Eighteenth Amendment within six years after the League formally launched its campaign for national prohibition. Though the League was less successful in retaining the victory it had won, its influence was respected and feared by many.[6]

The adoption of prohibition is a prime example of Protestant influences on the political system, while Catholics have an analogous influence with reference to birth-control legislation. Since Catholic doctrine maintains that any "artificial" interference with conception is inherently evil and sinful, the Catholic Church has worked long and hard to resist attempts to repeal or modify existing laws that prohibit the sale of birth-control devices

[4]Leo Pfeffer, *Church, State, and Freedom* (Boston, MA: Beacon Press, 1953), p. 200.
[5]Quoted in ibid., p. 200.
[6]Ibid.

or dissemination of information regarding their use. Earlier in American history Catholics were not alone in this stance—the "Comstock law," actually a set of laws passed by Congress in 1873 prohibiting mailing, transporting, or importing "obscene, lewd, or lascivious" materials, had support that also included Protestants and some groups that were at least ostensibly secular. Birth-control information and devices were interpreted as being included among the prohibitions detailed by these laws. Soon thereafter twenty-two states passed "little Comstock laws" that imposed strictures ranging from New York's restriction on physicians' freedom to prescribe lawful contraceptives (and then only "for the cure or prevention of disease"), to Massachusetts's ban on the publication of information and the distribution of material dealing with contraception, to Connecticut's absolute ban on birth control extending even to the private use of contraceptive devices.[7]

More recently we have seen attempts, largely unsuccessful as yet, by a variety of religious groups to influence legislatures and the Congress to repeal the liberalized abortion legislation that was passed and tested in the courts during the 1970s. Supporters of the "Pro-Life Amendment" to the United States Constitution are prominent protagonists in this area. Religious groups provide the major base of support.

THE ALLIANCE OF RIGHT-WING RELIGION AND POLITICS

The forays of conservative religious groups—frequently called the New Christian Right (NCR)—into the political arena have been much in the news over the last decade and a half. The NCR has been credited with playing a significant role in defeating five of six targeted "liberal" U.S. Senators in 1980; they have supported the candidacy of a televangelist for President of the United States (Pat Robertson); they have led the movement to overturn the *Roe* v. *Wade* decision of the U.S. Supreme Court on abortion.

But, while much in the news, the perspective represented by the NCR is actually not new. In fact, it goes back to the beginnings of the nation. But it was not until the last third of the nineteenth century that the people and groups that are today labeled Fundamentalists, Evangelicals, and the New Christian Right began to become conscious of themselves as part of a movement within Christianity in which they shared a perspective on political life and moral issues with some other religious groups. In fact, what they might have assumed earlier was that the dominant world view in the United States

[7]David M. Kennedy, *Birth Control in America* (New Haven, CT: Yale University Press, 1970), p. 218.

was being seriously challenged by a variety of groups that would, if allowed, undermine the traditional Christian principles of this nation.

The Beginnings of Fundamentalism

The primary stimuli for the emerging fundamentalist concern were, first, what they viewed as increasing secularism in the society. This is tied up with the advancement of science and the increasing confidence in the inductive scientific method of attaining truth—at the expense of deduction from a standard repository of truth such as the Bible. Of concern to them also were such developments as the dissemination of the Marxist social philosophy, the spread of the accounts of Darwin and others concerning the evolution of people and their world, and the increasing independence of society's institutions from religious influence. In short, the traditionalists, or Evangelicals as they are commonly called, were disturbed by the erosion of religious influence throughout the rest of the society and its institutions. Second, they felt that the Christian religion was being betrayed from within. The increasing emphasis on social service and the social gospel by individuals and groups within the broad Christian community was a significant part of their concern. For one thing, they felt that when social service was emphasized, the traditional emphasis was of necessity neglected, or at best put in a secondary position. For another, they felt some were rejecting the traditional message of Christianity altogether and substituting the social gospel in all particulars. This was liberal ideology as opposed to their conservative religion—this was liberal Christianity that attempted to incorporate secular values into the Christian structure. What further alarmed the Evangelicals was the development of a form of biblical scholarship known as *higher criticism*, an approach to the Bible asserting that it is a collection of human documents subject to the same principles of textual criticism as any other group of documents—a perspective that originated in German theological schools and universities in the mid-1800s and was subsequently adopted at many leading seminaries in the United States.

In an effort to combat this "creeping liberalism" and restore Christianity to what they regarded as its original nature and message, many of the Evangelicals coalesced around the publication, beginning in 1910, of their orthodox manifesto in twelve volumes titled *The Fundamentals*. As Stewart Cole says, "In this action the historian finds the clear emergence of fundamentalism."[8] This publication was the capstone to a series of Bible conferences held by conservatives throughout the country between 1876 and 1900, which Gasper views as "embryonic stirrings" of the fundamental-

---

[8]Stewart G. Cole, *The History of Fundamentalism* (Hamden, CT: Archon Books, 1963), p. 53.

ist movement.[9] At the most significant of these conferences, held in 1895 at Niagara, New York, a declaration was formulated that anticipated the famous "five points" of fundamentalist doctrine as expounded in the twelve volumes of *The Fundamentals*. The five independent points of traditional Protestant Christianity agreed upon at the Niagara Conference were (1) the inerrancy of the Scriptures, (2) the virgin birth of Jesus Christ, (3) the deity of Jesus Christ, (4) the substitutionary atonement (Jesus taking the punishment for sin in people's place), and (5) the physical resurrection of Jesus Christ and his anticipated bodily return.[10]

The five points of fundamentalist doctrine enunciated in the first volume of *The Fundamentals* were almost identical: (1) the verbal and inerrant inspiration of the Bible, (2) the virgin birth of Jesus Christ, (3) the substitutionary atonement of Jesus Christ, (4) the bodily resurrection of Jesus Christ from the tomb, and (5) the imminent second coming of Jesus Christ. Four closely related doctrines that could more or less be inferred from these basic five were (1) the deity of Jesus Christ, (2) the sinful nature of humanity, (3) salvation by faith through the free grace of God, and (4) the expectation of the bodily resurrection of true believers on the Last Day.[11] Much attention was also paid to refutation of errors, such as the theory of organic evolution and higher criticism of the Bible, and to ways of relating to such heretical religious groups and movements as Roman Catholics, Mormons, Jehovah's Witnesses, Christian Science, and Spiritualism.

Fundamentalism became more conscious of self when the assumptions of conservative Protestantism (which had served as the dominant, pace-setting religion throughout the previous two and one-half centuries of American history) began to be threatened. First, many immigrants—particularly Roman Catholics and Jews—arriving in the last half of the nineteenth century created a sense of uncertainty for the fundamentalists. At the same time, industrialization and the erosion of the farming and small business patterns that had prevailed during the first two and one-half centuries of the country's existence were having an impact. Until this time, fundamentalists, while not terribly conscious of their political nature, were nonetheless comfortable with notions of this as a Christian nation that puts Christian principles of morality and civility into practice.

Speer describes such devolution of fundamentalism between 1870 and 1920 as movement from a "church" to a "beleaguered sect."[12] But following

---

[9]Louis Gasper, *The Fundamentalist Movement* (The Hague: Mouton, 1963), p. 11.

[10]Ibid.

[11]*The Fundamentals: A Testimony to the Truth*, Vols. 1–12 (Chicago: Testimony Publishing Company, n.d. [c. 1919]).

[12]James A. Speer, "The New Christian Right and Its Parent Company: A Study in Political Contrasts," in *New Christian Politics*, eds. David Bromley and Anson Shupe (Macon, GA: Mercer Press, 1984), p. 30.

this period of adjustment and consolidation of its concerns, fundamentalism came back with a flurry of activity following World War I, opposing the teaching of evolution in schools and supporting prohibition. In fact, fundamentalism probably reached its zenith in 1925. This was the date of the Scopes "monkey trial," in which the fundamentalists hoped that their political spokesman and three-time candidate for the presidency, William Jennings Bryan, would defeat religious modernism as epitomized in the teaching of evolution in the public schools. Even though Scopes was found guilty, the farcical nature of the trial and the "bad press" the prosecution received turned the legal victory of the fundamentalists into a public relations defeat, and the cohesiveness of the movement began to dissipate. By the following year attendance at their annual meeting had fallen off. By their 1930 convention "none of the scheduled speeches contained any reference to modernism or evolution."[13] They began to fight among themselves, and a host of subgroups formed.

The Post World War II Fundamentalism Revival

Following World War II many evangelicals/fundamentalists joined the anti-Communist crusade that linked them with right-wing political groups. These political groups supported the reckless inquisition by Senator Joseph McCarthy and the destruction, or at best long interruption, of careers for many people. The movement was based on such ideas as opposition to communism and socialism in most any form; support for traditional free enterprise and capitalism and its corollary limited government; commitment to traditional morality, which would exclude and condemn such persons as "liberated" women, homosexuals, and civil libertarians; and frequently an expression of anti-Semitism as well. The Radical Right and its history in the United States is a fascinating topic in itself. But what is of primary interest to us in this text is the relationship and intermingling of radical right political philosophies and activities with fundamentalist Protestant religion. Particularly intriguing is the intimate association of fundamentalist Protestant theology with right-wing politics among many of the anti-Communist crusaders in the 1950s and 1960s. As Janson and Eismann state:

> Ultraconservative leaders have had considerable success, simply by preaching anticommunism, in rallying not only religious fundamentalists concerned about heresy but also political, economic, and social fundamentalists concerned about the liberal trends that are threatening their values.[14]

[13]Norman F. Furniss, *The Fundamentalist Controversy, 1918–1931* (New Haven: Yale University Press, 1954), p. 56.

[14]Donald Janson and Bernard Eismann, *The Far Right* (New York: McGraw-Hill, 1963), p. 239.

Some of the radical right groups tried to remain aloof from religion—Robert Welch's John Birch Society, for one. Welch did not reveal his personal religious convictions, if any, and said that he did not care what religion a person was. His ultimate appeal was not to religious beliefs but to what he viewed as fundamental American values. Other prominent right-wing political groups, however, made an intimate connection between the two. Fred C. Schwartz's Christian Anti-Communist Crusade, Billy James Hargis's Christian Crusade, and Carl McIntire's "20th Century Reformation Hour" were major groups with deep roots in Protestant fundamentalism. As Hargis has said, "I fight Communism . . . because it is part of my ordination vows, of my creed."[15] In his publication *Christian Crusade*, he states:

> Christian Crusade's fight against Communism is Christ's fight. Christ is using this Movement. The very fact that Christian Crusade has existed through fourteen years of opposition from powerful forces in high and low circles is proof that it is of God. . . . I know we are on the right track, getting the job done for Jesus.[16]

In discussing the connection between religion and politics that tends to exist among radical right groups, Murray Havens states that most of these groups "would substitute for religious tolerance an insistence on uniform acceptance not only of Christianity but of their particular highly dogmatic version of Christianity."[17] Their urging of Protestant fundamentalism merges smoothly with appeals for maximum cultural conformity based on small-town and rural America, an explicit antiintellectualism, and a defense of the status quo so far as economic and racial disparities are concerned.

It is interesting that while most authors who have analyzed radical right groups note the congruence and close association between right-wing political views and fundamentalist Protestant religion, seldom do they carry out much analysis of the relationship. One important exception is John Redekop, who discusses several intimate connections. One is a simplistic dualism. The fundamentalist sees only two categories, good and evil, with nothing in between. The radical right-winger sees fellow citizens as either Americans or Communists, one or the other. Tolerance is only for those who do not believe strongly in anything. Hatred of evil is therefore perfectly logical, and heresy hunting perfectly legitimate. Another characteristic of both fundamentalism and radical right philosophy is a conspiratorial view of the world. Satan conspires to detour people from the path of righteousness;

---

[15]Billy James Hargis, television address, KAIL-TV, Fresno, California, October 25, 1964. Quoted in John H. Redekop, *The American Far Right* (Grand Rapids, MI: William B. Eerdmans, 1968), p. 17.

[16]Billy James Hargis, *Christian Crusade*, January–February 1962, p. 3. Quoted in Redekop, *The American Far Right*, p. 18.

[17]Murray C. Havens, *The Challenges to Democracy* (Austin, TX: University of Texas Press, 1965), pp. 82–83.

communism does the same. Communism actually becomes the Devil personified—or better, politicized. As a result, all political discussion takes on a strong moral fervor. Politics thus becomes a crusade, and one's patriotism proof of a mature Christianity.

A third connection is the individualistic emphasis in fundamentalism (individual salvation) and a corresponding disapproval of social action and public welfare programs, which matches the radical right's laissez-faire economic and political ideology. Individuals are more important than society and are capable of satisfying their wants and needs in the free enterprise marketplace. Governmental intervention here is morally wrong. Communism is therefore readily viewed as the epitome of evil.[18]

Although Murray Stedman is likely correct when he contends that "there is no apparent dictate in the inner logic of fundamentalism that would necessarily predispose its followers to political authoritarianism"[19]— that is, not all fundamentalists are or will become radical right-wingers— there is nevertheless a ready alliance between the two. When they coincide, as they frequently do, the connection is easy to understand, for the religious and the political views reinforce one another. It should be noted that this connection had been highly explicit in an earlier generation as well. In the early 1920s the spellbinding evangelist Billy Sunday convinced a lot of people that there was an extremely clever satanic plot afoot in the world that true fundamentalist Christianity had to combat. The world conspiracy consisted of kaiserism (the First World War had just ended), bolshevism (the Communist Revolution in the Soviet Union occurred in 1917), evolutionism, higher criticism (modern biblical scholarship), and liberal theology in general—a mixture of certain theological, political, and scientific elements—all evil in their own right according to Billy Sunday and his followers.[20]

But as interest by citizens in the shrill variety of anti-Communism of the 1950s declined, fundamentalism turned again to spiritual matters and an emphasis on personal regeneration.

The New Christian Right—Recent Developments

Nonetheless, by the mid-1970s the political aspirations of fundamentalism were again stirring in the wake of new developments in technology that were seen as opportunities to affect profoundly both individuals and the corporate body of the nation. Such a waxing and waning of fundamentalist

[18]Redekop, *The American Far Right*, Chapter 10.

[19]Murray Stedman, *Religion and Politics in America* (New York: Harcourt Brace Jovanovich, Inc., 1964), p. 129.

[20]Erling Jorstad, *The Politics of Doomsday* (Nashville: Abingdon, 1970), p. 24.

interest in political action expresses an inherent ambivalence among these religious groups. This ambivalence is best understood by the juxtaposition of two important themes in Calvinism, which is the religious parent of fundamentalism. One is that the individual should separate oneself as much as possible from the evil world because it can contaminate and infect one spiritually. Politics is particularly suspect in this regard. Therefore, Calvinists concentrate on regeneration and making the people in a society moral, attempting to perfect the society one person at a time. The other theme is that of theocracy. That is, if a group of well-informed believers can achieve God's design for humanity by controlling the governance of a social system, then they should do it.

The so-called "New Christian Right" is an expression of the latter view. Fundamentalists and evangelicals saw opportunities to have a profound effect on the nation through controlling the outcome of elections which could set the stage for later legislation of morality.

As the 1980s began, two developments came together to enhance very substantially the impact of the conservative or Fundamentalist-Evangelical segment in American religion and carry to a new level and to a new generation the linkage of right-wing politics and religion.

The first of these developments was the fast growth of what has come to be known as the "electronic church." This refers to the rapid expansion of preachers and groups, particularly from the fundamentalist wing of Protestantism, into a television ministry. It is of course true that religious broadcasting has existed since the beginnings of radio and television. In the early days, however, the programs were either extremely localized, or they were broadcast as part of the free public service obligation of the broadcasting media, which tended to put them at non-prime times such as the "God hour" on Sunday mornings. What is different today is (1) the widespread outright ownership of radio and television stations by religious groups, (2) the full-time religious broadcasting on these stations, and (3) as a corollary of this, the greater volume of religious broadcasting on radio and TV. In 1980, 1,400 radio stations and 60 television stations were wholly owned by religious groups. These stations produced thousands of hours of religious programming each week and generated up to $500 million in nontaxable revenue annually.

While we do not wish to underestimate the significance of the electronic church (in fact, we are trying to feature not only its contemporary importance but even more its potential influence), the extent of its audience and influence has been overplayed by the mass media themselves. William Martin assembled some of the extravagant reports from recent books and popular magazines.[21] In a recent book by Ben Armstrong called *The Electric*

---

[21]William Martin, "The Birth of a Media Myth," *The Atlantic* 247, no. 6 (January, 1981), 7–16.

Church (Nashville: Thomas Nelson, 1979), one reads about almost 130 million people drawn on Sundays to religious programs on TV and radio. The *Wall Street Journal* (July 11, 1980) credits a weekly audience of 128 million viewers for Oral Roberts, Pat Robertson, and Jerry Falwell. An article in *New York* magazine (October 6, 1980) not only sets membership in the electronic church at 130 million but asserts that contributions to teleministries total in the billions—a figure far in excess of the $500 million that is commonly credited to the combined fund-raising efforts of both radio and television ministries. Actually, many of the preachers for the electronic church are themselves becoming more modest in their claims. For example, whereas Rex Humbard's press materials once claimed an audience of "up to 100 million," his recent promotional literature says only 1.4 million.[22] There are still those at the other extreme, however. Martin notes, for example, the claims by the radio preacher Bert Clendennen, who has often told his hearers that his program reaches "one out of every two people on the face of this earth."[23]

But we do not need to rely on guesswork or projections based partly on public relations motivations, partly on a self-confident and optimistic outlook on one's work. The two major rating services for the broadcast media, Nielsen and Arbitron, have independently surveyed the audience for religious broadcasting that constitutes the electronic church. A. C. Nielsen found in 1980 a maximum audience for one TV preacher, Oral Roberts, to be 2,351,000.[24] Others, such as Robert Schuller, Rex Humbard, Jimmy Swaggart, and Jerry Falwell scaled down from there. The total for the top ten programs was only 13,767,000.[25] We say "only" because there is no doubt that there is considerable overlap in the audiences of these programs. That is, one person will watch several and get counted several times. Martin suggests that there may be 7 to 10 million individual persons who watch these programs. Even that figure is probably on the generous side.

The upshot of this quick look at the numbers that might be involved in the electronic church is that although many of the popular claims of tens of millions of viewers and participants are significant overestimates, a substantial core and base remain.

Such statistics in themselves, while perhaps impressive, do not necessarily have much significance beyond the expanded religious outreach they represent. However, they loom much more significant, particularly in the political context, when we realize that an explicit goal of many contemporary religious broadcasters is political influence. While not new, this second development—interest in political influence—has been revived. The epit-

---

[22]Ibid., p. 10.
[23]Ibid.
[24]A. C. Nielsen Company. Reported in Martin, "The Birth of a Media Myth," p. 11.
[25]Ibid.

ome of this phenomenon and trend is the "Moral Majority" and its program for the 1980s and beyond.[26]

In June, 1980, the Reverend Jerry Falwell founded Moral Majority—an organization with at least five primary messages and emphases: (1) America is in a state of terrifying moral decline; (2) moral decay in this country will result in the fall of America and the rise of atheistic dictatorships if not stopped; (3) this nation is a chosen instrument of God for good in the world; (4) Christian citizens have a moral obligation and duty to vote; (5) as they vote they are to put into office candidates who pledge to support the religious principles of the Moral Majority. It was reported that within sixteen months Falwell's group claimed to have signed up 72,000 ministers and 4 million lay members with chapters in every state, and had expectations of raising $5 million for support of political campaigns in 1980 alone.[27]

In addition to coming out foursquare in support of the Republican candidate Ronald Reagan and the Republican platform he represented (they had a hand in building it), the New Right groups collectively opposed three major developments: the legalization of abortion-on-demand, the spread of pornography, and the tolerance of homosexuality. Three causes they championed were as follows: providing for prayer and Bible reading in public schools, nullifying the Equal Rights Amendment, and defeating liberal senators and members of Congress who were viewed as aiding and abetting moral decay. These groups set as one target for 1980 the defeat of six liberal senators.

Five of them did indeed go down to defeat in November, 1980: George McGovern of South Dakota, Frank Church of Idaho, John Culver of Iowa, Birch Bayh of Indiana, and Gaylord Nelson of Wisconsin. Only Alan Cranston of California retained his seat in the Senate. During the campaign, not necessarily with the endorsement of the national organization, epithets such as "baby killer" and accusations of promoting homosexuality were commonplace at the local level. Birch Bayh's comment is typical of those concerned about the New Religious Right movement. He said, "The cause of liberty is not served by organizations that brand public officials as being immoral or anti-God simply because they may hold different views. . . . These hate groups now have tasted blood. . . . Step out of line one time, and they'll chop your head off."[28]

Many have referred to the platform of these groups as "single issue politics." While "single issue" may be an overstatement, at most their plat-

---

[26]While the Moral Majority is technically a political organization, not a religious group, its major leadership, membership, and support come from the New Religious Right.

[27]George J. Church, "Politics from the Pulpit," *Time*, 116 (October 13, 1980), 28.

[28]"Religious Right Goes For Bigger Game," *U.S. News & World Report*, 89 (November 17, 1980), 42.

forms include but a few items. What they overlook is the broad array of political issues a member of Congress or a president is called upon to deal with. Further, critics point out that with their emphasis on abortion or homosexuality or prayer in public schools, there is total silence with respect to providing justice for all, care for the needy, protection of minorities, and the like. Various religious groups have gone so far as to condemn publicly or at least raise questions about their tactics and program. Among others, these include some Methodist and Lutheran groups, the National Council of Churches, the American Jewish Committee, and the Jesuit publication *America.*

In all fairness, however, it should be pointed out that more liberal church people and the groups they represent, although not so well-financed or perhaps with as much support, have also been known to wage single issue campaigns—anti-Vietnam War protesting, antinuclear demonstrations, participation in the 1960s civil rights movement and joining the Sanctuary movement are examples of these campaigns. The New Religious Right (sometimes called the New Christian Right) is certainly not the first coalition of religious groups to attempt to influence voters and the political structure of a country, the United States of America included.

In addition to such specific goals as mentioned earlier (legislation against abortion, pornography, and homosexuality, and defeating the Equal Rights Amendment and liberal members of Congress), there are other in one sense more important themes in the message of the New Christian Right. It is these themes that provide the initial "hook" that brings people in. Jeffrey Hadden and Charles Swann have summarized them as follows. First, they communicate the impression of absolute certainty about anything and everything. The elimination of ambiguity is central. Second, a positive attitude toward life is of crucial importance to success and happiness. Norman Vincent Peale's *Power of Positive Thinking* from the 1950s gets daily repetition and updating. Third, it is all right to look out for yourself. It is OK to seek success and reward, and to attain them.[29]

The message would seem to be much like the following: "And now that we've got your attention, have you been noticing what's going on around you? Have you sensed how far we've degenerated as a nation? Have you noticed how sinful we've become? And perhaps even worse, have you noticed how tolerant of sin we've become? Won't you help us do something about it?"

But what is really fascinating about the new Religious Right and in particular what conspired to make them loom significant sociologically is not simply their message. That is not really new. Preaching against sin, trying to improve the morality of people, and providing simple answers to complex

---

[29]Jeffrey K. Hadden and Charles E. Swann, *Prime Time Preachers* (Reading, MA: Addison-Wesley, 1981), pp. 101–102.

issues and problems are far from new ideas on the American religious scene. What is new is the pair of technological advances that the proponents employ: (1) television, and (2) direct mail technology that could come of age only with the storage and pinpointing capabilities of the computer. These two advances in technology give the potential not only of reaching millions of people in a short time but also of mobilizing masses of fairly ordinary church members who hold conservative opinions and values in the religious sphere as well as in the political and social spheres.

In terms of potential support, John Simpson notes that a full 30 percent of Americans, although not necessarily members of the Moral Majority, hold to a set of four convictions espoused by the Moral Majority, that is, opposition to abortion, homosexuality, the Supreme Court school prayer decision, and a "modern" role for women outside the traditional homemaking, childrearing functions.[30] In addition, Simpson suggests that as many as 70 percent of Americans can be classified as conservative in terms of the socio-moral platform of the Moral Majority. That is, while not necessarily supporting all points of the platform, they can be attracted to support a Moral Majority position on particular issues and combinations of issues (they espouse the Moral Majority position on at least two of the four issues identified above).[31]

But already, as we have come to expect, the New Christian Right has begun a recession. Its candidate for president, Pat Robertson, did not become popular with the voters and withdrew during the primaries in 1988; several of NCR's prominent televangelists were discredited (Jimmy Swaggert and the Bakkers); the Moral Majority, founded in 1980 and renamed the Liberty Federation in 1986, ceased to exist in 1989; and national interest in prayer in the public schools declined. But one primary issue remains. It will not be submerged. That is the abortion issue. This debate continues vigorously and is in the forefront of political debate. It remains a vital issue because it is not only a concern of fundamentalists. Significant numbers of other religious groups, particularly Roman Catholics, share both concern and position with the fundamentalists on this issue.

CIVIL RELIGION

As we continue to look at the relationship between religion and politics, we need to consider a concept that has had wide attention among those trying to understand how religion and politics affect one another. That is the con-

---

[30]John H. Simpson, "Is There a Moral Majority?" Paper presented at the joint annual meeting of the Society for the Scientific Study of Religion and the Religious Research Association, Baltimore, Maryland, October 30, 1981.

[31]Ibid.

cept of *civil religion*. Briefly, the idea of civil religion refers to the view of some people that the foundation of their society and the events that mark its progress through history are parts of a larger, divine scheme of things; the political structure and the political acts that flow out of that structure have a transcendental dimension—God is at work in our nation, and as such we have a destiny.

Robert Bellah introduced the term and describes civil religion as a substratum of common religious understandings that are quite pervasive in society, American society in particular.

> Although matters of personal religious belief, worship, and association are considered to be strictly private affairs, there are, at the same time, certain common elements of religious orientation that the great majority of Americans share. These have played a crucial role in the development of American institutions and still provide a religious dimension for the whole fabric of American life, including the political sphere. This public religious dimension is expressed in a set of beliefs, symbols, and rituals that I am calling the American civil religion.[32]

Bellah goes on to point out that America's civil religion is certainly not Christianity in anything like the specific sense such as would necessitate belief in Jesus Christ and the Atonement, but rather it is more "unitarian" in the sense of regarding God as a sort of single supernatural being. But this God is not to be understood simply in the deistic tradition of an aloof Maker who set the world in motion and then left it to shift for itself. No, "he is actively interested and involved in history, with a special concern for America."[33] At the heart of civil religion within the United States is the idea that America is the promised land God has led people to—out of the land of bondage (Europe). Thus, this nation is to be dedicated to order, law, and justice as God would have them carried out. Bellah quotes extensively from Washington and Jefferson, as well as from John Kennedy and Lyndon Johnson, pointing out the idea of America as charged with a divinely ordained mission to fulfill in bringing about God's will for humankind. Out of the trauma of the Civil War emerged new themes of sacrifice and rebirth. Lincoln's Gettysburg Address was replete with Christian symbolism without being specifically Christian (for example, "that those who here gave their lives, that the nation might live"). Lincoln's own "sacrificial" martyrdom enhanced the concept. Memorial Day ceremonies and to a lesser extent the ceremonies of the Fourth of July, Veterans Day, Thanksgiving Day, and Washington's and Lincoln's birthdays provided ritual vehicles for the civil religion.

Coleman formalizes a definition of civil religion and lists three central characteristics of American civil religion. He defines *civil religion* as "the set

[32]Robert N. Bellah, "Civil Religion in America," in *Religion in America*, eds. William G. McLoughlin and Robert N. Bellah (Boston, MA: Houghton Mifflin, 1968), pp. 5–6.
[33]Ibid., p. 9.

of beliefs, rites, and symbols which relates a man's role as citizen and his society's place in space, time, and history to the conditions of ultimate existence and meaning."[34] Three characteristics, according to Coleman, typify American civil religion. (1) The nation is the primary agent of God's meaningful activity in history. This belief gave rise to the doctrines of manifest destiny and world obligation. (2) The nation is the primary society in terms of which individual Americans discover personal and group identity. Like the historic church, through the doctrine of the melting pot, America was called to be "catholic." (3) The nation also assumes a churchly feature as the community of righteousness.[35]

In the 1950s and 1960s, many writers, most with a strong theological orientation and commitment, reacted strongly against what Bellah subsequently called civil religion and constituted much of the so-called religious revival of the 1950s. Martin Marty's criticism of what he calls the "religion of democracy" or "state Shinto" is typical. Marty states that in American state Shinto, "democracy becomes the ultimate, religion the handmaiden."[36]

Whether critical of such a religion of democracy as a perversion of Christianity or not, most who have analyzed the phenomenon would agree that civil religion in America is differentiated. That is, neither state nor church is in charge of it. Coleman sees this as a new development. He suggests that much of the furor in the 1950s over a sellout of Christianity to secularism and the substitution of a new American Shinto was implicit recognition that control over civil religion had fallen out of religious hands. His view is that such differentiation is "healthy for both the state which does not place itself in opposition to the church and the church which remains free to perform a prophetic religious function."[37]

Others have suggested quite a different perspective—the rejuvenation and encouragement of civil religion, and the active involvement of organized religion in that process. A writer such as J. Paul Williams sees this as the future task of religion, although he does not use the concept *civil religion* and his proposals predate Bellah's introduction of the concept. Actually, Williams blends in a most interesting way a couple of sociological ideas—the idea of religion as an integrating, functional entity in society and the widely held view of the decline of institutional religion.

Williams calls the integrating factor *"societal"* religion. This is distinguished from *"private"* religion, which an individual shares with only a few other intimate persons, and *"denominational"* religion, which is simply the denominational phenomenon we have discussed several times before. Williams points out that although denominational religion has changed in

[34]John A. Coleman, "Civil Religion," *Sociological Analysis 31*, no. 2 (1970), 76.
[35]Ibid., p. 74.
[36]Martin E. Marty, *The New Shape of American Religion* (New York: Harper & Brothers, 1958), p. 78.
[37]Coleman, "Civil Religion," p. 76.

response to social change, societal religion has remained quite uniform over the decades. Its essence is commitment to the democratic way of life. He quotes A. Powell Davies's description of the democratic faith or way of life, which asserts that people were meant to be free, that they can improve their level of life through the power of reason and discussion, and that human rights such as liberty and justice are by their nature universal. In summary, Davies states: "God and history are on the side of freedom and justice, love and righteousness; and man will therefore, be it soon or late, achieve a world society of peace and happiness where all are free and none shall be afraid."[38] The central idea here is that the core values of America, which are almost by definition nearly universally accepted by Americans, are essentially religious values that in turn constitute the societal religion.

Williams deeply believes that since American democracy and the societal religion that undergirds it face threats of various kinds, they need buttressing. Such support, he feels, ought to come from denominational religion. "Americans must be brought to the conviction that democracy is the very Law of life."[39] To accomplish this, "democracy must become an object of religious dedication. Americans must come to look on the democratic ideal (not necessarily American practice of it) as the Will of God or, if they prefer, the Law of Nature."[40] William's proposal is simply this: "The churches and synagogues should not only promulgate their own denominational values, but in addition should support those broader values which are essential to the continuance and betterment of society as a whole. . . . In America the churches and synagogues should teach faith in democracy as one item of their creed."[41]

Williams is suggesting implicitly that all would be better off if religion in America would lose much of its denominational character and get on with the important business at hand of creating and maintaining a true democracy—that is, if religion would return to its true social purpose of enhancing the integration of society. It hardly needs pointing out, however, that his proposal has not caught on in a particularly striking fashion. Many religious groups would reject it out and out—conservatives because of its tendencies to dilute traditional religious tenets and to blur the distinction between church and state, and liberals because it appears to them too uncritical of existing political arrangements and of the manner in which democratic principles are expedited. Certainly, many secularized Americans would raise serious questions about William's proposal in this day of political and intellectual dissent and criticism, when many can find no honest way to give democracy (as it obtains in the present, at least) such unqualified support.

[38]Quoted in J. Paul Williams, *What Americans Believe and How They Worship* (New York: Harper & Row, 1969), p. 481.
[39]Ibid., p. 491.
[40]Ibid., p. 484.
[41]Ibid., p. 488.

RELIGION AND POLITICS IN THE THIRD WORLD

Although religious issues periodically surface as political issues in every society of the world, a politico-religious phenomenon virtually unknown in the United States but fairly common in the Third World (the developing nations of Asia, Africa, and Latin America) is the emergence of religious political parties—that is, political parties whose constituency is a particular religious group and that pursue both religious and political ends. Donald Smith distinguishes three kinds of Third World politico-religious parties.[42] There are first of all the *communal parties*, such as the Hindu Mahasabha, the Jana Sangh, and the Sikhs in India, which exist within a national context of religious pluralism. Their self-styled function is to "protect and promote the largely secular economic and political interests of their respective communal groups."[43] Such political parties are organized manifestations of communal conflict and violence of the sort that might erupt between Hindus and Muslims if the latter were alleged to have killed sacred cows or if a Hindu procession was accused of disturbing Muslims in their mosques at prayer—violence of the sort paralleled in the West by the protracted Protestant-Catholic conflict in Northern Ireland. An excellent example of the Third World communal party is the Freedom party led by S. W. R. D. Bandaranaike that pledged itself to restore Buddhism to its rightful place in the national life of Sri Lanka (formerly Ceylon). The focus of its attack was Christianity, particularly the Roman Catholic Church, which was felt to be favored by governing authorities. Bandaranaike succeeded in becoming prime minister in the election of 1956 but was assassinated three years later. The subsequest administration under his wife found its power considerably weakened through expedient compromises with Marxists.

The second type of religious political party is the *sect-based party*. Smith cites the Ummah in the northern Sudan as a prime example. Although the northern portion of the Sudan is solidly Muslim, the Ummah is a minority political party that derives its constituency from the Ansar sect within that branch of Islam. In other words, unlike the interreligious conflict inherent in the communal parties, here intrareligious conflict between a sect and the parent religious group finds expression in political action and party formation.

The third type is the *ideological religious party* that, Smith notes, functions in societies in which religious minorities are politically unimportant. Such parties are not oriented to conflict with other religious groups but desire to speak to the ideological assumptions that undergird and shape the society. They may be conservative and attempt to preserve traditional patterns, such as many Latin American conservative parties, particularly of

---

[42]Donald E. Smith, *Religion, Politics, and Social Change in the Third World* (New York: Free Press, 1971), pp. 140–169.

[43]Ibid., p. 440.

thirty and more years ago. Or they may be modernizing or reforming as they challenge aspects of the fundamental societal ideology. Examples of the latter are the Christian Democrats in Chile and the Masjumi in Indonesia.

The point to appreciate in this extremely brief look at religion and politics in the Third World is the widespread tendency of citizens in these societies to refuse to relegate religion solely to the private sphere of individual faith and practice. The politico-religious conflict that ensues is aided by the onrush of social change and the inevitable challenges to traditional ideologies that social change involves. Such developments may upset traditional delicate compromises and stalemates among religions, which may lead to intergroup conflict, or religious groups may organize themselves politically to uphold traditional values in some cases or promote other values in other cases. The point, then, is that in many Third World societies religion and politics are less clearly separated than in, say, the United States.

A prime reason for this, as Smith points out, is that Third World societies began much more recently to question the view of government as ordained by God and of governmental leaders as gods or direct agents of God.[44] These societies have not become as secularized as most societies of the West, though this process seems to be accelerating. It is thus unlikely that religion will remain the political force that it has represented in the recent past. An important reason for this is that in many Third World countries religion has become intimately associated with nationalistic sentiments and activities. With political independence already a fact in many of these societies, a major purpose of the politico-religious parties has been all but eliminated. Furthermore, as Smith points out, participation in the political process itself has an important secularizing effect.[45] The political party with an Islamic ideology, for example, may work within a pluralistic ideological milieu and find itself making deals that are politically expedient but that implicitly deny the absolutist, inviolable precepts of orthodox Islam. They compromise their ideology to capture minority votes. Smith notes that in the long run, "particularistic ideologies such as Islam give ground before universalistic ideologies such as socialism."[46]

[44]Ibid., pp. 1–2.
[45]Ibid., p. 4.
[46]Ibid.

8

Religion and the Economy

In line with an underlying principle made explicit throughout this book, namely, that religion is in a continuous reciprocal and interdependent relationship with society and its institutions, we now turn to one of society's most important institutions (some would say, *the* most important)—the economy.

We can initially observe that religion, although often legitimately viewed as a semiautonomous social system (societal institution) paralleling other institutions, is itself in various ways a part of the inclusive economic system of a society—it is an employer; it buys and sells; it owns property; it contributes to the gross national product (the amount spent annually on all goods and services). A brief look at religion as an active participant in the economy constitutes the first section of this chapter. The major section that follows looks at religion's influence on economic relationships in a society. We will, then, in a third section, conclude with an assessment of how and to what degree religion has an impact on the economy and vice versa.

RELIGION AS AN ECONOMIC INSTITUTION

Two obvious ways in which organized religion plays an economic role in most societies is as an employer (providing the economic livelihood for religious professionals and their families) and as an owner of property and a builder of facilities. Although there are no precise figures available concerning the number of persons employed by religious organizations, we do know that as of 1987 there were at least 530,763 members of the clergy in the United States.[1] But even this figure is not comprehensive, inasmuch as not all religious groups report statistics to the National Council of Churches. Conservatively, we would therefore estimate that there are at least 550,000 clergy members in the United States alone. Add to this the members of Catholic monastic orders; the tens of thousands of church secretaries, janitors, and sextons; employees of religious publishing companies; parochial-school teachers as well as clerical and secretarial staff for area, state, regional, and national denominations and ecumenical organizations; social workers employed by religious welfare agencies; and the like—and a total of 800,000 or more families deriving part or, for many, all of their family income from religious organizations would be a conservative estimate.

In 1957, church property and endowments in the United States were valued at $13.7 billion.[2] Although there was some decline in new construction by religious groups between 1965 and 1975, the value of expenditures for such new construction has increased each year since 1975, even when inflation is taken into account. Total new construction in 1987 was $2,753 million ($2,340 in 1982 adjusted dollars).[3]

Probably even more impressive are the figures for contributions to religious groups. In 1984, the American Association of Fund-Raising Councils estimated contributions to religious groups at $35.56 billion, or 47.9 percent of the total estimated amount of charitable contributions that year of $74.25 billion.[4] While it is not the biggest business in this country or the world, religion is nonetheless a significant element in the economy as an owner of great amounts of property and as an agent for the collection and distribution of billions of dollars annually.

Religious organizations also engage in economic activities and enterprises that are not intrinsically religious—they own and derive income from apartment and office buildings, parking lots, factories, and of course stocks and bonds held as endowments by local congregations, national denominations, and church workers' pension funds. Until 1969, many of such "for

[1]National Council of Churches of Christ in the U.S.A., Office of Research and Evaluation, *Yearbook of American Churches*, 1987, ed. Constant H. Jacquet, Jr. (Nashville, TN: Abingdon, 1987), p. 247.

[2]David O. Moberg, *The Church as a Social Institution* (Englewood Cliffs, NJ: Prentice-Hall, 1962), p. 169.

[3]National Council of Churches, *Yearbook*, p. 280.

[4]National Council of Churches of Christ in the U.S.A., Office of Planning and Program, *Yearbook of American Churches, 1986*, ed. Constant H. Jacquet, Jr. (Nashville, TN: Abingdon, 1986), p. 256.

profit" enterprises owned by churches went untaxed because religious groups were unique among incorporated organizations in not being required to pay income taxes on "unrelated business income."[5] But the Tax Reform Act of 1969, which was actively supported by such associations as the National Council of Churches and the U.S. Catholic Conference, closed this infamous loophole. Most "horror stories" of tax preferences and abuses predate 1969 and the five-year grace period that followed. But even before the federal law went into effect, most religious groups, particularly at the local level, held no investments beyond the buildings and property in which they worshiped and performed their educational functions. They earned no "unrelated business income."

With respect to taxes on the property owned by churches, there is great variation by state and municipality. Generally, property used primarily for religious worship and education is not taxed, though some churches contribute a sum annually in recognition of the police and fire protection accorded them by the community. Land used to turn a profit for the church is often placed on the property tax rolls.

RELIGION AS A SHAPER OF ECONOMIC ATTITUDES AND BEHAVIOR

Throughout history, religious groups have faced a dilemma with regard to attempting to influence economic attitudes and behavior. On the one hand, churches have tended to treat poverty as a virtue and discourage the faithful from becoming encumbered by material goods and concerns. Certainly the Bible extols poverty in such statements as "Blessed are the poor for they shall inherit the earth," or "How hard it is for a rich man to enter the kingdom of heaven." Buddhism extols the mendicant monk who travels light and remains free from economic concerns in order to engage in a life of contemplation.

Yet any religious group, particularly as its organization begins to get the least bit complex, requires funds to operate. The group then begins to get involved in economic affairs, whether it wants to or not. It finds itself grateful for substantial contributions from wealthy members. It may exact a tithe from its adherents. As at least some members rise out of poverty, it does not kick them out but perhaps even extols them for their industry and frugality. It is this tendency of religious groups to become fairly actively engaged in economic activities that is one of several stimuli to the formation of sects. We observed in Chapter 5 that sects tend to turn poverty into a virtue. This is what Max Weber calls a "theodicy of disprivilege" or

---

[5]Dean M. Kelley, *Why Churches Should Not Pay Taxes* (New York: Harper & Row, 1977), pp. 17–18.

"theodicy of escape,"[6]—that is, a rationalization and justification of one's disprivileged economic and social status as an advantage so far as salvation is concerned. True riches and enhanced status will accrue in the hereafter, when it really counts—when it is for eternity, not just sixty or seventy years of toil and trouble on this earth.

Just as children say, "That's the dumbest toy I ever saw—I didn't want that crummy old thing anyway" of the toy they grab from another child but have to return after a stern parental reprimand, so the sectarians of low socioeconomic status are likely to define what is denied them as evil, or at least as unimportant and undesirable. Wealth, fancy clothes, "highfalutin" manners and language? Who needs them! Actually Weber identifies three different forms that release from earthly disprivilege might take: the expectation of a better life in the hereafter (paradise or heaven); hope for oneself, or at least for one's progeny, in a new world to be created by God for the faithful called the Messianic Age or the millennium; hope for another life or rebirth in this world that will be better or higher than the present one (the concept of transmigration of souls in Hinduism, for example).[7]

On the other hand, there is the "theodicy of good fortune" identified by Weber. Here there is theological justification for superior economic and social status. "The fortunate is seldom satisfied with the fact of being fortunate. Beyond this, he needs to know that he has the *right* to his good fortune, . . . that he 'deserves' it."[8] Good fortune wants to be "legitimate" fortune. Religion legitimates the favored conditions of "religious men, the propertied, the victorious, and the healthy. In short, religion provides the theodicy of good fortune for those who are fortunate."[9]

Here we find ourselves drifting into the perspective in which religion is seen as influenced by forces outside itself—in this case, by economic factors, which are seen as influencing religious doctrine. There is of course much evidence supporting this point of view, and we will look at the matter more closely in the third section of this chapter. But first let us examine how and to what extent religion affects economic attitudes and behavior.

David Moberg mentions several ways in which religion to varying degrees of intensity and significance affects economic attitudes and behavior. First, insofar as such personal and business virtues as honesty, fair play, and honoring one's commitments are essential in economic life, and to the extent that religion is successful in inculcating such virtues in its members, religion has an impact on the economy. Second, religion on occasion stimulates consumption. Religious holidays implicitly encourage material con-

---

[6]Max Weber, *The Sociology of Religion*, trans. Ephraim Fischoff (Boston: Beacon Press, 1963), p. 113.

[7]Max Weber, "The Social Psychology of the World Religions," *From Max Weber: Essays in Sociology*, ed. and trans. H. H. Gerth and C. Wright Mills (New York: Oxford University Press, 1958), p. 275.

[8]Ibid., p. 271.

[9]Ibid.

sumption by followers, even if it is only special candles to light and special foods to eat. Third, in emphasizing one's work as a "calling," religion (Protestant Christianity in particular) has glorified and elevated work at one's job, however menial it may be. To the extent that people internalize this view it is likely to increase productivity. The individual worker may think along the following lines: "I'm working for God, not just for my employer or for myself. Therefore, I'd better put out a little more and do the best job possible."[10]

Vogt and O'Dea provide interesting evidence related to this point.[11] Although located in the same natural environment, the communities of Homestead and Rimrock (fictitious names) evidence quite different social systems. Rimrock, which stresses cooperative community effort and achieves great productivity as a consequence, appears to be strongly influenced by the Mormon ideology held by most of its citizens. Homestead, with its individualistic orientation and less successful farming endeavors, evidences the influence of competitive and divisive Protestant denominationalism that inhibits community-oriented cooperative efforts.

A fourth way in which religion may influence the economy is by explicitly endorsing certain economic systems or certain types of economic or business activities. For example, Liston Pope notes that religious leaders were influential in helping establish the cotton mill industry in Gaston County, North Carolina, around the turn of the twentieth century. This was accomplished directly through supportive sermonizing and pronouncements that helped create public approval of the textile enterprise. Religion also indirectly influenced economic endeavor in Gaston County by supporting Prohibition. With the advent of Prohibition, economic capital that had been invested in distilleries was released for investment in the textile mills. Also, mill workers were slightly more likely to appear for work Monday mornings in good condition now that weekend "benders" were more unlikely. Above all, religion helped the mills (and thus influenced the economy) by exerting moral influence over the workers, encouraging them to do a good day's work and to do what the boss told them.[12]

Weber's Protestant Ethic and the Spirit of Capitalism

Probably the greatest single contribution to the discussion of the impact of religion on the economy is Max Weber's seminal study *The Protestant Ethic*

[10]Moberg, *The Church*, pp. 170–174.

[11]Evon Z. Vogt and Thomas F. O'Dea, "A Comparative Study of the Role of Values in Social Action in Two Southwestern Communities," *American Sociological Review 18*, no. 6 (1953), 645–654.

[12]Liston Pope, *Millhands and Preachers* (New Haven: Yale University Press, 1942), Chapter 2.

and the Spirit of Capitalism (1905), which has stimulated massive amounts of research and discussion over the past half-century. Weber's thesis is that Calvinistic Protestantism as a theological belief system exerted an important influence on the emergence and growth of capitalism as a mode of economic organization. Quite explicitly Weber was trying to answer Karl Marx's assertion that society's normative system, including such phenomena as religious values and principles, in fact consists of epiphenomena produced, or at least conditioned in a primary way, by factors in the economy. Weber was essentially saying that at the very least the influential relationship between religion and the economy is a two-way street. Accordingly, he set out to show how religion, as embodied in Calvinism, affected the economy, as represented by capitalism.

The Prime Elements in Calvinistic Theology

In order to see the relationship hypothesized by Weber, we first need to understand a bit of Calvinistic theology. At the center of Calvinistic theology is the concept and goal of the *glory of God*—everything people do should somehow add to God's glory. Since God does not exist for people, but people for God,[13] it is not too surprising that an early Calvinist theologian has been quoted as saying that he would eagerly and joyfully be damned in hell if that would somehow glorify God.

A second central doctrine of Calvinism is that of *predestination*. This teaching speaks of the foreknowledge and above all the foreordaining by God of all people either to eternal salvation or eternal damnation. In Lutheran theology the attempt had been to use this doctrine as a source of comfort and encouragement to the believer. The emphasis was on God's foreknowledge. God knows in advance who will become a true and faithful follower and believer and who will not. Those whom He foresees as believing, He then predestines to heaven. God does not, however, explicitly predestine to hell those whom He foresees as rejecting Him of their own free will; rather, they seal their own fate, so to speak, by rejecting opportunities to become a believer.

In Calvinism, however, God appears a bit more arbitrary. With less emphasis on God's foreknowledge, Calvinism sees God as assigning some to one fate, some to the other. An important implication of Calvinism's version of predestination was that a person has to proceed all alone down the path of life to meet the destiny decreed for him or her for eternity.[14] No priest, no church, no sacrament, nothing human can avail to the contrary. This is

---

[13]Max Weber, *The Protestant Ethic and the Spirit of Capitalism*, trans. Talcott Parsons (New York: Scribner's, 1958), pp. 102–103.

[14]Ibid., p. 104.

because what God has decided beforehand cannot be changed. Of course, someone who is damned should still belong to a church and observe the sacraments, because in such activities God is glorified. This is one's obligation as a human being. But it will not do the person any good so far as his or her eternal destiny is concerned. Such activities will not change God's mind. This is so because Christ died only for the "elect" (those predestined to salvation).[15] Obviously this view is a radical departure from Catholicism, which emphasized the church, the sacraments, and the priesthood as channels of God's gifts of hope and salvation to humankind.

A social consequence of this combination of predestination and obligation to glorify God was the encouragement of a rather extreme kind of individualism. Not only are you on your own in the sense that no other individual or group can help you change the direction of your predestined end, but you must be careful lest your relationships with people become too strong and important. You must not get carried away in involvement with and commitment to husband, wife, children, or friends. Your primary task is to glorify God.

We now add one more element to complete the basic theological ingredients, as Weber saw them, that provided the foundation for the Protestant (Calvinist) ethic—the concept of the "*calling.*" This is a concept, elaborated by Luther, which emphasized using one's secular occupation, whether farmer, artisan, soldier, king, or housewife, to glorify God and to help your neighbor by doing a good job and faithfully carrying out your tasks. This concept taught people not to despise or belittle their job or role in life—it taught them instead to see their work as a "calling" by God. Calvinism picked up this concept and placed even greater emphasis on hard work; whatever your calling, you must carry out its duties to the best of your ability and with your last ounce of energy.

Implications for the Individual

We have to realize that the Calvinist was placed in a rather uneasy position with the combining of these three theological elements. He or she was to glorify God by working to the fullest in his or her calling, all the while aware that he or she had been predestined—yet not knowing whether to heaven or to hell. Hence a highly important question in the person's mind was, Is there any way I can know or at least infer that I'm one of the elect? Catholics had little problem with this question. If they were members of the church and performed at least the minimal ritual and confessional requirements, they had nothing to worry about. Lutherans also were little worried about predestination. Since predestination was viewed as based on God's

[15]Ibid.

offer of salvation, they had every reason to believe that they were numbered among the elect. Furthermore, they were promised the inner working of the Holy Spirit, who would develop in them a consciousness and conviction that they were specially chosen by God. True, they could "fall from grace"— but only if they lost their faith and rejected God's offered hand of deliverance. So as long as one believed and did not reject, one did not need to worry.

The Calvinist, however, did not have such assurance. She or he could not truly know or be convinced. But the Calvinist could make inferences from essentially empirical evidence—evidence of an ability consistently to perform well, of success in his or her calling, of the feeling that God seemed to be providing him or her with opportunities and was working through him or her. Would God be likely to choose to work through someone who was not one of the elect? The upshot was that the three theological elements mentioned earlier, in combination with a desire to know whether one was predestined to salvation, produced a tremendous drive toward action. This resulted in what Weber calls "ascetic Protestantism"—a life of strict discipline. Hard work in one's calling is the best discipline. Work is not only the best prophylactic against a sensual, immoral life but also the best means for glorifying God. Time, then, becomes infinitely valuable. Thus, one must avoid idle conversation, unproductive recreation, or more sleep than absolutely necessary in order to have maximum time for work.

Now, if you work harder than people around you, if you put in more hours at your job, if you live frugally and ascetically, you will likely be economically more successful than those around you. This is not bad. In fact, it is good—in two ways. First, this might be inferential evidence that you are one of God's elect. Second, God is being glorified. In the meantime, however, you may become rich. Now what? Such wealth dare not be used for personal sensual pleasure—to buy wine, sexual favors, and frolic. It should not be used to buy early retirement from one's calling. What alternative is there, then? The answer is *investment*—investment of capital to produce more goods, which create more profits, which in turn represent more capital for investment, ad infinitum—which is the heart of entrepreneurial capitalism. The option of giving away the surplus in philanthropic activity was seldom recommended inasmuch as the poor might then be distracted from doing their duty in their calling to menial but important tasks.

Implications for Economics

This returns us to Weber's thesis regarding the effect of religious norms and patterns on economic relationships and institutions. Attempting "to ascertain whether and to what extent religious forces have taken part in the qualitative formation and the quantitative expansion of [the] spirit of capitalism over the world," Weber concludes that Calvinism was indeed just such a force. However, Weber is quick to warn that no one should be so foolish as to maintain that capitalism or the spirit of capitalism could therefore only have developed as a result of the Reformation or that it is a direct product of Calvinism.[16] Rather, he essentially maintains that Calvinism served an important stimulating and reinforcing function for capitalism. Calvinism did not create capitalism nor was it even absolutely necessary for the triumph of capitalism. Rather, Calvinism encouraged capitalism and, if nothing else, hastened its development in those societies where Calvinism wielded an influence.

Weber was much more careful than some of his followers in hypothesizing about the relationship between Calvinistic Protestantism and capitalism, a point not always appreciated by those critics who represent him as arguing that the former "caused" the latter.

Alternatives to Weber's Hypothesis

At this point we will briefly consider some of the alternatives to and modified versions of Weber's thesis that have been suggested. Kurt Samuelsson cites four early objections to Weber's position raised by Felix Rachfahl four years after Weber first made it public in a series of articles in 1905. Rachfahl first questions the validity of representing ethical-religious motivation as a crucial factor in economic activity. More reasonable factors, he suggests, are such things as the desire to enjoy life, solicitude for the family, and the urge to work for the common good, or for the nation and its welfare. Second, Rachfahl points to several limiting conditions imposed by Calvin on economic activity that taken together do not at all condone a free-for-all capitalism. Third, the differences between Catholicism and Calvinism with regard to economic activity should not be exaggerated. Catholic monastic orders such as the Franciscans and Jesuits were not so different from Calvinism in this respect. Fourth, Weber's distinction between Catholic and Protestant countries and cities with regard to economic activity are not so neatly associated with one religion or the other as Weber seems to suggest. Some supposedly Protestant capitalistic cities, for example, had strong Catholic influence.[17]

R. H. Tawney also emphasizes Rachfahl's fourth point, observing that capitalism had clearly existed in medieval Italy and Flanders (both Catholic areas) and that the capitalistic spirit was "only too familiar to the saints and sages of the Middle Ages." He goes on to point out that Catholic cities were

[16]Ibid., p. 91.

[17]Kurt Samuelsson, *Religion and Economic Action: A Critique of Max Weber*, trans. E. Geoffrey French (New York: Harper & Row, 1961), pp. 8–9.

the chief commercial capitals of medieval Europe and Catholic bankers its leading financiers.[18]

Another hypothesis is that the social situation of Calvinists rather than their theology encouraged their entrance into capitalistic ventures. Calvinists constituted a religious minority almost everywhere except Geneva, and in some countries and communities they were barred from governmental positions and professions such as medicine and law. Where else to turn but to business enterprises? Thus, we observe a process similar to that affecting Jews during the Middle Ages, who undertook money-lending and money-handling positions partly by default—because Christians did not want to "dirty their hands" with such activities or break the church's laws against usury. Just as it did not mean that Jews had some kind of genetic advantage over Gentiles so far as financial matters were concerned, so there was nothing particularly significant in Calvinist theology that was more conducive to the development of capitalism than Catholic, Lutheran, or Presbyterian theology.

Personality factors might also be suggested. Perhaps the very persons who were most energetic and independent, who were most willing to take business risks, were those most attracted by Calvinism as a theological system because of its stress on individualism and effort. That is, perhaps at least some people choose a religion because it meshes with their own value system and commitments. As such, it would be incorrect to suggest that religion produced particular economic attitudes, for example.

Tawney, questioning Weber's concept of capitalism itself, does not see Calvinism fitting into the free-for-all capitalism of the eighteenth and nineteenth centuries. Rather, Tawney credits Calvinism with providing a business ethic to a "world of small traders and handicrafts."[19] The huge fortunes required and created by capitalism were not produced merely by thrift, Tawney notes, but by exploitation and by deliberately creating "opportunities."

As one scans four centuries of Calvinist theological writing, one is impressed with the dilemma mentioned earlier in this chapter—the dilemma of a fundamental distrust in wealth and a belief in its likely insidious undermining of fundamental Christian principles such as "keeping oneself unstained by the world" as opposed to the religious group's need for money in order to survive and the need to justify its members' accumulation of wealth. In this connection, some have stressed the distinction between early and later Calvinism—the theology of Calvin himself contrasted with that of later followers and interpreters. John McNeill points out that John Calvin had a profound mistrust of economic success, and he suggests that to argue that Calvin characterized the prosperity of believers as inferential proof of

[18]R. H. Tawney, *Religion and the Rise of Capitalism* (Gloucester, MA: Peter Smith, 1962), pp. 84, 316.
[19]Tawney, *Religion*, p. 31.

their election to heaven is to misinterpret completely the evidence we have of Calvin's thought, as reflected in such statements as "Wherever prosperity flows uninterruptedly its delight corrupts even the best of us. . . . The faithful are more miserable than despisers of God. . . . Prosperity like wine inebriates men. . . . Property is like rust or mildew."[20]

Indeed, only later did Calvinists rationalize economic success and interpret economic gain as a sign of virtue. It is interesting that Weber quotes extensively from Richard Baxter, a late seventeenth century Puritan-Calvinist theologian writing approximately 150 years after Calvin. Weber also quotes Benjamin Franklin, who was not only considerably removed in time from Calvin but was not a Calvinist theologian at all. Thus it was Baxter, not Calvin, who made such statements as, "Be wholly taken up in diligent business of your lawful calling. . . . It is for action that God maintaineth us. . . . Keep up a high esteem of time and be every day more careful that you lose none of your time. . . . [and] if vain recreation, dressings, feastings, idle talk, unprofitable company, or sleep be any of them temptations to rob you of any of your time, accordingly heighten your watchfulness."[21]

Toward a Resolution of the Issue

While still other critiques of Weber's hypothesis could be introduced, enough have been summarized to make the point that the link between Calvinism and capitalism, if one exists at all, is far from a unitary causal one. Of course, Weber himself spoke not of cause but of strong encouragement and support—what we today tend to call *reinforcement*. Actually, most of Weber's critics grant some such supportive role for Calvinism. This is the position taken by Tawney, who says that the "capitalistic spirit," though "as old as history, found in certain aspects of Puritanism a tonic which braced its energies and fortified its already vigorous temper."[22] And Rachfahl, the first to criticize Weber's hypothesis, points out several indirect ways in which the doctrinal positions of Protestant theologians influenced economic matters. He concludes that despite important weaknesses in Weber's interpretation, the basic contention that Calvinism had an important influence upon economic activity is valid.[23] Rachfahl's observations are the following:

1. Protestantism permitted the intellect to be devoted to worldly pursuits, whereas in Catholic countries many of the best minds went into the priesthood.

---

[20]John T. McNeill, *The History and Character of Calvinism* (New York: Oxford University Press, 1954), p. 222.

[21]See Weber, *The Protestant Ethic*, pp. 262, 260, 261.

[22]Tawney, *Religion*, pp. 226–227.

[23]Quoted in Samuelsson, *Religion and Economic Action*, p. 10.

2. Protestantism introduced education to the masses.
3. Protestantism reversed the tendency toward indolence and distaste for work associated with Catholic renunciation of the world.
4. Protestantism encouraged independence and personal responsibility for one's fate—something downplayed in Catholicism.
5. Protestantism created a "higher type of morality" than did Catholicism.
6. Protestantism distinguished politics from religion more clearly than did Catholicism. This freed persons to engage in more diverse economic activities and, by tolerating a greater diversity of views, ultimately resulted in economic change.[24]

Although some of these points tend to make false or at least strained comparisons, in combination they constitute the essence of the observation made more recently by Hammond and Demerath. These writers suggest a way of salvaging Weber's thesis without having to accept all that he says. They note that the advent of Protestantism—that is, the fact that it appeared at all—implies a weakening and ultimate breakdown of medieval Catholic control, resulting in greater freedom to experiment with new political and economic forms, one of which was capitalism.[25] In other words, there is a third variable out there, or a whole set of other variables, that affected *both* Calvinism and capitalism and provided fertile soil in which both could grow.

In a very real sense, then, the success of Protestantism represented the destruction of the church type of religious organization (discussed in Chapter 5) and the introduction of religious pluralism, which is intimately associated with political, and ultimately with economic, pluralism as well. That is, people were beginning to face options and make choices—political and economic choices as well as religious ones. The positive influence of Protestantism on capitalism is, of course, only an indirect one and must take second place to primary developments—the discovery and colonization of the New World, the expansion of trade, the second agrarian revolution that increased food production and thus resulted in a labor surplus available for commercial and manufacturing occupations, the Enlightenment, political revolutions, and ultimately the Industrial Revolution itself.

Guy Swanson analyzes the relationship of Protestantism and capitalism along somewhat the same lines as Rachfahl and as Hammond and Demerath by seeing the general "loosening" of the social structure as the important ingredient. But for Swanson, religion is essentially the middle variable in a three-variable chain that begins with political structure and ends with social structure, of which capitalism is only one aspect. Comparing the social structures of various European states in late medieval Europe, he notes that

[24]Ibid.
[25]N. J. Demerath III and Phillip E. Hammond, *Religion in Social Context* (New York: Random House, 1969), p. 150.

important differences in political structure preceded and served as a base for different religious commitments (Protestantism or Catholicism). Thus, societies that remained Catholic had one primary source or center of decision making. By contrast, Protestantism was more likely to appear in those societies in which there were a variety of decision-making sources. Thus, political diversity encouraged Protestantism, and together they encouraged capitalism.[26]

Whether one agrees with Samuelsson that there is "no support for Weber's theories" and that "almost all the evidence contradicts them,"[27] or with others who hold out for at least an indirect relationship of some kind between Calvinistic Protestantism and the growth of capitalism, one conclusion seems clear: Although religion has some impact on the economy, it is likely to be indirect and to be effective only as a supportive, reinforcing ingredient in concert with others in a complex causal chain.

AN ASSESSMENT OF THE RELATIONSHIP BETWEEN RELIGION AND ECONOMICS

It is clear that religion is, among other things, an economic institution—in the sense that it participates in the economy and is an economic "force" as a buyer and seller of goods and services, in the sense that it is an employer, and in the sense that it influences the buying habits of believers. Even in such relatively simple, small ways as creating a market for devotional and "peace of mind" literature, and supporting industries that produce religious artifacts such as religious vestments, statues, medallions, church pews, and baptismal fonts, religion has an impact on the economy of the society.

Religion's Influence on the Economy

It is important to realize, however, that the economic influence or impact of religion is seldom radical or revolutionary. It is unlikely to send the economy in new directions. The buying-and-selling and economy-stimulating role of religion in the society is both stable and predictable. It creates few new markets and demands few innovative products. Religion is a relatively stable employer that neither stimulates nor retards economic swings of recession, depression, or inflation. It does, however, tend to respond to economic change. During the Great Depression of the 1930s in the

[26]Guy E. Swanson, *Religion and Regime* (Ann Arbor, MI: University of Michigan Press, 1967).

[27]Samuelsson, *Religion and Economic Action*, p. 154.

United States, thousands of seminary graduates of all denominations went without calls to religious vocations because congregations could not afford to hire and pay them and denominations could not afford the cost of establishing new congregations that would need clergy leaders. During the period of economic expansion beginning in the late 1940s and continuing through the 1950s, when new congregations proliferated and when established congregations expanded their membership and programs, seminaries could not launch enough graduates into the religious sea. Demand was greater than supply.

Of course, some religious leaders occasionally exert a significant influence on the economy of the society. A prime example, though not consciously directed toward economic change, consists of the attempts by religious groups to reinforce traditional moral values. Sometimes religious groups or persons attempt to ban the sale of certain "immoral" books or curtail the distribution of pornographic films. When this happens, an obvious indirect influence on the economy is made. The most dramatic and economically influential instance of this in recent times is the movement leading to enactment of the Prohibition amendment in 1919. Conservative religious forces are generally credited with pushing this amendment through the states. The economic impact upon specific segments of the economy (liquor producers, wholesalers, retailers, bootleggers, and the like) was significant, though the impact on the overall economy was not that great. Eventually, minor readjustments by subunits in the economy were required, not major changes in its direction or form.

A more recent example involves the use of moral suasion by religious leaders in an attempt to influence the corporate policy of large organizations in favor of the objectives of the civil rights movement. Some attempts have been made by religious leaders to encourage, even force, organizations to divest themselves of stock in companies that blatantly discriminate against blacks and other minorities. Primary attention has been focused on corporations that do business with the Union of South Africa and thus implicitly support the apartheid policies of that country's government. Although success has been neither overwhelming nor immediate, and although religious groups are not the only ones working in this area, some noticeable change has occurred. At least four denominations (Reformed Church in America, Church of the Brethren, United Church of Christ, and Unitarian Universalist Association) have adopted strong divestment policies both for themselves and as recommendations to others: churches, corporations, banking institutions, and retirement funds. Perhaps the greatest success has been with North American banks, many of which have refrained from automatic rollovers on loans to the Union of South Africa. Further, the Sullivan Principles that urge foreign corporations operating in the Union of South Africa to abide by a set of fair employment practices were written and championed by an American minister, Leon H. Sullivan, of the

Zion Baptist Church in Philadelphia. Many corporations have adopted them and are now being urged to proceed another step by way of engaging in what Sullivan calls "corporate civil disobedience." This would involve challenging apartheid laws and practices by such acts as buying apartment buildings for corporate employees that would violate existing "white only"/ "black only" restrictions.[28]

The Economy's Influence on Religion

Although we have been concentrating in this chapter on ways in which religion impinges on the economy, we do not mean to imply that there is no relationship between religion and the economy that proceeds in the opposite direction. In fact, many have suggested that the primary or most frequently observed relationship between religion and the economy is that of the economy influencing religion. Probably the most extreme view along these lines is the familiar perspective of Karl Marx, who saw religion—and all normative features of society, for that matter—as growing out of and reflecting economic factors and relationships. For Marx, religion was little more than a tool in the hands of the society's elites for pacifying the masses and maintaining prevailing economic patterns and the respective relationships of owners and nonowners to the means of production. First, there is the economy and a stratification system that reflects the relationship of various people to the means of production within that economy; then comes religion, both reflecting these economic relationships and reinforcing them. Although we do not subscribe to the whole of Marx's point of view, some of this perspective is implicit in Chapter 5's discussion of the importance of lower socioeconomic status in sect formation. Certainly differential economic status is associated with different needs of all kinds, religious needs included. We need only recall Weber's distinction between the theodicies of escape and of good fortune to see a relationship between economic status and religious perspective and expression.

It can hardly be accidental that most religious groups in a society implicitly, and often explicitly, support prevailing economic norms and institutional patterns. For example, one would hear few if any sermons on any given Sunday in the United States of America decrying capitalism. Social norms—in this case, economic norms—get absorbed into all institutions and most groups in a society, religious groups included. Although one could find as many precedents, examples, and specific injunctions in the New Testament for communal ownership, sharing of wealth, and giving to the

---

[28]*Christianity Today* 30, no. 13 (September 19, 1986), p. 55, and Jim Cason and Mike Fleshman, "Profit without Honor: Divesting from Apartheid," *Christianity and Crisis*, 46, no. 9 (June 16, 1986), pp. 212–217.

needy till it truly hurts as one could find for a capitalistic economic structure and private accumulation of wealth, it is not by chance that Christian churches in nonsocialistic lands usually support a capitalistic ideology. Very simply, the dominant economic norms of a society tend to be reflected by religion in that society.

We have referred before to Liston Pope's *Millhands and Preachers*. He provides some fascinating documentation of the impact of economic factors on religion. For one thing, he discovered that religion prospers as the economy prospers and expands—new churches are founded, old ones add members, and all groups tend to prosper as the economic base of the community expands, attracts workers, and provides wages for those people. Pope observes that in the mill towns in Gaston County the mills provided land and built churches for the workers and often subsidized ministers' salaries, but at a price. Mill management expected and usually received religious support and reinforcement of their policies and ideology. At the very least, the mill churches and clergy kept silent on economic issues, sticking to "religious" concerns, thereby of course implicitly supporting economic policy and practice.[29]

In summary, we must repeat that although religion is definitely involved in, and a part of, the economy of the society in which it exists, its overall impact is relatively slight. Primarily, it reinforces economic norms and patterns through participation as one among many buyers and sellers of goods and services. Although occasionally religion challenges specific aspects of economic relationships or the activities of specific economic units, its challenges tend to be of slight impact in the long run.

[29]Pope, *Millhands*, Chapters 8 and 9.

9

Religion
and the Class System

In Chapter 5 we introduced the topic of the relationship between religion and social class (social stratification) in outlining differences between denominations and sects. In fact, we observed that one of the dominant features of sectarian religion is its close association with lower- or working-class problems and life situations, together with the responses of persons of low social status to those problems and situations.

In generalizing from investigations into the relationships between religion and social class, sociologists have made the primary observation that there are important differences in religious meaning related to social class. That is, religion tends to perform at least somewhat different functions for people in different classes. Or, put another way, people tend to seek or construct different things in religion depending on their social class position.

Such assertions that stress the importance of social class with regard to religion should not really surprise us, inasmuch as nearly every beginning student of sociology becomes aware that one of the most significant variables in social life is social class. Although not strictly determinative, one's social-class position dramatically influences one's behavior, attitudes, and aspirations—that is, both what one thinks and what one does throughout life. Depending upon peoples' social-class origins and lifetime position in the stratification system, they will find their lives affected in a multitude of ways—voting propensities, likelihood of psychosis, amount of travel, attitudes toward social issues, age upon marriage, size of family, sexual behavior, even life expectancy. Small wonder, then, that important relationships between social class and religion have also been found. Differences by social-class levels can be seen in differential affiliation with various religious groups, type and degree of involvement in the activities of religious groups, perceptions of the purposes and functions of religion for people, motivation for joining and belonging to religious groups, religious knowledgeability, and the like.

DIFFERENCES IN RELIGIOUS MEANING AND EXPRESSION AMONG SOCIAL CLASSES

A classic distinction regarding differences in the functions of religion by social class is that made by Karl Marx. In defining religion as the "opium of the people," he was actually drawing an implicit distinction between the religion of the bourgeoisie (property-owning capitalist) and that of the proletariat (working class). For the proletariat, in Marx's view, religion is a sedative, a narcotic that dulls people's sensitivity to and understanding of the plight of their life situation; it provides an escape from the harshness of reality. But more. As Marx wrote: "Religion is the sigh of the oppressed creature, the mind of a heartless world, as it is the spirit of unspiritual conditions. . . . the removal of religion as the illusory happiness of the people is the requirement for their real happiness."[1]

By way of contrast, for the bourgeoisie and elites in society, Marx contended, religion serves both as a tool of oppression—a means of placating and keeping the proletariat in line—and as a rationalization and justification for the elite's own position of power and privilege. Inasmuch as Marx viewed the normative aspects of social life as deriving from the most fundamental fact and relationship in society—namely, the economy—religion becomes really nothing more than an expression of prevailing economic relationships and thus, in the capitalistic economy, a means of preserving and reinforcing existing class distinctions. The intertwining of capitalism and prevailing religions is so complete, and the alienation of people from their true destinies so truly reflected in religion, that Marx's associate Engels could predict that religion would disappear when the prevailing capitalistic economies disappeared.[2]

[1]Karl Marx and Friedrich Engels, *Toward the Criticism of Hegel's Philosophy of Right*, trans. Glen Waas (Paris, 1843), quoted in Robert Freedman, *Marxist Social Thought* (New York: Harcourt Brace Jovanovich, Inc, 1968), p. 230.

[2]Friedrich Engels, *Anti-Dühring (Moscow: Foreign Language Publishing House, 1954), pp. 438–440*, quoted in Freedman, *Marxist Social Thought*, p. 228.

Although Max Weber objected to the unidirectional nature of the relationship that Marx portrayed between the economy and social norms and values (including religion), and although he wrote *The Protestant Ethic and the Spirit of Capitalism* in large part to refute or at least modify or offer an alternative to Marx's theory, Weber actually held much the same view of differential functions of religion for the various social classes. We have already spoken of Weber's distinction, between the religion of the disprivileged and that of the privileged, underlying the concepts "theodicy of despair or escape" and "theodicy of good fortune."[3] In the first case one thinks of the proletariat, for whom religion promises release and some kind of eventual "salvation" if they can only endure and remain eternally faithful. Interestingly, according to Weber, the need for compensation and hope in the face of an adverse existence is relatively seldom colored by resentment or rebellion. In other words, some of the disprivileged appear to be satisfied that hell is reserved for wealthy sinners (recall our earlier discussion of the sect in Chapter 5). The privileged classes, however, learn and express religious justification of their good fortune and emphasize their "blessings" as evidence of the favor with which God looks upon them. Wealth and privilege for them are not a detriment to salvation, but an indication not only that all is going well for them now but that it is likely to continue to do so in any future life.[4]

Liston Pope discovered similar differences by social class in his study of Gaston County, North Carolina. This county became an important textile mill center in the 1920s and 1930s and attracted thousands of unskilled and semiskilled laborers for the mills. Quite early during this period, a division of residents between "uptown" people and mill workers was made—a distinction corresponding roughly to Marx's bourgeoisie and proletariat and to Weber's privileged and disprivileged. Religious behavior and ideology differed rather markedly among these two major segments of the population. Pope describes the religion of the mill worker as follows:

> In the theology of the mill worker, the world is a great battlefield on which the Lord and the Devil struggle for each individual soul. The "blood of Jesus" and the reading of the Bible turn the tide of victory toward the Lord. As one mill minister summarized it, "You have to carry a bucket of blood into the pulpit to satisfy these people." The principal sins, in the eyes of mill villagers, are such uptown "worldly amusements" as playing cards, dancing, gambling, drinking, and swimming with members of the opposite sex.
> . . . But the worker also looks to his church to find transvaluation of life, which may take the form of reassurance or of escape, or both. By affirmation of values denied in the economic world, the church provides comfort and ultimate assurance; in its religious services it often affords escape temporarily

[3]See Chapter 8.
[4]Max Weber, "The Social Psychology of the World Religions," in *From Max Weber*, trans. and ed. Hans Gerth and C. Wright Mills (New York: Oxford University Press, 1958), p. 276.

from the economic and social situation in which workaday life must be spent. The difficulties of life for the mill worker in this world help to explain the noteworthy emphasis on otherworldliness in his churches. Most of the hymns and sermons in village churches point toward a more placid state and have little concern with mundane economic or social relations. . . . A well-loved stanza, typical in ideas of many others, says:

> While some live in splendid mansions,
> And have wealth at their command,
> I'm a stranger and a pilgrim
> Passing through this barren land.[5]

In short, religion for mill workers provides a relief or escape from the harshness of their lives. For an hour or two, once or twice a week, they can transcend the mundane, and focus on a future that promises to be far better than the present.

Pope points out, by way of contrast, that "if religion in the mill churches is largely an escape from economic conditions, religion in the uptown churches is to a considerable degree a sanction of prevailing economic arrangements."[6] Pope reports that major sins for the uptown church members include sexual immorality, breaking one's word, not paying one's debts, engaging in "shady business," and failing to carry out one's civic and social obligations.[7] Although religion attempts to invade the personal life of the mill worker, religion is not to meddle in the private lives of the middle- and upper-class town residents. Pope suggests that "greater economic security breeds personal independence."[8] Such independence and individualism are also major features of the religion of the bourgeoisie according to Emile Pin. Pin states that individualism characterizes essentially every aspect of the life of the bourgeois, "who has reached, through his own efforts, a worldly 'salvation,' does not depend on religion to regulate his existence, but rather appeals to it only to assure the continuation of this salvation in the other world."[9]

Pope points out that for the privileged classes in Gaston County, religion is for the most part a specialized sphere of life. Their religious attitudes, as he observes them, are:

> that a man ought to belong to a church, and should attend as often as convenient, and should bear his part of the financial burden,
>   that churches are essential to the welfare of the community,

[5]Liston Pope, *Millhands and Preachers* (New Haven: Yale University Press, 1942), pp. 88–90.

[6]Ibid., p. 92.

[7]Ibid.

[8]Ibid.

[9]Emile Pin, "Social Classes and Their Religious Approaches," in *Religion, Culture, and Society*, ed. Louis Schneider (New York: John Wiley, 1964), p. 411.

that there is no use in getting all wrought up or emotional about religion,

that if a person lives as decently as he can, that's all that God can expect of him,

that a minister ought to be a good fellow in his private life, joining civic clubs, attending baseball games, and the like,

that a minister ought to be a leader in all community enterprises, such as projects sponsored by the Chamber of Commerce,

that religion ought not to meddle in politics, except where moral issues, such as prohibition, are involved,

that Holy Rollers are ignorant, and are to be pitied,

that mill churches meet the needs of mill workers very satisfactorily.[10]

Pope summarizes by saying, "The role of the uptown minister, and of his church, is not to transcend immediate cultural boundaries but to symbolize and sanction the rightness of things as they are."[11]

DIFFERENTIAL DENOMINATIONAL AFFILIATION BY SOCIAL CLASS

As would be expected, differences in the meaning and expression of religion by social class are reflected in denominational affiliation—that is, denominations differ in their social class composition. An indication of class differences is suggested in Table 9-1. From National Opinion Research Center data gathered in the 1960s we see there are dramatic differences by denomination in the proportion of members who have attended college for at least awhile. Jews and Episcopalians are almost three times as likely as Baptists and Lutherans to have attended college.[12]

More recent and more detailed data gathered from National Opinion Research Center samples in the 1970s and 1980s confirm the differences suggested in Table 9-1, but appear less dramatic. The data in Table 9-2 include the three most commonly used empirical measures of status: level of education attained, level of occupational prestige, and level of income. On each measure there are significant differences relative to denominational affiliation. The members of some religious groups, such as Jews, Episcopalians, and Presbyterians, on the average, have attained more education, have higher prestige jobs, and earn more money than others (see Table 9-2).

The factors underlying such class differences among denominations are many. In part it is a self-selection process of like seeking like—of people affiliating with a church whose current members are reasonably similar to

[10]Pope, *Millhands and Preachers*, pp. 93–94.

[11]Ibid., p. 95.

[12]While not by itself a perfect indicator of social class, education, particularly if it involves attendance at college, reflects class differences fairly well.

TABLE 9-1   Proportion of Denominational Membership Who Have Attended College

DENOMINATION	PERCENT COLLEGE
Jew	60%
Episcopalian	59
Presbyterian	51
Methodist	32
Catholic	29
Baptist	23
Lutheran	22
All Americans	32

Source: The SuperNORC composite samples taken between 1963 and the early 1970s by the National Opinion Research Center of the University of Chicago. Reported in Andrew M. Greeley, William C. McCready, and Kathleen McCourt, *Catholic Schools in a Declining Church* (Kansas City: Sheed and Ward, 1976), abstracted from Table 3.2, p. 44. Copyright 1976 by Andrew Greeley, William C. McCready, and Kathleen McCourt. Reprinted with permission of Sheed and Ward, 115 E. Armour Blvd., Kansas City, MO 64141-0281. All rights reserved.

TABLE 9-2   Status Differences Along Three Dimensions among Selected Religious Groups

RELIGIOUS GROUP	AVERAGE EDUCATION ATTAINED (IN YEARS)	AVERAGE LEVEL OF OCCUPATIONAL PRESTIGE	PERCENT OF FAMILIES WITH INCOMES OVER $20,000
Jews	13.9	46.7	50%
Episcopalians	13.8	45.6	44
Presbyterians	13.0	43.9	42
Congregationalists*	12.8	42.7	43
Methodists	12.2	41.2	32
Roman Catholics	11.9	38.9	34
Lutherans	11.9	39.5	31
Southern Baptists	10.9	37.3	23
Nazarenes	11.1	36.2	19
Churches of God	9.7	33.2	27

Source: Abstracted from Wade Clark Roof and William McKinney, *American Mainline Religion* (New Brunswick: Rutgers University Press, 1987), pp. 112-113.
*Now a part of the United Church of Christ.

themselves. There is the theological dimension also—the theological celebration of success in this world in some religious groups versus the emphasis on otherworldly salvation in others. In large part the class differences by denomination are a product of history. The highest status denominations in Tables 9-1 and 9-2, with the exception of the Jewish groups, have been well established in this country for the longest periods. Thus their members have had greater opportunities to accumulate family wealth and enhance their status. On the other hand, Lutherans and Roman Catholics are composed of more recent arrivals in this country who have had less opportunity for upward mobility. The Lutherans also are predominantly rural in their constituency and hence likely to rank lower on such dimensions of status as education, cash income, and occupational prestige. Sectarians, we have earlier noted, are almost by definition more likely to be of low socioeconomic status than members of established denominations.

Probably the biggest change in the past twenty years has been the movement upward of Roman Catholics. They have moved past both Lutherans and Baptists in education, and past Lutherans, Baptists, and Methodists in family income, although thirty years ago they ranked behind them all on these dimensions. Only in occupational prestige do they still rank behind those groups. It should be noted that there is substantial variation within Roman Catholicism on the basis of ethnicity. For example, Irish Catholics rank at the 12.7 level in education, while Spanish-speaking Catholics rank at 10.3.[13]

It is clear though that no religious group is completely class-exclusive—that is, there is a range of classes represented in every religious group. Class exclusiveness, however, is often more pronounced at the local congregational level. Thus, if a third of all Congregationalists, for example, are lower class we would not infer that a third of all the members of every local Congregational church, or even of a majority of them, are from the lower class. What it does mean is that there are some congregations with a majority of lower-class members, others with a majority of middle- and/or upper-class members. This should not be surprising inasmuch as congregations tend to attract a majority of their members from the neighborhoods in which they are located, and neighborhoods tend to be fairly class-exclusive.

This phenomenon is clearly in evidence in Pope's study of Gaston County. In 1939, Pope tallied thirty-four rural churches, only five of which had a significant minority (a minimum of 20 percent) of mill workers and none of which had a significant minority of uptown members. Similarly, of seventy-six mill churches only one had a significant minority of rural members and only eight a significant minority of uptown members. Uptown churches were less likely to be so predominantly of one class. Yet in only seventeen of thirty-five were even 20 percent of the members mill workers, and in only three were there significant minorities of rural members. In total, only 23 percent of the churches in Gaston County had significant minority membership, and only 6 percent lacked a majority group of at least 66.6 percent.[14] Clearly, then, a religious group is very likely to represent the class constituency of the geographic area in which it is located.

Demerath has pointed out that although there may be a mixture of social classes in a national denomination and even in its local congregations,

[13]Wade Clark Roof, "Socioeconomic Differentials Among White Socio-religious Groups in the United States," *Social Forces* 58, no. 1 (September, 1979), pp. 280–289.

[14]Ibid., pp. 70–71.

the members of these classes may not be looking for or receiving the same things out of their affiliation and participation.[15] Demerath first reports Fukuyama's 1961 study demonstrating differences in religiosity among Congregationalists by social class. Fukuyama's data, reported in Table 9-3, show that the higher social classes are more likely than the lowest social class to express their religion in cultic and cognitive ways, whereas the lowest social class is more likely than the others to express religion devotionally (the differences along the creedal dimension are not significant). Demerath dichotomizes the possible relationship to one's religious group for his sample (Lutherans) into "churchlike" and "sectlike" religiosity. Some of his findings are included in Table 9-4, which indicates quite clearly that the lower Lutherans' social-class position, the less likely they are to exhibit a

TABLE 9-3   Proportion of Congregationalists Scoring High on Selected Measures of Religiosity, by Social Class

MEASURE	Socioeconomic Status		
	HIGH	MEDIUM	LOW
Cultic	53%	43%	35%
Cognitive	28	24	15
Creedal	27	28	31
Devotional	16	23	32

Source: Adapted from Yoshio Fukuyama, "The Major Dimensions of Church Membership," *Review of Religious Research* 2, no. 4 (1960), 159.
Note: Cultic = measure of church attendance and organizational participation
Cognitive = measure of knowledge of religious doctrine and congregational affairs
Creedal = measure or personal allegiance to traditional doctrine
Devotional = measure of personal prayer and expression of reliance on religion beyond the church itself

TABLE 9-4   Churchlike Religiosity among Lutherans, by Social Class

DEGREE OF CHURCHLIKE COMMITMENT*	Socioeconomic Status			
	UPPER	MIDDLE	WORKING	LOWER
High	51%	45%	32%	24%
Moderate	20	20	19	19
Low	29	35	48	57

Source: N. J. Demerath III, *Social Class in American Protestantism* (Chicago: Rand McNally, 1965), p. 87.
*Based on frequency of church attendance, participation in parish organizations, and membership in outside organizations.

[15]N. J. Demerath III, *Social Class in American Protestantism* (Chicago: Rand McNally, 1965).

churchlike attachment to religion. As would be expected, a corresponding opposite relationship is observed with respect to sectlike commitment. The progression for high sectlike commitment from the upper through the middle, working, and lower classes is 10 percent, 15 percent, 25 percent, and 35 percent respectively.[16]

All these data indicate that social status appears to have an effect upon the meaning and expression of religion for people. This is not only evidenced by the fact that people of one status level tend to be members of particular denominations or sects, but people within a particular denomination and even within a local organization are both looking for and finding different things.

That the meaning of religion and participation in religious activities varies among social classes is of course not unique to Western Christianity. Such differences are noted particularly in Hinduism. The division into social classes of Brahmins, Kshatriyas, Vaisyas, Shudras, and "outcasts" or "untouchables" correlates quite closely with differences in the historical meaning and expression of Hinduism as a religion. The fact that originally only the two upper classes were literate and could read and become familiar with the holy books predetermined important differences. For example, even today the upper classes tend to be monistic—they believe in one Absolute, with all other gods a part or expression of the One. The common people tend to be polytheists and believe in many local gods and spirits, tend to identify the image or statue itself with the divine living reality, and believe in a heaven and hell, which the higher classes do not. The upper classes believe more firmly in the doctrines of samsara (the transmigration of souls), karma (the principle of cause and effect—what you sow you reap), and dharma (the standard of determining whether you move socially upward or downward in the next life). The upper classes are more firmly committed to the belief that if you follow the rules of your caste you can move upward, from one life to another. This could be all the way to an ultimate goal of being released from the nearly endless cycle of transmigration of souls and realizing unity with the Brahman or Absolute (attaining Nirvana). Noss notes that the masses have never had a clear conception of the finer points of Hinduism such as the various "ways" of salvation and release from the miseries and responsibilities of life (Way of Works, Way of Knowledge, Way of Devotion). He says that the masses go about being religious in the traditional manner of their local area. They practice and reflect animism, fetishism, shamanism, demonolatry, animal worship, and devotion to local spirits and godlings, often without the "higher" worship of the supreme deities in the Hindu pantheon.[17] Noss goes on to say that in some areas Hinduism can

[16]Ibid., p. 88.
[17]John B. Noss, *Man's Religions* (New York: Macmillan, 1949), p. 243.

hardly be recognized as such; a primitive animism takes its place. This sub-Hinduism is common among the millions of "untouchables."[18]

Along a similar vein, Buddhism in its original form found little response among the masses. But they gradually became interested, as Noss observes, not in the theologian Gautama Buddha, but in the man.[19] Worship of the person and the idea of salvation through various saviors became popular with the lower classes.[20] In fact, some of the untouchables, in trying to improve their degraded lot in life, adopted Buddhism, which promised some relief and release from the desperate, unredeemable character of their existence.

If we look a little more closely at the religious situation in India, we discover that Hinduism and Indian culture (including its caste system) are almost one and the same. Hinduism is a comprehensive religion in the sense that there is really nothing that the Hindu does of a cultural nature—whether brushing one's teeth, preparing food, encountering people in the street, or any other act—that does not have religious significance and some kind of religious prescription wrapped around it. "Hinduism is a culture and a religion at the same time . . . religion and life are synonymous."[21]

At least this is the heritage of India's past—a caste-based society in which strict separation of classes was both a cultural and religious dictum. In 1950, however, the Democratic Republican Constitution of India was adopted. This constitution, much like that of the United States, emphasizes justice, liberty, and equality—and not just in a political sense but in a social sense as well. Article 15 of the Constitution states that caste cannot be a basis for discrimination or any restrictions on access to stores, restaurants, village water sources, and the like. Further, any traditional practices based on untouchability are categorically forbidden.

However, castes continue to be identified, and such a system, though in a somewhat modified form, will continue for many years to come. This is so and will continue to be so in part because the caste system is so deeply embedded in Indian culture and society that it is a primary source of identification for people. As such it is a rallying point, a source of members of caste-restrictive political parties, a power bloc for economic and political action, an audience for caste journals and newspapers, the body of membership in particular craft unions, and the constituency of voluntary associations of various types. Such goes on quite irrespective of religious sanctions one way or the other and of a constitution that prescribes that caste be ignored and transcended.

[18]Ibid., p. 244.
[19]Ibid., p. 171.
[20]Ibid., p. 188.
[21]Trevor Ling, *Buddha, Marx, and God* (London: Macmillan, 1966), p. 211.

It is worth noting too that with respect to the origin of caste the role of religion is almost assuredly one of reinforcement rather than cause. While there is not now and probably never will be total consensus on the precise cause or causes of caste in India, it is likely that several factors together provided the basis. While a common belief among the populace is that the castes "issued from the mouth, arms, thighs, and feet of Brahma," it is also widely understood that race has played a part. Sir Herbert Risley states that in Eastern India "a man's status varies in inverse ratio to the width of his nose."[22] Others emphasize occupational sources of caste. That is, various occupations were status ranked differentially by the people themselves; subsequently, specific occupations and occupational categories became castes. Still others point to the separateness of ancient tribes as well as the differences between invaders and the conquered as early sources of castes. And so on. But the point is simply that cultural and highly sociological factors have contributed to a rigid class (caste) system that, while integral within Indian religion, is not necessarily of religious origin. Further, a democratic constitution and continuous religious denunciation of caste today do not eradicate overnight or even in a generation or two what has been so integral a part of a society's political, religious, and social structure.

SOCIAL STRATIFICATION WITHIN RELIGIOUS GROUPS

If we define social stratification as a hierarchical arrangement or ordering of people in a group according to criteria or standards determined and accepted by that group—a definition implicit in this chapter so far—then it is easy to see that such stratification is an integral part of religion. Although many religious groups preach the equality of everyone before God, this often implies only equality among the specially favored people in their own group. Religious groups are historically notorious for their clear distinction between the "ins" and the "outs," the believers and the nonbelievers, the saved and the unsaved. Moreover, stratification appears even within the group itself. Stratification is endemic in two senses. First, there is the distinction between prophet and people, or leader and followers. Those who are considered to have special insights or are credited with special revelation are accorded elevated positions relative to those who listen and follow. The person with deeper knowledge of sacred things (rituals and writings)— the teacher or priest—is ranked higher than those who are his or her pupils and followers. Second, there is the recognition that even among the followers, some follow the norms of the group more closely than others and are

---

[22]Herbert Risley, "The Tribes and Castes of Bengal," quoted by N. Presad, *The Myth of the Caste System* (Petna: Prakashan, 1957), p. 26.

more holy, more knowledgeable, more dedicated than the "average" or "majority" of followers or members. Even though the majority of rank-and-file members may not personally aspire to such status, they tend to acknowledge its validity and give honor and respect to those who embody most perfectly the virtues and knowledge that the group has defined as praiseworthy. Such distinctions are readily observed in the panoply of saints in the Roman Catholic Church—persons who have gone an extra mile or two in perfecting the expression and application of the Catholic faith.

The great majority of Buddhists also recognize the elevated status of the numerous monks and "holy men" who have proceeded farther along the path in search of the ultimate goal—the elimination of desire—than has the ordinary follower of the Buddha.

Jehovah's Witnesses speak of the 144,000 higher-caste believers who will be rewarded with "heaven," while others will simply be inhabitants of "paradise." Although the sacred number of 144,000 appears to be taken more figuratively than literally today, particularly as the membership in the group has surpassed that number, the idea of a greater reward for the few who are most holy remains.

As Glenn Vernon suggests, probably the best known "celestial caste system" is that of the Roman Catholic Church, with its four levels of heaven, hell, purgatory, and limbo for persons after death—heaven for the purest believers, hell for the nonbelievers, purgatory for the believers who still need some "cleansing" before entering heaven, limbo a place to which people went before Christ's work of redemption was completed and from which he thereafter liberated them.[23]

Other groups talk of the visible church on earth—the voluntary association including not only sincere believers but also some nonbelievers and hypocrites who are professed but insincere members—as contrasted with the invisible church, which is composed of true believers whom only God can know by looking within their heart and assessing their sincerity.

We have already mentioned the religious stratification in Hinduism that is so intimately associated with the societal stratification as well. Lower-caste persons are not just lower-class socially but religiously as well. To move upward in successive lives through the process of samsara (transmigration of the soul) into higher castes in the social sense is to move upward religiously as well. One would thereby not only enjoy more and more of the amenities of life but would also come ever closer to the ultimate goal of union with or absorption into the timeless or eternal Brahman, thus finding release from the cycle of transmigration. In this connection Charles Eliot makes the point that it is the caste structure of Indian society that influences Hinduism, not vice versa. He states that many Hindu religious leaders have

---

[23]Glenn M. Vernon, *Sociology of Religion* (New York: McGraw-Hill, 1962), p. 380.

declared unequivocally that there ought to be no social distinctions among believers. But caste continually reasserts itself. Social structure and precedents, Eliot concludes, are stronger than theology.[24]

STRATIFICATION, RELIGION, AND RACE

We now turn to a somewhat extended example of how stratification and religion interrelate when a third variable, race or ethnic background, is introduced. Here again we shall see the reciprocal-interaction relationship between religion and other features of the society.

Although each of the major religions of the world has tended officially to welcome all comers into its fellowship of faith, in practice most have at some time or other discriminated against racial or ethnic groups living in the same society. Of course, we need to emphasize that the religious element in such discrimination is usually inextricably bound up with political and economic factors as well. This point will be amply demonstrated as we proceed.

One quick example before proceeding with our primary one. The interaction of political and religious factors is dramatically seen in India and Pakistan, where the centuries-old conflict between Hinduism and Islam culminated in the 1971 war over Bangladesh (formerly East Pakistan). When East Pakistan was still part of the larger nation, the government located in the Western portion, which has a Muslim majority, systematically discriminated against Hindus within both West Pakistan and East Pakistan, which has a Hindu majority. Thus a basic ingredient of the military and political conflict was the religious antagonism between Muslims and Hindus.

We need to think once again of the examples of religious conflict presented in Chapter 6—the Inquisition in medieval Europe, the Thirty Years' War in seventeenth-century Europe between Protestant and Roman Catholic forces, the continuing Protestant-Catholic conflict in Northern Ireland, and, along a somewhat different line, the prejudice and discrimination in the name of religion that has been directed against blacks throughout American history. We shall focus just a bit on this last phenomenon particularly, because it so well portrays the intimate connection of the three variables mentioned above—religion, race, and social class.

By definition, slaves in any society are at the very bottom of the stratification system. This is not an issue in itself in a society that tolerates slavery and includes it in its normative system—if we assume a society has the right

[24]Charles Eliot, *Hinduism and Buddhism* (London: Routledge & Kegan Paul, 1921), vol. 2, 176–178.

to determine such a structure in the face of universal human rights.[25] But the phenomenon of slavery presented a problem for the Christian religion. In fact, it became a dilemma in the sense that Christian theology had developed the principle that although slavery itself was not forbidden by God, a Christian should not hold another Christian in bondage. The dilemma arose when that principle came in contact with the conversion principle—that is, the mandate to "make disciples of all nations" and convert everyone possible.

The Early American Experience

Early in colonial American history the question arose concerning what to do about the religion of black slaves. One mandate said: Convert them to Christianity. But the other said: You should not hold a fellow Christian as a slave. Therefore, what to do? Some slaveholders quite expectedly opposed the conversion of slaves. Unconverted they presented no problem, since the slaveholder would not be keeping a fellow Christian as a slave. But theologians and clergy members said it was the Christian's obligation to teach the slaves Christianity and convert them. Some Southerners resolved the issue by defining blacks as less than human. We do not convert dogs, kudus, or zebras; therefore, we do not need to convert blacks—as a lower animal form, they lack a soul to be saved.

And so the controversy went on. Ultimately a compromise was reached. Religious leaders abandoned their original position and said that the church would no longer maintain the position that conversion required emancipation. This meant that the church could save souls and the slaveholders their investment. This compromise led to substantial missionary activity among slaves, who were rapidly converted to Christianity. The mass conversions of slaves occurred in significant part, of course, because once the owners decided their slaves should espouse Christianity the slaves themselves, as property and with essentially no personal or civil rights, had little choice in the matter.

The process of this religious about-face is well documented for the Methodist Church and merits a somewhat extended examination as an example of social-class and economic influences on religious ideology and practice. In its beginning, American Methodism quite naturally looked to its English founder John Wesley for guidance on the issue of slavery. They did not look in vain. Among Wesley's *General Rules*, prepared in 1739, was a rule

---

[25]This is not the place to discuss whether norms that condone slavery run counter to "human nature" or violate fundamental human rights to such things as life, liberty, and the pursuit of happiness. Although we happen to agree that involuntary servitude is in direct violation of universal human rights, we need not debate the issue to understand the sociological points that this chapter is making.

forbidding "the buying or selling of the bodies and souls of men, women, or children with an intention to enslave them."[26] And in 1772 he denounced the slave trade as "the sum of all villainies."[27] Accordingly, the Methodist Episcopal Church, organized in Baltimore in 1784, proposed and adopted the following six special rules designed to destroy slavery among its members:

1. Every slave-holding member, within twelve months, was required to execute a deed of manumission.
2. All infants who were born after these rules went into effect were to have immediate freedom.
3. Members who chose not to comply were allowed to withdraw within twelve months.
4. The sacrament of the Lord's Supper was to be denied to all such thenceforward.
5. No slaveholders were to be admitted thereafter into church membership.
6. Any members who bought, sold, or gave slaves away, except on purpose to free them, were immediately to be expelled.[28]

This, then, was the official stand of the Methodist Church on the question of slavery.

Thus during these early days of Methodism in the United States there appeared to be no great problem with slavery. Apparently no members were slaveholders, and, moreover, Wesley's principles were in force. Slavery, however, seems to have found its way into the Methodist Church during the Revolutionary War, probably without the knowledge of John Wesley or his American assistant Francis Asbury.[29] It seems to have entered gradually and unobtrusively. In this connection it is important to note that rather lax church administration prevailed at this time. By 1778 every English missionary preacher had returned to the mother country except Asbury, and the latter restricted himself primarily to the small state of Delaware. The job of expanding the church was thus committed to young, inexperienced, poorly educated men. Almost all of these young ministers had been born and reared in a slave culture and appeared to have no clear understanding that slavery was wrong. DeVinne states that the forty-eight preachers who had been received into the ministry during the Revolutionary War belonged almost exclusively to this class.[30] Further, the early work

[26]Quoted in W. W. Sweet, *The Methodist Episcopal Church and the Civil War* (Cincinnati, OH: Methodist Book Concern Press, 1912), p. 15.

[27]Quoted in Charles Swaney, *Episcopal Methodism and Slavery* (Boston, MA: R. G. Badger, 1926), p. 1.

[28]Sweet, *The Methodist Episcopal Church*, p. 16.

[29]Daniel DeVinne, *The Methodist Episcopal Church and Slavery* (New York: F. Hart, 1857), p. 12.

[30]Ibid.

of these Methodist preachers was primarily in the slaveholding states. Out of a national membership of about fourteen thousand, only about two thousand resided in non-Southern states.[31]

It is not surprising, then, that the formal resolutions of Methodist conferences and conventions during the last decade of the eighteenth century, although disapproving slavery, became ever more modified in tone.[32] Mattison reports that by 1808 "all that related to slaveholding among private members [that is, laypersons] was stricken from the Methodist body of rules and regulations and the following put in its place: 'The General Conference authorizes each Annual Conference to form their own regulations, relative to buying and selling slaves.' "[33] It is important to note that it was the buying and selling of slaves that each conference was to regulate, not the holding of slaves. Apparently, the possession of slaves, at least by laypeople, now had the church's tacit approval. By 1840, the ownership of slave property was extended to ministers.[34]

A crisis developed in 1844 when a bishop of the Methodist Church, the Reverend James Andrew, was found to be a slaveholder. This necessitated a clear decision. Either do something with Bishop Andrew or openly tolerate slaveholding in the highest positions of the church. Was the Methodist Episcopal Church a slaveholding church, or was it not? The issue was essentially resolved that same year when the Methodist Episcopal Church split into what amounted to Northern and Southern branches—the former condemning slavery, the latter citing Scripture to support it.

What we observe quite clearly here is the influence of social and situational factors upon the institution of religion. To summarize briefly: Early American Methodist activity and growth were in the South where the question of slavery and slaveholding became an issue almost by definition. As the plantation system grew and as it became economically profitable to own slaves, Methodist laypeople, preachers, and finally bishops acceded to the practice. Bishop Asbury, residing in Baltimore, had little knowledge of or control over his fellow Methodists scattered throughout the South. Also, the Methodist ministers during this period were little educated, poorly informed, and Southerners by background, orientation, and ways of thinking.

And so, quite apart from official theological statements or the moral convictions and commitments of church leaders, social factors exerted their influence on the religious group. Economic pressures, organizational features, and characteristics both of the members and lower-level leadership

[31]Ibid.

[32]Lucius Matlack, *History of American Slavery and Methodism from 1780 to 1849* (New York: Lucius Matlack, 1849), pp. 33 ff.

[33]Hiram Mattison, *The Impending Crisis of 1860* (New York: Mason Brothers, 1859), p. 30.

[34]Ibid., p. 34.

combined to override theological and moral mandates. Because religion exists in society and in the subcommunities and regions of that society, it finds itself influenced by the norms and structure of that society and its subunits.

American Presbyterians followed a similar route. Murray states that most colonial Presbyterians viewed slavery as permitted by God and tended to accept the customs of the areas in which they settled.[35] As slaveholding became more economically significant, the battlelines between North and South were more clearly drawn. This was true of religious groups no less than other groups and institutions in the society. Actually, although some southern Presbyterians vigorously opposed slavery, it was not only the issue of theological liberalism but also the controversy over slavery that resulted in the "schism of 1837" between "old-school" and "new-school" Presbyterians.[36] This schism was sealed by the coming of the Civil War, as the Northern and Southern Presbyterians went their separate ways.

With the outbreak of the Civil War in 1861, all the major Protestant denominations either officially split into Northern and Southern branches or allowed local political policy to dictate the church's position. For example, C. F. W. Walther, leader of what is now known as the Luthern Church, Missouri Synod, saw the slavery issue as a matter for government, not churches, to decide. In doing so he relied on a strict interpretation of the principle of separation of church and state: Church members are to respect and abide by the laws established by the political process in the governmental units of which they are citizens.

Into the Present

Slight variations of this principle appear to have guided much religious thinking on the slavery issue and thus set the stage for the relative noninvolvement of religious groups in civil rights struggles following the Civil War. Most religious groups at both the national and local levels remained on balance silent on the issue of black civil rights for nearly ten decades. It was a stand of aloofness which relegated first the issue of slavery, then equal rights for blacks, to the political and social realm and asserted that it was "not the business of the church" to interfere in such social and political (that is, nonreligious) matters.[37] It is in fact this very silence which prompts our excursion into the question of the relationship of white Christianity in the United States to black Americans. White churches have tended to reinforce the class and caste gap between whites and blacks, sometimes by lending

[35]Andrew E. Murray, *Presbyterians and the Negro—A History* (Philadelphia, PA: Presbyterian Historical Society, 1966), p. 12.

[36]Ibid., pp. 103 ff.

[37]Ralph Moellering, *Christian Conscience and Negro Emancipation* (Philadelphia, PA: Fortress Press, 1965), p. 76.

active support to claims of blacks' inherent inferiority and to justifications for their second-class citizenship, but most often by remaining silent and thereby giving tacit approval to racial segregation, discrimination, and prejudice. Furthermore, racial or ethnic differences, which became closely associated with class differences, were reflected in religious differences. In other words, white churches were for whites, black churches for blacks. Kyle Haselden asserts that "long before the little signs—'White Only' and 'Colored'—appeared in the public utilities they had appeared in the Church."[38]

In the 1950s and 1960s, however, nearly every major religious group issued official statements and passed resolutions at their national conventions favoring equality for blacks and calling for an end to discrimination and segregation, although not always issuing clear calls for integration as such. Also during this period white faces in clerical collars became highly visible in sit-ins, marches, and demonstrations, as numerous white clergy and some laypeople as well provided leadership and helped fill the ranks of participants in the civil rights struggle. They sincerely wanted to tell the nation and the world that the white Christian churches were concerned and committed, and they wanted by example and exhortation to bring their fellow white church members along. Yet their voices and presence do not seem to have been representative or typical of the churches from which they came.

A strong antiblack animus remained within the white Christian denominations. In a nationwide survey as recently as 1967, nearly half (44 percent) of the white respondents registered basic disapproval of the black civil rights movement in this country.[39] Of significant interest, this proportion compares with from only 4 to 8 percent of clergy (some slight differences by denomination) who disapprove of the movement.[40]

Actually, it is generally believed that the 44 percent of laypeople who expressed disapproval of the civil rights movement represented a decline from earlier periods. Paul Sheatsley of the National Opinion Research Center believes that various polls conducted since the 1940s indicate a steady, unambiguous increase in positive sentiment toward civil rights issues.[41] While an improvement over attitudes expressed in earlier polls, a Brink and Harris poll in 1966 found that 52 percent of white Americans would be upset if blacks moved into their neighborhood, and 76 percent of whites who live in neighborhoods into which blacks would like to move would be

---

[38]Kyle Haselden, *The Racial Problem in Christian Perspective* (New York: Harper & Row, Pub., 1959), p. 29.

[39]Jeffrey K. Hadden, *The Gathering Storm in the Churches* (Garden City, NY: Doubleday, 1969), p. 127.

[40]Ibid., p. 104.

[41]Paul B. Sheatsley, "White Attitudes Toward the Negro," *Daedalus* 95, no. 1 (1966), 217–238, quoted in Hadden, *The Gathering Storm*, p. 130.

upset at such a development.[42] More recent data from Gallup polls (1978) suggest continuing improvement in such attitudes. For example, in response to the question, "If blacks came to live next door, would you move?" only 4 percent said they definitely would move (with an additional 9 percent saying that they might move). A full 84 percent said they would not move (the remaining 3 percent expressed no opinion).[43] A follow-up question that posed a more threatening situation elicited more willingness to move. Fifty-one percent of white respondents said they either would definitely or might move if blacks came to live in great numbers in their neighborhood. Yet 45 percent said they would not move.[44] A further question asked respondents if they would vote for a qualified black candidate for president if nominated by their political party. A full 77 percent said they would—a proportion that has been steadily growing from the 38 percent who said they would vote for such a candidate when this question was first asked in 1958.[45]

Religion, Social Class, and Racial Attitudes

Quite obviously religion in the United States has not reversed, even to the degree it has tried, its long history of maintaining major class distinctions between whites and blacks. There are, however, important differences in this regard among major religious groups. Jews, for example, express far less suspicion of and animosity toward blacks than do Protestants and Catholics, with Catholics slightly less likely than Protestants to express such suspicion and hostility. For example, Jeffrey Hadden found in the mid-1960s that only 43 percent of Jewish laypersons would be upset if their rabbi participated in civil rights activities; but 68 percent of Catholic laypersons and 77 percent of Protestant laypersons would be upset if their priest or minister joined in civil rights activities such as marches or sit-ins. Similarly, 59 percent, 30 percent, and 27 percent respectively of Jewish, Catholic, and Protestant laypersons agreed that Martin Luther King was an outstanding example of making Christianity relevant and meaningful.[46]

The social class of respondents also appears to be extremely relevant here. It appears that traditionally the lower the social class of people, the more likely they have been to express suspicion and resentment toward blacks. Using level of educational achievement as the independent measure of social class, we observe some dramatic contrasts in Hadden's sample. For

[42]Reported in Hadden, *The Gathering Storm*, p. 130.

[43]George H. Gallup, *The Gallup Poll: Public Opinion 1979* (Wilmington, DE: Scholarly Resources, 1979), p. 214.

[44]Ibid., p. 215.

[45]George H. Gallup, *The Gallup Opinion Index*, no. 160 (Nov., 1978) p. 26.

[46]Hadden, *The Gathering Storm*, pp. 136–137.

example, the proportion of respondents who believed that "clergy should stick to religion and not concern themselves with social, economic, and political questions" declines rapidly with increasing amounts of education. Specifically, while 63 percent of those with only "some high school" agreed with the above view, the proportion declines to 47 percent of high school graduates, 38 percent of those with some college, and only 23 percent of those who had graduated from college.[47]

One must note, of course, that not all religious persons of low educational attainment or low social status are opposed to black progress or express measurable prejudice against blacks. In fact, David Harrell has noted that some Southern whites of working- or lower-class social status and some religious sects whose members are primarily of working-class status have related well to blacks at the same class level, express little or no racial prejudice, and engage in integrated religious activities.[48]

It has frequently been suggested that part of the reason for prejudice against blacks, particularly by whites of at least moderately low socioeconomic status, is the latter's fear of economic threat and of a potential undermining of their only "claim to fame," so to speak—namely, having higher status than at least one other category of people (the blacks around them). Christian antagonism toward Jews has some of this same flavor—not strictly a class phenomenon, but an uneasiness and resentment in the face of Jewish economic, educational, and political success and influence, which is frequently seen as disproportionate to their numbers in the population.

Recent data suggest, however, that former differences in white racial attitudes that were related to educational level of respondents have been reduced, perhaps to the point of disappearance. From the 1978 Gallup polls mentioned earlier we note that the difference between the college educated and those with only a grade school education who definitely or might move if blacks came to live next door was only two percentage points (13 percent of the college educated, 14 percent of those with a high school diploma, and 15 percent of those with only a grade school education).[49] On the more threatening question about whether the respondents would either definitely or possibly move if blacks came in great numbers to live in their neighborhood, the contrast between the college and the grade school educated people is seven percentage points, but in *the opposite direction* (50 percent of college educated, 43 percent of grade school educated).[50]

While such data do not prove that a reversal has taken place, at the very least we must look carefully at what has been a traditional relationship be-

[47]Jeffrey K. Hadden, *The Gathering Storm in the Churches* (Garden City, NY: Doubleday, 1969), p. 145.

[48]David E. Harrell, Jr., *White Sects and Black Men in the Recent South* (Nashville: Vanderbilt University Press, 1971).

[49]Gallup, *The Gallup Poll*, p. 214.

[50]Ibid., p. 215.

tween education and attitudes in the particular area in question. We need additional data and more intensive, focused research. It just could be that many lower-status whites have by now come to terms with improved educational, job, and housing opportunities for blacks. On the other hand, as opportunities continue to improve for blacks, middle-class whites might feel psychological threats to their status and security that until recently have been rare.

10

Women and Religion

In an age of turmoil over the roles and rights of women, it is small wonder that religious organizations worldwide have themselves become microcosms of the women's role and rights debate. An examination of the sociological relationship of women and religion from both a historical and contemporary perspective will be the focus of this chapter.

By way of a beginning, we need to explore in at least an introductory way the context within which women have had and continue to have their relationship to religion, and within which they express themselves religiously. This is, of course, the society and the subgroup context within which both women and the religious institutions themselves live out their lives.

THE RELATIONSHIP OF WOMEN TO RELIGION IN HISTORICAL PERSPECTIVE

The Societal Context

As we try to reconstruct life in early hunting and food gathering societies, at least one characteristic appears to be universal: The contribution of women to the food supply and hence their importance to the community was equal to and perhaps greater than that of men. As such, the power and status of women were not appreciably lower when compared with men. Further, female participation in and responsibility for what we would today call "religious" activities were on a fairly equal plane with men.

While it is true that biological gender factors determine that at least some of women's work will almost assuredly be different from men's work, such work was not usually seen as less important. Because of recurrent pregnancies that were in most cases necessary and desirable in hunting and gathering societies in order to replenish a population continually devastated by a high death rate, a woman's work needed to be close to camp and hut, and she herself needed to be accessible to nursing children. As such, her activities centered around gathering edible plant life—roots, fruits, and berries—in the vicinity of the camp, as well as caring for the children and carrying out routine camp chores. The men hunted and traversed the more distant territory of the society's domain. While each contributed to the food supply, the women's contribution was usually the more stable and predictable portion and as such was almost by definition the most important. Thus, her status was usually essentially equivalent to that of men.

As horticultural societies evolved, following the discovery of the cause-effect relationship between seed planting and harvest, women's role receded but little. The gardens that had now been created fell most often upon the women to tend (the gardens were, after all, on the edge of the village), while men continued to wander in search of game. Even today in the rural areas of developing countries, women and girls provide 60 percent of household food. Again, the stability of women's contribution to the food supply contributed to their maintenance of status. Concomitantly, matrilineal lines of descent were nearly as common as patrilineal, and sexual freedom, whether prenuptial or postnuptial, was frequently as great for women as for men. In short, there was relatively little status differentiation by sex.

With the domestication of animals and eventually the invention of the plow, men's roles in the food production process began to exceed those of women. For one thing, the arduousness of breaking and tilling the ground, as well as breaking and controlling the large animals that provided the energy, required the greater physical strength of men.

Eventually, as technology expanded and as industrialization transformed society, women became increasingly economically dependent upon men. Although they played important roles in childbearing and childrearing and in food preparation and home management, they were drawn further away from direct access to the means of production. Not only did they not own the means of production, they participated only minimally in the production process. As such, their economic dependency increased, and their status decreased.

Although the beginnings of industrialization in the form of cottage industries brought women back, at least for awhile, into the mainstream of the productive process, the persons involved—the men, the women, and the children alike (remember that abuses in the area of child labor began in the home cottage industry, not the factories, mines, and mills that followed after)—were all sufficiently enslaved by the cottage industry process as to do little for the status of these women. They were all members of an exploited class, dependent for bare subsistence upon the middlemen who provided the raw materials and accumulated the finished products for resale and their own profit.

It was only later, as the work of at least some women was moved out of the home—first in the textile industry, then in primary education[1]—that women began to participate in a more direct and obvious way in economic production. However, such a shift involved sufficiently few women, and jobs were sufficiently economically exploitative, that there was still no significant improvement of women's status. However, it is in these early days of industrialization that the pioneer voices of women's liberation could be heard. The first major feminist tract, *The Vindication of the Rights of Women*, was published in 1792. The first American feminist convention, led by Lucretia Mott and Elizabeth Cady Stanton, well-known nineteenth century feminists, was held in 1848.[2]

But before we get too close to the present and too far away from our quick overview of the past, we want to parallel the relationship of women to religion and their roles in the religious patterns and institutions with the various stages of societal evolution.

THE HISTORIC PATTERNS

There is considerable archeological evidence that a great mother goddess was the supreme deity in a great many ancient societies. In fact, Merlin Stone states quite categorically: "At the dawn of religion, God was a woman."[3] Although evidence is insufficient to be certain that such was indeed true *everywhere*, a great deal of supporting evidence does exist.

The anthropologist Edwin James documents the prominent position of female deities throughout the ancient world from the Indian subcontinent and Mesopotamia, through all of the Near East and Greece and Rome, to Western Europe and the islands of the Mediterranean.[4] There were female creator gods in China, Australia, Africa, Babylon, and Egypt. Legends in

---

[1]Jo Freeman, *The Politics of Women's Liberation* (New York: D. McKay, 1975), p. 14.

[2]Ibid., p. 13.

[3]Merlin Stone, *The Paradise Papers* (London: Quartel Books, 1976), p. 17.

[4]Edwin O. James, *The Cult of the Mother-Goddess* (New York: Barnes & Noble, 1959)

Japan identify the sun goddess Amaterasu Omikami as the supreme deity and founder of the Japanese imperial family.[5]

Egypt is one of the better-known ancient societies in which female deities not only appeared early but remained prominent. Already by 3,000 B.C. the goddess Nut—probably derived from the more ancient Nekhebt, a goddess in early Upper Egypt—was described as having existed before anything else appeared in the world and as actually having created all else that has come into being. In fact, she first placed the familiar sun god, Ra, in the heavens.[6] At the point of recorded history, however, Ra (Re) appears to have become first among a pantheon of gods.[7] Ra represented the sun in all its fullness, combined all the forces of nature, and held absolute control over the Nile valley. Yet he appears to have been preceded by a powerful and creative mother-goddess, as we have mentioned.

It was Nut's daughter, Isis, who became the most popular and important goddess in Egyptian history—a highly beneficent deity who personified all that was vital in motherhood—a goddess who remained important for a long period of time.[8]

It is also worth noting that in early Egypt the queen was intended to have greater power than the king, and in marriage the wife was to have authority over the husband, with husbands agreeing to be obedient to their wives.[9]

What appears to have been the most important deity to the various Eskimo tribes was Sedna, a female deity. Tales relate how she sent her children across the seas to become ancestors for other cultures, what we know as European cultures in particular. When her father tried to sacrifice her to appease an evil spirit by throwing her into the sea, even cutting off her fingers as she grabbed at the side of the boat, her fingers became the seal and walrus and other sea animals crucial to the Eskimos' survival. As Sedna sinks to the bottom of the sea she becomes "Mother of the Sea Animals." One can readily infer her supreme importance from such depictions when one realizes the centrality of the seal and walrus to the Eskimo food, clothing, and tool supplies. When taboos are perceived to have been violated and she withholds the sea animals, shamans must get very busy performing appropriate rituals to appease her.[10]

---

[5]Dorothy Robins-Mowry, *The Hidden Sun: Women of Modern Japan* (Boulder, CO: Westview Press, 1983), p. 5.

[6]Stone, *Paradise Papers*, p. 52.

[7]Jacquetta Hawkes and Leonard Woolley, *Prehistory and the Beginnings of Civilization* (New York: Harper & Row, 1963), p. 724; E. O. James, *The Ancient Gods* (New York: Putnam's, 1960), p. 71.

[8]James, *The Ancient Gods*, p. 85.

[9]Reported by Diodorus and quoted in Stone, *Paradise Papers*, p. 53.

[10]Adolph Jensen, *Myth and Cult among Primitive People* (Chicago: University of Chicago Press, 1963), pp. 141–44.

mehhel

Even in the region of Palestine, where Old Testament Judaism ultimately triumphed and not only excluded female deities (without even having a vocabulary word for "goddess") but severely restricted women's participation in religious activities, mother and other goddesses abounded in prehistoric times. Prominent among them were Anat, the "Lady of the Mountain" and consort and sister of Aleyan-Baal; Asherah, the arch rival of Anat, who with the god El bore seventy gods and goddesses; and Astarte, a Philistine goddess of procreation and fecundity.[11]

That the female should be so prominently featured and credited with primary religious responsibilities in the earliest societies should not really surprise us if we remember observations made at the beginning of this chapter. For one thing, the female bears the most obvious productive responsibility. It is she who actually bears the children. Thus, from mother of children to "mother of the tribe," "mother of humankind," and so on would be fairly logical and easy extensions. Further, some reinforcement for the importance and centrality of "mother" would be observed in those societies that were uncertain concerning the source of conception in the first place, not really perceiving the male role and the serial relationship among coitus, conception, and birth. Men were most often perceived to be very much on the fringes of this process of reproduction and birth.

As hunters and gatherers discovered horticulture and as they began to rely increasingly on cultivation and gardening for their food supply, female goddesses continued to be prominent in the religious thought systems of these people. This is likely related in a significant way to the fact that women were in most societies the principal gardeners. However, the male gods did begin to assume greater prominence in horticultural societies. Many of the female goddesses became merely consorts and assistants or specialist supervisors over particular functions. The primary gods gradually became male—Ra in Egypt, Elyan and Bel in Syria, Yahweh in Israel, Zeus in Greece, and so on.

We have entered a time period when the religious roles of men began to wax, those of women to wane. That is, while there still were positive roles for female deities and for ordinary women as members of the religious community as well, the role and view of women and religion became ambivalent. An excellent summary of the ambivalence, the change, and the ultimate subjugation of women religiously can be seen in India. In early Indian religion at the time of the Vedas (roughly 1,000 B.C.) there were not only numerous female goddesses, but women generally enjoyed comparative freedom of movement and participation. However, by 500 B.C. and the flowering of classical Hinduism, women as a category had clearly been relegated to second-class status. There was even a common belief that no

---

[11]James, *Cult of the Mother-Goddess*, pp. 69–77; Hawkes and Woolley, *Prehistory and the Beginnings of Civilization*, p. 736.

woman of any caste could as a woman gain salvation through the attainment of Nirvana. In a later life she would first have to be born a man.

For a time in the early years of Buddhism, women's status saw a beginning of modest restoration. Buddha himself (born 563 B.C.) preached the Four Noble Truths and the Eightfold Path to all who would listen, including women. Falk reports that women received a great deal of respect in the home, were allowed to manage property, give it away, and probably inherit it as well.[12] They were not forced into marriage—certainly not into child marriages as was later so common in Hindu practice. Nor did either societal or religious dictum force women to become recluses if widowed. "Most important, they were able to leave the world, study the sacred teachings of Buddhism, [and] become preachers and teachers in their own right. . . ."[13] The reference here is to female monastic orders. These were established fairly early, and monasticism became an alternative to marriage for some Indian women. But there was a fascinating ambivalence, and Buddhism changed within three to four centuries to closely mirror Hinduism. On the one hand, the Buddhist teaching on karma—with the goal of spiritual perfection, which would eliminate the differences among living beings—maintained that continued spiritual development should result in a gradual sloughing off of sexual differences and limitations. To such goals monks and nuns alike would strive. They had virtually identical spiritual paths and charges, and dressed alike as well.

But another sexual model dominated in the society (the Hindu conception of dharma)—an image of everything "in its place" and following its "nature," role, and order. Failure to coincide with one's dharma invites disaster for all concerned. The woman's dharma is to be a childbearing wife and mother. Thus, for a woman to follow a monastic role was to violate her dharma. Consistent with such a view was the positive portrayal within Buddhism of laywomen who were mothers. Their deeds and virtues could be recounted and extolled because they were following their dharma. And so, Buddhism, Hinduism, and the society itself all agreed that women's proper role was domestic.

Carmody suggests that the change is associated with the view of women as dangerous temptations—one side of the ambivalent view of women which we shall discuss later. Women in the monastic orders, even though in separate ones, were viewed by some as threats to male celibacy.[14] Buddhist literature at the time warned against the ravenous sexual appetites of women and the obstacle to the perfection of male monks that they

[12]Nancy Falk, "An Image of Woman in Old Buddhist Literature: The Daughters of Mara," in *Women and Religion* (revised edition), eds. Judith Plaskow and Joan Arnold (Missoula, MT: Scholars Press, 1974), p. 105.

[13]Ibid., p. 105.

[14]Denise Carmody, *Women and World Religions* (Nashville: Abingdon, 1979), pp. 49–50.

represent.[15] Thus, what Carmody calls a "deeply misogynistic strain"[16] infects both Hinduism and Buddhism. "Unless a woman is neutralized by marriage to a controlling man, Hindu imagination conjures up for her such images as the snake, death, the underworld, hell's entrance, the prostitute, and the adulteress."[17]

The record of Confucianism and Taoism in China is much like that of Hinduism and Buddhism in India. There is evidence of early respect for women generally, together with female goddesses and opportunities for women to participate in religious activities. But by the time of Confucius (500 B.C.) women were relegated to a distant second behind men.

In Japan it appears that women were provided a little more formal religious involvement and for somewhat longer than in the other ancient Asian societies. There is considerable evidence to suggest that early Japan was actually a matriarchy, with female shamans playing a prominent role in religious activities.[18] However, with the importation of the Confucian ethic the depreciation of women began, and women eventually lost their civil rights. It is interesting to note, though, that a curious ambivalence so far as the ideal of womanhood remained. On the one hand there was the ideal of the court lady who epitomized elegance and romance and presided over a mannered, erotic, leisured, and artistic court life.[19] On the other hand, some women were urged to overcome their female frailty and match males' fortitude and bravery.[20] They were trained already as children to repress their emotions and be able to use the dagger they were given at the onset of puberty.[21]

Once all of the major religions had reached their maturity[22] they all strongly resembled one another both in their depiction and treatment of women and in the degree and type of religious involvement granted their female adherents. Women were defined as inferior to men and dependent on them; the religious tasks open to them were peripheral or at best serving in nature.

Even to this day Orthodox Jewish men can be heard to repeat a morning prayer which says, "Blessed art thou, O Lord our God, King of the Universe who has not made me a woman." Jewish women have traditionally been discouraged from studying the holy Torah or even learning Hebrew.

---

[15]Ibid., p. 50.
[16]Ibid., p. 51.
[17]Ibid., p. 51.
[18]Ibid., p. 84.
[19]Ibid., p. 82–83.
[20]Ibid., p. 84.
[21]Ibid., p. 84.
[22]By "maturity" we mean only a further point along an evolutionary plane and intend no value judgment whatsoever.

Women have not counted in the minyan (the quorum of ten males required for public religious services), cannot read Torah publicly or lead public services, and must frequently sit in special locations in the synagogue separated from men.[23]

Within Christianity, building as it did on a Jewish base, we find a long history of second-class citizenship for women. St. Paul sets the stage and tone for nineteen centuries that follow as he says:

> A woman must be a learner, listening quietly and with due submission. I do not permit a woman to be a teacher, nor must woman domineer over man; she should be quiet. For Adam was created first, and Eve afterwards; and it was not Adam who was deceived; it was the woman who, yielding to deception, fell into sin.[24]

Closely associated with the Pauline view of women as inferior to men are other themes that were enunciated early in the Christian tradition and reinforced throughout much of its history.

1. Celibacy, continence, and virginity are the better ways for persons of both sexes.
2. Sexual drives, if sexual restraint is not possible, must be released only within marriage and then for the procreation of children.
3. Women tempt and seduce; they are below man, yet they drag him down by their sexual attractiveness and wiles.
4. Women, as inferior to men, are to stay in the background of religious activities. (Note again Paul's assertions in I Tim. 2:11.)
5. Women who want to be religiously active can join specific religious orders established for that purpose. As celibates they can come closer to God, thereby benefitting both themselves and the men around them by withdrawing from interactions that could lead to infractions of God's moral code.
6. Leadership and decision making are reserved for men.
7. Preaching and interpretation of the Scriptures are reserved for men.

In fairness to Christianity it needs to be noted that Jesus himself treated women and men more evenhandedly than many of his followers did. His recorded miracles include women as well as men as recipients—the daughter of Jairus and Peter's mother-in-law benefitted no less than the man born blind or the man possessed by demons, for example. Women were singled out for their expressions of strong faith as frequently as men (for example, the woman with a hemorrhage, the Samaritan woman, and the beggar woman). Although Jesus did not practice affirmative action in the selection of his twelve disciples, he did number several women among his close friends. He violated the Sabbath to help women (for example, Luke 13:10–

---

[23]Gail B. Shulman, "View from the Back of the Synagogue: Women in Judaism," in *Sexist Religion and Women in the Church*, ed. Alice L. Hageman (New York: Association Press, 1974), pp. 147–49.

[24]I Timothy 2:11–14. *New English Bible* (New York: Oxford University Press, 1976).

13), and he rejected one taboo after another in speaking to the Samaritan woman at the well (John 4:7–30)—taboos against associating with impure persons (in this case doubly so—both as a woman and a Samaritan)—and then using her as a religious messenger to her townspeople. Carmody summarizes by saying:

> Jesus treats men and women simply as individuals who need his help, or as coworkers, or friends. He offers women no separate but equal way of works; he compiles no segregating list of feminine virtues. In the face of considerable opposition, and with the consequence of provoking scandal, Jesus associates with the outcasts and marginal people of his day; the poor, sinners, tax collectors, lepers—and women.[25]

That there is this model in the New Testament as a contrast to the Pauline reinforcement for the established societal model of second-class citizenship for women is probably a primary reason that many women continue to work for reform within the Christian denominations—one of the options or routes being followed by women today (to be discussed later in this chapter). In fairness to Paul, however, there are many scholars who would attribute the New Testament books that tend to subjugate women and urge their second-class nature to writers other than Paul. Many scholars would suggest that only Romans, 1 and 2 Corinthians, Galations, and Philemon are genuinely authored by Paul. It should be noted that these books are least likely of the nonhistorical books of the New Testament to support inferior status for women. In fact, a favorite text for sermons preached at ordination services of women candidates for the ministry continues to be the text chosen by the Reverend Luther Lee at the ordination service of the first woman ordained in the United States (Antoinette Brown) in 1856—Galations 3:28: "There is neither Jew nor Greek, there is neither slave nor free, there is neither male nor female; for you are all one in Christ Jesus." The second of the dual texts used by Reverend Lee was the prophecy in Joel 2:28, which was quoted by Peter in the story of Pentecost and recorded in Acts 2:17: "Your sons and daughters will prophesy."[26]

By way of a brief summary of the roles of women in traditionally religious societies, we turn again to Carmody. She notes first a subordinate role, as a woman gained status only through her relationship to a man—"by being the daughter of this father, the wife of this husband, the mother of that son."[27] Second, there is the dependent role. Carmody notes that Buddhist nuns were expected to serve even the newest and youngest monk; Christian wives were instructed to be silent in the churches and obedient to their husbands, as their "heads," just as Christ is the head of the Church;

[25]Carmody, *Women and World Religions*, p. 115.

[26]Rosemary Skinner Keller, "Women and Religion," in *Encyclopedia of American Religious Experience*, eds. Charles Lippey and Peter Williams (New York: Charles Scribner's Sons, 1988), p. 1555.

[27]Ibid., p. 16.

Muslim women were veiled through purdah from the eyes of all but their own husband.[28] Third, there was assumed intellectual inferiority. For example, Jewish women were denied opportunity to study the Torah; Chinese women did not study the Confucian classics; Hindu women did not study the Vedas.[29]

THE CHALLENGES TO TRADITIONAL PATTERNS

As we look at the contemporary religious scene so far as the responses and participation of women are concerned, we see a broad array of options that are available—challenges, if you will—all of which have proponents, all of which are in process and practice, all of which have precedents as well.

In an attempt to provide some organization to what might at first glance seem a bewildering and unrelated set of options, we would suggest that there are three primary categories of response on the part of women to the question of their relationship to religion. Each category of response has in turn at least two subcategories.

The first we shall call the tradition-affirming response. Here we encounter two major subtypes: (1) The subordinate female religious role along the lines of the New Testament admonition for women to "keep silent" in the church and refrain from having any religious authority over men; and (2) the specialized religious role for women as best typified in the female monastic orders within Roman Catholicism.

Second, there is the tradition-reforming response, in which there is continuing strong commitment to the religious institution, but at the same time there is a call for significant change (reformation) with respect to the traditional role and functions of women. Here two particular movements or emphases stand out. One is the movement to open ordination to the ministry to women. The second is a position that is newer and somewhat more inclusive than the ordination issue. That is the "radical obedience" position articulated by the women's rights leader and theologian Rosemary Radford Ruether by which she urges rethinking and reforming the traditional roles and perceptions of women but without either destroying the church or pulling women out of the institution.

Third, there is the revolutionary response that calls for such change in the substance of religion as traditionally expressed and organized as to be truly revolutionary. Here we include two subthemes. First, the call to "exodus" from traditional religious institutions as expressed by the Roman Catholic writer and theologian Mary Daly. Second, the proclamation of female superiority and the rejection of male dominance and direction of reli-

[28]Ibid., pp. 16–17.
[29]Ibid., p. 17.

gious patterns through the resurrection of ancient practices and beliefs of witchcraft.

Tradition-Affirming Responses

With respect to support for traditional patterns of religious involvement for women we have to observe that they are certainly the most highly supported of all the options. That is to say, female religious orders continue to gain novices, and ladies' guilds and societies in both denominations and sects continue to flourish. This is not to say that membership in religious orders is not down from past numbers (actually membership has declined at a dramatic rate), or that ladies' guilds and women's missionary societies are flourishing at their peak post-World War II levels. But it nonetheless remains true that because of the inertia of tradition, if nothing else, great numbers of women continue to express themselves and find some level of satisfaction in avenues of religious expression that have been sanctioned by longstanding tradition.

We earlier mentioned the option for women of monastic orders, particularly with reference to Buddhism. The viability of this option within Christianity for a great many centuries is of course well known. The provision of a structure through which women could perform distinctly "feminine" tasks, such as nurturing and healing the sick, caring for the poor and needy, or teaching the young in schools, was well suited to use women's skills and energy in constructive ways and yet did not challenge one whit the established religious patriarchy. One might even suggest, at the risk of sounding facetious, that these women, celibate as they were required to be, were therefore not only closer to God but constituted that many fewer temptations to the men in society.

We referred earlier to the high regard for virginity and celibacy that existed in the early centuries of the Christian Church. This resulted already in the second century A.D. in the consecration of young women to remain unmarried and live either with the parental family or occasionally alone to fulfill a life of contemplation and devotion. Some widows were consecrated as deaconesses to live lives of service. Gradually communities of these celibate women developed and what we would properly think of today as a monastic order or convent emerged. This occurred at least as early as the fourth century A.D. Both male and female monastic orders began to multiply and we encounter such founders and advocates as Saint Antony, Saint Pachomius, and Saint Basil in the fourth century, and Saint Augustine, Saint Benedict, and Saint Caesarius in the fifth century. Their female counterparts and contemporaries were the sisters of Saint Pachomius and Saint Benedict, Bathilde at Chelles, Rodegund at Poitiers, Joan at Bourges, and Bridget in Sweden. They opened houses of learning, work, and devotion that were based on various elaborations of the three universal vows of chastity, poverty, and obedience.[30]

New orders continued to be established throughout the world. Taking vows of a nun (sister) became in the Roman Catholic Church and much later in a few Protestant denominations a goal for young women that was highly valued by both the women themselves and their fellow church members. Thus, for millions of women down through the centuries the celibate, impoverished, obedient life of the nun has been a highly legitimate religious route for women to follow. Although the number of women entering such orders continues to dwindle,[31] the life of the nun endures as a legitimate religious road for women to walk. It is of course, without question, about as traditional a choice as there is—chaste, virginal women doing "women's work" of teaching, healing, serving the needy, and baking bread.

The other traditional religious role for women is one with which the reader is probably very familiar. This is the role which for all but a very few has placed women in the background of religious activities—in most Christian denominations, for example, without vote in congregational matters and excluded from the pulpit and from behind the communion rail, women have typically been in charge only of chicken dinners and the pre-Christmas bazaar. This traditional role within Christianity, as well as some flavor of a contemporary woman's reaction to that traditional role *vis-à-vis* the traditional male role, is ably described in the following excerpt from Sharon Emswiler's essay "How the New Woman Feels in the Old Worship Service." She describes her participation in a typical worship service in a Protestant church.

I enter the sanctuary and am directed to my seat by an usher, always male, except on "Ladies' Day," that one day in the year when women are given the opportunity to "play usher." As I sit and meditate I listen to the organ prelude. If the church is a small one, I notice that the organist is a woman. However, if the church is a large, prestigious one, with an expensive organ, the position of organist is most often filled by a man.

The minister (or ministers)—male, of course—then appears to begin the service, accompanied by a lay person (male) acting as the liturgist of the morning. The call to worship is given, setting the worship service in motion. One such call to worship that sticks in my mind from a service I attended contains the line, "To be is to be a brother." Hearing those words, I instantly carry them to their logical conclusion: "I am not, and never will be, a brother. Therefore, I am not. I do not exist." The service is off to a great start!

The congregation now rises for the first hymn and I find myself singing a song such as "Men and Children Everywhere" (I wonder in which group I am to include myself), "Rise Up, O Men of God," or "Faith of Our Fathers." If it is

[30]Suzanne Cita-Malard, *Religious Orders of Women*, trans. George J. Robinson (New York: Hawthorn, 1964), p. 15.

[31]In the United States the decline in the number of nuns in just ten years has been 18 percent—from 128,378 in 1979 to 104,419 in 1989. Cf. Felician A. Fay, ed., *1990 Catholic Almanac* (Huntington, IN: Our Sunday Visitor Publication Division, 1990), p. 427.

near Christmas, the selections might be "God Rest Ye, Merry Gentlemen" or "Good Christian Men, Rejoice;" while the Easter season offers such choices as "Sing with All the Sons of Glory" or "Good Christian Men Rejoice and Sing." Other possible hymns in the service might include "Once to Every Man and Nation," "Now Praise We Great and Famous Men," "Brother Man, Fold to Thy Heart," "As Men of Old Their First Fruits Brought," or "Turn Back, O Man."

If the service is of a more contemporary style, I go in the hope that the hymns will speak to me in a way that the traditional ones do not. But here, too, I discover that while the folk tunes have a great appeal to me, I am asked to sing songs with titles like "Be a New Man," "Sons of God," "Come, My Brothers," "Brothers, Get Yourselves Together," and "Brother, How's Your Love."

As I sing I try to imagine that these songs are speaking to me, but I am not accustomed to thinking of myself as a "man" or a "brother;" and the identification is difficult, and most often impossible. The only way I can find to identify with these masculine words is to attempt either to deny or set aside my femininity. But I do not want to deny that part of my personhood; I want rather to affirm it. I want my femaleness recognized and affirmed by the Church also. As the worship progresses through the prayers, creeds, and sermon, the same language form keeps recurring—always the masculine when referring to people; always the masculine when referring to God. While I sing and during prayer I change the word "men" to "people;" "mankind" to "humankind;" "sons" to "children;" "Father" to "Parent," but I feel as though I am outshouted by the rest of the congregation. My words are swallowed up by theirs.

Listening to the minister preach his sermon for the morning, I am aware that he is not really attempting to address me or my sisters in the congregation. His illustrations all revolve around men and speak overwhelmingly to the masculine experience in our society. Suddenly, I feel as though I am eavesdropping on a conversation labeled "For Men Only." Or worse yet, I feel that the suspicion I had after the call to worship is true. I do not exist! I look down at my hands and arms and feet. I can see them; they are very real to me. But I feel that somehow I must be invisible to this preacher who has designed this service and now stands in front of me, speaking of "the brethren" and telling his congregation to be "new men."

Following the sermon, the worshippers are invited to participate in the celebration of the Lord's Supper. As the large group of male ushers marches down the aisle to receive the communion elements and distribute them to the congregation, I am suddenly struck with the irony of the situation. The chicken suppers, the ham suppers, the turkey suppers in the church are all prepared and served by the women. But not the Lord's Supper! Yes, it is prepared by the women, but the privilege of serving the Lord's Supper in worship is reserved for the men. This particular morning I find it very difficult to swallow the bread and drink the wine, knowing that within the Body of Christ, the Church, the sisters of Christ are not given the same respect and privileges as are his brothers.[32]

[32]Sharon Neufer Emswiler, "How the New Woman Feels in the Old Worship Service," in *Women and Worship*, A Guide to Non-Sexist Hymns, Prayers, and Liturgies, eds. Sharon Neufer Emswiler and Thomas Neufer Emswiler (New York: Harper & Row, 1974), pp. 3–5. Copyright © 1974 by Sharon Neufer Emswiler and Thomas Neufer Emswiler. Reprinted by permission of Harper & Row, Publishers, Inc.

Such a "men only" or "men first" pattern is, as mentioned earlier in this chapter, not unique to Christianity. It has been characteristic, in some cases to an even more extreme degree, in all the major world religions. Nor is it dead. Far from it. For one thing, a great many women continue to assume such female subordinate religious roles and postures as proper and divinely ordained. Entire denominations continue to espouse such perspectives and make them tenets of doctrinal assent. In fact, a resurgent movement within many fundamentalist and conservative church bodies and congregations calling for a return to the "Christian family" holds as the ideal family structure a patriarchial one in which women and children assume nurturing and obedient roles respectively behind a dominant, decision-making, sanction-disseminating husband-father. Consistent with this perspective, though not necessarily essential to it, was the "total woman" concept espoused by Marabel Morgan and made popular in the 1970s.[33] The central ideas of the total woman concept were that a woman could expect a much happier and more satisfying life if she worked hard at pleasing "her man" and remained in the traditional niche set aside for women.

But there is also evidence on the other side of this issue. In many denominations women have been and are assuming both more visible and more significant roles in religious life. Ordination to the ministry and receiving calls to be pastors, priests (Episcopal), and rabbis constitute dramatic evidence of this (to be discussed later in the chapter). But even short of ordination, women in some denominations serve on church boards, become deacons and elders in local churches, and assist in the distribution of holy communion.

Thus, what we have referred to as the traditional secondary and subordinate role for women in religious activities is certainly not extinct. In fact, one could hardly even say it is dying. While, as we will document in the concluding two sections of this chapter, there are numerous challenges and alternatives to such traditional views of women's religious roles, and a significant number of women have adopted alternative definitions and modes, such challenges have actually at the same time stimulated a resurgence of support for traditional female religious roles. A quick browsing through any religious bookstore that specializes in conservative, fundamentalistic or "born again" Christian literature will immediately reinforce this observation.

Reformation Responses for the Female Religious Role

Here we shall look particularly at two ways in which women want to continue within the traditional religious organizations but at the same time

---

[33]Marabel Morgan, *The Total Woman* (Old Tappan, NJ: Fleming H. Revell Company, 1973).

are dedicated to reforming those organizations and their traditional patterns. Parallel to a grand tradition in British politics, these would be women of the "loyal opposition." That is, they want to remain members in good standing of a standard religious group, yet are equally committed to changing certain aspects, tenets, or practices of that group, in their terms, "updating" them.

Any woman who seeks to change a local congregation's constitution that prohibits women from voting on congregational matters, serving as an elder or deacon, or assisting with the formal worship service in any visible way is part of this reformational response. Any woman who lobbies within her denomination for change in that religious group's stand on abortion or birth control is part of this response. But in the interests of brevity, we shall focus briefly on but two emphases—first, the movement toward the ordination of women as bona fide "clergymen," and second, the perspective espoused by the women's rights leader and theologian Rosemary Radford Ruether and identified in her own terms as "radical obedience."[34]

The ordination of women issue, though not brand new, is certainly of relatively recent origin so far as the span of history is concerned. As we mentioned earlier, the first American women to be ordained into the ministry was Antoinette Brown, a Congregationalist, in South Butler, New York, in 1856.[35] Olympia Brown followed in 1863. But such nineteenth century ordinations were rare. In fact, it has not been until this century, and very recently at that, that any significant number of religious groups have allowed the ordination of women. For example, it was not until 1956 that the United Presbyterian Church in the United States began to ordain women. The Church of the Brethren ordained its first woman in 1960. The Lutheran Church in America approved of the ordination of women in 1970. The first Jewish woman in Reform Judaism in the United States to become a rabbi, Sally Priesand, was ordained in 1972. The first female rabbi in Conservative Judaism was not ordained until 1986. And it was not until 1974 that the first women were ordained in the Episcopal Church in the United States. The Church of England is still debating the issue.[36] It did, however, vote in 1987 to develop guidelines on how to open the priesthood to women.

A logical consequence of the ordination of women is consideration of their consecration as bishops in faiths that have such roles—namely, Roman Catholicism, Eastern Orthodoxy, and Anglicanism. In the Episcopal (Anglican) Church in the United States that action occurred for the first time in

[34]Rosemary Ruether and Eleanor McLaughlin, "Women's Leadership in the Jewish and Christian Traditions: Continuity and Change," in *Women of Spirit*, eds. Rosemary Ruether and Eleanor McLaughlin (New York: Simon & Schuster, 1979), p. 19.

[35]Margaret B. Crook, *Women and Religion* (Boston, MA: Beacon Press, 1964), p. 235, and Keller, "Women and Religion," p. 1555.

[36]Kenneth Slack, "Women's Ordination: The Fight Is On," *The Christian Century* 102 no. 38 (December 4, 1985), 1108–09.

February, 1989, when Barbara Harris was consecrated as a bishop in Boston. Ms. Harris is not only a woman, but she is black as well. Neither the Anglican Church of England nor the Roman Catholic Church sent formal representatives to the rites, though 60 American Anglican bishops were present.

The provocation for raising the question of the ordination of women has been largely a social one. It is clear that when women participating in the antislavery movement in the 1830s to 1860s discovered that while their leadership and oratory were often eagerly sought out, they were not allowed to use a pulpit or church platform as a place from which to speak, their consciousness as well as their level of indignation were raised. Women such as the Grimke sisters (Angelina and Sarah), Margaret Prior, Lucy Stone, and Lydia Child led the way. When Lucretia Mott and Elizabeth Cady Stanton were excluded on the basis of sex from the World Anti-Slavery Convention in London in 1840, they began to lay plans for a new movement devoted to the cause of women.[37]

As feminism generally, and the woman's suffrage movement in particular, gained momentum at the end of the nineteenth and beginning of the twentieth centuries, culminating in the Nineteenth Amendment in 1920, some religious groups saw the incongruity and permitted women to head churches as ordained ministers (primarily in Baptist, Methodist, and Pentecostal churches). But probably more common was the alternative of being a female religious entrepreneur who possessed charismatic leadership qualities and gathered bands of local followers in sectarian groups, particularly in urban settings. Some of these women attained national and international notice and followings. Note such women as Mary Baker Eddy, founder of Christian Science, and the evangelist Aimee Semple McPherson.

Nonetheless, the door to ordination and religious leadership remained closed to most women. As we have mentioned, it was only very recently that the barriers have been knocked down in many of the major religious groups. Continuing in opposition are such major religious groups as the Orthodox Churches, The Lutheran Church—Missouri Synod, the Roman Catholic Church, and over a hundred of the 262 official denominations in the United States that report statistics to the National Council of Churches. Of course, none of these is without both male and female voices that challenge the sex-based restrictions to ordination. Even such a stronghold of religious patriarchy as the Roman Catholic Church is beginning to discuss the topic. Books, papers, and special conferences are beginning to accumulate.

With respect to those women who have been ordained in the United States, three sets of data are instructive. First, there continue to be relatively

---

[37]Dorothy C. Bass, "Their Prodigious Influence: Women, Religion, and Reform in Antebellum America," in *Women of Spirit*, eds. Rosemary Ruether and Eleanor McLaughlin (New York: Simon & Schuster, 1979), p. 296.

few ordained women. The 1960 United States Census listed 4,727 women as "clergymen." This was 2.3 percent of all clergy. This proportion compares with 3.7 percent of all lawyers and judges, and 7 percent of physicians and surgeons. By 1970 the proportion of clergy who were women had increased to 2.9 percent. But lawyers-judges and physicians-surgeons categories had increased even more—to 4.9 percent and 9.7 percent, respectively. In the 1980 census the increase of women clergy was more substantial. Their increase was an even doubling of their proportion of all clergy—from 2.9 percent in 1970 to 5.8 percent in 1980 (from 6,674 to 16,434). Again, this increase still lagged behind that of women lawyers and judges by a considerable margin. Women lawyers-judges grew in proportion of all lawyers-judges from 4.9 percent to 14 percent—nearly tripling their share. The number of women physicians also grew, but not by as much on a percentage basis: from 9.7 percent in 1970 to 13.4 percent of all physicians in 1980.

Data on female Protestant clergy collected by Constant Jacquet for the National Council of Churches in 1977 and again in 1986 provide excellent documentation of change. During this ten-year interval the number of female clergy in Protestant denominations more than doubled (from 10,470 in 1977 to 23,730 in 1986).[38]

Such an increase is dramatic. But within that substantial increase is a great deal of variation so far as individual denominations are concerned. Some denominations actually lost ground in the ten-year period. For example, the Wesleyan Church's female clergy ranks declined by 33 percent, and the Church of the Nazarene and the International Church of the Foursquare Gospel both declined by 17 percent. At the other extreme, the Reformed Church in America increased its women clergy by 4100 percent! Specifically, that involved growth from one in 1977 to 42 in 1986. Others also showed substantial growth largely because they had only recently begun to ordain women in 1977 and have had significant increases in women clergy since then. The American Lutheran Church (from 18 to 306—a gain of 1600 percent) and the Episcopal Church (from 94 to 796—an increase of 747 percent) fall into this category.[39]

But percentage gains, often involving fairly small numbers, are not the only statistics to review. Despite the fact that about eighty denominations now ordain women, female clergy are still clustered in preponderant numbers in a few denominations. The two religious groups with the greatest number of female clergy—the Assemblies of God, with 3,718 female clergy, and the Salvation Army with 3,220—are neither very large nor at the core of mainline American denominationalism. On the other hand, the only other groups with more than a thousand female clergy are mainline denom-

---

[38]Constant H. Jacquet, Jr., *Women Ministers in 1986 and 1977: A Ten Year View* (New York: National Council of Churches, 1988), p. 4.
[39]Ibid.

inations—the United Methodist Church (1,891), the Presbyterian Church U.S.A. (1,519), and the United Church of Christ (1,460). The proportion of females to the total number of clergy in various denominations is still low, except for the Salvation Army (62 percent of Salvation Army clergy are women). Of mainline Protestant denominations, only the United Church of Christ at 14.5 percent is above 10 percent, and most are in the 4–6 percent range (Methodists, Episcopalians, American Baptist, and Lutherans).

The second set of data show that of the ordained women at work in the denominations that permit them, the proportion in the parish ministry is quite low. In 1951, only half (51.8 percent) of the ordained Protestant women were serving as pastors of churches (including those in an assistant minister capacity). Of the 13 denominations that have over 100 female clergy and provide sufficient data, the proportion of female clergy serving in a pastoral capacity within a local congregation had not increased much by 1986. Data abstracted from Jacquet's study show only 55 percent, with a range that runs from 20 percent (Church of the Nazarene) to 99 percent (the Christian Congregation denomination).[40] But actually, the overall percentage of 55 percent is not so out of line as it might at first appear. The total proportion of all clergy in the denominations that report statistics to the National Council of Churches who are in the parish ministry is only 61 percent.[41] Although female clergy are included in that proportion, the proportion for males alone is barely above 62 percent. Of course, the male clergy who are not parish pastors when interviewed have in most cases been pastors at one time. Although they are now hospital or military chaplains, seminary professors, executive secretaries of denominational agencies and commissions, directors of religious social service organizations, and so on, in most cases they started out in the pastoral ministry.

What might be suggested here is a moderate tendency to separate or isolate women clergy into specialized roles, much like the more radical clergy were, according to Hammond and Mitchell's study,[42] and to assign them to nonparish roles such as the campus ministry or to various administrative roles within denominational and ecumenical bureaucratic structures. Another partial explanation may be that the role of parish minister has been a male role for so long that women may find some difficulty in filling it without at least some redefinition of the role taking place. That women can fill the role well, though with perhaps some redefinition of the role required to take place, is well attested in Priscilla and William Proctor's book, *Women in the Pulpit.*[43] Chaim Waxman notes that even in Reform Ju-

[40]Ibid., p. 7.

[41]Constant H. Jacquet, Jr., *Yearbook of American and Canadian Churches, 1987* (Nashville: Abingdon Press, 1988), p. 247.

[42]Philip E. Hammond and Robert E. Mitchell, "Segmentation of Radicalism—The Case of the Protestant Campus Minister," *American Journal of Sociology* 71, no. 2 (September 1965).

[43]Priscilla and William Proctor, *Women in the Pulpit* (Garden City, NY: Doubleday, 1976).

daism the "ordination of women . . . can provide the necessary title but it does not guarantee a job."[44] And that's in the most liberal branch of Judaism. There are no ordained female rabbis in Orthodox Judaism, and hardly any in conservative Judaism. Waxman also notes the turning of some of the few ordained Jewish women to Jewish communal service in the face of no pulpits being open to them.[45]

With respect to predicting the future of women filling the clergy role and finding acceptance by laypersons, studies in several denominations are now available. We shall look briefly at three. First is Larry Kersten's study of Lutherans in 1968 before any Lutheran women had been ordained in the United States. Kersten found that a substantial majority of laypersons in the two more liberal Lutheran denominations (73 percent of the Lutheran Church in America and 68 percent of the American Lutheran Church) were in favor of women being allowed to become ordained ministers.[46]

In a study of attitudes toward women clergy, using a representative sample of United Presbyterian laypersons, Edward Lehman found a generally favorable attitude toward women clergy, but with some qualifications. For example, although fully 82 percent of laypersons said that a woman's temperment was as well suited to the ministry as that of men, a third of the sample still tended to think of women pastors in a stereotypical way with respect to carrying out the dual functions of pastor and wife-mother.[47] Also, nearly two-thirds of the respondents indicated that in the face of local church resistence to calling a woman as pastor, they would choose a man over a woman,[48] i.e., ignore affirmative action principles. A number of factors correlate with this bias: sex (men were more likely than women to express such bias), age (older members more likely than young), education (higher the education the more open), church size (the larger the more likely to be biased), and involvement (the greater involvement by members the less supportive of women clergy).[49]

There is clear evidence that once a female minister is allowed to carry out the activities of a minister people generally evaluate the performance as satisfactory. Yet two-thirds will still say they prefer a man, even going so far as to believe that their female minister is an atypical success—a woman with very special abilities.[50]

[44]Chaim I. Waxman, *America's Jews in Transition* (Philadelphia: Temple University press, 1983), p. 217.

[45]Ibid.

[46]Lawrence L. Kersten, *The Lutheran Ethic* (Detroit: Wayne State University Press, 1970), p. 125.

[47]Edward C. Lehman, Jr., *Women Clergy: Breaking Through Gender Barriers* (New Brunswick, NJ: Transaction Books, 1985), p. 31.

[48]Ibid., p. 51.

[49]Ibid., pp. 80–109.

[50]Ibid., pp. 274–275.

Lest the reader come away with a negative conclusion with respect to how people view female ministers, we next hasten to note that Lehman concludes that while there are negative and stereotypical views of women in the ministry in churches and a "resistent minority has a powerful voice in the current debates,"[51] still the predominant response of church members to women in ministry is positive.[52] And Lehman concludes: "If women are allowed to function as ordained clergy in local congregations, they will succeed as fully as men."[53]

Jacquet provides some interesting data regarding opportunities for female clergy to serve as sole or senior pastors of congregations. Nationally, only 20 percent of female clergy are serving in the traditional parish ministry as "head pastor," whether alone or in charge of one or more other ministers in a large congregation. The range is almost incredibly wide: from 2 percent (21 of 860) of female clergy as head pastor in the Reorganized Church of Jesus Christ of Latter Day Saints, to 99 percent (289 or 290) of women clergy in the Christian Congregation denomination.[54] It is of interest to note that the denomination with the greatest number of female clergy (the Assemblies of God, with 3,718 women clergy) has a very low proportion of its women clergy as heads of pastoral staffs—only 7 percent.[55] The denomination with the second highest number of female clergy is the Salvation Army, which also has a low proportion of its female clergy as heads of pastoral staff—only 18 percent. Actually, the denomination with the second highest proportion of female clergy acting as head pastor is the Lutheran Church in America (now merged with the American Lutheran Church to form the Evangelical Lutheran Church in America) with 55 percent. All other denominations are below 50 percent, with most in the 23–32 percent range.[56]

With respect to satisfaction so far as their ministries are concerned, Hale, King, and Jones found in a study of 900 Methodist clergywomen a great many with feelings of acceptance, success, and satisfaction. Yet, for 15–20 percent, the ordained ministry has confronted them with serious problems and provided them with little satisfaction.[57] Actually, a third of Methodist clergywomen reported "considerable" to "much" difficulty at all but one of seven stages in reaching a mature ministry. The least problematic

[51]Ibid., p. 285.

[52]Ibid., p. 284.

[53]Ibid., p. 294.

[54]Constant H. Jacquet, Jr., "Women Ministers in 1986 and 1977: A Ten-Year View," in Constant H. Jacquet, Jr., ed., *Yearbook of American Churches, 1989* (Nashville: Abingdon Press, 1989), p. 262.

[55]Ibid., p. 263.

[56]Ibid.

[57]Harry Hale, Jr., Morton King, and Doris M. Jones, *Clergywomen: Problems and Satisfactions* (Lima, OH: Fairway Press, 1985), p. 13.

was handling the course of study at seminary (only 22 percent reporting at least "considerable difficulty").[58]

Further indications of the future increase in women ordained to the ministry come from seminary enrollment data—our third set of data. From 1972 to 1987 the enrollment of women in Protestant seminaries in the United States and Canada increased 356 percent. The corresponding change for males was only 36 percent. The number of women enrolled in Protestant seminaries increased from 3,358 in 1972, when they accounted for 10.2 percent of seminary enrollees, to 15,310 in 1987, when they constituted 27 percent of enrollment.

When we look at individual denominations, the increase in female seminarians is even more dramatic. For example, in the American Baptist (Northern) seminaries, the increase in Master of Divinity enrollments—the traditional route taken to become a minister for a local congregation—for males was only 7 percent between 1970–71 and 1979–80. But for females the increase was 570 percent! The percentage of females enrolled in American Baptist seminary Bachelor of Divinity programs was 6 percent in 1970–71. That percentage of the total increased to 29 percent in 1979–80.[59] It is very likely that we won't be very far into the next century before women will constitute a majority of candidates for the ministry. Already women are over half of the seminarians at some Protestant, nondenominational seminaries.

We referred earlier to a second reforming approach so far as the relationship of women to religion is concerned. That is the approach of "radical obedience" urged by Rosemary Radford Ruether. The term is Ms. Ruether's own. She remains within the Christian Church (Roman Catholic), speaks out explicitly against some of the more radical options espoused by some women, the feminists among them in particular, (options that we shall discuss in the final section of this chapter), yet wants reformation of existing structures, not their dissolution and death. We shall neither attempt nor pretend to present fully Rosemary Ruether's position and advice, but will offer a few summary indications of her position.

While appealing for reform rather than revolution and rejection of the core of Christianity, Ms. Ruether notes how women have in the past exercised some leadership and made contributions "from within" the body of the church.[60] Religious orders of nuns and sisters who are set apart for special religious work constitute an example known by everyone. But also, martyrdom has not been sex exclusive, and women have been recognized as

[58]Ibid., p. 15.

[59]Edward C. Lehman, Jr., "Organizational Resistance to Women in Ministry," *Sociological Analysis* 42, no. 2 (1981), p. 114.

[60]Rosemary Radford Ruether, "Women's Leadership in the Jewish and Christian Traditions: Continuity and Change," in *Women of Spirit*, eds. Rosemary Radford Ruether and Eleanor McLaughlin (New York: Simon & Schuster, 1979), pp. 19–28.

contributing prophetic gifts in this process. Further, at times when reform movements such as millenialism have gained popularity, women could step into leadership positions because the very nature of the movement called into question some of the traditional expectations and patterns of family, religious organization, and society. She also mentions the important difference between religious organizations that have stressed lay leadership in contrast to formally trained and sanctioned clerical leadership as in the Roman Catholic Church. She notes that those "who have the gifts, rather than those authorized by the traditional institutions, are acclaimed as leaders. In this situation women too can emerge as leaders."[61] Further, she notes that the pentecostal groups and traditions have provided more opportunities for women because the "gifts of the Spirit" could come to anyone, male or female. As such the person and the message should have been heeded without particularly noting the sex of the person who was seen as a vehicle for the Holy Spirit.

Her conclusion at this point is that women should appropriate such patterns and precedents from history to vindicate their moving forward within religious institutions in the present in order "to reshape and enlarge the vision and life of the church today."[62]

Integral to this "reshaping" must be reevaluation of both traditional and contemporary Mariology (the theology surrounding the Virgin Mary within Roman Catholicism).[63] Here she speaks of the need to excise the concept of passive femininity in which women are made to be "specialists in self-abnegating, auxiliary modes of existence,"[64] while men remain dominant and superordinate. Nor is it enough for men to adopt a "feminine side," particularly when such a feminine side is viewed as in the "nature" of women, but only auxiliary and supplemental to men.[65]

While Ruether is here enunciating in almost a classic manner the contemporary feminist demand for a true balance and transposition of so-called male and female qualities, rights, and expectations, she continues her assertions and appeals for action within the context of *reform*, "radical" for some though it may be.

Revolutionary Responses

Among various proposals for resolving the issue of traditional inferior roles and status for women in the major world religions, and Christianity in

[61] Ibid., p. 21.

[62] Ibid., p. 28.

[63] Rosemary Radford Ruether, *New Woman/New Earth* (New York: Seabury Press, 1975), pp. 56–59.

[64] Ibid., p. 57.

[65] Ibid., p. 57.

particular, we shall focus on what seem to be the two major options at the moment: (1) the religious exodus proposal, and (2) the resort to witchcraft.

The principal spokesperson for the religious exodus proposal is Mary Daly, who first caught public attention in 1968 with the publication of her book *The Church and the Second Sex*. In the book she was highly critical of the sexist perceptions, views, and practices of Christianity (Roman Catholicism in particular). But she called for reform, not revolution in the sense of destroying the old to inaugurate a new order. Fairly quickly she has moved to the point not of revolution in the strictest sense of the term, perhaps, but of *exodus* from the institution—turning one's back on the old and marching out to establish something new. She articulated this position already in 1971 in her now famous Harvard Memorial Church Sermon in which she spoke of the women's movement as an "exodus community." She speaks of women building a new community as they are bonded in sisterhood. This sisterhood includes a number of qualities that lead eventually to the exodus. It is revolutionary as it destroys the credibility of sex stereotyping. It is revolutionary as it creates new definitions of God and invalidates patriarchal religion. It is antichurch in the sense that the institution called church remains sexist and wedded to patriarchal religious concepts. It is church itself as it becomes a community "with a mission to challenge the distortions in sexually unbalanced society, to be a counter force to the prevailing sense of reality by building up a new sense of reality."[66] It is, finally, an exodus community that goes away from the land of its fathers. In that sermon Daly then called to women to follow what had probably already been a spiritual break by giving physical expression to their exodus community by leaving, that is, literally walking out of the church building.

In her book *Beyond God the Father*, Mary Daly calls for the death of God as he has been known within the Judeo-Christian tradition—that is, as male. This concept should be replaced with one of God more like that proposed by theologian Paul Tillich—ultimate meaning and reality, a process more than a "person."

She then makes even more clear what she means in her "postchristian" introduction to a second printing of her first book *The Church and the Second Sex*. In a fascinating review of her own book of seven years earlier she describes how far she has moved from those embryonic beginnings, how she had referred to her sisters in the movement as "they," not "we," and above all had viewed the movement as one of *reform*, not the exodus-revolution she has now come to espouse. In a more recent book, *Gyn/Ecology*,[67] she refers to her first book as written by a "reformist foresister" (herself) whose

[66]Mary Daly, "The Women's Movement: An Exodus Community," *Religious Education* 67 (September/October 1972), p. 332.

[67]Mary Daly, *Gyn/Ecology: The Metaethics of Radical Feminism* (Boston: Beacon Press, 1978), p. xi.

work she had to refute. Her current position appears to be quite clearly summarized when she says that women "whose consciousness has been raised are spiritual exiles whose sense of transcendence is seeking alternative expressions to those available in institutional religion."[68] Or again, "When you can say 'No' to the institution you can begin to say a clearer and more effective 'Yes' to real movement, the movement of your sisters—past, present, and future."[69]

Another revolutionary expression so far as the relationship of women to religion is concerned is articulated by Naomi Goldenberg. Like Mary Daly, Ms. Goldenberg traces the rapid evolution of her own perceptions. She identifies her problems with traditional religion beginning when she tried to visualize women as rabbis, priests, and ministers, but suddenly wondered how they as women would or could represent a male god.[70] She saw this as an impossible incongruity. She now sees in witchcraft a solution to the ancient problem of the subordination of women religiously and otherwise.

In witchcraft traditional historic religion is essentially turned upside down. Female is defined as superior; although goddesses have male consorts, and although those male beings are called gods, the goddess is more highly valued and ranks higher in prestige and power.[71] What makes witchcraft very different from most religions, particularly in the West, is not only the superiority of women it upholds, but the radical break it makes with the view of religion always implying an "other"—a god or other supernatural force or power that is "out there," so to speak. Witchcraft places divinity within—not a new idea at all of course (one thinks of pantheism, deism, Reform Judaism, to only begin a long list). Its radical, revolutionary nature is in the substitution of inner divinity for any and all traditional religious systems and expressions.

Some of the flavor of this inner divine power residing within the female and superior to that in the male, as well as a feel for some of the rage and defiance against traditional religion that women in the witchcraft movement feel, is found in Goldenberg's description and analysis of an evening service of the first national conference on women's spirituality held in Boston on April 23, 1976, attended by several hundred women. Goldenberg's description is as follows:

> The keynote speeches and opening rituals were held in a church in the heart of Boston. After listening attentively to two addresses on the theme of "Wom-

[68]Mary Daly, "Theology after the Demise of God the Father," in *Sexist Religion and Women in the Church*, ed. Alice L. Hagemen (New York: Association Press, 1974), pp. 126–127.

[69]Mary Daly, *The Church and the Second Sex* (New York: Harper & Row, Pub., 1968, 1975), p. 39.

[70]Naomi Goldenberg, *Changing of the Gods: Feminism and the End of Traditional Religions* (Boston: Beacon Press, 1979), p. 3. Copyright © 1979 by Naomi R. Goldenberg.

[71]Ibid., p. 103.

anpower: Energy Re-Sourcement," the audience became very active. In tones ranging from whispers to shouts, they chanted, "The Goddess Is Alive— Magic Is Afoot." The women evoked the Goddess with dancing, stamping, clapping and yelling. They stood on pews and danced bare-breasted on the pulpit and amid the hymnbooks. Had any sedate, white-haired clergyman been present, I am sure he would have felt the Apocalypse had arrived.

This episode during the Boston conference cannot be described as joyful. Women felt angry and bitter in a church that represented the worship of a male god. It did not matter that this particular denomination had a more liberal outlook than most. In fact, the women were angry at all religions of the fathers and took this opportunity to mock and defy those religions in a church they had rented for the occasion. The anger was not pretty but it certainly was justified. Why not be enraged with the whole Judeo-Christian tradition for centuries of degradation of the bodies and images of women? Why not display your breasts in a place that has tried to teach you that they are things to be ashamed of, features that make you unlike God or His son? Proclaiming that the "Goddess Is Alive" in a traditional church setting is proclaiming that woman is alive, that being female is divine. The women in Boston were raising up their images as fleshly female beings to defy their culture's image of God as an immaterial male spirit. At this opening of the Boston conference the Goddess represented fierce pride in female physical presence and fury at the abuse that presence has taken from male religious authorities. The Goddess was never symbolized as an idol or a picture in this or any other ritual. Instead, She was seen as the force which had motivated each woman to be present at the first national gathering in Her honor.[72]

While the above discussion of revolutionary proposals so far as the role of women in organized religion is concerned might suggest their recency, we should be aware that these are not brand new voices. There were witches of old, of course. But there were other voices of religious revolution over the years. For example, early Shaker teaching (late 1700s) viewed God as both male and female and said that Ann Lee, the founder of Shakerism, was co-savior with Christ.

CONCLUSION

Without belaboring issues or repeating ideas that have already been presented, one additional remark by way of conclusion seems appropriate. That is an insight contributed by Denise Carmody. She notes that there has been a world-wide tendency to view women as either much better or much worse than men, implying that only men have normal, mid-range humanity. So women have been placed on pedestals of purity, loveliness, and virginity. Correspondingly they have been denounced as evil witches, seducing

---

[72]Goldenberg, *Changing of the Gods, Feminism and the End of Traditional Religions*, pp. 92–93. Copyright © 1979 by Naomi Goldenberg. Reprinted by permission of Beacon Press.

sirens, and treacherous whores.[73] She adds, "What they have not been, historically, is equal sharers of humanity whose social and religious offices have been determined principally by their talents."[74] In a neat nutshell this seems to be the central issue for society and the central issue for religion as well.

[73]Carmody, *Women and World Religions*, p. 17.
[74]Ibid.

11

Major Historical Developments

[handwritten: Intolerant Beginnings]
[handwritten: Frontier Challenge]
[handwritten: Ordeal of ~~Orthodoxy~~]
[handwritten: Pluralism]

[handwritten: 6 themes]

In this chapter, we will discuss six specific themes or developments in the history of American religion, proceeding roughly chronologically. Moreover, this discussion can be viewed within the context of two more general themes that the reader will find helpful to keep in mind as we proceed—first, that the outward manifestation or pattern of religion has constantly changed during the nearly four centuries since the initial European settlement of this country, and second, that the relationships between religion and other features of the social structure have also changed.

INTOLERANT BEGINNINGS

The first theme or stage in the history of religion in America we call the period of intolerant beginnings. Many of the early colonists were themselves religious dissenters and minorities extolled by our history books for their courage and principles in struggling for religious freedom and liberty, even to the extent of making perilous voyages in search of a place where they could practice their religious convictions unhampered. Yet many of these same seekers of religious freedom were inclined to deny to others what they demanded for themselves. Those who asked that others be tolerant of their views were themselves intolerant of the divergent religious views of still others.

During the colonial period the settlers, though speaking of a new world and a new age, had reproduced an ancient pattern of officially established religion that was supported by law and governmental authority. The state-church pattern predominated. Nine of the thirteen original colonies recognized officially established religious systems. Persons who dissented were frequently expelled from these colonies or at best accorded only second-class citizenship if allowed to remain.

The situation is well summarized in the following excerpt from the U.S. Supreme Court's opinion in the historic 1947 *Everson* decision:

> Catholics found themselves hounded and proscribed because of their faith; Quakers who followed their conscience went to jail; Baptists were peculiarly obnoxious to certain dominant Protestant sects; men and women of varied faiths who happened to be in a minority in a particular locality were persecuted because they steadfastly persisted in worshipping God only as their own consciences dictated. And all of these dissenters were compelled to pay tithes and taxes to support government-sponsored churches whose ministers preached inflammatory sermons designed to strengthen and consolidate the established faith by generating a burning hatred against dissenters.[1]

These examples were particularly obvious in Massachusetts Bay Colony and Virginia. As the Puritan settlers in Massachusetts established what for all intents and purposes was a state church, the colonial government was expected, as part of its service to its citizens, to support the Congregational Church and its clergy. The Congregationalist meeting house was used for both governmental and religious activities. Colonial law compelled all people to attend church services regardless of their personal beliefs and denied equal rights to the "unorthodox." Citizens were subject to trial by the colonial government for what the church called sins but the government called crimes—heresy, blasphemy, and idolatry.

Anne Hutchinson, whose history is one of the better-known examples of such victimization, was interestingly enough not a representative of a dissenting or deviant religious group in the Massachusetts Bay Colony where she resided. Although what she taught was defined as deviant, heretical doctrine, she was technically a Congregationalist, like all the other (acceptable) residents of Boston. Her heresy lay in her stress on a "covenant of grace"—a religion in which a person could have direct access to God's love and grace—in opposition to the "covenant of works" that stressed obedience to the laws of church and state. In 1638, both she and her doctrines were tried and condemned—her teaching as heresy and she as a blasphemer of God and seducer of the faithful.

---

[1]*Everson* v. *Board of Education*, 333 U.S. 1.

Earlier, in 1636, Roger Williams and four companions, having been banished from the same colony, settled in "Rogues' Island" (that is, Rhode Island) and established a community there as a haven for Quakers, Baptists, and other deviant and dissenting religious groups. Even in this tolerant colony, however, approximately a century later a law was passed restricting both citizenship and eligibility for public office to Protestants.[2]

Quakers were particularly obnoxious to the colonists in Massachusetts, as reflected by laws there specifying that any of that "cursed sect of heretics" who entered the colony were to be jailed, whipped with twenty stripes, and then expelled from the colony. Four Quakers were even hanged. Some were branded or had ears cut off. In at least one case, the children of Quaker parents were sold into slavery upon authorization of a Boston court.

In Virginia, Anglicanism was established as the official church, but in a somewhat different form than Congregationalism was established in Massachusetts. Whereas in Massachusetts the church tended to control the government, in Virginia the government tended to control the church. In Virginia, all citizens were required to attend Anglican services and were taxed to support the Anglican church, no non-Anglican religious group could hold services, no Catholic or Quaker could hold public office, and no one who did not believe in infant baptism could even become a citizen of the colony.[3] Early Virginia laws, later reduced in severity, specified that anyone convicted a third time for failure to attend religious services was to spend six months in the galleys and that a third offense of working on the Sabbath was punishable by death.

THE CONSTITUTIONAL COMPROMISE

With the Revolution and the adoption of the Constitution, the colonial pattern became subject to forces resulting in drastic change. In the First Amendment, American society took the official stance that "Congress shall make no law respecting an establishment of religion, or prohibiting the free exercise thereof." As such, the early pattern of state churches and their implicit intolerance was repudiated. It is interesting to note, however, that it was not until the passage of the Fourteenth Amendment in 1868 that this limitation was applied at the state level. Theoretically, any state could have had an official state religion up to that time; but none did after 1833, when Massachusetts rescinded its state-church commitments, the last state to do so.

[2]Evarts B. Greene, *Religion and the State* (New York: New York University Press, 1941), p. 51.

[3]Anson Phelps Stokes and Leo Pfeffer, *Church and State in the United States* (New York: Harper & Row, 1964), p. 7.

In significant part, this change from state churches to religious tolera-
tion and pluralism occurred because no single religious group could claim
anything near the majority of supporters throughout the thirteen states
necessary to establish it as the officially sanctioned religion of the new nation. Not that particular groups (Congregationalists, for example, who
probably had the greatest number of members of any group) would not
have wanted such status; it was simply that none had sufficient numbers to
gain a majority vote. Every state had a goodly number of dissenters and
minority-religious-group members; there were even substantial numbers of
"free thinkers" who professed no formal religious affiliation. Therefore,
only one practical solution appeared feasible, and that was to cut off
churches both legally and financially from government support. Hence the
clause in the First Amendment specifying that "Congress shall make no law
respecting an establishment of religion."

Looking at the situation from a slightly different angle, every religious
group, whether dissenting or firmly established, now found itself occupying
a minority status in the context of all thirteen states, and so each was quite
naturally concerned with keeping government from interfering with what it
wanted to do and teach religiously. What if another religious group should
later gain a majority—what would happen to us? Hence the second clause
dealing with religion in the First Amendment stating that Congress shall
make no law "prohibiting the free exercise thereof."

With disestablishment came voluntarism and the rise of denominationalism. People could join any religious group of their choice, or they could
choose to join none at all. They could even form antireligious groups. Thus,
religious groups now had to find ways of becoming self-supporting. Competition for members and for scarce resources developed, and religious innovation was implicitly encouraged as a consequence.

It is difficult to overstate the significance and the dramatic impact of
this severance of religion from state auspices. Sanford H. Cobb, an expert
on the history of religious liberty, maintains that the American pattern of
religious freedom was "the most striking contribution of America to the science of Government."[4]

As dramatic and innovative as the Constitution was with respect to the
social organization of both religion and government, it appears that these
arrangements provoked relatively little struggle. Martin Marty notes that in
only three of the thirteen original states was there much resistance to these
First Amendment provisions.[5] Further, "in most other colonies the change
was made as if with a sigh of relief, in a spirit of tidying up, and with only
whimpers of reactions."[6]

[4]Quoted in Martin E. Marty, *Righteous Empire* (New York: Dial Press, 1970), p. 36.
[5]Ibid., p. 37.
[6]Ibid.

This is not to suggest of course that the First Amendment resolved all the issues. Part of the problem is its brevity and vagueness. As Joseph Tuss-man states:

> The First Amendment in its attractive brevity leaves much unstated and seems to take much for granted. Even its spirit is elusive. Is it a practical expression of "a religious people"? Or is it a tolerant statement of commitment to a secular experiment? Does it indeed put us "under God"? What is "establishment" and what is an "exercise" of religion? The Amendment does not explain itself.[7]

Although it would be of great help, it is impossible to "get into the mind," so to speak, of the framers of the Constitution and discover their intentions. Were they flaunting sociological realities? Or were they acknowledging them? That is, were they trying to do something that cannot be done—namely, separate religion from politics and government in society? Or, recognizing that interaction and overlap between the two is inevitable, were they simply trying to avoid excesses as the two spheres commingled?

Although throughout our history people have pointed to the First Amendment as evidence of an "official endorsement" of religion and have suggested that we are therefore fundamentally a religious people, it is not all that clear that the Founding Fathers were so much encouraging religion as they were trying to place some limitations on its power and influence. Clearly they did not want a repetition of early Massachusetts Bay Colony or Virginia at the national level. We need to remember that many of the Founding Fathers and framers of the Constitution were freethinkers, deists, and sons of the Enlightenment who doubted, if not rejected, much of traditional Christian orthodoxy. Further, at the official birth of the new nation relatively few of its citizens were formal members of churches.[8] Quite clearly the early emphasis seems to be one of limitation of religious power and influence rather than support and encouragement of such influence. If this is so, it represents quite a shift from the strong religious (Christian) influence in the early days of the colonies. Yet note the action of the Supreme Court fifty years later (1844) as it interprets the First Amendment. In 1831, Stephen Girard, a wealthy Philadelphian, provided in his will for the establishment of a college for orphans—on condition that although the orphans were to be taught the "purest principles of morality," no clergy members representing any religion whatsoever were to teach at, hold office in, or even visit the proposed institution. Daniel Webster, in challenging the will, stated: "No fault can be found with Girard for wishing a marble college to bear his name forever, but it is not valuable unless it has a fragrance of

[7]Joseph Tussman, *The Supreme Court on Church and State* (New York: Oxford University Press, 1962), p. xiii.

[8]According to the first U.S. Census in 1790, only 5 percent of U.S. citizens reported being members of churches.

Christianity about it. . . . A cruel experiment is to be made upon these orphans to ascertain whether they cannot be brought up without religion."[9]

The Supreme Court upheld Girard's will interpreting it as bearing no animosity to Christianity, but only to clergy, since nonclergy were left free to teach Christian principles. In fact, regarding the requirement that teachers in the school "instill into the minds of the scholars the purest principles of morality" the Court commented: "Where can the purest principles of morality be learned so clearly or so perfectly as from the New Testament?"[10] In other words, Christianity should be taught—by lay Christians instead of clergy if necessary. Quite clearly there was a Christian bias abroad in the land, and it was certainly encouraged by the Supreme Court's interpretation of the Constitution.

Two summary observations can be made at this point: First, despite the constitutional prohibitions against the establishment of a state church, the history of our society evidences strong favor toward religion—Christianity in particular. Second, opinion regarding how and to what extent the state is to be allowed to exercise its support for religion has fluctuated. Although we lack the space to document this point in detail, some semblance of a pendulum motion has been in operation throughout our history in terms of degree of involvement in and support for religion on the part of the state and political elements.

The United States' original Protestant-Christian bias was challenged and broadened by waves of Roman Catholic and Jewish immigrants in the nineteenth and early twentieth centuries and later by agnostics and secularists. Mormons demanded the right to practice polygamy as a free exercise of their religion, but ultimately they were denied it. John T. Scopes taught evolution in a Tennessee high school in contradiction to fundamentalist Christianity and although a loser in court, was granted by many a "moral" victory because of the national publicity and lampooning of the prosecution by the press. Prohibition came and went. Oregon required that every child be educated in its public schools, but the Supreme Court declared religious (parochial) schools a valid alternative (1925). And so the pendulum has swung. To a great extent the problem centers around balancing the requirement of nonestablishment of religion and its inherent neutrality stance, on the one hand, with providing opportunity for free exercise of religion on the other. When the state emphasizes neutrality, its action is interpreted by some as antagonism. When the state encourages free exercise, it is accused of establishment. For example, if the state says it cannot allow observance of Christmas in public schools lest it thereby favor Christianity, objectors claim that their freedom to act out their religious convictions wherever they may be is infringed upon. If Christmas observances are

[9]Quoted in Tussman, *The Supreme Court*, pp. 5–6.
[10]Quoted in ibid., p. 6.

allowed, members of non-Christian religions or those with no religious affiliation or commitment cry "foul" and "establishment of religion." Quite obviously, the First Amendment provides the political system with a built-in dilemma that will never be fully resolved. And so the problem of separating religion from other social phenomena, which we earlier branded as sociologically impossible in the first place, is now merely compounded.

THE FRONTIER CHALLENGE

We mentioned in the preceding section that the Constitution's disestablishment of religion demanded innovation on the part of religious groups if they were to thrive—or perhaps just to survive. This need to innovate was significantly compounded by the opening of the frontier and increased westward migration. In a sense, the frontier almost immediately presented opportunities for religious groups to "test their mettle," so to speak. Here was territory. Here were people. And no one religious group had a monopoly on either.

Frontier Conditions

A number of characteristics of the frontier and the people who ventured there are of direct relevance both to the response and to the success or failure of religious groups in the frontier environment. One obvious feature was a sparse population located in small, widely separated settlements. This situation fostered among frontier settlers loneliness and the need for emotional outlets. These factors gave rise to an essential requirement of frontier life—a spirit of independence and self-sufficiency. If frontier settlers were going to make it, they had to do it on their own. Further, in the absence of external restraints, of social-control mechanisms for monitoring people's behavior, the task of checking antisocial behavior fell to control mechanisms internal to the individual. Overarching all this was another factor—namely, the constant threat of physical danger and insecurity, whether from disease, accident, inadequate food supply, Indian raids, or fellow citizens turned brigand. A final feature of the frontier worth mentioning is the fact that the frontier effected selective migration. Those who traveled westward were not a representative cross section of the inhabitants of the eastern seaboard. Rather, the roads west tended to fill up with those who had less at stake on the east coast—specifically, those of lower socioeconomic status and with little education. Not all of the latter traveled west of course, but primarily those with an adventuresome spirit, a willingness to work, and long-range aspirations.

Responses by Organized Religion

The established social institutions on the east coast, particularly the churches, were generally ill equipped to meet the combination of challenges that were described. The established eastern churches, which were of the denominational type, tended to require a trained, professional full-time clergy member to head a self-supporting congregation. They were used to meeting in a specially dedicated, permanent facility containing the standard accoutrements—pews, hymnbooks, a pulpit, and perhaps a keyboard instrument. Transplanting this pattern to the frontier was infeasible, if for no other reason than a sparse population with little ready cash could not support such a standard religious organization.

Recognizing this problem, some eastern ecclesiastical leaders and organizations turned to sponsoring revivals and camp meetings (occasional gatherings of large groups of people at a central location for several days of spiritual exhortation and instruction)—techniques that were actually better suited to such emerging sectarian groups as the Methodists and the Baptists. Nevertheless, as a result for a brief period after the Revolution there occurred what came to be known as the Second Great Awakening. (The First Great Awakening began in 1734 in New England with the evangelistic preaching of Jonathan Edwards, George Whitfield, and others, and spread through the colonies in the 1730s to 1750s). This general religious revival was epitomized in the Cane Ridge, Kentucky, camp meeting of 1801, which 20,000 persons are estimated to have attended. Considering the sparse population of "the West" at that time, this is an impressive number that says a great deal about the eagerness of people for human contact, for an emotional outlet, and probably for many if not most, for religious participation and expression as well. The Second Great Awakening was relatively short-lived, however, and produced no durable institutional forms.

The Baptist and Methodist Solutions

So far as religion was concerned, the Methodists and the Baptists became the inheritors of the frontier, for they were better able than the established churches to meet the challenges and brave the conditions of the frontier by innovative strategies. Thus, the Methodists, who had numbered approximately 9,000 in 1776, grew to become the largest religious group in the country by 1850. Baptist growth was nearly as great. There is no doubt, then, about their rapid success. But why? What exactly did they do? The answer is basically twofold: (1) Both groups developed innovative organizational structures for reaching widely scattered people and (2) as sects they had rejected many traditional denominational patterns and seemed capable of adapting to and growing up with the frontier. As a consequence, they enjoyed a response among frontier settlers that the established denominations could not elicit.

First, regarding strategy, the Methodists employed the technique of the *circuit-riding preacher.* Initially these were men with some theological training who were commissioned as missionaries to the frontier by John Wesley in England or by Bishop Asbury, John Wesley's representative in the colonies and then in the states. Their strategy was simply to go from house to house preaching the Gospel within the family setting, delivering sermons from a tree stump or wagon bed when a larger group could be gathered, creating "Methodists" as they went. They asked little more than food and shelter from those who received them. Periodically they would return on their circuit to rally the faithful, solemnize marriages, and conduct baptisms. They traveled thousands of miles a year along circuits that took a minimum of three to four weeks, and often a month or two, to complete.

The Baptists settled on a different, though equally successful, approach—the *lay preacher,* a farmer or craftsman for six days, a preacher for one. The success of this technique required only a concentration of a few families on adjoining farms or in a small village. The genius of the Baptist plan was that it required no recruitment from the outside. Anyone with a "call" from God to preach and with some oratorical and pedagogical ability could do it. The people whom such lay preachers gathered together began to think of themselves as Baptists.

And so the Baptist and Methodist sects grew. But these groups had more going for them than their strategies for overcoming the problem of sparse populations. The preachers were like their flocks—largely uneducated and independent of spirit—and knew "where the people were coming from," so to speak. They could communicate. And they encouraged emotional response and involvement in everyone. Religion for them was not a spectator sport. Revival services were frequent and they were popular, for they met people's need for emotional release. The democratic slant of these sects—which included the concepts that anyone could interpret Scripture as God directed him (no women were in the clergy role yet) and that parents were responsible for the spiritual welfare of their own children between visits by the circuit rider or Sunday gatherings for worship—agreed with the individualism and self-sufficiency of the frontier settlers. The typical emphasis of these sects on internal controls in the face of all manner of temptations to sin meshed well with the need for such internal controls in the absence of external ones.

Later Religious Responses

As the harshness of the frontier waned, as towns developed, and as social structures became more stabilized, further developments arose in the religious life of the frontier. For one thing, the Methodists and the Baptists consolidated their gains, for as people improved their lot and their communities became more firmly established, they did not suddenly forsake the religious group that had been serving them well. In great part such continuity was maintained because the Methodist and the Baptist religious groups evolved and developed along with the frontier. Originally sects, they became full-fledged denominations. More attention was paid to theological training, colleges and seminaries were established throughout the Midwest, circuit riders became resident clergymen, part-time Sunday preachers became full-time ministers.

As more middle-class business and professional people came west, the established eastern denominations followed and built their churches in the growing towns. Some of the upwardly mobile early settlers joined these "higher-status" Episcopalian, Presbyterian, and Congregational churches, though not in sufficient numbers to erode seriously the membership gains the Baptists and Methodists had already made.

As the nineteenth century neared and passed midpoint, groups of Lutherans from Germany and the Scandinavian countries came to settle and tame the farmland of the Midwest and the north-central United States. They brought their churches with them and by virtue of different language and religion remained relatively isolated from those Protestants who had preceded them. Catholics came also in substantial numbers and established their ethnically oriented churches in both urban and rural areas. Thus, the frontier was becoming religiously diverse primarily through the immigration of groups from outside the United States.

A pair of unique frontier phenomena need yet to be mentioned. One was the emergence of two new denominations that were born essentially as denominations and did not follow the sect-to-denomination evolutionary route. These were the Disciples of Christ and the Churches of Christ. Both groups downplayed denominational differences and stepped into the developing towns and cities as the frontier moved ever westward, picking up some of the people left behind as many of the Methodist and Baptist preachers moved on to follow the scattering pioneers. These groups formed what today are often called "community" churches or "nondenominational" churches that preach an "average" Protestantism and express little interest in the denominational "brand name" a member may have had before. Many of these preachers were dissident Methodists, Baptists, and Presbyterians who did not wish to be regarded as comprising yet another denomination but did so nonetheless.

The other unique frontier religious phenomenon was the Church of Jesus Christ of Latter-Day Saints (Mormons), founded by Joseph Smith in western New York State in the early 1840s. This group, regarded by some outsiders as neither Protestant nor even Christian, experienced serious opposition from an alliance of established Protestant denominations and growing Protestant sects who otherwise only competed among themselves. To escape harassment that often reached violent proportions, the Mormons moved from New York to Ohio to Missouri to Illinois and finally to Utah. But even the Mormons, which were probably best viewed as a religious cult in the beginning, evolved. Today the Mormon church is generally acknowledged to belong among the ranks of standard religious denominations, even though it is more aggressive in proselytizing than many of the latter.

THE ORDEAL OF PLURALISM

Anti-Catholicism

Although there had really never been much doubt, by the beginning of the nineteenth century the new American nation saw itself as definitely a Protestant domain. Probably this is one important reason why citizens generally accepted so graciously the radically new concept of separation of church and state enunciated in the First Amendment. Of the approximately four and one-half million citizens at the birth of the nation, estimates suggest there were only about twenty thousand Roman Catholics—a small minority indeed. Not that they were ignored. In fact, they were almost universally mistrusted. Small wonder, then, at the chagrin, uneasiness, and outright fear many citizens experienced and expressed as substantial immigration of Roman Catholics from Ireland, Germany, and Eastern Europe began in the 1830s.

The First Amendment's protection of the free exercise of religion was now to be put to its first serious test. The concept of *religious pluralism*, of freedom of religious expression and conviction and of tolerance of religious diversity to which Protestants had paid lip service, now became a bitter pill for the many spokespeople for and supporters of the view that the United States was God's Protestant kingdom on earth. Not only were substantial efforts expended in trying to amend immigration laws to keep Catholics out of this country or, failing that, to convert them to Protestantism and thereby dilute their "poison," but the society witnessed several decades of physical abuse directed against Catholics in the middle of the nineteenth century.

Martin Marty points out that the anti-Catholic agitators had deep reservoirs of suspicion from which to draw. He summarizes the historical setting as follows:

> The original colonists had felt themselves beleaguered, with French Catholics to the north and Spanish-Portuguese Catholics to the south. They had emotionally protected themselves against Catholic intrusions into the thirteen colonies. Where possible they isolated the Catholics, mostly in Maryland. Where necessary they began to accept them, as in the case of prestigious families like the Carrolls. But with few Catholics on the scene, it had been easy for colonial

parsons to exaggerate stories of Catholic superstition and horror; no one was around to refute them. People could thus constantly reaffirm the prejudices their fathers had brought with them from England and elsewhere across the Atlantic.

As the 20,000 or 25,000 colonial Roman Catholics grew to a body of 40,000 at the beginning of the [nineteenth] century and multiplied forty times by 1850 to 1,606,000, there were ever-increasing levels of animus and threat in the Protestant rhetoric.[11]

Reacting to this dramatic upsurge in Catholic immigration, a few outspoken propagandists—such as Samuel F. B. Morse, who painted visions of a foreign conspiracy based in the Vatican to take over America—were able to render Protestant Americans ready to believe almost anything. By midcentury the nativist Know-Nothing political party was formed with anti-Catholicism as one of its unifying themes. At this point we observe the blooming of what R. A. Billington terms the "Protestant Crusade."[12] At the heart of this "Crusade" were Protestants who felt threatened by the waves of Catholic immigration and were willing to believe most any accusation or innuendo about Catholics. Occasionally they reacted both impetuously and violently. There was, for example, Louisville's "Bloody Monday"—August 5, 1855—in which more than twenty persons were killed and several hundred wounded. This was a conflict between Protestants and Catholics—the former having been aroused by a "no-popery" campaign carried on by the *Louisville Journal*, all within the context of the notoriously anti-Catholic Know-Nothing political party and philosophy. The Philadelphia riots of 1844 represented an earlier case of anti-Catholicism that saw Catholic churches destroyed and the homes of Catholics burned, not to mention considerable bloodshed.

It appears that Roman Catholics in this country may have unwittingly and quite coincidentally provided some fuel for the Protestant fires that were smoldering. Consider, for example, the Philadelphia trustee conflict of the 1820s within the Roman Catholic church, which revolved around the question of whether church property should be controlled by trustees representing laypeople or by the bishop of the diocese. The issue dated back to 1808, when St. Mary's Cathedral had been erected by the congregation and control of the property had been vested in a board of lay trustees instead of the bishop, as was usual. The long battle, during which the priest of the congregation was excommunicated, ended in 1830. The church was placed under an interdict, which caused members to abandon it for other churches and thus forced the trustees, left without financial support, to submit to the bishop.

[11]Marty, *Righteous Empire*, pp. 127–128.
[12]Ray Allen Billington, *The Protestant Crusade, 1800–1860* (Gloucester, MA: Peter Smith, 1963).

This Philadelphia controversy did American Catholicism much harm. It attracted the hostile attention of the entire nation, inspired a great deal of "bad press" and negative literature, and left the impression in the minds of many Protestants that Catholicism was the sworn enemy of democratic institutions and thus a dangerous influence in the United States.[13] Ironically, the Philadelphia episode in fact marked an attempt by Catholic laypeople to pattern their church after typically American Protestant autonomous churches and to establish an independent Catholic church in America.[14]

Opposition by Catholics to the reading of the "Protestant" King James Version of the Bible in New York public schools, Protestant resentment and suspicion of the Catholic parochial schools as "un-American" and subversive, Catholic bloc voting as evidence of considerable political strength, "native American" resentment of "cheap" Irish Catholic labor—all are factors that have contributed to anti-Catholicism in this country.

By the Civil War, anti-Catholic sentiment had lost much of its intensity. And the war itself certainly diverted energy and attention away from the issue. After the war, Catholic immigration proceeded steadily and then soared in the late 1800s with the arrival of waves of southern and eastern European Catholics. By now, lacking evidence of any "papal plot," American Protestants established a somewhat uneasy but workable peace with their Catholic fellow citizens. The flames of conflict have been kindled sporadically ever since, however, over such issues as public aid to parochial schools, birth control and abortion, and official government or presidential representation to the Vatican. But as we will observe in Chapter 13, the animosities have been greatly reduced.

Anti-Semitism

The issue of religious pluralism and the challenge to Protestant domination was not limited to Catholic-Protestant relations. Significant numbers of Jews also immigrated to the United States between 1880 and the First World War. Until that time there had been relatively so few Jews in this country—in 1815, for example, there were only about three thousand—that they were not regarded as a threat to established Protestantism. Although Jews had been excluded from full political participation in some of the colonies (for example, Virginia) by Trinitarian belief requirements, and although the depiction of Jews in the denominational literature of that period would today properly be termed anti-Semitic, the small number of Jews elicited little explicit reaction from their fellow citizens. Anti-Semitism in this country began in earnest with the substantial immigration of Russian

[13]Ibid., pp. 38–40.
[14]Will Herberg, *Protestant, Catholic, Jew* (Garden City, NY: Doubleday, 1956), p. 140.

Jews in the 1880s, when the Ku Klux Klan made anti-Semitism one of its major stances. Many of the Jews who immigrated to the United States after 1880, although often quite secularized (and sometimes politically radical), retained their ethnic identity, settling almost exclusively in urban areas and engaging in mutual assistance in establishing business enterprises. Other ethnic groups and Protestant "native Americans" began to resent their presence, and anti-Semitism began to surface. Jews thus found it necessary to establish various defense organizations, of which the Anti-Defamation League of the B'nai B'rith is the best known.

Anti-Semitism came to be a significant feature of American life—one that though significantly diminished is still alive today. Anti-Semitism probably reached its zenith in this country in the 1920s and 1930s, when anti-Semitic newspapers and radio columnists proliferated and reached out into many American homes. Such strident anti-Semitism has been relegated to the fringes of our society today, and many of the most blatant forms of anti-Semitic discrimination in housing, education, employment, and voluntary-association membership have been eliminated. Yet as recently as 1960, during a two-month period, 643 incidents of anti-Jewish swastika painting on synagogue walls, vandalism against Jewish property, and beatings of Jews were recorded in the United States.[15]

Studies by Glock and Stark and Bernard Olson have shown a connection between conservative Protestant theology and anti-Semitism, though the nature of this connection and its intensity is not clear.[16] A serious difficulty arises in trying to separate what we might call *social anti-Semitism*—hatred of Jews as social beings, as persons—from *religious anti-Semitism*, which from the conservative Christian viewpoint is the concept that Jews need salvation and that it will be denied them until they accept Jesus as Savior. Unfortunately, these two "types" of anti-Semitism, although undoubtedly intermingled in many cases, are not adequately distinguished in existing measures and indexes of anti-Semitism.

Other groups, of course, come in for their share of aspersion and harassment. We have already mentioned the Mormons, who were literally forced to flee for their lives to new territory, ultimately standing their ground in the Utah Territory. Similar though not so violent harassment has been directed against Jehovah's Witnesses in many communities. It is interesting from the sociological perspective to note that both these groups traditionally engage in vigorous conversion and missionary activities. That is, they implicitly reject the pluralism concept that includes respect for every other group's autonomy and right to be and do as it chooses. Whereas adherence to the spirit of pluralism demands that one accept diversity—in

---

[15]Charles Y. Glock and Rodney Stark, *Christian Beliefs and Anti-Semitism* (New York: Harper & Row, 1966), p. xi.
[16]Ibid. and Bernard Olson, *Faith and Prejudice* (New Haven: Yale University Press, 1963).

fact, that one champion it—these groups actively seek to bring everyone into their ranks—an aggressive stance that undoubtedly encourages resentment. Even German Lutherans who during World War I persisted in using the German language in their worship services and conversation were harassed in some communities.

The outcome of the religious pluralism controversy in this country has, however, been the triumph of pluralism and the peaceful acceptance of religious diversity by nearly all. This of course has not stopped many religious groups from actively proselytizing and openly criticizing the theology of other religious groups. But the practice of taking the process a step further by associating what appears theologically inadequate or incorrect from one's religious perspective with "un-Americanism," inferior citizenship, subversion, and the like has been significantly reduced.

RELIGIOUS SOCIAL CONCERN

The second half of the nineteenth century marked the beginning of a highly significant controversy within American Protestantism that continues today—a fundamental argument over the proper focus of Christianity. In simplest terms, should the focus be the salvation of souls or the improvement of society? Although few if any proponents of either alternative would have asserted that Christianity should exclusively be devoted to one or the other goal, the controversy tended to place most Christians, theologian and layperson alike, into one camp or the other.

This period is known for the emergence of the so-called *social gospel* and the rise of such proponents of socially concerned Christianity as Horace Bushnell, Walter Rauschenbusch, and Washington Gladden. These were people who argued that Christianity is neither fulfilled nor true to its origins and history unless and until it immerses itself in alleviating the world's miseries and social pathologies—social problems that emerged with advancing industrialization, increasing urbanization, and the appearance, already then, of decay in portions of the mushrooming cities. These spokesmen contended that their emphasis on social responsibility was the old, authentic emphasis of the Bible. They pointed to the prophets in the Old Testament Scriptures and to Jesus in the New Testament Gospels, who evidenced great concern for the physical and social needs and problems of people. On the other side, those who stressed the more individualistic, salvation-centered focus for Christianity tended to stress the emphasis of the New Testament Epistles of Paul on the atonement of Jesus and his rescue of people from the wrath of a just and judging God.

Although we will look more thoroughly into this controversy in its present-day form in Chapter 14, we want at least to highlight at this point the emergence of the "new" emphasis in Christianity (or, as many contended, the resurgence of the original one) that loomed so significantly during the last century. Although it did not turn American religion completely around, for some individuals and groups it did radically change the focus and purpose of religion; at the very least, it added a new dimension.

The establishment of hospitals, orphanages, and settlement houses, and the formation of groups such as the Salvation Army occurred after the Industrial Revolution was solidly under way and many of the latter's excesses and abuses were clearly seen adversely affecting great numbers of people. It is important to note, however, that the emphasis of religious people during the period of western industrialization was primarily an individualized one. That is, the primary concern of religious leaders was with helping individuals. First of all, they wanted to save the individual's soul. But then, out of compassion for those persons living a materially disadvantaged existence, they began establishing institutions and mechanisms for the purpose of helping the body. But again, just as the concern was for the souls of individual people, so the concern was for individual bodies. The social service activities of salvation-oriented religious groups, already begun in the 1820s, continued into the early part of the twentieth century. The emphasis was essentially that of John Wesley in the eighteenth century—concern for individuals, that is, replacing individual vices with individual virtues, changing the direction of individuals from hell to heaven, making physically healthy bodies out of ill and broken ones.

Later, other religious leaders, such as the aforementioned Bushnell, Rauschenbusch, and Gladden, began to direct primary attention away from salvation and toward physical and social well-being; above all, they began to shift the focus from individual vices to societal ones. That is, they saw the locus of social problems not in individuals but in society and in institutional structures and patterns beyond the immediate control of individuals. To these social reformers the goal was one of "Christianizing" the social order, of applying the teachings of Jesus to the social and economic institutions of the society, of reforming the social environment in which people lived and worked. They expounded what came to be known as the social gospel.

Those who followed in the footsteps of the earlier, individual-oriented religious leaders became increasingly uneasy with the social gospel, which they felt operated at the expense of individual salvation—the preeminent responsibility of Christianity, in their view. Influential evangelistic preachers who emphasized individual salvation such as Dwight L. Moody and Billy Sunday thus began challenging the social gospel and in fact essentially carried the day so far as rank-and-file preachers and church members were concerned. Martin Marty reports how the flamboyant evangelist Sunday took on the most noted advocate of the social gospel still at work in the parish ministry, Washington Gladden:[17]

---

[17]Most of the social-gospel advocates were seminary professors, editors, authors, and the like who remained largely unknown to the rank-and-file church member.

The setting of their encounter was Columbus, Ohio, where Gladden had piled up a record of achievement in a socially oriented ministry over three decades. But when Sunday came to town to carry on one of his pro-evangelistic and apparently "antisocial" revivals, Gladden quietly opposed him, and after the revival, Gladden was more outspoken over the meager returns he saw garnered from Sunday's raucous efforts. But Gladden was attacked by the vast majority of Columbus's ministers of all Protestant denominations. They rose to the defense of Sunday's approach and clearly identified with the conversionism of the revivalist.[18]

In their attempts to discredit the social gospel, the individual-oriented evangelists began to pull back from and react against social service and welfare activities that they had earlier engaged in and rededicated themselves to efforts to win souls and raise levels of individual morality by means of such tactics as emphasizing the evil of "demon rum" and supporting the Prohibition movement. The social-gospel wing of American Christianity did not disappear, however. It continued with minority support in the major denominations and through the various agencies of the Federal Council of Churches (now the National Council of Churches) that had been founded in 1908 primarily by social-gospel forces.

Thus, the social-gospel movement did not wither away; in fact, it has continued to exert significant influence in American religion up to the present. It enjoyed a resurgence with its involvement in the civil rights movement in the 1950s and 1960s and in the war on poverty of the 1960s and 1970s, although with what still appears to have been a minority of church member support. There will be more on this issue in Chapter 14.

Reconciling the great diversity of opinion and practice regarding social versus individual emphases is of course not uniquely a problem of religious institutions. Religious groups have in fact always reflected the historical ambivalence in American society at large regarding rugged individualism, self-sufficiency, and individual responsibility versus social concerns, welfarism, and mutual responsibility for one's fellow human beings. This could hardly be better exemplified than in the recent memory of the reader as religious and political conservatives push to slow down and remove welfare and aid programs of many types, put curbs on minority rights and funding for abortions and sex education, and promote other actions championed by the so-called Moral Majority, which was renamed the Liberty Federation in 1986.

THE POST-WORLD WAR II REVIVAL

Following the Second World War the United States experienced what came to be known as a religious "revival." Beginning in the late 1940s and extend-

[18]Marty, *Righteous Empire*, p. 183.

ing into the 1950s, church membership and attendance soared, contributions to religious organizations poured in, literally thousands of new congregations were established and quickly became self-supporting, and the value of new construction by religious groups increased dramatically, year after year. Some data will document this growth. Between 1940 and 1950 membership in churches rose from 49 to 57 percent of the population, and by 1959 had reached 63.6 percent.[19] Gallup poll data show a comparable increase in church attendance—whereas only 36 percent of the sample in 1942 reported having attended a church service during the week preceding the interview, by 1957 the figure had risen to 51 percent.[20] The value of new construction of religious facilities totaled $28 million in 1935, during the depth of the Depression, and had increased to $59 million by 1940. But the really big increase was still to come—in 1950 the value of new construction was $409 million, and by 1965 the figure reached $1.2 billion. The religion business was indeed a booming one.

Further, there developed what William Lee Miller has called our national "piety along the Potomac," which included Bible breakfasts, congressional prayer groups, and a president named Eisenhower who made numerous religious allusions in his speeches and was himself baptized in the White House following his inauguration.[21] Postage stamps and folding money suddenly began to include "In God We Trust" on their faces. We inserted the phrase "under God" in the Pledge of Allegiance. Popular music and movie extravaganzas followed religious themes. Books of a religious, devotional, or inspirational nature proliferated, and many even made the best-seller lists.

The opening passage of this section referred to a religious "revival." At least this is what many called it. Many churchmen who saw their churches filling up, who saw massive building programs quickly underwritten with cash and pledges, who noted their denominations annually opening new mission congregations numbering in the dozens and even hundreds can hardly be blamed for speaking in such terms. Finally their sermons and various other efforts in a lifetime of dedication to religion were bearing some tangible fruit. Religion was really "catching on" and getting through to people. Observing these phenomena sociologically, however, we should be more cautious in assessing what was going on. As A. Roy Eckardt observes, there was "a manifest upsurge of *interest* in religion."[22] Whether this reflected a true revival in the sense of increasing dedication and commitment is difficult if not impossible to determine.

---

[19]Benson Y. Landis, ed., *Yearbook of American Churches 1964* (New York: National Council of Churches in the U.S.A., 1964), p. 290.

[20]Ibid., p. 283.

[21]William Lee Miller, "Piety Along the Potomac," *The Reporter*, August 17, 1954, p. 25.

[22]A. Roy Eckhardt, *The Surge of Piety in America* (New York: Association Press, 1958), p. 17.

What we do know is that the period following World War II found many more people within our national boundaries, as millions of service-men and women returned home and as the baby boom of the 1940s got underway. A fantastic building boom accompanied the population growth as many new and some older families moved to the suburbs in search of a place to start a new life. Church facilities that had barely sufficed during a Depression and a world war (when there was relatively little new construc-tion) clearly came up short in the face of population and residential expan-sion. New church facilities were built where the new people now were. In some cases this meant a net gain, as the old facilities in the city remained and new facilities were built near the edges of the spreading suburban frontier. In other instances it was a trade. The downtown and inner-city churches were abandoned for the new, as a majority of the people moved out, or the former were sold for a few cents on the dollar to the sects that emerged to serve the migrants (primarily blacks) who replaced the mobile, more afflu-ent whites who left—a prime example of human ecological succession.

We do know that the United States was trying to piece itself together again after a long, harsh Depression and an expensive, grief-filled war. No doubt countless people were seeking moorings, eternal verities upon which they could start building something new. Paul Hutchinson wrote in 1955 about the "cult of reassurance," which he described as

> a flocking to religion, especially in middle-class circles, for a renewal of confi-dence and optimism at a time when these are in short supply. It is a turning to the priest for encouragement to believe that, despite everything that has hap-pened in this dismaying century, the world is good, life is good, and the hu-man story makes sense and comes out where we want it to come out.[23]

Further, there was in the postwar years the unsettled state of mind caused by the specter of the atomic bomb and the uneasiness of what was termed the "menace" of communism. Many people were undoubtedly seek-ing a firm base on which to stand and a clear perspective from which to evaluate what was happening.

Yet we cannot help but return to our prior comments about the grow-ing population, and above all the suburban migration trends. Without a doubt something quite sociological and not particularly religious was going on as people got involved in building churches and attending them once they were built. These people were in a new place; they had left their neigh-borhoods of many years, perhaps even of their childhood; they were tem-porarily without friends or voluntary-association outlets and involvements; they were looking for human contact. A ready place which developed early in the suburban development to resolve some of these needs and problems was the church. In a real sense, the idea of religion as an integrating mech-

[23]Quoted in ibid., p. 28.

anism in society has definite meaning and relevance here—religion provided social contacts, outlets, and activities for people that were quite apart from strictly religious functions or concerns.

At the height of the religious "revival" Will Herberg suggested another partial explanation for the rise of religious interest. His suggestion revolves around the third-generation hypothesis, which says that while the children of immigrants strive to deny their heritage in their struggle to "match up" to what they perceive to be true American standards and characteristics, the grandchildren (the third generation), quite secure in their Americanism, look for further identity, for a heritage and a link with the past. This, Herberg feels, is available for nearly all Americans in religion, specifically the three equally alternative religions of our contemporary society—Protestantism, Catholicism, and Judaism. Since in the latter half of the twentieth century we in the United States constitute essentially a nation of third-generation or later-generation Americans, it is therefore not surprising to see a renewal of interest in religion—a heightened interest not strictly for "religious" reasons, but for social and psychological reasons as well, as people try to identify what they are besides "just an American."[24]

Certainly some reservations are in order concerning how paramount religious identity is for the majority of people. If asked, "What are you?" would not more people respond in terms of their occupation rather than their religion? It is nevertheless likely that, for some people at least, religious identity has come to serve as an important link with the past and as a source of present identity.

At this point we refer the reader back to our discussion in Chapter 4 and a problem inherent in the measurement of religiosity. Most of the discussion of religious revival has centered around rather low-powered measures, such as church attendance and membership. There has been little assessment of changes in intensity of religious feeling or meaning, or changes in what people believed in and are committed to (ideological dimension), or changes in behavior as a result of religious influences (consequential dimension). Thus even if we could agree that a religious revival occurred in the United States from approximately 1945 to 1965, we may be referring to little more than what Eckardt noted—an increased *interest* in religion. And this may be somewhat of an overstatement. For example, what does an increase in church membership mean? In part it reflects the fact that requirements for church membership have in many groups become progressively less demanding and restrictive. That is, it appears to be easier to become a church member. Further, the high degree of geographic mobility of people during this period in our history, coupled with the tardiness of most local congregations to clear their membership lists of dropouts and people who have moved away, have undoubtedly resulted in some—in certain cases per-

---

[24]Herberg, *Protestant, Catholic, Jew*, pp. 272–275.

haps considerable—duplication hidden in comprehensive church membership figures. That is, it is likely that some people were counted two or three times within a given year's totals.

There is no point here in going further in expressing our uneasiness with unqualified assertions of a postwar religious revival, for we have made our basic point.[25] That is, although there appears to have been a definite upswing in religious interest in the post-World War II period, the upswing may not have been so great or significant as some have supposed. In a sense, religion became more highly visible. It was no longer contained solely within the walls of religious organizations. It hit the jukeboxes, the movie theaters, and the drugstore paperback bookracks. Religion was popularized, and it impinged on everyone's consciousness—much as any fad does. Just as any fad, however, some of the glitter and popularity began to fade. Glock and Stark even suggest that, solely in response to wide publicity given church membership growth in the late 1940s, there was "generated a commercial interest in producing and promoting religious literature, songs and plays with a religious motif, and commodities having religious connotations."[26] That is, commercial interests saw a new market, and the resultant visibility of religion through commercial exploitation tended to exaggerate the level of religious interest actually felt and expressed by people.

Although we could now proceed to examine developments in American religion following the postwar religious "revival" and thus bring our discussion up to date, we shall delay such an examination until Chapter 14. In that chapter we shall go into greater detail concerning the contemporary religious scene and what developed out of the postwar religious "revival" period. We now proceed in the next chapter to discuss unique religious patterns on the American scene, namely, black religion and native American religion.

[25] Additional questions are raised by Charles Y. Glock, "The Religious Revival in America?" in *Religion and the Face in America*, ed. Jane Zahn (Berkeley: University Extension, University of California, 1959); Seymour Martin Lipset, "Religion in America: What Religious Revival?" *Columbia University Forum* 11, no. 2 (1959); and W. H. Hudson, "Are Churches Really Booming?" *Christian Century* 72, no. 51 (1955), 1494–1496.

[26] Charles Y. Glock and Rodney Stark, *Religion and Society in Tension* (Chicago: Rand McNally, 1965), p. 78.

12

Black and Native American Religion in America

In Chapter 9, we introduced the subject of religion and the black American. We focused both on the historical issue once facing American Christians of whether to convert black slaves to Christianity and on the more recent issue of the relationship of white churches to the black civil rights movement. In the present chapter, we wish to pick up at the historical point when the issue of the conversion of slaves had been resolved and trace the development of the black church as a social institution. In doing so we will work within three major sections: an overview of the historical development of the institution; an examination of the role of militancy versus social pacifism so far as the black church is concerned; and a discussion of contemporary religious issues and developments within the black church and the black community, together with an assessment of the continuing role of religion in the black community. We will then review the impact of white colonization on Native American religion, consider some dominant features of Native American religion, and review the forms Native American religion has taken today.

THE HISTORICAL DEVELOPMENT OF THE BLACK CHURCH AS A SOCIAL INSTITUTION

Following the consensus in the United States around the turn of the nineteenth century that slaves should be converted to Christianity and still remain slaves, the early pattern of worship services found black slaves and whites in the same congregations—the blacks usually occupying the balcony, the whites the main floor. Such joint worship was deemed advisable because white masters could then keep an eye on their "possessions" and be reassured that their slaves were not listening to a different message—such as a call to insurrection.

The Deculturation Process

Whether slaveholders were always conscious of it or not, for blacks conversion to Christianity and joint worship served as part of the deculturation process. At the very least, religious conversion served as a useful follow-up and capstone to the deliberate efforts by slave traders and owners to deculturate the slaves, to strip them of their African culture and heritage. This was accomplished by such tactics as breaking up families and prohibiting any two slaves from the same African village or tribe to be sold to work on the same plantation. One highly significant concomitant of this tactic was that the slaves usually shared no common language and thus could only converse in the English language that they had to learn. In short, much of the original culture of these people was stripped from them in less than a generation.

Obviously, slaves could not very successfully preserve and practice many shared religious patterns either. Christianity, which was substituted for the ancient religions, itself became an agent for subduing and pacifying the slaves. What slaves heard preached was submission to authority, obedience, obligation to perform one's duty, commitment to nonviolence, and promise of splendid eternal rewards in heaven for all who led proper lives and made appropriate commitments during one's earthly sojourn. "Some God has made to be masters, some to be slaves. But we'll all receive a grand reward in the hereafter"—this is what has been waggishly referred to as "pie-in-the-sky by and by."

Kenneth Stampp has summarized well the use to which religion was put with regard to controlling the behavior of slaves:

> Through religious instruction the bondsmen learned that slavery had divine sanction, that insolence was as much an offense against God as against the temporal master. They received the Biblical command that servants should obey their masters, and they heard, too, that eternal salvation would be their reward for faithful service, and that on the day of judgment God would deal impartially with the poor and the rich, the black man and the white.[1]

Stampp also mentions a book titled *Suggestions on the Religious Instruction of the Negroes in the Southern States* written by Charles C. Jones and published by the national Presbyterian Board of Publication. Stampp cites Jones as

[1] Kenneth M. Stampp, *The Peculiar Institution* (New York: Knopf, 1956), p. 158.

advising missionaries to ignore the "civil condition" of slaves and to pay no attention to complaints against their masters. In preaching to slaves, ministers should condemn "every vice and evil custom," urge the "discharge of every duty," and support the "peace and order of society." They should, in sum, teach the slaves to give "respect and obedience [to] all those whom God in his providence has placed in authority over them."[2]

Emerging Independence of the Black Church

The early pattern of joint worship of masters and slaves in the same church did not remain the common one, probably in large part because the white masters wanted one message for their slaves, another for themselves. Therefore, another early pattern on the larger plantations was for the owner to provide special religious leaders and preachers for the slaves. These were not always white preachers, but occasionally trusted slaves who had a "gift" for preaching. Also fairly early, the Baptists and Methodists began missionary activities among the slaves, and they enjoyed considerable success—for many of the same reasons that they succeeded with white settlers on the frontier (see Chapter 11). Thus, the early pattern of joint worship in the same congregation was gradually replaced by segregated worship in white and black "congregations." Strictly speaking, except in the North and in a few border cities, slaves did not form their own independent congregations, largely because of laws forbidding slave assemblies. Informally, however, on many plantations essentially autonomous slave churches developed under "trusted" slave ministers. Of course, their services and activities were carefully monitored by the master or his overseer. Nevertheless, such congregations of slaves set the stage for the eventual emergence of the black church as the major formal group or organization over which blacks, after Emancipation, had essential control. Thus, we can begin to understand the importance and centrality that black religious organizations have assumed in the black community to this day.

Although for various reasons whites began to tolerate separate religious groups and activities for blacks, it was not without some apprehension. Richard Wade points out that as late as 1847 "many citizens" in Charleston expressed their discomfort over permitting religious institutions for blacks, particularly as it resulted in separate congregations. They feared the independence, the absence of the control and authority of the master, the taste of freedom it provided, and the opportunity for black leaders to emerge and learn skills.[3]

---

[2]Quoted in ibid., p. 160.

[3]Richard C. Wade, *Slavery in the Cities: The South, 1820–1860* (New York: Oxford University Press, 1964), p. 83.

In the North, after some initial integrated worship, free blacks began to pull out and form their own congregations and, soon, their own denominations. In fact, the earliest all-black denominations, the African Methodist Episcopal Zion Church and the African Methodist Episcopal Church, organized in 1796 and 1816, respectively, were founded by free blacks who had experienced harassment and "balcony segregation" in white congregations.

The Functions of the Black Church

After the Civil War and Emancipation, with most legal restrictions against black assemblies lifted, there occurred a mass withdrawal of blacks from racially mixed congregations and even denominations in order to form their own churches. What had begun as an outlet or escape and a focal institution for their lives under slavery continued to serve the same functions after Emancipation. Although the following evaluation by Richard Wade concerns the functions of religion for blacks under slavery, the pattern then established continued after Emancipation.

> Slavery had stripped [blacks] of any meaningful pattern of life beyond that of the master and their bondage. The family could furnish none. No tradition could provide roots into a history without servitude. Neither today nor tomorrow offered any expectation of a life without the present stigma. Deprived of nostalgia for the past and unable to discover any real meaning in the present, the blacks sought relief and consolation in a distant time. In the church, with their own kind, amid songs of redemption and the promises of Paradise, a lifeline could be thrown into the future.[4]

The prominent black leader and sociologist W. E. B. Du Bois states that once blacks assumed complete control over their church following Emancipation, the local black church became the center of its members' social life, the primary medium of communication and information exchange, and even the organizer of entertainment and amusement. With regard to the last function, he lists such activities and functions as concerts, suppers, socials, fairs, literary exercises and debates, cantatas, plays, excursions, picnics, and celebrations.[5]

Gunnar Myrdal describes the black church as a "community center par excellence."[6] In most black communities, the church was the only institution where blacks not only enjoyed autonomy and freedom from the prying eyes of whites but also had access to facilities in which to conduct social activities.

---

[4]Ibid., pp. 162–163.

[5]W. E. B. Du Bois, *The Philadelphia Negro* (Philadelphia: University of Pennsylvania, 1899), p. 201.

[6]Gunnar Myrdal, *An American Dilemma* (New York: Harper & Brothers, 1944), p. 938.

But to note such a function as this is only to begin to list the important roles of the religious group or institution in the life of black Americans. First there is the economic function: "A study of economic co-operation among Negroes," Du Bois has stated, "must begin with the church group."[7] Many black churches early formed mutual-aid or "beneficial" societies designed to help members survive financial crises associated with illness or death of family members. These were actually incipient insurance companies. In rural communities, the emphasis seemed to be particularly on burial "insurance" to provide the members with a "decent Christian burial."

The black churches have also played a significant role in education over the years. Frequently, black ministers established a school along with a church. Just as the original purpose of slave education had been to communicate the Christian Gospel and enable slaves to read the Bible, these minister-educators sought to raise the spiritual understanding of their people. When the Julius Rosenwald Fund aided in building over 5,000 schools for blacks in the South during the first third of the twentieth century, black churches played an important role in supplementing those funds—E. Franklin Frazier notes that southern blacks contributed 17 percent of the total cost of $28 million (Rosenwald Fund, 15 percent; white friends, 4 percent; taxes, 64 percent), and that they raised much of their share through church suppers and various other church-sponsored programs.[8]

There was also impetus among the black denominations following the Civil War to erect educational institutions independent of white philanthropy. This plan was primarily motivated by the desire to provide a better-educated ministry—a project Frazier feels was not eminently successful, since the black denominational schools "never attained a high level as educational institutions . . . [and] have generally nurtured a narrow religious outlook and have restricted the intellectual development of Negroes."[9] Frazier also notes that the authoritarian demeanor and antiintellectualism exhibited by many black ministers have tended to inhibit the black churches from making a strong, positive contribution to education.[10] In other words, although certainly contributing to educational advancement for blacks, the black church has not been as significant an influence in this sphere as it might have been.

Supporting the significance of the black church's role in educating blacks, however, Wade mentions that some of the pre-Emancipation opposition to independent black churches—or, for that matter, to Christianity for blacks at all—centered around the observation that some blacks were

[7]W.E.B. DuBois, *Economic Cooperation Among Negroes* (Atlanta: Atlanta University Press, 1907), p. 54.
[8]E. Franklin Frazier, *The Negro Church in America* (New York: Schocken, 1963), p. 40.
[9]Ibid., p. 41.
[10]Ibid., p. 42.

becoming literate in the process of their religious instruction. Many whites feared black literacy as much as black independence in their religious activities.[11]

A third area of influence and involvement on the part of the black religious institution has been politics. During the Reconstruction period several black ministers and bishops in the South became federal and state officials, state legislators, and U.S. congressmen, and one was elected a U.S. senator. With the end of Reconstruction and the resumption of white supremacy, however, blacks were virtually eliminated from public political life, and the black church then became, as Frazier observes, "the arena of . . . political activities" for black citizens.[12] As the sole major institution over which they had complete control, the church became the major context within which ambitious individuals could aspire to leadership and achieve distinction and status. In particular, the black church turned out to be the most likely source of power, upward mobility, and economic success for black males. Black churches thus soon overflowed with aspiring ministers, apprentice ministers, and "jackleg preachers" who literally waited in the wings for a chance to preach, prove their ability, and gather a following or congregation for themselves.

In the South, the church also presented the only outlet of political expression for the black rank and file, which was denied the franchise in local, state, and national elections. The only place they could vote and make significant choices was in their church—as they elected local officers and denominational representatives and engaged in debate over policies for their local church.

We must note also that as the franchise was granted or returned to blacks, particularly in the North, black churches became more politically involved than most of their white counterparts. Candidates for political office were frequently invited to speak in black churches during or after Sunday services, ministers urged their followers to vote for particular candidates, and partisan campaign literature was made available in church buildings—all to a greater extent than in white churches, most of which counseled keeping politics and religion separate.

Although no hard data on the frequency with which black churches were involved in politics are available from the distant past, 1963 data on black clergymen in Detroit reveal that 45.5 percent allowed political candidates access to their churches, 62.7 percent permitted distribution of campaign literature from their churches, 67.8 percent explicitly encouraged their members to work with the political parties in their neighborhoods, and 30.5 percent even told their members for whom they should vote. Further,

[11]Wade, *Slavery*, pp. 173–177.
[12]Frazier, *The Negro Church*, p. 43.

24.4 percent of black clergymen in Detroit had at some time actively worked for a political party at the local level.[13]

It is important to note that the more militantly committed a black cleric is to the civil rights movement and its goals, the more likely he or she is to engage in the political behaviors just cited. We will focus on important differences among contemporary black clergymen later in this chapter. At this point, we simply wish to document that the black church has been and continues to be a fairly active political organization. Although no comparable hard data for white churches are available, every indication is that, on the average, white churches have traditionally not been so politically involved. There has been some change here recently, as we have seen some clergy and churches become politically active over the abortion issue.

Finally, we must say that permeating all of the preceding functions of the black church is the fundamental function of representing what Frazier calls "a refuge in a hostile white world."[14] The black church has provided a structural context for interaction in which blacks could not only express their deepest feelings and longings but also attain some measure of status (in God's eyes, if in no one else's). Earlier, religion provided black slaves some catharsis as well as hope for eventual freedom, even though they were now in temporal bondage. Later, in a similar way, the "emancipated" blacks, after a brief opportunity to participate somewhat freely in the wider society during Reconstruction, were soon again excluded from participation in the white person's world except as inferiors. They were disfranchised, given a skimpy and inferior education, and accorded far less than justice by a court system that operated with a double standard of justice. These "emancipated" blacks needed escape and hope as much as their enslaved parents and grandparents before them. Where could a black find refuge amid such hostility and discrimination? The place was predominantly the church, which whites left alone.

Most of what we have been describing in the foregoing paragraphs applies most appropriately to the black church since the days of Reconstruction. During slavery, when the black church had to be the "invisible institution," there were many calls for freedom in black religion. Although it is difficult to distinguish whether calls for freedom in black slaves' religion were for ultimate spiritual freedom in heaven, or for temporal freedom from bondage, or perhaps a subtle and even unconscious combination of both ideas, there is evidence that black religion did encourage slaves' hopes of physical freedom. The leaders of the better-known slave uprisings, for example, used ample biblical imagery and justification for their actions. Consider, for example, the rebellion led by Nat Turner, himself a black

---

[13]Ronald L. Johnstone, "Militant and Conservative Community Leadership among Negro Clergymen" (Ph.D. dissertation, University of Michigan, 1963), pp. 126–127.

[14]Frazier, *The Negro Church*, p. 44.

minister. Moreover, some of the northern black churches composed of freed blacks stood squarely for slaves' freedom as they worked for the Underground Railroad.

But following the Civil War, when the issue was no longer slavery but the pervasive racism that securely kept blacks "in their place," whatever small amount of past protest and calls for freedom there had been receded in the face of escapist and otherworldly emphases. It is this post-Civil War pattern of black religion that nurtured the stereotype of the black church that so many whites cling to—the revivalist or sectarian emotionalism and escapism that an accommodating Uncle Tom, albeit a fiery and eloquent preacher, supervised and promoted. Here one sees the subservient, peacemaking, don't-rock-the-boat style of black ministers who knew only too well that their job was to keep their place, encourage submission and fatalistic acquiescence on the part of their congregations, and preach an otherworldly gospel. If they did their job well, their choir would receive an invitation to sing in white churches during the year, and they could look forward to a little free coal for the church and parsonage in the winter.[15]

The black church became overwhelmingly a haven where blacks could exercise autonomy but where there appeared to be little challenge to the status quo. In fact, the following observation by an anonymous black preacher probably conveys even more truth than humor: "Come weal or woe, my status is quo." Rare was the black minister who took up the banner of change or social revolution at the risk of losing a fairly comfortable position whose advantages included high personal status and power and income as great if not usually greater than most other blacks. Black ministers were also occasionally accused of being "bought off" by elements in the white power structure as they were accorded the courtesy of speaking for or representing the black community and serving as the funnel for the table crumbs of white philanthropy.

With little impetus for challenge and change coming from black ministers, who did reasonably well for themselves under a system of racism, and with the rank-and-file black church members finding solace, escape, recreation, and temporal autonomy in the black church, it is not surprising that the black church proceeded through the decades of segregation and discrimination tacitly approving, or at least certainly not openly challenging, prevailing social structures and patterns. Not that there were no voices of protest coming from the black church and its clergy. Not that black religion was totally acquiescent in the face of a dominant racism. On the contrary, there were definite protests and other forms of aggressive reaction in the name of religion. In fact, although we have been stressing the accommodating, other-worldly, withdrawal response of black religion—essentially the

[15]See Ronald L. Johnstone, "Negro Preachers Take Sides," *Review of Religious Research* 11, no. 1 (1969), 81.

sect approach—in the face of white racism and exclusion from the society's mainstream, there has always been a mildly aggressive and persistent reaction stemming from within the ranks of black religion.

MILITANCY IN THE BLACK CHURCH

The Father Divine Style

Four types of black religious aggressiveness in the face of racism can be distinguished.[16] One is typified by the Father Divine Peace Mission that flourished in the 1930s and early 1940s. Here was a religious group that provided blacks with food and occasional job opportunities during the Great Depression as many blacks migrated to northern cities in search of employment. Although the Father Divine Peace Mission presents a fascinating study in theology (Father Divine was viewed as God himself), our interest here is in the group's commitment to a social-service type of action that fed and housed thousands of needy persons over a period of years. Although of course this approach did not strike significantly at the root causes of problems facing black Americans and worked only at the remedial level of treating symptoms, there was here and in similar groups a clear manifestation of aggressiveness in the name of black religion. We are forced to conclude, however, that the net impact of such food and lodging efforts benefited only a few needy blacks.

The Black Nationalism Style

Another example of aggressiveness in the name of religion in the black community is similar to the foregoing, but more far-reaching and enduring. That is the self-help philosophy and activities of black nationalist religious organizations, best represented (most recently, at least) by the Nation of Islam (Black Muslims). Here is a group dating back to the early 1930s that stresses black supremacy, advocates racial separation, and maintains rigid membership requirements (religious dietary laws and moral discipline). Major emphases are to pool economic resources, "buy black," secure an education, learn skills, work hard, cultivate self-discipline, and in general engage in cooperative self-help—all in the name of religion (in this instance a version of Islam whose validity other branches of Islam tend not to recognize). Considerable credit has been given the Black Muslims for their success in rehabilitating ex-convicts and improving the economic welfare of

---

[16]*Aggressiveness* is understood here and in the discussion that follows in a very general sense of direct action of some kind that is perceived as likely to improve the condition of oneself or one's group.

their adherents. While the movement has not attracted hordes of blacks into its ranks, its success with the few it has attracted is worthy of attention. Again, our point here is simply that in the name of religion some American blacks have been aggressive with respect to improving their life situation.

The Individual Aggressive Style

A third example of black aggressiveness in the name of or from the ranks of religion would be the numerous examples of individual black ministers from the more standard black denominations who either took it upon themselves to extract philanthropy from the white community or became involved as individuals in political activities that concerned blacks. An excellent example of the latter activity is seen in Detroit in the late 1930s and early 1940s during the bitter labor struggle to unionize the Ford Motor Company. Using various ingenious techniques, Henry Ford and his aides had long kept a substantial contingent of blacks out of the labor movement. Although Ford as early as 1910 established the policy that at least 10 percent of his employees would be blacks, every prospective black employee needed a letter of recommendation from a black minister attesting to his or her moral fiber and (at least implicitly) antiunion commitment. Black ministers were expected to emphasize not only what a benefactor Henry Ford was to blacks, but what a disaster unionization would be for black workers. By a system of judiciously placed contributions and periodic visits, Henry Ford kept many black clergy "in line." Three "maverick" black ministers, however, became outspoken leaders of the unionization movement and acted on the conviction that unionization would benefit their fellow blacks. The Reverends Horace White, Charles Hill, and Malcolm Dade were convinced that accommodation and an otherworldly gospel should be replaced or at least supplemented by challenges to existing structures and concern with the problems and opportunities of this world. Such religious leaders in the black community appear to have been rare, yet their presence merits noting in our summary of aggressive social action emanating from black religious sources.

Organized Militancy

A fourth example of aggressiveness from the black church is more recent. As with the example just cited, the action centers in the clergy but is more organized and represents a greater proportion of black clergy. The emergence of black clergy organized for social protest action directed against institutionalized racism occurred at the height of the civil rights movement in the early 1960s. In various urban communities, such as Baltimore, Detroit, and St. Louis, black clergy organized what amounted to economic boycotts, called "selective-buying" campaigns, against firms that were guilty of blatant discrimination against blacks in employment and promotion and whose representatives refused to discuss the issue.

For example, the usual procedure in Detroit was for a committee of the larger clergy group that called itself The Negro Preachers of Detroit and Vicinity to request an audience with executives of the company suspected of discrimination to discuss their policies and to check into the proportion of blacks employed at various levels in the organization. Following this initial contact, the committee would return with specific requests. The hope was that the company would cooperate by hiring a number of qualified black workers at various levels within the organization as requested by the black preachers. The company was then given a few weeks to implement this proposal, after which time (they would be informed) an economic boycott of their product(s) would commence if compliance with the request was not forthcoming. If, after a three-to-four-week period, the company still delayed and resisted, the committee would contact every black preacher in the community and ask that they cooperate and help their black brothers and sisters in the community by reading a letter to their congregations the following Sunday morning. That letter urged their members not to buy the products of a specified company and said, among other things: "Our eyes are open! Never again will we stand by and see doors closed in the faces of our people. We cannot, therefore, in good conscience, remain silent while members of our congregations support a company's prejudice with our dollars."[17]

Types of Black Religious Leaders

Of course, not all the black clergy in the Detroit area participated in the boycott campaigns just described. And not everyone who participated did so to the same degree or in the same manner. In fact, Detroit's black clergy can be divided into three fairly distinct types: militants, moderates, and traditionalists. The *militants*, who constituted approximately 20 percent of the black clergy, were persons deeply committed to civil rights goals who demonstrated, marched, and picketed during the civil rights movement of the 1960s. They comprised the central planning unit of the boycott organization. These ministers tended to be young and highly educated, came from higher-than-average social-status backgrounds, tended toward theological liberalism, served larger-than-average black congregations, assumed an independent stance in their voting behavior, and emphasized social as op-

[17]Letter sent to black ministers in the Detroit area by the Negro Preachers of Detroit and Vicinity, dated November 22, 1961, in possession of the author.

posed to otherworldly concerns. It should be noted in passing that the designation "militant" as used throughout this chapter refers to aggressive action to secure constitutionally guaranteed civil rights in an integrated society, not the more separatist militancy espoused by some black leaders after 1964.

Second, there were the *moderate* black clergy. Though committed ideologically to improving the lot of blacks in American society, they were gradualists and were more conciliatory and accommodating than the militant black clergy. On the average they were likely to be older than the militants and not so highly educated (a third of the moderates had no formal education beyond high school). Moderates lent support to the Detroit boycott activities by reading the letters from the boycott committee to their congregations, but by and large they refrained from helping plan strategy. In Detroit, 27 percent of black religious leaders fit into this category.

The third category, the *traditionalists*, were passive with regard to challenging the prevailing social order and were spiritually rather than socially oriented: "My job is to preach the Gospel and do spiritual work." They tended to be older men who had very little formal education (approximately three-fifths did not go beyond high school), came from low-social-status backgrounds, and served small congregations, often only as part-time ministers. These preachers, who constituted slightly over half of all black religious leaders, actually served fewer people in their combined congregations in Detroit than did their militant counterparts; thus, although they were not directly supportive of the boycott actions, neither could they prevent a clear majority of black church members from hearing about them.

An obvious conclusion we can make on the basis of these observations about the three distinctive types of religious leaders in the contemporary black church (based on our Detroit data but likely applicable to at least the urban North if not the urban South as well) is that the traditional otherworldly pattern of black religion is being effectively challenged. Militant social-action- and civil-rights-oriented religious leaders and perspectives have emerged and gained substantial followings among members of black churches. Clearly, it would be both misleading and blatantly inaccurate to speak of *the* black church today. The range of internal diversity is great. Clearly, the militant civil rights perspective has made significant progress within black religious institutions. Yet it is equally important to note that the traditional black religious emphasis on otherworldliness and accommodation persists.

The Dilemma Posed by Black Militancy

Because of the rapid developments in the civil rights struggle and the emergence of countless "secular" local and national organizations combating racism and discrimination in various ways, the centrality and dominance of the black church have been challenged fairly seriously during the past thirty years. It has been noted that young blacks in particular are becoming increasingly disenchanted with the churches and are less and less likely to find satisfaction there. Increasingly they have turned to other types of organizations that appear to deal more directly with their life situations and with the social problems they face. We are reminded of Glock's theory, introduced in Chapter 5, concerning relative deprivation and various possible responses to it. Recall that in the cases of economic and social deprivation, according to Glock's theory, responses are more likely to be secular than religious if the causes of the deprivation are not only accurately perceived but deemed capable of relief and change. Such seems increasingly to be the case with blacks, with young blacks in particular, perceiving greater potential in secular organizations than in the traditional religious ones.

Such observations do not of course sound the death knell for the black church. For one thing, many people in a religious organization—whether black, white, or whatever—will remain there if for no other reason than simple habit—inertia. Also, for many, disaffiliating requires a more dramatic stand than they are willing to make. Furthermore, many people over time come to regard their associations and relationships with others in an organization (such as a church)—as well as with the organization itself—as so meaningful and important that these considerations alone prevent them from being readily convinced to substitute a new organization and commitment. Thus, the historic centrality and importance of the black church in the life of the black population and community alone makes it particularly unlikely that black church members will easily or quickly forsake this organization. Also, there still is a large proportion of the black population for whom the social environment has changed little despite the progress achieved by the civil rights movement and subsequent affirmative action programs. If the sectarian nature of much black religion has served in the past to provide release and escape for low-status blacks, it might be expected to continue to do so today.

Note, however, that such comments about continuity of function within organized religion do not necessarily apply to those young blacks who find escape in any of the three "strategies for survival" described by Lee Rainwater: (1) the expressive lifestyle of living "cool" and "working the game" on the people around you; (2) the violent strategy of more-or-less blindly striking back at the social structure that holds you down; or (3) the depressive strategy of withdrawal, perhaps into drugs—"I don't bother nobody; don't nobody bother me."[18] Nor do such functions seem to apply well to those blacks who in increasing numbers are escaping the ghetto, securing ad-

[18]Lee Rainwater, "A World of Trouble: The Pruitt-Igoe Housing Project," *The Public Interest* 8 (Summer 1967), 116–126.

vanced education, and entering previously closed or severely restricted occupations.

Observing young blacks' relative lack of enthusiasm for traditional
black churches prompted black writer Joseph R. Washington essentially to
predict, at the height of the civil rights movement in the early 1960s, the
eventual demise of the black church—although in 1967 he strongly urged
the black church to become involved with the black revolution because it
had the potential to be of significant help, since it still had contact with many
blacks.[19]

We have already shown a connection between at least a few black clergy
and militant civil rights activities. What connection is there between black
religion generally, particularly for laypeople, and involvement in civil rights
activities? In other words, so far as black Americans are concerned, does
religion in any way stimulate reform, or does it inhibit social change? Gary
Marx has phrased this question well in his book *Protest and Prejudice*, which
includes a chapter headed, "Religion: Opiate or Inspiration of Civil Rights
Militancy?"[20] Generally, Marx finds traditional otherworldly religion as expressed and practiced by blacks to be inconsistent with militant protest. For
example, militants constitute a significantly lower proportion of black sects
and cults than they do of black members of the more liberal Protestant denominations (15 percent among sects and cults, 43 and 36 percent among
black Episcopalians and Presbyterians, respectively).[21] Of course, there is
an important class bias affecting these data that eliminates virtually any possibility of making a valid inference regarding a cause-and-effect relationship between sectarianism and nonmilitancy; there is an association only.
But at least it is interesting to observe that one finds relatively few militants
in black sectarian religious groups as compared with the more liberal and
predominantly white Protestant denominations.

Other measures of religion add support to the observation that traditional black religion of the otherworldly variety is at best not conducive to
militancy and that the two approaches are "mutually corrosive kinds of
commitments,"[22] if not actually mutually exclusive points of view. Marx
found, for example, that the lower in importance black respondents regarded religion, the more likely they would be classed as militant in terms of
civil rights philosophy; whereas only 22 percent of those to whom religion
was "extremely important" fell into the militant category, 62 percent of
those who felt religion was "not at all important" were so classified.[23] Similarly, of those scoring high in orthodoxy, only 20 percent were militant,

[19]Joseph R. Washington, Jr., *Black Religion* (Boston: Beacon Press, 1964); idem, *The Politics of God* (Boston: Beacon Press, 1967), pp. 207–227.

[20]Gary T. Marx, *Protest and Prejudice* (New York: Harper & Row, 1967), Chapter 4.

[21]Ibid., p. 99.

[22]Rodney Stark, "Class, Radicalism, and Religious Involvement," *American Sociological
Review* 29, no. 5 (1964), 703, quoted in Marx, *Protest and Prejudice*, p. 105.

[23]Marx, *Protest and Prejudice*, p. 100.

while of those scoring lowest on the orthodoxy scale, 57 percent were militant.[24]

Although our point of emphasis here is that there is an inverse relationship between religious orthodoxy and civil rights militancy, yet it is intriguing that there are a few civil rights militants even among the religiously traditional and orthodox. In this connection, we should mention that many of the traditionalist ministers appear to harbor a secret respect for at least some aspects of the militant stance. In our Detroit sample, these ministers selected militants over fellow traditionalists as their opinion leaders by a ratio of six to one, even though they may not have known them personally.[25] It is also probable that the message of freedom and release in traditional black sectarian religion, which many have interpreted as heaven oriented, has been generalized by at least some to signify social and political freedom and release as well. There is consensus that the Jordan River in the black spirituals was not solely a symbolic hurdle to cross before entering the bliss of heaven but also was the Ohio River that separated the slave from freedom in the North.

NEW THEMES IN BLACK RELIGION

Although militant black clergy have issued calls for change and have had some successes in the attainment of civil rights goals among blacks, the black church as a whole appears to have had only limited influence in the civil rights area. There has been almost no challenge from the black community to the contention, expressed more than once in this chapter, that black religion has concentrated on "religious" matters and salvation concerns to the neglect of social action and reform. Thus, it is of more than passing interest that one black theologian, James Cone, has published a proposal for a "black theology of liberation" in which he contends that Christianity is in essence a religion of liberation and that the struggle of the oppressed for political, social, and economic justice is integral to Jesus Christ's message.[26] Cone condemns the black and the white Protestant churches in the same breath: "Both have marked out their places as havens of retreat, the one to cover the guilt of the oppressors, the other to daub the wounds of the oppressed."[27] Cone is calling for the reform of black theology and of the black church. The view that such reform is crucial in the face of social change is shared by Joseph Washington, who states in a review of Cone's

---

[24] Ibid.

[25] Johnstone, "Community Leadership," pp. 169–170.

[26] James H. Cone, *Liberation* (Philadelphia: Lippincott, 1970).

[27] James H. Cone, *Black Theology and Black Power* (New York: Seabury Press, 1969), p. 115.

first book that "the future of the black church is in its critical participation in the future of black power—which is, the future of black people."[28] Undoubtedly, there is less room today in the black church than in the white church for dual religious tracks—the one proclaiming traditional salvation goals, the other championing social reforms.

Cone chides the black church for emulating the white church and for feeling good when praised by whites. In reality, he asserts, the black church, just because it is black, is automatically among the rejected. He suggests that the black church must accept its true role as sufferer and follow the natural course of being black.[29] One thing this requires is excising the "most corrupting influence among the Black churches"—namely, "their adoption of the 'white lie' that Christianity is primarily concerned with an otherworldly reality. . . . The idea of heaven is irrelevant for Black Theology. The Christian cannot waste time contemplating the next world,"[30] for that reward is not a legitimate motive for action. In fact, it is a denial of the Christian faith, in addition to being a gigantic "put-on" devised by whites to keep blacks in their place.

The Reverend Albert Cleage, another black theologian, also expresses this view when he describes the gift of Christianity to the black slave by the white master:

> The religion which the master gave to his slave was designed for pacification and to support the authority of white supremacy. He said, "This is a picture of God. This is a picture of Jesus. They are both white as you can plainly see. Here are Biblical characters. They are all white. But they love you in spite of your evil Blackness, and they offer you salvation in the great beyond! You have to live such a life here on earth, that after death, when you cross over Jordan, there will be a reward for you. Sometimes you think that all the suffering that you are doing down here is passing unnoticed by God, but it is not! God is watching everything, every minute of every day. And every bit of suffering you have down here is written down in God's big book, and eventually on the other side of Jordan there will be a reward, milk and honey and golden streets." So Black people had only to accept the authority of the white world to inherit a glorious reward in heaven.[31]

The point emphasized again and again by Cone and Cleage is that the black church must purge itself of such otherworldly-reward perspectives and join the black power movement. Black pride and social justice must become the dominant guiding concepts both in the ideology or theology and in the activities of the black church. Integral to this process, at least for Cleage, is acceptance of the fact that the Jesus of Christianity was in reality

[28]Joseph R. Washington, Jr., review of *Black Theology and Black Power* by James H. Cone, *Journal for the Scientific Study of Religion* 11, no. 3 (1972), 311.

[29]Cone, *Black Theology*, p. 113.

[30]Ibid., pp. 121, 125.

[31]Albert B. Cleage, Jr., *Black Christian Nationalism* (New York: Morrow, 1972), p. xxviii.

black. Cleage defines Jesus as a revolutionary black leader seeking to lead a black nation to freedom.[32] But more than that, Cleage reflects the ideas of Marcus Garvey, who in the late 1920s organized the African Orthodox Church and developed an entire black hierarchy of black God, black Jesus, black Madonna, and black angels.[33] The Reverend Cleage is minister of the Shrine of the Black Madonna, formerly the Central Congregational Church, in Detroit.

Cone, too, speaks of God as black, but more in a figurative sense. God must be known as He reveals Himself in His blackness, by which Cone means that "either God is identified with the oppressed to the point that their experience becomes his or he is a God of racism."[34] Cone is referring, in other words, to total identification of God with black people and their plight. "Because God has made the goal of Black people his own goal, Black Theology believes that it is not only appropriate but necessary to begin the doctrine of God with an insistence on his blackness."[35] And again, "The blackness of God means that God has made the oppressed condition God's own condition."[36]

An intriguing observation applicable to the "radical" black theology of Cone and Cleage, though suggested earlier by Washington, is the conviction that the black church not only must reorient itself, but that it is capable of doing so. In one sense, such a belief or assumption appears sound inasmuch as the black church is still by far the largest social institution in the black community and is in contact with the greatest number of people. On the other hand, whether it can turn itself around and make a radical change in direction and focus is problematic. It is undoubtedly true that significant numbers of influential black preachers have at least begun the switch. It is also true, as Cone points out, that the black church and its clergy have retained some of the theme of freedom and injustice from their slave religion heritage.[37]

Actually, Peter Paris suggests that although most blacks even today reject the views of Cone as too radical and not true to the historic role of black churches,[38] it is simply not correct to say that black churches have retreated into a haven-of-rest mentality. Paris maintains that the traditional black churches are motivated by racial self-interest in a new way. He says that the members of black churches no longer feel that they are being unfaithful to

[32]Albert B. Cleage, Jr., *Black Messiah* (New York: Sheed & Ward, 1968), p. 4.

[33]Ibid., p. 8.

[34]Cone, *Liberation*, pp. 120–121.

[35]Ibid., p. 121.

[36]James H. Cone, *A Black Theology of Liberation* (Maryknoll, NY: Orbis Books, 1986), p. 63.

[37]Cone, *Black Theology*, Chapter 4.

[38]Peter J. Paris, *The Social Teachings of the Black Churches* (Philadelphia, PA: Fortress Press, 1985), p. 127, fn. 22.

"their ideal societal vision by working vigorously for such racial goals as political determinism, economic development, preservation of predominantly
black schools (private and public), and construction of senior citizens homes
in the black community."[39] In other words, the black militants portrayed by
the 1960s Negro Preachers of Detroit and Vicinity identified earlier is winning, so to speak, yet short of Cone and Cleage's black liberation theology.

This would certainly be consistent with Paris's contention that the mission of the black churches has always transcended their own constituency by
aiming at the reform of the larger white society, that is, causing the latter to
practice racial justice as an expression of genuine Christian understanding
and devotion. Their mission, therefore, has had both an internal and an
external dimension in that they have sought religious, moral, and political
reform in both the black and the white community, though not in the same
respect.[40]

Another black theologian, Olin P. Moyd, goes further by suggesting
that black theological themes not only speak to the situation of blacks but
can make important contributions to theological discussion and development generally. He suggests with pure sociological insight that principally
because American blacks have had a different experience than whites their
theology will be distinctive. He and others have further suggested that it is
such black theology that will move to the forefront of theological discussion
in the 1980s and 1990s. While Cone and others have talked about the black
theology of liberation, Moyd uses the term "redemption." In that term he
incorporates three ideas: (1) "liberation" in the sense of deliverance from
states of human-caused oppression, (2) "liberation" in the sense of salvation
from sin, and (3) "confederation" with other people in a covenant relationship with each other and with God.[41]

As black theologians have increasingly talked about "liberation" and
liberation theology, they have interacted widely with Third World theologians from Africa, Latin America, and Asia. James Cone notes that dialogue
with these theologians has greatly expanded American black theologians'
awareness. He notes that Africans brought knowledge of historic black culture; Latin American theologians expanded black awareness of the need
for class analysis; feminist theologians exposed the sexist base of much of
Christian theology, true also of black American theology; and other minorities pointed out the importance of a coalition to join in the struggle for
justice in America and throughout the world.[42] Cone notes further that in

---

[39]Ibid., p. 132.

[40]Ibid., p. 111.

[41]Olin P. Moyd, *Redemption in Black Theology* (Valley Forge, PA: Pudson Press, 1979).

[42]James H. Cone, "Black Religious Thought," in Charles H. Lippy and Peter W.
Williams, *Encyclopedia of American Religious Experience*, Vol. II (New York: Charles Scribner's
Sons, 1988), p. 1186.

return American black theology has been able to heighten significantly the awareness of Third World theologians concerning racism.[43]

The outcome has been an enrichment of the theology of liberation and a growing appreciation of the relevance of this theology for American blacks. In the process, "liberation" has taken on new meanings. Not only is it liberation *from* sin and slavery, as in the Negro spirituals of old, but it is liberation *for* change in society, as all who have been subjected arbitrarily to second-rank status (notably women and ethnic/racial minorities) gain freedom and equal opportunity.

NATIVE AMERICAN RELIGION

At the beginning of any discussion of Native American religion we need to observe that there really is no such thing as "Native American Religion." To try to speak of a religion that somehow represents Native Americans ignores the fact that this vast group comes from many dozens of nations and cultures. The idea that they are all "Indians" or even "Native Americans" is an alien notion thrust upon them by the Europeans who settled the land, and then, by Americans, who pushed westward to the Pacific. Native Americans were not one people or society. Therefore, it is understandable that they would not have one religion. We should remember, too, that as independent nations they also had separate languages. While they are not all totally different, there are nine language families, each with dozens of distinctive languages within it.

It should also be noted that these languages were oral only. They were neither preserved nor taught in written form. There was therefore little chance that a language spanning the continent on which the Native Americans lived would develop.

Examples of such variation and the importance of oral tradition are cited by Ake Hultkrantz, who states that on both sides of the Mississippi not only tribes and clans but also families had their unique oral traditions. By way of example, each clan among the Winnebago had its own myth of the origin of the world—not totally different, to be sure, but unique nonetheless.[44]

As we noted in Chapter 2 in describing the religions of preliterate people, Native American cultures rarely had a word for "religion."[45] What we call "religion" and see as a distinguishable entity that can be separated out of

[43]Ibid.

[44]Ake Hultkrantz, *Native Religions of North America* (San Francisco: Harper & Row, 1987), p. 16.

[45]It is very possible that the few tribes that do have a word for "religion" created the word only after contact with colonists, settlers, and missionaries. Cf. Ake Hultkrantz, *The Religion of the American Indians* (Berkeley: University of California Press, 1967, 1979), p. 10.

the rest of culture—separated from the economy, the educational system, industry, sports, and the like—most Native American societies did not have. Rather, their "religion" was woven into the fabric of life and prescribed activities that were accepted traditional components of life and reality. Therefore, at the moment we describe any activity, belief, or word as "religious," we have made it something different than it is because we have made it conform to our language and our conceptions of things.

What we do know is that many Native American nations say something about many things that other peoples such as ourselves speak of—what we call "religion"—how the world came into being, how we should treat our fellow human beings, what happens after death, how we become and remain one of God's chosen, and so on. Yet the basic difference remains: We talk about religion as one specialized slice of life, but Native Americans would simply say "life."

Further, we cannot ignore the fact that we are already over 300 years past the beginning of Christian missionary activity among Native Americans. Missionary work among Native Americans has been extensive—so much so that probably nothing in Native American religion is today in pure form. Nor were earlier accounts from 100 to 200 years ago much better. Not only had Christian missionaries already been very active, but those who observed and wrote about the Native Americans had strong biases toward Western culture and the Judeo-Christian heritage so that any observation about Native American religions was filtered through a lens composed of Christian perspectives and understandings of what religion was and should be.

Therefore, our task will not be to get back to all the beginnings of Native American religion and describe its manifestations as they existed in pure form. Nor will we even attempt to be inclusive of all there was or is of Native American religion. Rather, we shall look first at some of the more central ideas in Native American religion that, while not necessarily universal nor without nuances and variations from one Native American culture to another, are frequently present in Native American nations. Second, we shall look at changing emphases in Native American religion in response to influences from the surrounding American culture.

Time

With respect to time, our Western tradition tends to categorize events and history into past, present, and future. While we also recognize that some things are continuous and span past, present, and future, most of what we think and do occurs in a context of linear movement through time—that is what I did yesterday, this is what I'm doing now, those will be my activities tomorrow. Everything can be placed at a point on a line of time. But Native Americans are much more likely to concentrate on cyclical time. Emphasis is not so much on when an event occurred (yesterday, today, or tomorrow), as where on its recurrent cycle it is. Whereas linear time looks toward ends and points on a continuum moving toward the end, cyclical time concentrates on a core, a center that is always there and around which we move. Thus the Native American, as he or she saw the seasons of a year, he or she saw a progression in a familiar cycle and repeated familiar patterns. This is in contrast with the Western pattern of keeping track of the 365 days in a year that can be marked one-by-one on a calendar and keep accumulating for centuries and millennia—all moving toward some future end. Native Americans see time more as a recurring cycle of experiences. Hultkrantz notes that some Native American languages have no term for past and future. Everything is present.[46]

Circle

Such an emphasis on cyclical continuity makes the importance of the circle symbol among Native Americans quite understandable. A circle is the perfect visual representation of cycle and repetition. Black Elk, a Lakota Sioux, summarizes better than anyone what the circle means.

> You have noticed that everything an Indian does is in a circle, and that is because the Power of the World always works in circles, and everything tries to be round. In the old days when we were a strong and happy people, all our power came to us from the sacred hoop of the nation, and so long as the hoop was unbroken, the people flourished. The flowering tree was the living center of the hoop, and the circle of the four quarters nourished it. The east gave peace and light, the south gave warmth, the west gave rain, and the north with its cold and mighty wind gave strength and endurance. This knowledge came to us from the outer world with our religion. Everything the Power of the World does is done in a circle. The sky is round, and I have heard that the earth is round like a ball, and so are all the stars. The wind, in its greatest power, whirls. Birds make their nests in circles, for theirs is the same religion as ours. The sun comes forth and goes down again in a circle. The moon does the same, and both are round. Even the seasons form a great circle in their changing, and always come back again to where they were. The life of a man is a circle from childhood to childhood, and so it is in everything where power moves. Our teepees were round like the nests of birds, and these were always set in a circle, the nation's hoop, a nest of many nests, where the Great Spirit meant for us to hatch our children.[47]

---

[46]Hultkrantz, *Native Religions of North America*, p. 33.

[47]Black Elk, as told to John G. Neihardt, *Black Elk Speaks* (New York: William Morrow and Co., 1932), pp. 279–280. Reprinted in paperback by the Bison Series of the University of Nebraska Press, 1961. Quoted in Joseph E. Brown, *The Spiritual Legacy of the American Indian* (New York: Crossroad Publishing Company, 1982), p. 35.

Closely allied with the perspective of the cyclical nature of time is the Native American view of relationships, which links everyone in the family, the clan, the tribe, and the nation together with the animals and the land itself. Even the winds and the rain and the change of seasons share in the interrelationships with the land and its resources and with animal life.

The emphasis on such interrelationships is well illustrated by the arctic Indians or Eskimos who live a most precarious existence in a land that offers few resources. Nonetheless they believe that their greatest risk is not from subzero temperatures or lack of food but the omnipresent reality that their lives depend on taking the lives of other living things, whether fish and seal from the sea or four-footed land animals.[48] However, when appropriate norms and rituals are followed and the hunter is respectful of the rights of all parties, then the animals will present themselves willingly as sacrificial offerings to the hunter.[49]

The sacred pipe adds meaning to the interrelatedness of place, people, and animal life. As the pipe is passed from one person to another, each one inhales the breath of others, and, as the innumerable grains of tobacco represent all the creatures of God and thereby contribute to the unity, so each person smoking from the pipe is expressing and experiencing unity with all that exists.

In keeping with our earlier observations about the diversity among Native Americans, we need to emphasize that the tribes had varying points of emphasis, depending upon their means of making a living. Those with a hunting culture stressed their relationships with animals; those with a gathering culture emphasized their relationships with vegetation—the trees, shrubs, seeds, roots, and grasses.[50] In either case they wanted to live peacefully and in harmony with nature, disturbing it as little as possible. So, hunters kill only so much game as is needed and will be fully consumed. The gatherers pick up nuts and fruit from the trees and the ground around them without damaging the trees, and they use only fallen wood for building and burning.[51] One can thus readily understand the outrage of Native Americans induced by the mass shooting of buffalo by travelers aboard excursion hunting trains who left the animals to rot where they fell.

The ideas of harmony with nature and unity of all that exists is well illustrated by the reaction of the Shahaptin Indians of the Northwest to the suggestion by Indian agents to cultivate the ground and begin to farm.

> You ask me to plow the ground! Shall I take a knife and tear my mother's bosom? Then when I die she will not take me to her bosom to rest.

[48]Brown, *Spiritual Legacy*, p. 53.

[49]Ibid, pp. 6–7.

[50]Think back to Chapter 2 and Guy E. Swanson's high correlations between characteristics of the social structure and the beliefs and perspectives people hold.

[51]Ake Hultkrantz, *Belief and Worship in Native North America* (Syracuse, NY: Syracuse University Press, 1981), p. 121.

You ask me to dig for stone! Shall I dig under her skin for her bones? Then when I die I cannot enter her body to be born again.

You ask me to cut grass and make hay and sell it, and be rich like white men! But how dare I cut off my mother's hair?[52]

And thus do Native Americans see all that exists as interrelated and interdependent. Our task as human beings is to fit in and integrate with what is there—other people, other living things (both plant and animal), and inanimate matter and things—in a cooperative, mutually beneficial manner. Religious beliefs instruct us how to achieve that goal; religious ritual mobilizes us into appropriate activities and behavior.

Late in the nineteenth century something new in Native American religion emerged, and it became the focal point of a branch of Native American religion that continues until today, namely, the "peyote cult." Peyote is a small, carrot-shaped cactus that resembles a small pincushion when fresh, a coat button when dried. Both the "button" top and its root can be eaten for a mild hallucinogenic effect. Of its eight alkaloids, mescaline is its best known.

Peyote was not a new nineteenth-century discovery. It had been used within many Native American tribes for special purposes for centuries. Weston LeBarre discusses some nonreligious uses: to foretell the future, as a magic fetish to ward off evil, as a curative for wounds and snakebites, and to induce bravery in battle.[53] These uses were centuries old. The modern application that integrates peyote use with religion dates back to around 1870. This is a date commonly used to signal the end of the "Indian Wars" and the resignation of Native Americans to their subjugation to the white invaders of their lands.

Peyote has become an important adjunct to religious activity and worship for a substantial number of Native Americans from the Far West to the Middle West. Those who use it are participants in the Native American Church. While importation of peyote is outlawed in nine western states, its use for religious purposes is allowed. The function of peyote is not to induce visions, though on rare occasions people do experience them. Rather, as David Aberle suggests, its religious function is to provide the user with a sense of personal significance.[54] He adds that people also report improved health and experiencing a sense of power. On the medical side, peyote is a mild analgesic and modest stimulant as well. Many recipients will "feel better" for awhile when under the influence of peyote. Aberle discusses the power effect in terms of something external added to the individual. He

[52]James Mooney, *The Ghost-Dance Religion and the Sioux Outbreak of 1890* (Washington, D.C.: Bureau of American Ethnology, 14th Annual Report, 2), p. 721. Quoted in Hultkrantz, *Belief and Worship*, p. 129.

[53]Hultkrantz, *Belief and Worship*, p. 121.

[54]David F. Aberle, *The Peyote Religion Among the Navaho* (Chicago: University of Chicago Press, 1982), p. 6.

says of the Navajo, "When a person eats peyote, something external to him proves able to affect his thinking, his feelings, his perceptions, and his behavior, and to do so without his own volition."[55] Aberle summarizes the function of peyote as providing a feeling of personal significance, which heightens religious experience in the assembly, because it demonstrates that something is indeed being done to and for the person, and because it is felt to be a "power."[56]

The religious ceremony that involves peyote must find people gathered for a purpose, whether to cure illness, avert evil/promote good, or thank God for his blessings. It is a "communion" service in which one communicates with God and with the rest of the group. This communion is expressed by joint consumption of peyote at several points during the night, by the drinking of water at midnight and in the morning, and in the ceremonial breakfast at the end. The service begins at sundown and lasts all night and involves prayer, singing, drumming, and eating peyote.

While the adoption of peyote use by the Native Americans probably began in the 1870s and 1880s independent of Christian influence, by 1892 Christian elements were present.[57] The religious peyote cult spread rapidly after its probable origin among the Comanche or Kiowa Native Americans in Oklahoma. It had spread to at least sixteen tribes by 1899, and a total of seventy-seven tribes by 1955.[58] Areas where peyote ceremonies were common included the western provinces of Canada and most states west of the Mississippi. The religion of peyote did not formally incorporate until the Native American Church of Oklahoma formed in 1941; in 1945 it became the Native American Church of the United States. While opposed both by some Native Americans as an aberration from and rejection of traditional Native American beliefs and rituals, and by whites who disliked its incorporation of "drugs" and its sectarian or cultic nature, it has become quite popular among Native Americans, attaining an estimated membership of approximately 250,000 people.[59]

Native American Responses to Deprivation

With respect to why the peyote religion arose in the first place and why it appeals to many Native Americans today, we probably need to look no

[55]Ibid., p. 9.

[56]Ibid., p. 11.

[57]Ibid., p. 17.

[58]Membership varies considerably from one tribe to another. Aberle estimated membership among Navahoes to range from 12 to 14 percent in 1951. By 1965 he reports an increase to 35 to 39 percent (Aberle, ibid., pp. 110 and 124). Among Shoshoni, Hultkrantz estimates 75 percent in 1987 (Hultkrantz, *Native Religions*, p. 84).

[59]David Chidester, *Patterns of Power: Religion and Politics in American Culture* (Englewood Cliffs, NJ: Prentice Hall, 1988), p. 133.

further than the position of Native Americans in the broader American society. The first acceptance of peyote in the late 1800s followed closely the end of the Indian Wars, with Native Americans the losers on all fronts. Aberle suggests that many Native Americans looked for something special and unique, that would set them apart as something other than losers, inferior to the victorious white Americans.

We also know that Native Americans have as a whole not done well since then. They are not integrated into American society; many live in poverty; alcoholism and other drug addictions are common scourges. In short, Native Americans suffer significantly from deprivation. If you recall our discussion of the relationship of relative deprivation and the formation of sects in Chapter 5, and if we can identify a significant part of the deprivation of Native Americans after 1870 as social deprivation, then it is not hard to understand resorting to peyote as an escape and as a way of identifying those who see themselves chosen by God, even if such a quality is not recognized by white society. As Aberle suggests, participation in peyotism "assures some Navahos that Indians are at least equal to, and in some ways superior to whites—in knowledge, in wisdom, in spirituality, and in possession of a good religion."[60]

David Chidester, following Bryan Wilson, describes several distinct responses by Native Americans to the destruction of their traditional world and their displacement from it. First, there is the introversionist response. This reaction involves an attempt to resurrect and reaffirm traditional religious values of the tribe in the face of "overwhelming encroachment of white domination."[61]

Handsome Lake, an Iroquois, exemplified the introversionist response around the turn of the nineteenth century as he espoused a religion of the "good word" that involved ethical discipline, repentance, and mutual cooperation that would facilitate the survival of traditional Indian religious values in a new political environment.[62] Yet, while expounding traditional Native American values such as integrity, honesty, marital fidelity, and contributing a fair measure of one's labor for the good of all, the white man's religion was having its effect also. The very name "Good Word" is obviously reminiscent of Christianity's "good news" (gospel). The introversionist response tried to make the best of a bad situation and implicitly accept defeat. But through it all was the staunch conviction that they would retain a separate, continuing Iroquois identity and someday the old ways would return.

A second response was revolution. Herein lies the popular image of the fierce, fighting Indian doing battle with settlers, cowboys, and cavalry. The

---

[60]Aberle, *Peyote Religion*, pp. 193–194.

[61]David Chidester, *Patterns of Power*, p. 123.

[62]Ibid., p. 124.

religious aspects of this revolutionist response are best exemplified in the Ghost Dance religion. The basic premise is that Indians would be invincible in battle (a magical, powerful cloak would surround the warrior and it would repel enemy bullets and knives) if they were properly prepared by the Ghost Dance ritual. It was with this belief of Ghost Dance protection that Chief Short Bull led the Sioux into the disastrous battle of Wounded Knee in 1890 in which 370 Sioux were killed. They believed that their "ghost shirts" would shield them from harm. Joseph Jorgensen summarizes the Ghost Dance as a response of some Native Americans "to the deep poverty and ubiquitous oppression they had suffered during prolonged contact with whites."[63] They had suffered enormous losses in battle, from epidemics, and by starvation. They lost their land, were herded into reservations, and were forced into a way of life devoid of their traditional resources. Small wonder that the Ghost Dance theology would be attractive, even seductive. As Native Americans sought to transform their lives, Jorgensen suggests that not only had they rejected the status quo but they had some insight into the "enormous force necessary to transform things to what they should have been."[64]

And such is the religion of Native Americans. Nowhere has it remained even close to what it had been. This is in significant part because no people has seen more Christian missionary activity over the years than Native Americans. But Christianity did not soon triumph; nor in the end did it completely supplant the Native American religion that had come before. And certainly the reader would be correct to assume that Christian missionary activity would necessarily presume the eradication of Native American religion if Christianization were to be fully successful. Most practitioners of Christianity view it as the single true religion to the exclusion of all others. As such, "truth" has the right and obligation to cut out all that is "false."

This view was consistent with and reinforced by the effects of the Dawes Act, enacted by the U.S. Congress and effective in 1897. While the Dawes Act did not outlaw Native American religion per se, the clear purpose of what has come to be known as the "Allotment Act" was to "Americanize" the Indians. The widely held belief was that they would amount to nothing and would not fulfill their destiny until they were full-fledged Americans doing what most Americans did—they tended their farms and attended the Protestant church. By definition, to Americanize the Indians for their own good meant to strip them of their old culture of which religion was an important part and replace it with Protestant American values and culture. It was the clear, expressed intent of those promoting the passage of

---

[63]Joseph G. Jorgensen, "Religious Solutions and Native American Struggles," in *Religion, Rebellion, Revolution,* Bruce Lincoln, ed. (London: Macmillan, 1985), p. 102.

[64]Ibid., p. 107.

the Allotment Act that everything distinctly Indian was to be erased: Native American languages, religious and other communal ceremonies, drumming and dancing, and traditional funeral rites.

The core provision of the Dawes Act that was to accomplish all of the above was to split up the tribes by allocating 160 acres to each family head for the purpose of establishing a home separated from others, engage them in typical American agrarian pursuits, and make each family responsible for itself. Actually, the land was to be held in trust by the U.S. government for twenty-five years, after which the family would receive the deed to the land and full citizenship in the United States. The remainder of Indian reservation lands (and there was a lot left over after the allocation of 160 acres for each family, with lesser amounts for single persons), would go on the general market and be withdrawn from Indian control forever. But in addition, many of those Native Americans who received land were swindled out of even their small tracts. Acreage owned by Native Americans dropped from 140 million acres in 1887 to 78 million in 1900. In 1934 the amount owned had dropped to about 55 million, when the Wheeler-Howard Act, usually called the Indian Reorganization Act, was passed by Congress to rescind the Dawes Act.

Of course, after forty-seven years under the Dawes Act a great deal of damage had already been done to Indian culture. Yet some tribes had kept their traditional religion and ceremonies alive surreptitiously. Often their relative isolation on remote reservations helped in this regard. Vine Deloria cites another way. The Lummi tribe from western Washington preserved many ceremonies under the guise of celebrating the signing of their treaty with the United States.[65] Similarly, some of the Plains tribes kept ceremonies alive by ostensibly celebrating the Fourth of July—a grand joke on the conquering whites who did not really understand what they were seeing. The "patriotic" Indians were really preserving their religious customs. But also, after 1934 and the loosening of restrictions both of a formal and informal nature that had been imposed under the Dawes Act, there were still some old members of the tribes alive to remember and instruct in the former religious ways.

Nonetheless, despite somewhat greater freedom for Native Americans to practice the religion of their choice, there is relatively little authentic traditional Native American religion being practiced today. While there is great interest within the Native American communities in the old ceremonies, they stand and are practiced rather independently and are not serving quite the same religious function they once did. Most Native Americans are today what most other Americans are, namely some brand of Christian. It is of interest that Charismatic Christianity and Mormonism have had some

---

[65]Vine Deloria, Jr., *God Is Red* (New York: Grosset and Dunlap, 1973), pp. 251–252.

notable success among Native Americans since the early 1960s.[66] The Pentecostal groups, in emphasizing ecstatic experience and what some might call visions or trances, provide some opportunities for linkage with similar experiences that had been part of traditional Native American religious practices. Mormonism, with its emphasis on compiling accurate genealogical records going back many centuries in order to bring ancestors into the fold, will be attractive to Native Americans who in their emphasis on community have strong, personal feelings for those many members of their communities who have gone before.

In conclusion, while it is difficult to generalize, religion for some Native Americans, even when in Christian guise, continues to emphasize the importance of land and sacred space and place, the quest for power (mana) to deal with misfortune, and hope for an ultimate triumph—the final inheritance of themselves and all their ancestors who will rise up to populate and tend their land again when the white man is gone.

---

[66]Joseph G. Jorgensen, "Modern Religious Movements" in *Native American Religions*, Lawrence E. Sullivan, ed. (New York: Macmillan Publishing Company, 1987), p. 215.

13

Denominational Society

The necessity of devoting a full chapter to a discussion of the denominational phenomenon in American religion is reinforced by an observation by
the American sociologist Andrew Greeley to the effect that the United
States is nearly unique among world societies as a denominational society.[1]
By "denominational society" Greeley means one characterized by neither an
established church nor a protesting sect, but in which religion and the rest
of the society interrelate through a considerable number of essentially equal
religious organizations. These constitute a social organizational adjustment
to the fact of religious pluralism, and not a halfway house between sect and
church.[2] Greeley's emphasis, which is also this chapter's, is on the social organizational aspect of denominationalism. That is, we are observing here an
important social phenomenon, not simply a religious one—a type of social
organization that has significant impact on social structure and social interaction in American society.

---

[1] Andrew Greeley, *The Denominational Society* (Glenview, IL: Scott, Foresman, 1972), p. 1.
[2] Ibid.

THE MULTIPLICITY OF GROUPS

The denominational character of American society is of course rooted in the fact that ours is among other things a pluralistic society, particularly insofar as religion is concerned. As we pointed out in Chapter 11, the denominational society arose, not because everyone desired it, but because at the founding of our nation no one religion was sufficiently powerful to gain predominance and also because of the various philosophical perspectives and commitments of those who framed the Constitution. The result has been one of the most obvious features of denominationalism within American society—that is, the subdivision of religion in American society into a host of independent religious groups. A society could be designated as a denominational society with only a few different religious groups. But American society leaves no doubt as to its diverse denominational character, for it includes literally hundreds of religious groups. Note well that we are not referring here to the thousands of local congregations, but to larger groupings of individual congregations into more or less cohesive associations. That is, several, perhaps thousands, of local congregational units identify sufficiently with one another to stand under one umbrella, so to speak, to carry out some activities and functions jointly, to share perhaps a summary statement of belief and to think of themselves as united together and distinct from other associations of congregations who raise different umbrellas and fly different theological flags. Thus, we are talking about Baptists, Methodists, Episcopalians, Presbyterians, Lutherans, Roman Catholics, Mormons, Unitarians, Orthodox Jews, Jehovah's Witnesses, and other fairly familiar religious groups or denominations, as well as a plethora of lesser-known groups, such as the Pilgrim Holiness Church, the Plymouth Brethren, the Duck River Baptists, the Free Magyar Reformed Church in America, the Macedonian Orthodox Church in America, and so on.

There are over 300 such associations that maintain membership statistics and report them to the National Council of Churches. J. Gordon Melton has identified over 1,200 distinct religious groups in the United States.[3] In the main these are groups that consist of more than one local congregation, though Melton included single-congregation churches if they are large (2,000 or more members) or if they draw members from more than one state and beyond a single metropolitan area. In addition, there are literally thousands of individual local congregations that we might call entrepreneurial churches that are autonomous and begin and end with the entrepreneurial religious leader who founded them. These are particularly numerous in the sect-prone inner-city ghettos, though one sees such entrepreneurial groups elsewhere as well.

---

[3]J. Gordon Melton, *The Encyclopedia of American Religion*, Volumes 1 and 2 (Wilmington, NC: McGrath Publishing Company, 1978).

THE DIVERSITY OF GROUPS

Recognizing the multiplicity of religious groups in the United States is only an introduction to the great diversity among religious organizations that is a second prominent feature of denominationalism in this country. The differences among denominations can be seen along a variety of dimensions, some of which we have alluded to earlier in this text.

The Authority Dimension

At the level of structure and organization there is the basic distinction among episcopal, presbyterian, and congregational forms that we referred to in passing in Chapter 4. These terms refer to the structure of authority within the denomination and the relationship of the local congregation to the larger denomination with which it is affiliated. In the *episcopal* form, authority proceeds from the top down—from the heads of the denomination (pope, archbishop, bishop, and so on) down to local representatives. In the *presbyterian* form, authority rests more in the middle range, with elected representatives, both clergy and lay, at various levels from local to national holding regulatory and disciplinary authority over the levels below them. In the *congregational* type, authority lies, as the term implies, with the local group, with the national denomination having little authority, at least of a formal nature.

The Emotional Dimension

Another typology contrasts Apollonian with Dionysian religious orientation and worship style of liturgy.[4] The *Apollonian* style assumes that since the human being is basically rational and capable of controlling his or her biological and emotional urges, the person's communication with God should reflect such rationality and be characterized by moderation and gentility. The *Dionysian* emphasis rests on the observation that people are more than strictly rational beings. They have emotions and they need to express themselves individualistically. In fact, this orientation contends that an important, if not primary, feature of religion is the emotional dimension, including ecstatic, mystical experiences of the human with the divine. In religion one must and one does transcend the mundane rationality of life.

These descriptions of the Dionysian and Apollonian styles and orientations are likely to remind one of the religious sect and the denominational type of religious organization, respectively; and appropriately so. Yet nei-

[4]See Greeley, *The Denominational Society*, p. 23.

ther should be considered an exclusive association. Some groups most properly classified as denominations nevertheless exhibit Dionysian elements, either because they have only recently evolved to denominational status and retain vestiges of their old pattern or because religious leaders, particularly at the local level, are convinced of the importance of the Dionysian element in religion and encourage it. Note, for example, the recent increase in the phenomenon of "speaking in tongues" and related pentecostal elements in such highly Apollonian denominations as the Roman Catholic, Episcopal, and Lutheran Churches.

MAJOR DENOMINATIONAL FAMILIES

In an attempt to understand differences among the major denominations in America today, it is helpful to know the source and meaning of the broad popular categories Catholic, Protestant, Jew, and Eastern Orthodox. Each of these designations is a highly inclusive category in itself—inclusive in the sense that each has numerous subdivisions within it. We will explore some of that internal diversity in the coming pages. But here, just a few comments about the origins of these major categories.

Judaism is of course the oldest and is in fact the source out of which Christianity grew, first as Catholicism (later divided into the Roman Catholic and the Eastern Orthodox branches), and then Protestantism. Although we will add some detail later, we should mention here that Judaism in America is itself very diverse. There are six major categories of Jews: Orthodox, Conservative, Reform, Reconstructionist, Hasidic, and Cultural-Ethnic. Orthodox Judaism remains firmly rooted in historic Judaism, with a heavy emphasis on the Old Testament and its laws, restrictions, and rituals. Jews who can be called Reformed, as well as the Reconstructionists and those we call Cultural-Ethnic, are highly responsive to developments within contemporary society, assume that religion both does and should evolve, and have discarded much or all of the historical belief and ritual system of Judaism. Conservative Jews stand very consciously between the two extremes of Orthodox and Reform. Hasidic Judaism is a more mystical form of Judaism, truly in a class by itself.

Catholicism in its two major forms of Roman Catholicism and Eastern Orthodoxy came to be the designation for the religious group that was established by Jesus Christ and his followers in the first century A.D. and was a direct descendant of historic Judaism. It was the Christian Church that spread from Jerusalem throughout the Mediterranean world and beyond within a few generations following the death of Christ. Catholics believe that Christ's statement to the disciple Peter recorded in Matthew 16:18, "Thou art Peter, and upon this rock I will build my church" (King James Version), marked the true founding of the Catholic Church. Catholic tradition says that Peter journeyed to Rome late in life, preached there, became leader (bishop), and began to carry out Christ's directive to create one universal (catholic) church on earth. Both the catholicity and the unity were challenged by Eastern Christianity almost immediately, and in the Middle Ages[5] the Western (Roman Catholic) and the Eastern (Orthodox) Christian churches split and remain separated until this day. Actually, these divisions into Byzantine and Roman have existed from the beginning, were evident in the seven ecumenical councils, were enhanced by language differences (Greek in the East and Latin in the West), and found their political counterparts engaged in war (for example, when in 1204 the armies of the West during the Fourth Crusade sacked Constantinople, the center of the Eastern Church).

Protestantism is the newest of the major categories of American religion, originating as it did in the late Middle Ages with religious reformers such as John Huss (1369–1415), Martin Luther (1483–1546), Ulrich Zwingli (1484–1531), John Calvin (1509–1564), and John Knox (1513–1572), who wanted not so much to found new churches but to reform and restore what was already there, namely, the Roman Catholic Church. Thus, we have the term "reformation." And we have the term "Protestant," which refers both to the idea of protest against what some viewed as perversions and distortions of original Christianity within the Roman Catholic Church and, as the term came to be used in Elizabethan England, to the idea of affirming a particular set of beliefs, of "bearing witness" to a particular confession and point of view.

Jewish Denominations in America

We mentioned earlier that along religious dimensions there are six major subgroups of Jews in the United States. We will describe each briefly.

The most firmly rooted in historical Old Testament Judaism is that of Orthodoxy. Orthodox Jews very consciously try to maintain the teachings and rituals of the Torah (the first five books of the Old Testament) and perceive of themselves as the only legitimate bearers of Jewish tradition.[6] This means that they view themselves as the preservers of both traditional doctrine and ritual observances. There is a high emphasis on study of the

---

[5]There is no consensus among historians on either a date or an event to mark the formal division into a Roman Catholic and an Orthodox division of Christianity, though a prime candidate would be the ninth century mutual excommunication exchanged by St. Photius, patriarch of Constantinople, and St. Nicholas of Rome. Other suggestions range all the way to 1439 A.D., with a commonly accepted date being 1054, when another mutual excommunication took place. Cf. Arthur C. Piepkorn, *Profiles in Belief*, Vol. I (New York: Harper & Row, Pub., 1977), pp. 32–33.

[6]Charles S. Liebman, "Orthodoxy in American Jewish Life," in *The Jewish Community in America*, ed. Marshall Sklare (New York: Behrman House, 1974), p. 134.

Torah and the Talmud (the rabbinical commentary on the Torah) in the original Hebrew. The Torah is supreme and is believed to reveal that God has chosen the Jews to be His special people who will teach justice, peace, and love to the world. There is careful observance of festival days such as Yom Kippur and Passover. An unqualified obligation is the keeping of a kosher house and serving kosher meals by maintaining separate sets of dishes and utensils for meat and for dairy products, as well as using only those foods that have been slaughtered or prepared under approved rabbinical conditions. In observation of the Sabbath from sunset Friday to sunset Saturday the Orthodox Jew tries to put aside the secular world and enter a world of prayer and family activities that will not allow cooking, writing, buying and selling, and any number of other everyday activities that are avoided on such a special day in the week.

Reform Judaism emerged in nineteenth century Europe as a very conscious attempt by some Jewish intellectuals led by Abraham Geiger (1810–1874) in Germany to bring traditional Jewish Orthodoxy more up to date and in tune with modern realities. The movement rejected many traditional Jewish laws and substituted ethics for laws. The declaration of principles issued by the Frankfort Society of the Friends of Reform in 1843 is a fairly concise summary of their position.

> First, we recognize the possibility of unlimited development in the Mosaic religion. Second, the collection of controversies and prescriptions commonly designated by the name Talmud possess for us no authority from either the doctrinal or the practical standpoint. Third, a Messiah who is to lead back the Israelites to the land of Palestine is neither expected nor desired by us; we know no fatherland but that to which we belong by birth or citizenship.[7]

Isaac Mayer Wise (1819–1900), who is credited with establishing Reform Judaism in the United States when he founded the Union of American Hebrew Congregations in 1873, expressed confidence that this Reform Judaism would soon become the Judaism of all American Jews. While this did not happen, Reform Judaism did attract a substantial following and accounts for a little less than a third of American Jews.[8]

Conservative Judaism quite deliberately takes the traditionalism of Orthodoxy and the liberalism of the Reform movement and blends them. It is a distinctly American innovation for Jews who had immigrated to the

---

[7]Quoted from G. F. Moore, *History of Religions*, Vol. II (New York: Scribner's, 1946), p. 94.

[8]A Boston survey found 27 percent of Jews identify themselves as Reform, 44 percent Conservative, 14 percent Orthodox, 15 percent with no preference or consider themselves as nonreligious. Cf. Morris Axelrod, Floyd J. Fowler, and Arnold Gurin, *A Community for Long Range Planning—A Study of the Jewish Population of Greater Boston* (Boston: Combined Jewish Philanthropies of Greater Boston, 1967), p. 119. A survey in Providence, Rhode Island, found 21.2 percent Reform, 19.8 percent Orthodox, 54.1 percent Conservative, and 4.9 percent other self-designations. Cf. Sidney Goldstein and Calvin Goldscheider, *Jewish Americans: Three Generations in a Jewish Community* (Englewood Cliffs, NJ: Prentice-Hall 1968), p. 177.

United States some years earlier but were becoming highly accul-
turated—people who had moved out of the Jewish ghetto into neighborhoods that were predominantly non-Jewish, wanted to use English as their
religious as well as social language, yet did not want as complete a divorce
from historic Judaism with its host of customs and beliefs as Reform Judaism represented. The Conservative movement devised a Sunday school
program for children in conformity with the Protestants around them and
developed confirmation ceremonies, "Bas Mitzvah," for girls as a ritual parallel to the Bar Mitzvah for boys. Thus, Jewish children could maintain a
solid link with their past but also point out to the other children in their
neighborhood and school that although they were Jews they were not that
different.

Marshall Sklare points out that it became particularly difficult for truly
Orthodox Jews to maintain their orthodoxy when so much of their everyday life was outside the synagogue and its immediate community.[9] In other
words, it was much easier to be an Orthodox Jew in a Jewish ghetto in eastern Europe than in an American city where most of one's contacts and activities were with non-Jews.

The compromise that is Conservative Judaism quickly showed its practical wisdom as it became the largest Jewish religious organization. This
growth was particularly marked in the decades after World War II.

Reconstructionist Judaism is the newest of the Jewish denominations,
emerging to full-blown denominational status only in the late 1960s. Although the founder, Mordecai Kaplan (b. 1881), did not propose a new
denomination and wanted only to synthesize the best of all Jewish traditions
into a meaningful program of thought and practice for the contemporary
Jew, a new denomination emerged when Reconstructionists established
both their own seminary to train rabbis and a central organization to aid
congregations and propagate the faith. Doctrinally, Reconstructionist Jews
reject all ideas of supernatural power or person. Thus, no Torah was revealed to Moses on Mt. Sinai, no Messiah should be expected, and miracles
as recorded in the Bible never really happened. Instead they place heavy
emphasis on the unity of Jews with a common culture and heritage despite
denominational differences that separate them.

Sectarian Judaism consists of several small groups and movements, the
best known of which is Hasidic Judaism. A Hasid is a mystic. Thus, Hasidic
Judaism includes persons who consider themselves Orthodox but also possess an additional dimension of mysticism, emotion, and ecstasy. Their
counterparts within Protestantism in at least some ways would be the charismatic pentecostals.

The Hasidic movement arose in Poland in the eighteenth century and
spread rapidly to include nearly half of eastern European Jews in its

---

[9]Marshall Sklare, *Conservative Judaism: An American Religious Movement* (New York:
Schocken Books, 1972), pp. 45–46.

ranks.[10] Hasidic Jews are usually distinguished by their outward appearance. They will likely be dressed in black, wear large black hats sometimes of fur, be bearded, and have long curled earlocks. They are highly concentrated in circumscribed urban areas—the Labavitcher movement, for example, located predominantly in the Crown Heights section of Brooklyn, the Satmar community of about 1,200 families, most of whom are located in the Williamsburg and Borough Park sections of Brooklyn, and the Skvirer Hasidim in Rockland County, New York, that left Brooklyn to establish a separate community in which they could exercise greater internal social control.[11]

The final Jewish subgroup we would mention is not religious at all, strictly speaking. These are people of Jewish ethnicity who feel some kinship with others of Jewish origin but have rejected the religious elements of Judaism. Hence the designation we used earlier of "cultural-ethnic Jews." This designation would include the more than half of American Jews who are not affiliated with a local synagogue yet will probably identify themselves as Jews and might even claim affiliation with Reform Judaism if questioned about their religious identity.[12] In addition to the fewer than 50 percent who are not affiliated with a local synagogue, only about half participate at all regularly in synagogue services and activities.[13] And of that quarter of all American Jews, only about half go beyond celebrating Passover and Hannukah and regularly observe the Sabbath in any regularized way.[14]

Roman Catholicism

Roman Catholicism in the United States has suffered the effects of minority status since our country's beginning. Even when millions of immigrants from eastern and southern Europe and Ireland swelled the ranks of the Catholic Church in the nineteenth and early twentieth centuries, Roman Catholicism continued to be viewed with suspicion and distrust by other Americans. They saw Roman Catholic subjection to the Pope in Rome as an expression of a divided loyalty that made Roman Catholics at best only half American. They also saw Roman Catholics sending their children to Roman Catholic schools that were established explicitly to help members

[10]Martin Buber, *Hasidism and Modern Man*, ed. and trans. Maurice Friedman (New York: Harper & Row, 1958), p. 10.

[11]Marshall Sklare, *America's Jews* (New York: Random House, 1971), pp. 49–50.

[12]Charles S. Liebman and Eliezer Don-Yehiya, *Religion and Politics in Israel* (Bloomington: Indiana University Press, 1984), p. 9.

[13]Ibid.

[14]Ibid, p. 11.

"keep the faith," and they marked them as under suspicion. If one adds to the list of issues the opposition of Catholic theology to any kind of so-called unnatural birth control, the opposition to interfaith marriage and the requirement of a prenuptial agreement to educate any children in the Catholic faith if permission to marry outside the faith was granted at all, and a retention of many Old World customs in the many Roman Catholic ethnic enclaves, and Protestant Americans became even more suspicious. Quite expectedly, though hardly helping to improve the situation, many Roman Catholics developed an "inferiority complex" and found it difficult to relate on an eyeball-to-eyeball basis with their Protestant neighbors. However, with the election of the Roman Catholic John F. Kennedy as president, with clear signs of ecumenical openness in the person and message of Pope John XXIII, with signals of doctrinal innovation and change in the second ecumenical council, with fewer Roman Catholics isolating themselves in Catholic schools, with many nuns adopting average street clothing for their works of mercy and education, with the civil rights movement gaining acceptance for many minorities and not just black Americans, and above all with the practices of Catholic laypeople with respect to such traditionally important issues of marriage and birth control rapidly approximating those of other Americans—with all these changes we find that Roman Catholics have definitely joined and been accepted in the mainstream of American life.

Yet Roman Catholic doctrine continues to be distinctive. There continues to be a high regard for Mary, the mother of Jesus, who is still believed to have been immaculately conceived, have lived a sinless life, have given birth to Christ yet with her virginity intact, have bodily ascended to heaven before death and now is believed to serve as an intermediary between people and God. There continues to be a belief in papal infallibility over matters of faith and doctrine and an emphasis on penance paid by the faithful by way of partial atonement for their sinful acts. Yet on central doctrines of historic Christianity, such as the triune nature of God as Father, Son, and Holy Spirit, creation of the world by God, the existence of angels both good and evil, the sinful nature of human beings and their need for God's salvation, and salvation as coming only through the death and resurrection of God's Son, Jesus Christ, Roman Catholics join most Protestant and Orthodox Christians.

Yet many areas of doctrine and practice show great discrepancies between the official doctrine and the practice of Catholic laypersons. For example, Andrew Greeley found in a 1974 sample of Roman Catholics that only 17 percent practiced monthly confession and only 18 percent would accept the church's position on even two of three items that constituted a "sexual orthodoxy" scale (no divorce, no "artificial" methods of birth control, and no premarital sex). In each case there was a significant decline from only eleven years earlier, when 37 percent still practiced monthly confession and 42 percent followed the church's dictates on at least two of the three items in the sexual orthodoxy scale.[15]

We suggested earlier that such changed practices constitute one reason for greater acceptance of Catholics in the mainstream of American life. But probably more significant is the prediction that as a consequence of such changing practices doctrines will eventually change as well, although not overnight by any means. In fact, in the face of such changing behavior and practice there have been reactionary voices within Roman Catholic official-dom.

For example, although Pope John XXIII established a special commission in 1963 to investigate whether a change in the church's traditional prohibitions against birth control could and should be brought about, and although the commission voted 13 to 2 for change,[16] the closest advisors to the Pope (the Vatican Curia) persuaded the successor to John XXIII, Pope Paul VI, to conserve the traditional position of the church. His encyclical letter "Humanae Vitae," issued in 1968, reaffirmed traditional positions and was at odds with the liberalizing directions suggested by the Second Vatican Council (1962–1965). Andrew Greeley, whose data on changed attitudes and practices of Roman Catholics we reported earlier, finds the encyclical "Humanae Vitae" almost entirely to blame for the rapid decline of traditional Roman Catholic practice with respect to birth control in particular.

Pope John Paul II, although charming, diplomatic, warm, open, and well received by most, whether Catholic or non-Catholic, liberal or conservative, still felt obliged in the early 1980s to reaffirm traditional Roman Catholic positions in such areas as birth control, the ordination of women to the priesthood, and priestly celibacy. Furthermore, various groups of Catholic laypeople oppose many of the recent changes in doctrine and practice and urge a return to the old ways. Not only do they not want even to hear talk about the possibility of priests being allowed to marry, but they want Latin brought back as the language of the liturgy. They have declared Pope John XXIII an inauthentic pope and the Second Vatican Council an invalid assembly.

It is of more than passing interest that thousands of Roman Catholic laypeople are involved in this movement commonly referred to as "Catholic Traditionalism." William Dinges estimates 10,000 to 15,000 active participants. He reports that there are 230 locations throughout the United States where the old Latin Mass is celebrated regularly in violation of the man-

---

[15]Andrew M. Greeley, "Council or Encyclical?" *Review of Religious Research*, 18, no. 1 (Fall, 1976), 11.

[16]Andrew Greeley, "The Making of the Pope, Part Four," *Detroit Free Press* (August 17, 1978), p. 11a.

dated vernacular mass. Traditionalists support several parochial schools and have ninety priests to serve them.[17] Four organizations carry the banner of this Catholic traditionalism: the Catholic Traditionalist Movement in the United States, the Orthodox Roman Catholic Movement, Traditional Catholics in America, and the Society of Saint Pius X.[18] The last-named organization is the largest and most significant. As a religious order, it has organizational capabilities and continuity that many simple voluntary associations lack. It even has the authority to train and ordain priests to propagate the message of Catholic traditionalism (ordaining over twenty priests a year at present).[19] It should also be noted that the Catholic Traditionalism movement is both larger and more aggressive in Europe. The foremost figure in the movement, Archbishop Marcel Lefebvre, who heads the Society of Saint Pius X, began his work in France and immigrated to the United States a few years ago. He stated in his 1974 "Credo" that the reforms of the Second Vatican Council "spring from heresy and end in heresy."

We mentioned earlier that there have been some reactionary signs among Roman Catholic officialdom. In this connection, the authorization in 1981 by the Vatican of a broad study and evaluation of all 501 Roman Catholic seminaries in the United States has prompted a great deal of suspicion among more liberal Catholics. They see this as a fairly heavy-handed attempt to return to more traditional educational methods that will train more traditional priests who will stick to their traditional ministries and avoid political and social action involvement. Some heads of American Roman Catholic seminaries fear serious infringement on hard-won academic freedom gained since the Second Vatican Council.[20]

Further evidence of Vatican attempts to reaffirm the conservatism of the encyclical "Humanae Vitae" and discredit the Second Vatican Council came in the summer of 1986, when a Roman Catholic priest, Father Charles Curran, was dismissed from his post as a Professor of Moral Theology at Catholic University of America. He was dismissed by the Congregation for the Doctrine of the Faith at the Vatican for his liberal views on birth control, abortion, divorce, homosexuality, and euthanasia, among other issues.

It is clear that the Roman Catholic Church in America is not nearly so cohesive or unified as some common stereotypes would suggest. There are strong pressures from some constituencies to move in a more liberal direc-

---

[17]William D. Dinges, "Catholic Traditionalism in America: Sociological Aspects of a Value-Oriented Social Movement." Paper presented at the 1981 annual meeting of the Society for the Scientific Study of Religion and the Religious Research Association, October 30, 1981, Baltimore, Maryland.

[18]Ibid.

[19]Ibid.

[20]Harry Cook, "Is the Vatican Out to Change the Education of Its Priests?", *Detroit Free Press* (October 4, 1981).

tion; other constituencies push fervently back toward the past and a more conservative, traditionalist emphasis and practice. Roman Catholics are facing what Jews and Protestants have grappled with for a long time.

Eastern Orthodoxy

The Eastern Orthodox Church has its origins with the very beginning of Christianity, and its theologians played the leading roles in the seven ecumenical councils that were held during the fourth through eighth centuries A.D. As mentioned earlier, the Christian Church split into the Western (Roman Catholic) and Eastern (Orthodox) Churches in the ninth century A.D. But, while the Roman Catholic Church remained formally unified under the Pope in Rome, the Eastern Church recognized four primary Patriarchs—the religious sovereign and counterpart to the Pope—in Constantinople, Alexandria, Antioch, and Jerusalem. In addition, semiautonomous churches evolved in Greece, Albania, Bulgaria, Cyprus, Romania, the Soviet Union, and Yugoslavia. Immigrants to the United States from these countries brought their churches with them. The largest and best known are the Greek Orthodox Archdiocese of North and South America and the Russian Orthodox Church in America. Other Eastern Orthodox churches are the Albanian, the Bulgarian, the Romanian, the Carpatho-Russian, Serbian Orthodox, Syrian Antiochian Orthodox, the United Ukranian Orthodox churches, and many other very small groups for a total of 50 denominations that are in the Eastern Orthodox tradition.[21]

Although closer theologically to Roman Catholicism than is much of Protestantism, Orthodoxy differs from Roman Catholicism in several ways. It does not recognize the Pope in Rome as the supreme pontiff, but as only one bishop among many; it contends that the Virgin Mary was cleansed from original sin at the Annunciation rather than at her conception; it rejects the Roman Catholic doctrine of the Assumption of Mary and the doctrine of purgatory. The Orthodox groups differ from most Protestants in accepting apostolic succession, subscribing to seven sacraments (called mysteries), engaging in a dramatic liturgy, de-emphasizing the sermon, employing icons in their worship, and believing that there is a supernatural link between the icon and the person it represents.

The Orthodox churches have by and large successfully resisted the pressures of the surrounding society to "modernize" and "Americanize" their doctrine and practice. To step inside an Orthodox sanctuary is to take a longer step back in time and observe an older and more original tradition than would be the case in most any other American religious group except

---

[21]J. Gordon Melton, *Encyclopedia of American Religions*, Vol. 1 (Wilmington, NC: McGrath, 1978), pp. 57–87.

Orthodox Judaism. Consistent with such traditionalism and resistence to change, a religious feminist movement has yet to begin in the Orthodox churches.

Protestantism

The denominations and sects that comprise Protestantism are sufficiently different among themselves as almost to doom any attempt to generalize. Not only do their forms of organization run the full range from episcopal through presbyterian to congregational, but their assent to various central orthodox Christian doctrines is far from unanimous. While some say the Lord's body and blood are truly present in the bread and wine of the Lord's Supper, others believe the presence is only symbolized by the bread and wine, perhaps also insisting that the wine be grape juice. While some see the Virgin Birth as not only unimportant but untrue, others make the doctrine one of only a handful of the most crucial beliefs of all. While some believe God created the universe in six days of twenty-four hours each in length, others accept evolutionary theories that do not presume divine creation of any kind. For further specification of the diversity, note the great diversity among Protestant denominations and Roman Catholics on several standard Christian doctrines shown in Table 13-1. Note that these data reflect what members of these denominations believe and not necessarily what the denominations might officially stand for.

Although we have emphasized the vast diversity within Protestantism and have implied it is almost absurd to try to generalize, there are historical reasons for generalizing about Protestantism, and there are even a few generalizations that are reasonably valid today.

We suggested earlier that Protestants got their name by protesting against Roman Catholicism. In such protest there were some implicit similarities among the protesters—resentment against the Pope and religious control over political agencies, reaction against the imposition of indulgences, aversion against what amounted in many cases to worship of the saints, and the like. But there were important differences among the groups that gathered around the various reformers. For example, while someone like Martin Luther thought there was much in the Roman Catholic Church that should be retained, others such as Andreas Carlstadt (d. 1541) and Thomas Müntzer (d. 1525) insisted that everything that smacked of Romanism must go. So, while Luther thought organs and music and statues and paintings were important and must be integrated into worship and instruction, Carlstadt and Müntzer felt justified not only in keeping such ornamentations out of their churches but in destroying them when they could.

A more explicit tenet of all of Protestantism has been the right and the ability of individuals to be in touch with God, to learn religious truth, and to

TABLE 13-1 Proportion of Denominational Members Agreeing with Various Doctrinal Statements

STATEMENT	CONGREGA-TIONALIST	METHODIST	EPISCO-PALIAN	DISCIPLES OF CHRIST	PRESBY-TERIAN	AMERICAN LUTHERAN	AMERICAN BAPTIST	MISSOURI LUTHERAN	SOUTHERN BAPTIST	SECTS	ROMAN CATHOLIC
"I know God really exists and I have no doubts about it."	41%	60%	63%	76%	75%	73%	78%	81%	99%	96%	81%
"Jesus is the Divine Son of God and I have no doubts about it."	40	54	59	74	72	74	76	93	99	97	86
"Jesus was born of a virgin." (% saying: "Completely true.")	21	34	39	62	57	66	69	92	99	96	81
"Jesus walked on water." (% saying: "Completely true.")	19	26	30	62	51	58	62	83	99	94	71
"Will Jesus actually return to the earth someday?" (% answering, "Definitely.")	13	21	24	36	43	54	57	75	94	89	47
"Miracles actually happened just as the Bible says they did."	28	37	41	62	58	69	62	89	92	92	74
"There is a life beyond death." (% saying: "Completely true.")	36	49	53	64	69	70	72	84	97	94	75
"A child is born into the world already guilty of sin." (% saying: "Completely true.")	2	7	18	6	21	49	23	86	43	47	68

Source: Rodney Stark and Charles Y. Glock, *American Piety* (Berkeley: University of California Press, 1968), pp. 28, 33, 34, 36, 37, and 4U. Used by permission of the University of California Press.

worship God as individuals without the necessity of an intermediary or intercessor such as a priest or the Virgin Mary. Integral to this belief is the conviction that the Bible as the sourcebook for Christianity should not only be open and available to all believers but can be understood by them as well. This emphasis on the Bible has led to near idolatry by some Protestants, who make much of its "verbal inspiration" and authority as the perfect and complete revelation of God for all times.

Another generalization so far as Protestants are concerned is a restriction on the number of sacraments to two or fewer (Holy Baptism and the Lord's Supper), certainly far fewer than the traditional seven in Roman Catholicism (Baptism, Lord's Supper, Confirmation, Penance, Ordination, Matrimony, and Extreme Unction).

We have mentioned several times the great diversity within Protestantism. We will now, as we conclude our discussion of Protestantism in general terms, identify the major groupings of Protestant religious denominations in the United States.

The Anglican or Episcopal Churches   While it has been said that Anglicanism has no "theology" in the sense of a comprehensive summary of doctrine, actually in a practical sense Anglicanism has a very *comprehensive* theology in that it has very deliberately retained the traditional liturgical emphasis of the Roman Catholic Church while also incorporating an essentially Calvinist or Reformed set of beliefs. Its continuity with Roman Catholicism is reinforced by its emphasis on apostolic succession—the belief that its clergy are descendents in an unbroken line from the apostles. Furthermore, it is a sacramental church—meaning it believes that the two primary sacraments are central to the essence of the church. These Anglican churches might also be called "Christmas churches" in the sense that they stress that God became human at the birth of the God-man Jesus Christ (the Incarnation).

The Episcopal or Anglican churches originated in the English Reformation, which saw Parliament grant independence to the Church of England around 1530 during the reign of Henry VIII. The Anglican (English) Church was transplanted to the New World with the settlement of Jamestown, Virginia, in 1607. Following the Revolutionary War, the American Anglicans established their religious independence as the Protestant Episcopal Church in the United States.

The Lutheran Churches   The Lutheran faith might be said to have begun when Martin Luther nailed his ninety-five theses to the church door in Wittenberg, Germany, on October 31, 1517. However, it was not Luther's intent at that time to start a new church; he wanted reform of the Roman Catholic Church and had ninety-five issues or points he wanted to discuss and debate. The Lutheran movement spread rapidly through Germany and into the Scandinavian countries. It arrived early òn the American scene—Dutch Lutherans in New York in 1623 and Swedes along the Delaware River in 1638. The immigration of Lutherans continued steadily during the next three centuries and resulted in the establishment of many ethnic communities and churches. The Norwegians, Swedes, Danes, Finns, and Germans all established ethnic denominations—several denominations, in fact, within each ethnic group—and the Lutherans became in the process the most ethnically divided religious family in America.[22]

Several mergers within American Lutheranism have taken place within this century to reduce the number of Lutheran denominations to four major ones, though there remain ten other small ones—one with only five congregations totaling fewer than 400 members.

Lutherans constitute a "confessional" religious movement. That is, they place great stress on detailed bodies of doctrine that have become official interpretations of Scripture that are accepted because they correctly (it is asserted by Lutherans) interpret Scripture. Like the Roman Catholics and the Anglican-Episcopal traditions, they are sacramental churches. That is, they view the sacraments of baptism and the Lord's Supper as "means of grace" through which God works directly. As such, the sacraments are more than symbols; they mediate God's grace.

Their central confessional principle is the Latin expression *Sola Gratia, Sola Fide, Sola Scriptura*—by grace alone, by faith alone, by Scripture alone. Or to say it differently, but with another expression frequently used by Lutherans—justification by grace through faith. Like the Roman Catholics, Episcopalians, and Eastern Orthodox, they are liturgical churches. That is, Lutherans follow a fairly elaborate ritual and pattern in their worship services—one with strong historical roots and with great uniformity from one local congregation to another.

Reformed and Presbyterian Churches   These are the denominations that most directly followed the lead of John Calvin. The various Reformed bodies originated in Switzerland, Germany, and Holland; the Presbyterian bodies started in Scotland. Prominent themes within the Calvinist tradition are the sovereignty of God, the life of piety for God's people, and predestination or eternal election (cf. Chapter 8). Although they too use the two primary sacraments, they are seen more as symbolic acts that bring to remembrance God's acts in the past.

The first essentially Presbyterian Church was established in the Massachusetts Bay Colony in 1629. The Reformed Church in America goes back to 1621 when the Dutch West India Company placed Reformed ministers in the New Netherlands Colony along the Hudson River.

---

[22]Other ethnically identified religious groups would be the Dutch Reformed and informal subgroups within American Catholicism—Irish Catholics, Polish Catholics, Italian Catholics, Hispanic Catholics, and so on.

In many ways the Presbyterian-Reformed tradition is the most centrist, "average" expression of Protestantism in America. All the traditional orthodox doctrines of Christianity are there with little of an extreme nature, except perhaps the classic presentation of predestination. On the other hand, there are offshoots of this tradition that are not only highly conservative in theology but also in practice and have strong overtones of the Radical Reformation that we will introduce next. We are thinking here of such groups as the Dutch Reformed, Christian Reformed, Orthodox Presbyterian, and the Bible Presbyterian Church, among others.

Churches of the Radical Reformation   The major foundations and emphases of this tradition are articulated in the seven articles of the Schleitheim Confession of 1527.[23] These articles are as follows: baptism is for adults only; excommunication is an important means of keeping the group pure; the Lord's Supper is a memorial feast for adult members; the group must be separated from all evil such as Roman Catholic and any other worship services, as well as drinking establishments; the pastor must be a person of good reputation and integrity; church and state must be strictly separate, and individual Christians should not participate in the political process; oaths are forbidden.

In America, the original Puritans and the various Mennonite groups were direct practitioners of the Radical Reformation. Two major Protestant groupings today that might be surprises in a list of practitioners of this track of Protestantism because they seem to be such "normal," standard Protestant denominations are the Congregational Christian and the Evangelical and Reformed Churches that merged to become the United Church of Christ in 1957 as well as the various Baptist denominations. However, the Baptists, in particular, continue with the view of the sacraments expressed in the Schleitheim Confession and stress moral behavior that would often forbid such activities as card playing and drinking.

Methodist Churches   Methodism is certainly the youngest of the major Protestant denominations. Founded in the eighteenth century by John and Charles Wesley as a movement within the Church of England, it did not become a separate body until after John Wesley's death in 1791. Its origin was in the pietistic revival movement that swept Europe, the British Isles, and America in the early 1700s. Wesley held to the authority of Scripture and the centrality of faith but emphasized more than some Protestants the fruition of that faith in a life of love and good works. He talked much about the "life of perfection," which he believed was attainable by true Christians who felt God at work within them and had the experience of true conversion burning within them. Thus, knowing the moment of one's conversion became a trademark of Methodists. Also, the methodical attention in one's

[23] Arthur C. Piepkorn, *Profiles of Belief*, Vol. 2 (New York: Harper & Row, 1978), p. 363.

life to attain perfection became not only a trademark but the source of their name.

A *Life* magazine comment on the Methodist denomination, quoted by J. Paul Williams, although not totally complimentary, does catch the flavor of several major themes within Methodism:

> In many ways it is our most characteristic church. It is short on theology, long on good works, brilliantly organized, primarily middle-class, frequently big-oted, incurably optimistic, zealously missionary and touchingly confident of the essential goodness of the man next door.[24]

Holiness and Pentecostal Denominations   An outgrowth of Methodism in the late 1800s was the Holiness movement, which in turn provided the soil out of which the Pentecostal movement grew around the turn of this century. These are all Arminian groups with their theology rooted in the teachings of Jacob Arminius (1560–1609), who stressed both the universality of God's grace but also the freedom of people to choose for or against salvation—an emphasis implying a cooperative, human element in salvation that Lutherans and others viewed as undercutting the doctrine of salvation by God's grace alone.

The Holiness movement developed in classic sectarian form (cf. Chapter 8) as some among American Methodists felt that both the goal and method of attaining Christian perfection were being neglected. As Arthur Piepkorn says so succinctly, "[They] sought to recapture Wesleyan perfectionism in order to make American Methodists into holy people."[25] They stressed the sanctified life, renounced unholy practices such as the use of alcohol and tobacco and membership in secret societies, and encouraged continuation of the Methodist-inspired camp-meeting approach to instruction, conversion, and spiritual reinforcement.

The Pentecostal movement, in most simple terms, was holiness religion to which had been added the special gift of glossolalia (speaking in tongues) as evidence of Pentecostal experience. Although the holiness people as well as what we might call the classical Methodists were not pleased with the development of Pentecostalism, Ignacio Vergara's statement that "Pentecostalism is Methodism carried to its ultimate consequences,"[26] is quite accurate.

Other Religions

There are of course many other religious groups in America. We have discussed only the major ones—major in terms of numbers and visibility.

---

[24] J. Paul Williams, *What Americans Believe and How They Worship*, 3rd ed. (New York: Harper & Row, 1969), p. 286, quoted from an editorial, *Life* (November 10, 1947), p. 38.

[25] Arthur C. Piepkorn, *Profiles of Belief*, Vol. 3 (New York: Harper & Row, 1979), p. 3.

[26] Ignacio Vergara, *El Protestanismo En Chile* (1961), pp. 126–127, quoted in the Introduction by Vinson Syman to Arthur C. Piepkorn, ibid., p. xvi.

But there are others, including Asian religions such as Buddhism and Hinduism. We will say a little about them shortly.

But first we need to remind the reader of the many sects and cults that have always proliferated in America but have been particularly in evidence the past twenty-five years. We discussed the social form and character of sects and cults in Chapter 5, and will revisit them briefly in Chapter 14. Included would be the innumerable Christian sects that form in the inner cities of all major urban areas. And there are the highly visible and much-publicized cults such as Hare Krishna, Unification Church, Children of God, and so on, many of which have Asian leaders or at least have strong Asian religious influence.

But there are also groups of people who have transplanted local assemblies of fairly traditional Asian religions such as Hinduism, Buddhism, Shinto, and Sikhism, as well as the near-Eastern religion of Islam. Most of the growth of these groups has come in the decades since World War II. It has been largely the result of immigration of individuals and families who brought with them their religion just as earlier Poles brought their Catholicism, Swedes brought their Lutheranism, and Russian Jews brought their Judaism. But more recently the refugees from Vietnam and Cambodia have come, bringing their religion with them. Also many students from India and Pakistan have come to study and have stayed or have come back after a brief return to their country of birth. And immigrants from Lebanon, Turkey, Iran, and Yemen have come, just as millions of immigrants before them, looking for employment and a better life for themselves and their children. They have brought their Muslim religion with them.

It should be pointed out that the Muslim faith is probably the fastest growing non-Western religion in the United States. Since few of these groups keep and report membership statistics the way the long-established religious groups in the United States do, we lack precise figures. But we do see Muslim mosques and Muslim cultural centers either built or under construction throughout the country; we see ethnic concentrations of Muslims in such places as Dearborn, Michigan and Cedar Rapids, Iowa, in addition to the large metropolises of New York City and Chicago; and estimates of numbers of Muslims suggest at least 1,000,000 in the United States and 100,000 to 200,000 in Canada.[27] It may well be the fastest growing religion in North America at the present time.

Then, too, one could include the Black Muslim group, which has garnered a lot of press coverage over the last thirty-five years, but is of questionable validity so far as its stature as a Muslim group is concerned. They continue to receive publicity, whether it's the murder of a former leader, Malcolm X, or by following professional sports and learning that Cassius

---

[27]Newell S. Booth, Jr., "Islam in North America," in Charles H. Lippy and Peter W. Williams, eds., *Encyclopedia of the American Religious Experience*, Vol. II (New York: Charles Scribner's Sons, 1988), p. 726.

Clay became Muhammad Ali and Lew Alcindor became Kareem Abdul Ja-baar, or reading about Louis Farrakhan, the current Black Muslim leader of the reform group that is trying to restore the original Nation of Islam.

But although the Muslims are most numerous and fairly visible in their mosques and ethnic communities, there are Buddhist and Hindu "congregations" and temples also—as with Muslims, particularly in the urban ethnic communities. Many of the Hindus are Asian Indians who numbered 387,223 in the 1980 U.S. Census. The Population Reference Bureau estimates slightly over a million Asian Indians in the United States by the year 2000. Not all will be Hindu. Some will be Sikhs and a few Jains.

It needs to be observed that the numbers of avowed Muslims, Hindus, Buddhists, Sikhs, Shintoists, and other near-Eastern and Asian religions are already in the millions, and their numbers grow. While some inevitably will convert to Christianity and many gradually drift away from their traditional religious practices, the link of religion to ethnicity is strong enough that these religions will continue to be viable, will probably continue to grow, and will add many new dimensions to the meaning of religious diversity and pluralism in the United States and Canada.

ECUMENISM

Despite the theological diversity we have just scanned, American denominations have shown considerable facility at coexisting peacefully. This is true historically of Protestants with Protestants primarily. It has been suggested that, for Protestants at least, different denominations are regarded by most citizens as equally valid ways of being a religious American. In fact, the principal occasion for Protestant religious groups to become suspicious of other Protestant groups has been when the actions or beliefs of those others suggested less than wholehearted commitment to the American Republic. German Lutherans, for example, were prodded and occasionally harassed during World War I, as many of them continued to use the German language in their churches and schools and as some openly supported the German "fatherland." Jehovah's Witnesses have repeatedly felt legal and social pressure because of their stands against saluting the flag and serving in the armed forces. Amish fathers who refused to allow their children to attend school beyond the eighth grade were periodically jailed for their convictions until 1972, when the Supreme Court ruled in their favor. Choosing not to use the English language, refusing to salute the flag, and questioning the value of formal education raise doubts in many citizens' minds about a group's loyalty and commitment to basic American principles. It hardly needs mentioning that both the Jehovah's Witnesses and the Amish are sectarian groups that protest not simply against what they view as religious error but against prevailing social structures as well.

Despite some exceptions, such as those referred to above, we can say that for most of the United States' history most religious groups have felt relatively secure and have been able to pursue their business unhampered by government, other religious groups, or fellow citizens. In short, the constitutional provision for free exercise of religion has been in fairly effective operation.

There is, of course, a fairly certain way for a religious group to bring down the wrath of other groups upon itself, that is, to proselytize actively and seek converts from other religious groups. Actually, except for a few groups such as the Mormons and Jehovah's Witnesses and a few small conversionist sects, this has been no serious issue. Not that most groups have not been willing to make converts to their faith. But they have tended to concentrate on those who were not affiliated with any religious groups, those who voluntarily knocked on the door, and those with whom the group has been put in contact because of marriage with a group member. In fact, most major Protestant groups, concerned lest they inadvertently overstep the bounds of others and be accused of proselytizing, commonly establish comity arrangements with one another; particularly in expanding communities, denominations typically divide the territory among themselves so that each has designated areas in which to work and establish new congregations without competing with other denominations.

The context of cooperation and peaceful coexistence just described is an important background factor in the rise of *ecumenism*—not simply greater cooperation but joint efforts that might lead ultimately to the organic merger of two or more denominations. The ecumenical movement is essentially a phenomenon of the twentieth century and has involved much discussion and commentary. Yet despite the great volume of literature and discussion, relatively few actual mergers have taken place. There have been mergers among Lutheran denominations from various Scandinavian countries once the groups had become "Americanized," began conversing in English, and realized they all subscribed to the same confessional and creedal statements. Specifically, there have been four of these—the formation of the United Lutheran Church in America in 1917, the American Lutheran Church in 1960, the Lutheran Church of America in 1962, and the Evangelical Lutheran Church in America in 1988. In the last merger the Lutheran Church in America, the American Lutheran Church, and a smaller group, the American Evangelical Lutheran Church, joined forces and now constitute the largest Lutheran denomination in the United States.

In 1957 the Congregational Christian Churches merged with the Evangelical and Reformed Church to form the United Church of Christ. And in 1968 a merger was effected between the Evangelical United Brethren Church and the United Methodist Church. Stimulated by Eugene Carson Blake's dramatic suggestion in 1960 for a merger of most of the major Protestant denominations in the United States, discussions have been going on for nearly three decades within the Consultation on Church Union (COCU), which was formed to facilitate discussion and the possible ultimate merger itself. Twelve denominations originally entered the discussions of COCU. By 1972 four had withdrawn, the latest being the United Presbyterian Church, which, however, voted in 1973 to rescind its action of the previous year and rejoin the discussion. By 1980 there were nine denominations and one federation (the National Council of Community Churches) still involved in discussion and in supporting a small full-time staff. While no mergers have been brought about during its thirty and more years of existence, COCU sees itself as alive and well and continuing to facilitate the kinds of dialogue, interaction, and activity that could result in concrete ecumenical outcomes sometime down the road.

What those involved in COCU and other ecumenical discussions have been discovering is the extreme difficulty of blending religious groups that have unique histories, distinct theologies, and different social constituencies. Here, in a real sense, the theological differences reflected by the data in Table 13-1 become evident and important. Issues involving forms of church government (episcopal, presbyterian, or congregational), differing views of the ministry, the nature and function of the two most common Christian sacraments of baptism and holy communion (Lord's Supper), and a host of other issues make agreement and compromise extremely difficult to achieve.

But ecumenical discussion has not been limited to Protestantism. Increasingly after 1950, Catholics, Eastern Orthodox, and Jews were brought into the ecumenical discussions, and dialogues began taking place between all manner of combinations of denominations—various Protestant denominations individually, and occasionally jointly with Catholics, Eastern Orthodox, and Jews. Mostly the result has been greater mutual understanding, with occasional official recognition of agreement on certain issues. But to date there is no sign of significant progress toward actual organic unification of these diverse traditions. In fact, these broader ecumenical discussions appear to have reached their zenith in the late 1960s and early 1970s.

Certainly ecumenism has been an absorbing subject for religious leaders and groups. But sociologists have also been interested, for ecumenism is a sociological phenomenon, not simply a religious one. Sociological interest has focused less on what is going on than on why ecumenical interest has developed at all. What, if any, are the social sources of this phenomenon? Peter Berger has suggested that one primary reason is economic—that is, rising costs, particularly for buildings and staff, suggest joint effort and cost sharing.[28] It appears that denominations have become increasingly aware that duplication of effort is not only wasteful, but ultimately impossible to

---

[28]Peter Berger, "A Market Model for the Analysis of Ecumenicity," *Social Research* 30, no. 1 (1963), 77–93.

continue forever. Pooling resources, using one missionary governing board to supervise forty missionaries rather than two boards each supervising twenty missionaries, building one church edifice instead of two in a new subdivision—ideas such as these have begun to make economic sense to denominations. Such recognition would probably not have come so quickly had religious membership expansion continued past the early 1960s at its post-World War II pace. But as we will discuss in Chapter 14, by the 1970s membership growth in the major denominations had either ceased or in fact begun to decline. In the face of declining membership and a concomitant decline in contributions, denominations have been forced to become cost-conscious and to look for ways to economize and increase efficiency. At this point groups begin regarding the theological justification for ecumenism as more convincing than ever before.

A prime factor underlying the problem of stable or declining membership is that while church membership in this country has shown a fairly steady increase for nearly two centuries, the growth of churches was closely tied to population growth in the nation generally. It is very possible that denominations have "converted" and brought into their folds proportionately nearly all the people they can ever expect to. Few of those not yet convinced to join are likely to be convinced in the future. Thus one of the activities that before the mid-1960s absorbed much of the energy of local churches and of denominations—namely, home missionary activities (the establishment of new congregations to meet the demands of population shifts)—has declined and no longer commands the attention it once did. What, then, are church leaders at all levels within the structure as well as laypeople in the congregations to do by way of church work? What kind of religious frontier is left to explore and conquer? One option that excites the imagination of many is to try to break down ancient barriers that have kept denominations apart. A divided Christendom is defined as a "scandal." What with the recent emphasis in American society on overcoming prejudices, tolerating differences among people, and compromising old absolutes regarding what is good and what is evil, it is only natural that religious groups should begin to work at cleaning up their houses, so to speak, by relating to other religious groups. Ecumenical discussion and activity have become popular as a consequence. The challenge for the churches during what remains of the twentieth century will be for many the ecumenical goal of a united Christendom. Yet at this point we need to point out again that enthusiasm and commitment in theory to ecumenism have not been enough to effect much notable success since 1968.

Another factor that undoubtedly fostered ecumenism in the two decades following the close of World War II was the long-term trend toward autonomous bureaucracies in the major denominations. As numerous sociological studies have shown, those persons in high-level positions in organizations are the most tolerant, accepting, and understanding of competing organizations. High-level labor union officials, for example, often interact more harmoniously with their counterparts in management, from whom they will ultimately be trying to extract concessions to union demands, than they do with the rank-and-file union members they represent. It has been suggested that such leaders may even have difficulty demanding certain things that they have come to believe, through their contacts with management, the employer cannot afford. Similarly, officials of church bureaucracies tend to interact with comparable officials of other denominations, whom they find to be much like themselves. They find it easy to get along with them and therefore counsel that the denominations themselves ought to be able to get along as well. These church bureaucrats tend to be more liberal than the rank-and-file clergy in the denominations in the first place—a fact that may by itself go far in explaining why there is so much discussion of ecumenism by religious leaders but why little of a concrete nature in terms of denominational merger and extensive cooperation seems to occur. The local churches are likely not so interested or convinced as their representatives in the denominational bureaucracies.

Suffice it to say in summarizing our discussion to this point that ecumenism, at least during this century, has paralleled denominationalism. That is to say, both have thrived, even though this would seem to involve an inherent contradiction: Denominationalism appears to be as viable as ever, and ecumenism is also alive and at least fairly well. Part of the answer to this seeming contradiction is that in ecumenical conversations and activities denominations have found themselves looking more closely not only at others but at themselves, their heritage, and their uniqueness. This analysis may have led them to a new and stronger appreciation of themselves in their uniqueness. In fact, ours is a pluralistic society that today encourages its subgroups to celebrate and preserve their uniqueness as long as they support the fundamental values of the society. The upshot is that denominations may not be particularly ready to give up their identities. Yet they see much value in cooperation and certainly no value in cutthroat competition. Hence ecumenism remains viable also. While not going the whole ecumenical route and effecting outright organizational mergers, denominations feel free to cooperate and engage in joint tasks while each retains its identity.

THE CONTINUED VIABILITY
OF DENOMINATIONALISM

We now return more explicitly to the denominational phenomenon with which this chapter is concerned and discuss additional sociological reasons why the denominational phenomenon has remained so dominant a feature of American religion—of American society, for that matter. In the face of strong pressures, both theological and sociological, toward ecumenism, and given yet another unifying tendency (which we discussed in Chapter 7)— the phenomenon of civil religion, which at least implicitly would replace traditional religion with a religion focusing on the society itself—why is American society still divided into so many distinctive religious groups? It is not enough to point out, as we have already, that important doctrinal differences divide denominations, or that another factor keeping denominations distinct is the type of organizational tradition or liturgical emphasis, or the differences between Apollonian and Dionysian orientations. All of these are significant, and all represent a combination of theological and sociological factors and pressures. But there are two other factors, which are primarily sociological, that reinforce the denominational heritage that American society continually updates.

The Ethnic Factor

The first factor reinforcing denominationalism that we want to discuss—one strongly emphasized by Andrew Greeley—is the important ethnic function that religion in American society continues to serve. That is, one's religious affiliation represents for a great many people much more than commitment to a set of religious beliefs, symbols, and rituals. Religious affiliation may also become a means people use to define their identity— "who they are and where they stand in a large and complex society."[29] Greeley mentions that this definition and location of self may be the most important function religion performs for some people. For others it is intermixed with the belief system and ethical code that the religious group stands for.

The origin of religion as an American ethnic phenomenon rests with the fact that most of the nationality groups that immigrated into the United States brought their churches with them and transplanted them on American soil. The Norwegians, Swedes, Finns, and Danes brought their Lutheran churches. Some Germans brought their Lutheran church; other Germans brought their Catholic church; still others brought their Reformed church. The Irish brought their Catholic church; the Italians and Poles did likewise. The Vietnamese brought their Buddhist traditions, and so on. But there is more to it than that. The religious organization for these immigrants was immediately an important source of identification. In many cases it was a safe place for people to use their native tongue, and it linked them in their present insecurity in a new environment to a secure tradition or heritage. As the immigrants left the old cohesive communal relationship of the peasant village, with its primary relationships and awareness of who one was in relation to others, and entered a strange land of secondary rela-

---

[29]Greeley, *The Denominational Society*, p. 108.

tionships, they clung to their ethnic group in order to preserve some semblance of identity and a linkage with people who could provide empathy. Some of these people may not have been particularly "religious" before and perhaps would not have scored high on certain measures of religiosity in the new land, yet many found in the religious group an opportunity to meet those with whom they shared a heritage, people who spoke their language in both a literal and figurative sense. Andrew Greeley says that denominational membership makes available to Americans "a fellowship which is highly important in compensating for those intimate relationships of life which seem to have been lost when the peasant village was left behind."[30] Clearly, we see religion performing the "belonging" function emphasized by Max Weber and discussed in the chapter on religious origins (Chapter 2).

It should be noted that the opportunity for religion to serve an ethnic function, particularly for immigrant groups, was in part made possible by the religious pluralism that had existed in some of the American colonies and was reinforced in the Constitution. Religious diversity (pluralism) was valued and encouraged. Therefore, immigrants could turn to their religious group as a source of belonging without undue fear of reprisal. Not that the established Americans were always happy with the religious-ethnic enclaves. But they could do little about them and still be true to the American religious heritage and precedent. That resentment and suspicion did erupt in harassment and violence is attested to in the discussion of the "Protestant Crusade" in Chapter 11; the point to be made here is that not only was anti-Catholicism being expressed, but also anti-Irish and anti-cheap urban labor sentiments as well.

Acknowledging the ethnic nature and function of religion in the United States raises some serious questions about the melting-pot hypothesis—the idea that the United States has accommodated and homogenized peoples from a diversity of cultures and backgrounds. It is hardly even the triple melting pot of Protestants, Catholics, and Jews that some have suggested. Actually, historically it was Dutch Reformed, German Lutheran, Scottish Presbyterian, and so on for the Protestant immigrant groups; and Polish Catholic, Serbian Catholic, Irish Catholic, and so on for the Catholic groups. It was even to some extent Russian Jew, German Jew, and so on— not simply Jewish for the third major religious family in America. That is, Americans were not only ethnically "hyphenated" as citizens (Irish-Americans, German-Americans, Polish-Americans, and so on), but they were ethnically hyphenated as members of religious groups as well. The ethnic factor has thus been more important in patterning American religion than has often been recognized.

One final comment in connection with our discussion of the ethnic feature of religion in America is that the numerical strength of American reli-

---

[30]Ibid., p. 114.

gion is in significant degree related to the ethnic factor. Because the religious group was able to serve as an ethnic rallying point and to provide an identity for people and a sense of belonging to something more intimate and meaningful than the diffuse, cold, and distant society, people gained a religious commitment that, though perhaps less intense for many as the importance of ethnic identity fades for them, they are still reluctant to cut themselves off from completely. Religion has served and does serve an important social function as an ethnic community, which exists quite in addition to any strictly "religious" function it may serve. In many cases people have even been able to live out their entire lives while only rarely leaving the religious-ethnic community. Scattered throughout the land are ethnic-religious communities where nearly 100 percent of the citizens are of a single national origin and a single religious persuasion, and where the public schools become almost parochial ones. But one need not be a farmer or a shopkeeper in such a community to live out one's life in an ethnic subcommunity. One may be a city dweller and a medical doctor, or an accountant, or an attorney, or an academician—and still serve only or almost exclusively members of the ethnic community into which she or he was born.

The Social-Class Factor

The second additional factor that reinforces denominationalism in American society is social class. We spent considerable time in Chapter 9 discussing the relationship between religion and social class, and will therefore do little more than mention it again here. But it is of considerable relevance to our present interest in denominationalism. Religion does reflect the class structure. Denominations are disproportionately constituted of different social classes, sects are almost universally a lower-social-status phenomenon, and social mobility frequently results in change in religious group affiliation that corresponds more appropriately in the eyes of the community with one's newly achieved social status.

The fact that religion reflects the class structure of the society is of course not unique to American society. Differences in religious orientation and practice have been observed in less complex societies that have religious systems at an earlier stage on Bellah's continuum of religious evolution.[31] A distinctive feature of the "archaic" stage of religious evolution, according to Bellah, is a clearly stratified society and fairly distinctive religious expressions according to class level. The upper-status people who control the political and military power usually claim superior religious status as well. Bel-

---

[31]Robert Bellah outlines five states of religious evolution: the primitive, the archaic, the historical, the early modern, and the modern. Robert N. Bellah, "Religious Evolution," *American Sociological Review* 29, no. 3 (1964), 358–374, reprinted in idem, *Beyond Belief* (New York: Harper & Row, Pub., 1970), Chapter 2.

lah states that noble families are proud of their divine descent and often have special priestly functions.[32] We can point, for example, to ancient Greece where there appears to have been a fairly clear distinction between the religion of the plebians and that of the patricians. The plebians related to gods associated with agriculture, gods of local concerns, and gods related to magical animal symbols. The patricians were absorbed with the Olympian gods, such as Zeus, Apollo, Aphrodite, Athena, and Hermes, who oversaw broader areas of life, universal principles and emotions, and broader societal concerns. Another example is the Hindu religion. The major beliefs and practices associated with the Vedas and Upanishads and the concepts of Brahma and Brahman are largely unknown to the lower castes, who in fact have traditionally been deemed unworthy of being given the sacred truths. Instead, the lower castes learn the elemental Hindu ideas of samsara, karma, and dharma, and relate to a variety of local gods and spirits.

In American society we have fairly clear evidence of Weber's "theodicy of escape" and of Marx's and Freud's compensation-for-deprivation function of religion for the lower classes, on the one hand, and the "theodicy of good fortune" for the economically and socially successful members of the society on the other hand. The upshot is that various denominations and religious groups appeal disproportionately to different social classes. The fact that the United States has been and continues to be a highly stratified if somewhat mobile society has tended to reinforce and preserve denominational and religious diversity as different religious groups provide different things to different people.

Regional Differences

We must not leave our discussion of denominationalism and pluralism without a quick look at regional differences in denominational affiliation. While pluralism would suggest an idea perhaps of fairly equal dispersion of religious groups across the landscape as each tolerates the others, that is really not the way it is. There are in fact distinct regional concentrations of particular denominations. One is the Southern Baptist denomination in the South. The vast majority of counties in the southern states have 25 percent or more of the church membership affiliated with the Southern Baptist Convention, with many of those counties actually at 50 percent or more. The major exceptions are the southern tips of Florida, Texas, and Louisiana. Those exceptions show large concentrations of Catholics who also are dominant in most of the Northeast and in many urban centers. In addition, Martin Marty points out that in only five of the counties that border a Great

[32]Bellah, *Beyond Belief*, pp. 30–31.

Lake do Catholics not make up at least 25 percent of the religious population.[33] Lutherans show a distinct concentration in the upper Midwest—southern Wisconsin, Minnesota, the Dakotas, and in western Iowa and eastern Nebraska. And of course the most dramatic concentration is that of Mormons in the state of Utah (in no county are Mormons outnumbered by any other religious group). Their concentration extends also to contiguous areas: eastern Nevada, southern Idaho, western Wyoming, northern Arizona, and northwestern Colorado.

[33]Martin E. Marty, "The Career of Pluralism in America," in *Religion in America, 1950 to the Present*, eds. Jackson W. Carroll, Douglas W. Johnson, and Martin E. Marty (San Francisco: Harper & Row, 1979), p. 52.

14

The Future of Religion

Those who might have predicted in the past that by the late twentieth century religion would be a defunct institution would have to be quite surprised at what they can see almost anywhere in the world today. Not only are many traditional signs of religion in abundance, but new manifestations seem to emerge almost daily. In the United States not only does one continue to observe bumper stickers proclaiming Jesus Saves, political candidates mouthing religious clichés, evangelists like Billy Graham still "packing them in," and freshly painted church spires dotting both countryside and town, but one observes amazing new religious sights and sounds that daily bombard the consciousness. One sees smooth-headed young men in flowing saffron robes roaming the streets chanting "Hare Krishna . . . ," jazz and rock liturgies in traditional churches, a proliferation of Eastern mystical cults, so-called Moral Majority preachers and laypeople influencing elections and trying to move members of Congress in directions of their religious persuasion, and picketers and paraders on both sides of the abortion issue trying to solicit more popular support for what many define as a religious issue. In other words, there is a great deal of religious activity; there are numerous developments within religion. Some of these developments will give us clues as to what kind of future religion might have, particularly in the United States. Certainly they will influence people's thinking about the future of religion. Therefore as we try to look into that future we shall focus on several major religious developments that seem to have particular relevance.

LEVEL OF RELIGIOUS ACTIVITY

There are several fairly standard measures of religious activity that tell us something about the vitality of religion and of people's commitment to religion. These are church/synagogue membership, church/synagogue attendance, and the value of new construction of religious facilities. We see from the data on church/synagogue membership in Table 14-1 that although there was a steady decline between 1940 and 1982 when church/synagogue membership declined from 72 percent to 67 percent, membership appears to have stabilized in a narrow range of 65 to 68 percent. Actually, the overall pattern for the United States for half a century has been one of remarkable consistency.

The same can be said concerning the overall figures for church attendance. In the last fifty years the comparison between any period of up to ten years has never varied more than five percentage points. Also, the difference between attendance in 1940 and 1988 actually shows an increase of five percentage points. But if we look separately at Protestants and Catholics in data that go back only to 1958 (cf. Table 14-1) we note that while Protestants show a gain of a percentage point, Catholics show quite a differ-

TABLE 14-1   Church/Synagogue Membership and Attendance for Selected Years

YEAR	MEMBERSHIP	ATTENDANCE	PROTESTANT ATTENDANCE	CATHOLIC ATTENDANCE
1940	72%	37%	—	—
1952	73	—	—	—
1954	—	46	—	—
1955	—	49	—	—
1958	—	—	44%	74%
1965	73	44	—	—
1975	71	40	—	—
1978	—	—	40	52
1980	69	40	39	53
1982	67	40	41	51
1984	68	40	38	52
1987	69	40	38	52
1988	65	42	45	48

Source: George Gallup, Jr., and Jim Castelli, *The People's Religion: American Faith in the 90's* (New York: Maxmillian Publishing Company, 1989), Tables 2-5, 2-6, and 2-7, pp. 30-32.

ent pattern. Among Catholics there was a fairly precipitous drop in attendance from 74 percent to 52 percent in the twenty year period from 1958–1978 (a 30 percent decline). Since 1978, however, the rate of attendance for Catholics has been quite stable, ranging between 51 and 53 percent until 1988, when the rate was reported to be 48 percent. It is certainly interesting to note that whereas the difference between Catholics and Protestants was 30 percentage points (74 percent for Catholics, 44 percent for Protestants) in 1958, the difference has dropped to only 3 percentage points in 1988. We will make further comment about the reasons behind this decline in attendance among Catholics at the end of this section.

The third indicator from which to infer the vitality of religion is the value of new construction of buildings for religious purposes (cf. Table 14-2). Although the number of current dollars devoted to new construction was considerably higher in 1983 compared with 1968, standardized dollars show a decline, but a decline that has essentially leveled off. With church/synagogue membership not increasing, one would expect that new construction would also not be increasing.

The point we would make here is that while we should not assert that religion is on the ascendency and gaining in influence and support year by year, there is no clear evidence of a contrary trend either. Statistical measures such as we have presented reveal more stability than significant change.

But so much for total, national figures and trends. We have to consider also that there might be differences, possibly even substantial ones, among the various groups that in total constitute the summary figures. That is to say, some religious groups could be declining, perhaps dramatically; but others could be growing, perhaps as dramatically, or even more dramati-

TABLE 14-2 Value of New Construction of Religious Buildings in the United States in Current and Constant 1982 Dollars

YEAR	CURRENT DOLLARS	1982 DOLLARS
1968	$1,079 million	$3,336 million
1971	813	2,004
1975	867	1,543
1979	1,548	1,996
1981	1,665	1,746
1983	1,780	1,712
1985	2,409	2,161
1987	2,753	2,340

Source: U.S. Department of Commerce, *Annual Value of New Construction Put in Place in the United States: 1982 to 1987,* "Current Construction Reports, C-30, Value of New Construction Put in Place," Table 1.

cally than others are declining. If we find it is so (and it certainly is), then we are likely to ask another question as well: What are the reasons that might account for these differences—some churches growing, some declining?

GROWTH AND DECLINE OF MEMBERSHIP

By way of a very general summary we can observe that some of the standard, mainline Protestant churches have been declining fairly noticeably for two decades or so. For example, some of the most dramatic declines over the period 1960 to 1982 were registered by the Presbyterians (United Presbyterian Church in the U.S.A.) with a decline in membership of 28.1 percent, the Christian Church (Disciples of Christ) with a decline of 39.7 percent, and the United Church of Christ with a decline of 23.4 percent.[1] These were not the only losers, but these were the more dramatic losers.

On the other hand, several religious groups have not only been growing, but at a substantial rate. For example, between 1960 and 1982 the Church of the Nazarene grew by 62 percent, the Seventh-Day Adventists increased by 90.8 percent, the Church of Jesus Christ of Latter-Day Saints added 92.6 percent, and the Assemblies of God grew by 120 percent.[2] Others are of course in between, with only small fluctuations one way or the other, or alternating between small decreases some years but increases in other years.

In a controversial book published in 1972 (with a second edition in 1977), *Why Conservative Churches are Growing*, Dean M. Kelley analyzed the data on growth for some, decline for others and suggested that one explanatory factor stood out in particular: That was that the growing religious organizations were the strict ones. These demand high commitment and loyalty from their members; they exert church discipline over members' beliefs and lifestyles; they put missionary zeal into practice by carrying their message to outsiders; they tend to be absolutist and clear-cut about true and correct beliefs.[3] In fact Kelley has since said that although overruled by his publisher he had wanted as his title, not *Why Conservative Churches Are Growing*, but *Why Strict Churches Are Strong*.[4] These strict churches demand firm allegiance, tireless devotion to proclaiming the Gospel, obedience to authority, and stoic acceptance of ridicule from the outside.

[1]Percentages computed from data in Constant H. Jacquet, Jr., ed. *Yearbook of American and Canadian Churches* (Nashville, TN: Abingdon, 1984), pp, 246–47.

[2]Ibid.

[3]Dean M. Kelley, *Why Conservative Churches Are Growing* (New York: Harper & Row, Pub., 1972).

[4]Dean M. Kelley, "Commentary: Is Religion a Dependent Variable?" in *Understanding Church Growth and Decline: 1950–1978*, eds. Dean R. Hoge and David A. Roozen (New York: Pilgrim Press, 1979), p. 340.

In a similar vein is the explanation for conservative growth and liberal decline proposed by George LaNoue, who notes that the conservative churches offer people a scarce commodity for which religion is the nearly unique source—namely, salvation—while the liberal churches have been trying to offer a panoply of goods and services that are also available from a host of other sources—entertainment, intellectual stimulation, and discussion and activity centering around social issues, for example. Because many secular groups can often do a better job of delivering such goods and services within their areas of specialization, liberal religious groups are likely to lose out in the competition. Small wonder, then, that conservative groups that promise delivery of a scarce commodity should grow, and liberal groups that must compete with numerous secular groups in the same business, so to speak, should be shrinking.[5]

Innately appealing as these hypotheses concerning the differential growth and decline in conservative and liberal religious groups may be, we must introduce a couple of studies that trace the changing religious affiliations of people. The reason is that a distinct disadvantage of both Kelley's and LaNoue's work is that their data represent total membership figures only, and thus cannot be used to trace the movements of individuals from one religious group to another. In fact, we cannot necessarily infer from these data any movement at all. For example, if the birth rate were higher among members of the more conservative religious groups (which is quite likely, in fact), then the growth of these groups through natural reproduction alone might account for their increasing numerical advantage over the liberal denominations. Or again, perhaps the conservative groups are gaining strength by picking up the nonaffiliated person with little or no religious background, not necessarily the dropouts from liberal denominations.

As for studies tracing changes in religious affiliations, in Stark and Glock's San Francisco Bay Area study nearly half of the Protestant respondents (46 percent) reported having changed denominational affiliation at some time in the past.[6] In seeking patterns away from and toward certain denominations, Stark and Glock conclude that the general tendency for those who change religious affiliation is to move from more conservative bodies to those that are more liberal theologically.[7]

Samuel Mueller, analyzing the same data, reached different, though not diametrically opposed, conclusions. Through the application of factor-analytic techniques he found that switches of religious affiliation occur essentially without reference to the liberal or conservative stance of the

[5]Cited in Kelley, *Why Conservative Churches Are Growing*, pp. 92–93.
[6]Rodney Stark and Charles Y. Glock, *American Piety* (Berkeley: University of California Press, 1968).
[7]Ibid., p. 187.

groups involved, but are made in such a way as to preserve similarity along as many dimensions as possible; that is, people tend to affiliate with a religious group similar in a sociological sense to the one they are leaving. The relevant similarities do not seem to be so much doctrinal or creedal as they are related to such factors as social status and liturgy. In other words, people seem to look for another religious group that has members like themselves and that has a form of worship similar to what they have known and practiced in the past. Some of these religiously mobile people wind up in more liberal denominations, but usually for other than theological or doctrinal reasons or motivations. And the same is true for those who move to more conservative denominations.[8]

Where does this leave us, then, with regard to the issue of the relative growth and decline of conservative and liberal churches? And at an even more general level, where do these trends fit into the observation with which this chapter began—namely, that there has been a small decline in denominational religion in the United States since peaks of activity in the 1950s and 1960s?

For one thing, the analyses offered by Mueller and by Stark and Glock cast some doubt on Kelley's hypothesis. Since we do not know the source of the new members in the conservative groups for which Kelley gives data— whether they are defectors from liberal denominations, converts from irreligion, or simply a result of above-average natural reproductive increase— we cannot infer that doctrinal motivations cause the discrepancy between liberal and conservative denominational growth rates as both Kelley and LaNoue at least implicitly suggest. In fact, Stark and Glock's data, as well as National Opinion Research Center data that they also examined, suggest that denominational mobility proceeds in both directions between liberal and conservative groups—moreover it proceeds, according to Mueller's analysis, in a nearly random fashion insofar as theological stances of the gaining and losing denominations are concerned.

Wade Roof and Christopher Hadaway have more recently provided very helpful information on the issue, using National Opinion Research Center General Social Survey data from 1973 through 1976 that involved a merged sample of nearly six thousand adults. One important qualification of the earlier Stark and Glock findings is that many who defect from the mainline denominations do not move to the more liberal denominations as a sort of way station to religious agnosticism and dropping out altogether, but go directly from membership in mainline denominations to nonmembership in any religious group. For example, as high a proportion as 20.4 percent of former United Presbyterians describe themselves as religious dropouts. Corresponding proportions of Lutherans, Methodists, Baptists,

---

[8]Samuel A. Mueller, "Dimensions of Interdenominational Mobility in the United States," *Journal for the Scientific Study of Religion* 10, no. 2 (1971), 76–84.

and Disciples of Christ were 17.8 percent, 13.4 percent, 13.8 percent, and 9.1 percent respectively. Among the Presbyterians and the Lutherans those who dropped out constituted more than those who switched to any other particular religious group.[9]

But further, at least somewhat in line with what Kelley and LaNoue have been saying, Roof and Hadaway found considerable switching out of mainline Protestant denominations into what they term the "religious fringe"—the small Protestant denominations, sect and cult groups, Mormons, and various non-Christian, non-Jewish groups. By way of example, of Presbyterians who left the United Presbyterian Church, 16.8 percent went to small Protestant bodies, 9 percent to sectarian groups, and 3.6 percent to non-Christian groups; of Baptist defectors, 15.6 percent went to small Protestant denominations, 18.2 percent to sects, and 1.4 percent to non-Christian groups; of Methodist defectors, 14.7 percent went to the smaller Protestant denominations, 10.4 percent to various sects, and 1.0 percent to non-Christian groups.[10]

In a very substantial analysis of factors that might be involved in declining memberships of mainline Protestant churches,[11] various authors, looking both separately and collectively at mainline denominations, reach several similar conclusions. First, the more-highly-educated young adults who have moved in the direction of individualism, personal freedom, and tolerance of diversity appear not only to be less interested in maintaining membership in the denominations they grew up in, but are not much attracted to the even more-liberal Protestant groups either, preferring rather to defect from organized religion altogether. Dean Hoge describes a value shift among young people, particularly the more affluent and better educated among them, since the 1950s.

> The shift has been toward individualism, cosmopolitanism, and greater freedom in the areas of marriage, sexuality, sex roles, and personal morality. The total value shift has created some barriers between certain young people and the churches. Such broad contextual changes as these seem more important for explaining recent trends.[12]

If we add to this observation about defectors a second and third trend, the future of the mainline Protestant churches looks even more bleak. The two trends are the sharp decline in baptisms and shrinking enrollments in

[9]Wade Clark Roof and Christopher Kirk Hadaway, "Denominational Switching in the Seventies: Going beyond Stark and Glock," *Journal for the Scientific Study of Religion* 18, no. 4 (1979), 372.

[10]Ibid.

[11]Dean R. Hoge and David A. Roozen, eds., *Understanding Church Growth and Decline: 1950–1978* (New York: Pilgrim Press, 1979).

[12]Dean R. Hoge, "A Test of Theories of Denominational Growth and Decline," in *Understanding Church Growth and Decline*, eds. Hoge and Roozen, ibid., p. 197.

church schools and Sunday schools. Ruth Doyle and Sheila Kelly report that baptisms for all the major U.S. denominations that they studied (Roman Catholic, Southern Baptist Convention, United Presbyterian, United Methodist, Episcopalian, Lutheran Church in America, Lutheran Church–Missouri Synod, American Lutheran Church, and the United Church of Christ) declined from 1950 to 1975. They note that the declines have been especially dramatic since 1960 and, "in general, are disproportionately larger than the declines in church membership."[13] Not only do such declines result in fewer members right now, but a prime source of future members who would themselves bear children who would likely be baptized in the church are for the most part lost (some will of course come in on their own later as teens or adults).

Church school enrollment is, for most of the groups under study, a true disaster area. Of only four major religious groups that have outstripped the growth in population under age eighteen, only one is significantly ahead of that population increase over the twenty-five-year period from 1950 to 1975. That group is the Roman Catholic Church. But during the last ten years of that twenty-five-year period its gains too have fallen behind population growth. The other six denominations have fallen far behind population growth—actually declining from between 11.8 percent and 47 percent in church school enrollments between 1950 and 1975, while the U.S. population under age eighteen increased by 40.9 percent.[14]

The mainline Protestant churches all know that they are facing membership and participation problems. Several have conducted very substantial studies to analyze and try to reverse the pattern. But no clear answers have been forthcoming. There is an emerging consensus that from the religious perspective, growth or even holding steady so far as membership is concerned is not necessarily everything. That point is probably not more succinctly or well stated than by Robert K. Hudnut, a Presbyterian minister.

> But church growth is not the point. The point is whether the church is being true to the Gospel. And, in city after city, and town after town, it is. Indeed, because it is being faithful it is often losing members.
>
> Loss of growth in statistics has often meant increase in growth in the Gospel. The "dead wood" is gone. The "faithful remnant" remains.[15]

The famous neo-orthodox theologian Karl Barth raised such questions not only before the great post–World War II growth period in American

---

[13]Ruth T. Doyle and Sheila M. Kelly, "Comparison of Trends in Ten Denominations 1950–75," in *Understanding Church Growth and Decline*, eds. Hoge and Roozen, ibid., p. 151.

[14]Doyle and Kelly, ibid., p. 154.

[15]Robert K. Hudnut, *Church Growth Is Not the Point!* (New York: Harper & Row, 1975), p. ix.

religion became noticeable but certainly well before the decline in member-ship set in. In 1948 he said the following:

> What objection could we really make if it should please God to carry his work onward and reach his goal, not through a further numerical increase, but through a drastic numerical decrease of so-called Christendom? It seems to me the only question in this matter is: How can we free ourselves from all quantitative thinking, all statistics, all calculation of observable consequence, all efforts to achieve a Christian world order, and then shape our witness into a witness to the sovereignty of God's mercy ... ?[16]

Earlier in the chapter we introduced the reader to some significant changes in Roman Catholicism in terms of church membership and atten-dance. From the Catholic perspective this could be alarming. It would be particularly alarming to traditional, conservative Catholics because at first glance there appears to be a connection in timing between the decline in rates of Catholic religious participation and the pronouncements of the Sec-ond Vatican Council (Vatican II) in the early 1960s, which relaxed many traditional Catholic obligations. Vatican II moved the Catholic Church down a more liberal path. Garry Wills's analysis at the time was that Vatican II let the "dirty little secret" of Catholicism out of the bag, so to speak.[17] That secret was simply the admission that the Catholic Church could and does change.

While Vatican II certainly has had some influence, at least in the sense that the Catholic populace has been introduced to the possibility of change so far as some previously immutable doctrines are concerned, the immedi-ate cause likely has been the Humanae Vitae encyclical letter on birth con-trol issued by Pope Paul VI in 1968. This was a reiteration and reinforce-ment of very traditional Catholic prohibitions against "artificial" methods of birth control. It was an abrupt reversal of the direction that many Catholics saw their church taking following Vatican II.

This reversal "turned off" a great many Catholics. In fact, so much so that some dropped out and if not withdrawing their membership, ceased attending church services. Andrew Greeley says categorically: "Catholic church attendance declined because of birth control, ... "[18] Nonetheless, many continued to attend church, though not necessarily as frequently, out of old loyalties. Greeley describes the behavior of Catholics who would not accept the reaffirmation of traditional Catholic doctrine on birth control and were carrying out their own "quiet revolution" in which they decided to

---

[16]Karl Barth, "No Christian Marshall Plan," *The Christian Century LXV*, no. 49 (1948), 1332.

[17]Garry Wills, *Bare Ruined Choirs* (Garden City, NY: Doubleday, 1972), p. 21.

[18]Andrew M. Greeley, *Religious Change in America* (Cambridge, MA: Harvard University Press, 1989), p. 47.

remain Catholic "on their own terms."[19] Their loyalty stems in part from the minority status of Catholics in the Protestant-dominated United States for so many decades, as well as the close link of Catholicism with ethnic cultures and enclaves (Poles, Ukranians, and Italians, for example). The Catholic Church is more than *just* a church. It is a link with one's ethnic heritage and has been a place of refuge in an occasionally hostile Protestant society. Such loyalties limited the disengagement of Catholics. And so, many Catholics remain loyal to their church and continue to attend with some frequency, although privately they hold to a non-Catholic ethic on birth control and rationalize that God "understands" even if church leaders do not.[20]

It is of interest that the partial alienation from their church that is evident among the membership carries over into voluntary financial contributions. As recently as the early 1960s, Protestants and Catholics both contributed about the same amounts to their churches ($141 from Catholics, $138 from Protestants).[21] By the mid-1980s both groups had increased their contributions, but Catholics had fallen far behind Protestants ($320 from Catholics, $580 from Protestants). The proportion of contributions as compared to income had been 2.2 percent for both Catholics and Protestants in 1969, but by 1983 Catholics were giving half their former rate (1.1 percent of income) whereas Protestants contributed the same percentage as in 1969.[22]

CONTINUITY IN THE TRADITIONAL SOCIAL FUNCTIONS OF RELIGION

Here we wish to expand a little on observations made by Emile Durkheim (cf. Chapter 2) that much of the time and in most societies religion serves as an integrating influence in society. We refer to this observation again and in fact expand on it because we believe there are several important functions for society that religion will continue to provide in the future.

Normative Reinforcement

First, religion serves a reinforcement function in society to the degree that it teaches and emphasizes the same norms and values as the society at large. This may be at the very general level of teaching such values as human dignity and freedom, equality before the law, respect for legitimate

[19]Ibid.
[20]Ibid., p. 52.
[21]Ibid., p. 68.
[22]Ibid.

authority, and faithfulness to one's role. Or it may be more specific, such as, "Thou shalt not kill, steal, or procreate illegitimate children." In a direct sense, religion is here viewed as a socializing agent in the society. Although allowing that religious groups, just as all other kinds of groups, socialize their members into some norms unique unto themselves, we are here speaking of religion as one among several institutions involved in socializing citizens to the core norms of the society. Educational agencies, families, peer groups, mass media, and various voluntary associations are all involved in this process. Religion is but one such agent. But it is one that touches a majority of people with some regularity.

At a second level with respect to the reinforcement idea we observe that religion not only socializes people in the "thou shalts" and "thou shalt nots" of society in a reinforcing sense, but occasionally pushes those norms even farther. For example, society has norms against murder, but does not usually try to control what you think about your neighbors so long as you do not harm their persons or property or infringe on their rights. A religious system may go farther by teaching, for example, "Whosoever hateth his brother is a murderer," "Love your neighbor," and "Bless those who persecute you." If a religion is successful in inculcating norms more stringent than those the society imposes and thereby creates a "super-Christian" (or "super-Buddhist," or "super-Hindu," or whatever), to that degree one may also see a "supercitizen." That is to say, society would be even better off if people not only avoided destroying their neighbors but actually loved them and went out of their way to help them. The key here, of course, is discovering whether and to what degree religion actually produces such superior people. Undoubtedly there are some—they tend to be called "saints," and they may even be societal heroes and models for behavior. But there is no clear evidence that, on the average, religion produces a great number. Yet we must again observe: To the degree that it happens, the society would benefit and would be getting citizens with a level of commitment and dedication that they might not have in the absence of religious influence and training.

Integration into Meaningful Relationships

An exceptionally important function religion performs is that of bringing individuals into meaningful relationships with others in a group. Religious groups bring immigrants, social isolates, various minorities, and some socially maladjusted persons into a group where they are in contact with others. Not that religion reaches every such person or is successful in integrating all of those with whom it establishes contact. Nor is religion unique in performing this task or function for society—so do labor unions, fraternal lodges, newcomers' clubs, political parties, and innumerable other voluntary associations and groups of all sizes, constituencies, and purposes. However, religious groups, in large part because of their reputation for being concerned about life purposes and adjustment as well as for raising a person's sights beyond current mundane problems, attract relatively large proportions of persons in need of meaningful interpersonal contact. Society needs such groups to do this. Society needs members who can function well in their roles. People function better when they feel they have some personal worth and have meaningful, satisfying relationships with other people. To the extent that religious groups provide this service to some who feel isolated and who are not being relieved of their anxieties and problems elsewhere, religion is serving the society.

Catalyst and Symbol for Reaffirming Societal Values

Another way in which religion contributes to the integration of society is by serving as a focal point or symbol—in a sense, as a catalyst—for the society to reaffirm some of its basic values. Religion everywhere does this through festivals. Think, for example, of what happens in our society in connection with the religious festival called Christmas. Although there is plenty of growling about gifts yet to buy, overdrawn checking accounts, and crass commercialism conspiring to do us all in, there is something else as well. There is a pervasive spirit in the air of good will and joviality. There are increases in gifts to charities. There is more attention given to those less fortunate than the majority. Not that what emerges is particularly enduring. Yet periodically, through such rites and festivals that reach out beyond the religious group itself, some of the fundamental values of the society are dramatized for people, and they reaffirm them at least intellectually and momentarily. Certainly not every Scrooge does an about-face, much less one that lasts beyond the festival itself; yet some do, and most citizens are at least temporarily affected.

Aid in Adjusting to Personal Crises

Another integrating function of religion that some feel is actually getting close to the fundamental purpose or essence of religion itself is the help it gives to people facing various crisis situations in their lives. To the degree that religion helps people grapple with emotional crisis, with death and bereavement, with uncertainties and disappointments of all kinds, religion is performing an important service for society. We introduced the idea of relativizing suffering and crisis in Chapter 2. Religion attempts to relativize human problems by placing them in an eternal perspective, interpreting events as God's will ("All things work for good to those who love God"), and providing "answers" for irrational events. Whether the answers and explanations are "true" is for our purposes—and for society's—beside the point. What is important is whether people feel better as a result of what religion does for them in periods of crisis and imbalance. The society needs functioning members who fill their social roles with skill and attention. Society cannot afford to have great numbers of members incapacitated for extended periods of time. To the extent that religion helps with this task, society is greatly aided.

Source of Social Welfare

A final fairly major function religion performs in society is its service as a welfare institution. Religious groups were in the forefront of the nineteenth-century movement for establishing orphanages, schools for the deaf, blind, and mentally retarded, adoption and family-service agencies, hospitals, and similar welfare and service institutions. Earle E. Cairns has documented the significant impact of numerous Christian religions on drives for prison reforms, the abolition of slavery, humane treatment of the mentally ill, and improved working conditions for industrial workers in the wake of the Industrial Revolution.[23] Even today lists of United Way agencies include organizations that either retain a religious name or were founded by a religious organization. Today most of these agencies derive the major portion of their monetary support from nonreligious sources through fees, voluntary contributions and solicitations from the general public and governmental subsidy. But initially they were religiously motivated and funded and represented a direct response of religious groups to human need. Although the majority of funds in social-welfare areas are today collected and distributed by the government, much of the original stimulus and efforts in these directions were religious.

This transfer of charitable and social service functions from religious groups to governmental agencies is cause for concern on the part of Robert Wuthnow. He questions whether, as the governmental bureaucracy expands into activities that had earlier been the responsibility of religious groups and other voluntary participation agencies, "more and more of the society's policies will be determined behind closed doors rather than through open public discussion. . . . "[24] He notes too that such substitution of governmental responsibility reduces the raison d'être of voluntary organizations such as churches.

Similarly, from quite another direction, the commercial, profit-making sector has moved into providing social services as part of their "product lines"—the very activities that had been principally within the arena of reli-

---

[23]Earle E. Cairns, *Saints and Society* (Chicago: Moody Press, 1960).

[24]Robert Wuthnow, *The Struggle for America's Soul* (Grand Rapids, MI: William B. Eerdmans Publishing Company, 1989), p. 13.

gious and other voluntary groups. The establishment and administration of hospitals and rest homes by private and corporate enterprise, with the aim of profit, has become common.

There is also significant disagreement among religious groups over what is appropriate practice on their part—should their emphasis be on spiritual matters or on social concerns? We will pursue this topic later in this chapter. Now we must consider the concept of "secularization." It may well be that the changing responsibility for dealing with social welfare is but one manifestation of a fundamental change in society called secularization.

THE FACTOR OF SECULARIZATION

A concept that has been widely discussed for several decades and must be understood if we are to hope, at one level, to make sense out of contemporary developments in religion, and at a second level, to project the future of religion, is that of *secularization*. As this concept is commonly understood and used it is assumed that there has been a displacement of religious interpretations of reality and religious orientations toward life by an orientation that seeks explanations for and justifications of human behavior and other phenomena in scientific and rational terms. One has undergone a secularization process if, for example, instead of asserting that marriages are made in heaven and for eternity, he or she says that marriages are made by human beings, in time, on the basis of propinquity, and in response to biological and psychological needs. The results of secularization are that, instead of more or less automatically "explaining" much that happens—death, floods, plane crashes, drought, war, peace, or whatever—as "God's will," more and more people are seeking explanations in the laws of physical science and in the social scientific "laws" of human interaction. In other words, secularization is as much a state of mind as it is a specific, measurable development.

Andrew Greeley is very much on target when he says that secularization as discussed in the United States today means essentially that religion is less important now than it was in the past.[25] If this is in fact what people mean when they refer to the secularization process at work in American society, then the decline of religion in general, and not just in its institutional manifestations, is an empirical question that clamors for sociological investigation and documentation. Much will rest on how religion is defined—whether in terms of its "essence," or as a particular traditional package of beliefs and principles (such as "our Judeo-Christian heritage"), or in

---

[25]Andrew M. Greeley, *The Denominational Society* (Glenview, IL: Scott, Foresman, 1972), p. 127.

terms of the vitality of its institutional forms (membership, attendance, new construction, and so on).

This problem of achieving a consensus so far as a definition of religion is concerned surfaces in many discussions of the issue of secularization where one person's understanding of religion does not coincide with others' understandings. Larry Shriner implies as much when he shows how secularization has been defined in a half-dozen ways in recent discussions.[26] Although each of these definitions has its own nuances, two basic connotations of secularization can be distilled from them all. First, many see secularization as a process of *replacement* of religious faith with faith in scientific principles. This concept goes back to the beginnings of modern Western science, when scientists first dared to set aside religion's view of reality, at least temporarily, in order to consider and evaluate data objectively. Thus Copernicus and Galileo were secularists in that they repudiated the belief—then a religious doctrine—that the earth is the center of the universe.

The logical extreme of secularism, in this view, is refusing to grant credence to any assertion about people, the world, or the universe that cannot be empirically verified. While some view with alarm and others with joy such a displacement of religious faith with faith in the scientific method, many on both sides see such secularization as a trend in which people evidence less and less interest in sacred and supernatural phenomena, as religious doctrines and institutions lose prestige and influence, with the possible ultimate result of a religionless society emerging.

Note, however, that no simple dichotomy exists of secular scientists hailing the replacement of religious faith with scientific faith versus religionists decrying such replacement. The popular Protestant theologian Harvey Cox, for example, welcomes secularization and sees it as a fulfillment of biblical themes and sources. He defines secularization in terms of "emancipation"—as the "liberation of man from religious and metaphysical tutelage, the turning of his attention away from other worlds and toward this one"[27] Cox's view may thus be regarded as a distinct variation on the "secularization-as-replacement" theme, one in which fulfillment is emphasized as a form of replacement.

The second general understanding of secularization is that it is a process of increasing differentiation between the religious and the secular (nonreligious) spheres of life—a process, moreover, coinciding with and perhaps in part resulting from increasing specialization within society as it grows and becomes more urbanized and industrialized.[28] Some who hold to

---

[26]Larry Shriner, "The Concept of Secularization in Empirical Research," *Journal for the Scientific Study of Religion* 6, no. 2 (1967), 207–220.

[27]Harvey Cox, *The Secular City* (New York: Macmillan, 1965), p. 17.

[28]Talcott Parsons, "Christianity and Modern Industrial Society," in *Sociological Theory, Values, and Socio-Cultural Change,* ed. Edward A. Tiryakin (New York: Free Press, 1963), pp. 33–70.

the differentiation definition of secularization cite the increasing "privatiza-tion" of faith—the process of compartmentalizing the religious and the sec-ular, of regarding religion as a mystical, personal, phenomenon that one does not share with others.

The haunting question that pervades the above discussion and a myr-iad of other allegations of spreading secularization is whether such signs reflect gains by "secular" forces and points of view at the expense of reli-gion, or whether religion in its basic sense has remained essentially unaf-fected. Conceivably the essence of religion may be enjoying greater strength and influence today than during the heyday of the church type of religious organization in Europe or the early days of state churches in the United States. Further, "privatization" of religion need not mean that reli-gion is not in evidence in people's actions, attitudes, and decisions. Also, many former public manifestations of religion that are no longer in evi-dence may have been ritualistic, pro forma actions that signified little and influenced people even less.

The point we are making is that before undertaking any analysis of secularization, one must specify one's operational definitions of the vari-ables under discussion, for the conclusions one reaches about secularization are inevitably influenced by what one regards as the valuable features of religion and whether these features are perceived as threatened or disap-pearing, as well as by what one understands religion to be in the first place. That is, is the focus and concern on the preservation of the institution as presently constituted? Or is one concerned about what might be happening to the "essence" of religion, apart from its institutional manifestations?

But all we wish to do at this point is raise the issue of secularization, not resolve it. For one thing, we need the information and discussion in this chapter to "flesh out" the issue before trying to answer the question. Sec-ond, establishing operational definitions of religion and secularization will be more helpful in understanding both the current status and the future of religion in the United States than will premature conclusions about secular-ization.

One reason that definitive conclusions about secularization are so diffi-cult to reach is that contemporary American religion evidences numerous seeming paradoxes. While total church membership has declined somewhat from mid-1960s highs, and many mainline denominations have been expe-riencing membership losses, some religious groups have been advancing with firm strides if not leaps and bounds so far as membership is concerned. There is evidence of growing disenchantment with traditional religious forms among young people, yet a broad-based attempt to recapture the "real Jesus" and "authentic Christianity" constitutes the Jesus movement—a movement primarily of young people. In 1966 many Protestant theologians were busy proclaiming the "death of God," yet by 1980 some religious lead-ers were organizing to take over political parties and processes as they joined the Moral Majority and other groups like it. Finally there is much emphasis within denominations on employing modern techniques of management, cost accounting, and computer technology, yet one observes little progress in eliminating duplication of effort by putting ecumenical ideology into practice. Such paradoxes (or seeming paradoxes) simply highlight the importance of one's decisions regarding which phenomena to consider in reaching conclusions about secularization on the one hand or "religionization" on the other. We do indeed have to be concerned about both what operational definitions and what measures of these concepts we adopt.

One of the best descriptions of secularization from the differentiation perspective is Robert Bellah's in his account of the historical evolution of religion through five stages. A dominant theme within this evolutionary process, according to Bellah, is the process of making increasingly more sophisticated differentiations between the sacred and the secular. This process has culminated, in the fifth stage (the modern period), in a breakdown of the dualistic distinction between the sacred and the secular, and its replacement by a multidimensional view of life and reality.[29] At this final stage, everything, including religion, is seen as revisable (though not all people see it this way, of course). Removed, or in the process of being removed, are such "either-or" dualistic descriptions of reality as *this world-other world, sacred-profane, good-evil, salvation-damnation*. Absolutism is replaced with relativity. The search of people for meaning is no longer confined within religious institutions or limited to traditional religious formulations. Such concepts as *situation ethics* and *process theology* typify the modern period. Certain traditional concepts and approaches from the past (*orthodoxy, sin*, and *moral law*, for example) are nevertheless retained by some and appear not about to disappear completely in the near future. This latter observation, of course, only reinforces Bellah's point, for a diversity of approaches and expressions and a broad range of views and interpretations are characteristic of religion in the modern period.

It is of interest that in Bryan Wilson's extended discussion of secularization[30] he suggests that denominational diversity has itself promoted secularization by providing for people a diversity of religious choices and in providing institutional expression of social differences and diversity. This can be seen as support for the view of secularization as differentiation. That is, it is not that the ideas or values of religion have necessarily become less important, but that there is increasing competition among those ideas, values, and religious systems. And there is a great deal of choice, with some traditional religious systems losing adherents and proponents that in an age

[29]Robert N. Bellah, "Religious Evolution," *American Sociological Review* 29, no. 3 (1954), 358–374.

[30]Bryan Wilson, *Religion in Secular Society* (London: C. A. Watts & Co., 1966), p. 30.

gone by could have been considered guaranteed members by parentage and culture.

Consistent with this view is Wilson's suggestion that ecumenism is a manifestation, not of religious vigor, but of secularization (in a sense, weakness). Perhaps we should say, not a "manifestation of secularization," but another outcome of or response to secularization by which religious groups hope to recoup some lost influence. Or, as Wilson suggests, ecumenism can become a new focus of attention (a "new faith") when other facets of theology and faith are challenged or debunked.[31]

THE CONFLICT OVER THE PURPOSE OF RELIGION

A fourth feature of contemporary American religion which adds a dimension to our consideration of the future of religion is the controversy over its purpose. Is it for the personal benefit of its practitioners—that is, for the sake of their possible ultimate eternal salvation, in addition to their feelings of well-being, comfort, and reinforcement of lifestyle? Or is religion primarily a vehicle of social change as it tries to combat poverty, discrimination, sexism, and other social ills?

This debate over religion's functions and purposes, pitting social service versus self-service, is certainly not brand new. It represents a dilemma in American society at least as old as the Social Gospel movement that emerged in the last half of the nineteenth century and the counterchallenge by fundamentalism that followed. Yet the issue has been updated. Not that either perspective or emphasis ever disappeared. Both have remained viable, and in fact have in many instances coexisted within the same denomination. But the original social-gospel or social-service emphasis became institutionalized, in the sense that denominations established specialized commissions, boards, and subsidiary institutions to handle that aspect of their work. It may have been a part of the annual budget of both the local congregation and the national denomination and called "benevolences." It supported orphanages, hospitals, schools for the physically or mentally handicapped, and the like. Or it may have been supported through annual fund-raising drives as peoples' hearts were touched by an emotional appeal and they made a contribution. In any case, once a religious group's social-service and welfare concerns became primarily the responsibility of specialized personnel and agencies operating in the group's name, these same concerns were easily relegated to a peripheral dimension of most church members' lives.

However, with the emergence of the civil rights movement in the late 1950s and early 1960s, with the intensified American involvement in the

[31]Ibid., p. 126.

war in Southeast Asia, and amid growing publicity and concern over such domestic social issues as poverty, capital punishment, abortion, nuclear power, and environmental pollution, individual church members and ad hoc religious groups began involving themselves in the issues. They urged their religious groups to become similarly involved and in a real sense forced an issue that had long lain dormant. Protestant, Catholic, and Jewish clergy began participating in civil rights marches, sit-ins, and demonstrations; administrators of denominational social-service programs began to urge more substantial support for existing and additional programs; Martin Luther King, Jr., challenged church people of all colors to support the struggle of black citizens for freedom and dignity. Seminaries intensified their efforts by offering new courses in social ethics and concerns and by implementing social action fieldwork programs. Denominations began issuing position statements supporting, at least in general terms, the rights of minority and disprivileged groups. Young seminary graduates assuming the leadership of congregations began preaching a gospel that included more than personal comfort and salvation. A "new breed" began to enter the ministry.

The outcome of all this was a crisis of direction or purpose so far as organized religion was concerned. That is, organized religion was caught in the middle of the agonizing confrontation of individual versus social concerns, personal comfort and salvation versus social welfare and help for the disprivileged.

Not that those who championed the social-concern emphasis always saw these as polar alternatives. Certainly most people who emphasized social service in the name of religion spoke of it as a concomitant of traditional individual salvation and comfort emphases, though some at least implicitly urged social-service emphases at the expense of individual ones. It all became an issue when the idea left the seminaries and the resolution-forming conferences and conventions and began confronting the local congregations. Then the allegations and accusations implied by such book titles as *The Suburban Captivity of the Churches* and *The Comfortable Pew* became meaningful.[32] The message of these and similar analyses of organized religion in the 1960s was that churches not only were self-serving but probably would not change. The direct implication was that large numbers of both laypersons and clergy sought to retain the individual emphasis of the church at all costs—perhaps out of ideological commitment to the idea that salvation is the only true concern of churches, or perhaps because of inertia related to the comfort and security and meaningful interpersonal relationships the church provided many people.

---

[32]Gibson Winter, *The Suburban Captivity of the Churches* (Garden City, NY: Doubleday, 1961); Pierre Berton, *The Comfortable Pew* (Philadelphia: Lippincott, 1965).

In *The Gathering Storm in the Churches* (1969), Jeffrey Hadden provided data from various studies to support his contention that a wide gap existed between many laypersons and growing numbers of clergy on the salvation versus social-service issue. Centering his discussion on support for the civil rights issue, Hadden pointed out that although a great majority of Americans interviewed in one study (86 percent) agreed that "the best mark of a person's religiousness is the degree of his concern for others," nearly half (49 percent) of the same sample felt that "clergy should stick to religion and not concern themselves with social, economic, and political questions." Further, nearly three-fourths (72 percent) admitted they would be upset if their minister, priest, or rabbi were to participate in a picket line or demonstration. Only slightly more than a third (37 percent) professed being "basically sympathetic with Northern ministers and students who have gone to the South to work for civil rights." By way of contrast, on this last issue 64 percent of the clergy interviewed expressed sympathy for such active civil rights involvement.[33]

Such data reflect not only the conflict over the purpose of religion and the proper aims of the church, in which denominations have tended to lean strongly in one direction or the other, but also the conflict between clergy and laypeople within a given denomination, particulary those denominations that have tended to emphasize salvation. As a result of the latter conflict, Hadden feels, the traditional authority of clergy is gradually eroding and laypeople are beginning to "think for themselves" when their personal views of the purpose of religion are challenged. Such intradenominational conflicts are not new in themselves. Because the number of people involved may be greater, however, the traditional techniques religious groups have used for handling internal diversity may no longer be adequate. Agencies, "special ministries," and monastic orders with a social-service emphasis no longer seem to provide enough openings to accommodate the number of clergy and serious laypersons committed in this direction. Thus the "segmentation of radicalism" technique that Phillip Hammond and Robert Mitchell suggest has been widely used by religious groups can no longer contain the challenge to tradition as it has in the past.[34] While radicals at one time could be "kicked upstairs" into administrative positions or directed into campus ministries where contact with rank-and-file laity in standard congregations was minimal, such tactics are less effective today. It is interesting that falling back on such options assumes the group is not particularly interested in facing very directly the problems that the challengers are raising.

[33]Jeffrey K. Hadden, *The Gathering Storm in the Churches* (Garden City, NY: Doubleday, 1969), pp. 132, 134, 136.

[34]Phillip E. Hammond and Robert E. Mitchell, "Segmentation of Radicalism: The Case of the Protestant Campus Minister," *American Journal of Sociology* 71, no. 2 (1965), 133–143.

In general, however, the "crisis" of the salvation versus social concern issue seems to have abated somewhat. Many of the major objectives of the civil rights movement have been achieved, at least regarding legislation; the Vietnam War has ended; social problems and solutions that appeared simple have been recognized as complex; considerable backlash against social-welfare programs has set in; and new issues continue to surface that make a dichotomy of salvation versus social concern not so simple to maintain. Concentrating on a single, specialized issue such as women's rights, gay rights, or abortion reform need not place a protagonist at total odds with a congregation that pursues its own comfort, especially if she or he does not expect much participation or commitment from the congregation.

The whole issue of why there has been a reduction of such pressures is exceedingly complex, however, and thus the following observations are perhaps only a few of the factors that need to be considered:

1. Social-service-oriented clergy have made up the bulk of those who have left the ministry—and their numbers have been substantial in all faiths—apparently feeling that they could "do their thing" better in a secular setting. Moreover, the departure of such ministers may itself indicate that the salvation emphasis is still dominant.

2. Financial pressures have forced denominations to eliminate some of the administrative positions that formerly served as sources of and encouragement for dissidence.

3. The halt of growth in church membership (see Table 14-1) has tightened the job market for clergy. Not only are clergy less horizontally mobile within the denomination, but the job market outside is also less open. Such a constriction may have prompted some clergy, perhaps quite unconsciously, to accommodate themselves to the attitudes, both spoken and unspoken, of the congregations they serve.

4. In some denominations controversy has shifted to more traditional theological issues.

5. Some laypersons who objected most strongly to what they defined as at best a dilution and at worst a perversion or betrayal of the proper purpose of the church have left their denominations for more conservative ones that still emphasize salvation and personal goals.

6. A well-organized countermovement, of which the so-called Moral Majority is a prominent example (cf. Chapter 7), has arisen within the ranks of Christian denominations. Such groups explicitly aim to undo some of the earlier efforts of more liberal religious social-service efforts in the areas of welfare and abortion reform, liberalization of rights for homosexuals and women, and curtailment of the military machine.

It appears that the first wave of the most recent salvation versus social action controversy is past. There is some indication that the interest in social concerns has fallen victim to the mood of the nation, as people have become more concerned with such urgent personal goals as keeping a job when others are losing theirs, maintaining financial solvency while inflation forges ahead, and staying healthy as new dangers from cancer-inducing agents are made public constantly. Further, the stridency of many of the victims of social inequities who have shouted "Black Power," "Gay Rights," and "Women's Liberation" has tended to discourage some of the more faint-hearted—they did not intend to go to "war," but only to help the helpless.

It is of more than passing interest that the "social-service" churchpeople of a liberal stripe and the "Moral Majority" churchpeople of a conservative stripe, though far apart ideologically and theologically, proceed from a similar premise. That is, religious organizations can be used to apply political and social pressure to help bring about the social change the group desires.

As we mention again the New Christian Right, it is important to note that a new twist to the salvation versus social action issue has been added only very recently. It is the new combination of conservative religion and social views of the New Christian Right, with highly explicit attempts to influence social action. That social action has included (1) high-powered urging of voters to elect some and defeat others who were running for high public office; (2) attempts to influence members of Congress and the president and advisors all around to pass constitutional amendments and other forms of legislation that would ban abortion, permit if not require prayers in public schools, and restrict the civil rights of homosexuals; (3) a campaign to discredit the candidacy of the first female justice of the U.S. Supreme Court, Sandra Day O'Conner, on the basis of assessment by representatives of the New Christian Right of her stands on such issues as abortion.

NEW RELIGIOUS MOVEMENTS AND CULTS

If the proverbial "person in the street" knows anything about current developments on the religious scene, he or she is likely aware of new groups that appear and behave in somewhat unusual if not bizarre ways. We may see members of the Hare Krishna movement with their shaven heads and saffron robes. We see notices and advertisements about this or that guru touring in the United States to extol the benefits of his Eastern religious philosophy. We may encounter young people in the neighborhood who talk freely about being really "turned on" to Jesus and who take pride in the designation "Jesus freaks." We may know of someone in a traditional mainline Protestant or Catholic church who talks about his or her fantastic experiences with the Holy Spirit and how he or she has the gift of "speaking in tongues."

While one might be tempted to observe that offbeat and unconventional religious expressions are certainly nothing new, such an observation would not do justice to the proliferation of "new" religious expressions in the United States today. Although there is probably nothing in the "new" religious expressions and forms that has not appeared in another age or culture before, some of it is new to the American religious heritage.

That American society—world society, for that matter—is in a changing, fluid, uncertain state is a truism that is obvious to most and appears incredibly trite on the printed page. Yet this observation is fundamental to any discussion of new religious movements and cults. As contemporary people have begun to sense the serious, perhaps disastrous, repercussions of their past and present actions upon the future, they have become extremely discomfited. Unplanned and unlimited procreation appears to be leading to unbearable population pressures. Uncontrolled and expanding use of natural resources portends not only their disappearance but also a polluted and potentially unviable environment. Securing a college education and specialized academic training has produced a surplus of labor in a host of career fields. Blind faith in a political system and entrusting national leadership with virtually limitless power has resulted in the scandal of Watergate. For many, the cultivation of suburban lawns and the accumulation of gas-powered vehicles has resulted in less satisfaction and fulfillment than was confidently expected. Managed economies have on the average produced little more personal economic security than unmanaged ones. The unresponsiveness of governmental bureaucracy to personal cries of anguish, whether over undeclared wars or impoverishment and discrimination, has provoked both rebellion and cynicism, both strident assertiveness and navel-contemplating despair.

Both as a consequence and as a concomitant of these and other factors, traditional religious forms, answers, and solutions have for many become unsatisfying, even empty, and certainly quite irrelevant. Even the "civil religion" that Bellah cites as having been a unifying factor in American society almost from the founding of the nation has broken down.[35] One consequence of the dissatisfaction with traditional religious forms that many people have expressed has been that religious organizations have made attempts at restructuring and reforming themselves. Yet another consequence has been individual and small-group experimentation with new religious forms, ideologies, and structures. Most of the "new" religious activity centers around personal quests for meaning, purpose, and roots in an unsettled and quavering, if not fractured, social environment. Who am I? Where am I going? Where do I—and my whole world, for that matter—fit vis-à-vis both the history of this planet, and the cosmos itself? These are basic religious questions of personal identification and relationship with forces that affect both personal and societal destinies. One result of trying to answer them has been increasing experimentation with both new and rediscovered religious forms and emphases.

This is where we find what has been popularly called "New Age Religion." The teaching and practices of New Age Religion are aimed at raising the consciousness of people to have a more harmonious relationship to a

[35]Robert N. Bellah, "Civil Religion in America," *Daedalus* 96, no. 1 (1967), 1–21.

higher reality or self. The objective is to become synchronized with the higher self, which is the appropriate linkage to other people, to the cosmos, and to God. Activities that encourage self-discipline—for example, meditation, yoga, deep breathing, and crystal concentration—help people reach such goals.

A key concept is that of holism (wholeism). This is the belief that all things are really one, and that oneness is God. Accordingly, people are god; nature is god; right thinking is god. Access to this oneness is from mystical experiences. One of the objectives of New Age seminars and workshops is to induce experiences of this unity or wholeness.

Neopentecostalism

We shall focus on two general types of new religious forms. The first, which appears to be as much an adult as a youth phenomenon, is the *charismatic* or *(neo-)pentecostal movement* that has emerged within both Catholic and mainline Protestant denominations. The quest for special experiences with the Holy Spirit and his special gifts in the form of glossolalia ("speaking in tongues"), trances, miraculous healing, and bodily expression in dancing and spirit-possession is not at all new. A solid tradition within Protestantism that goes back to its beginnings in the fifteenth and sixteenth centuries has developed parallel to the dominant denominational Protestantism. The healing evangelists of the type of Oral Roberts and scores of other contemporary examplars are known to most everyone. The "snake cults" in Appalachia in which the special spiritual gift of handling poisonous serpents and quaffing poisonous strychnine without harm periodically hit the public press. But middle-class denominational Catholicism and Protestantism have habitually dismissed such activities as appropriate only for lower-class persons in need of some bizarre form of escape in order to adjust to their life situation, but hardly satisfying behavior for middle-class and upper-class types.

Thus what is new, and from certain perspectives surprising, is the emergence very recently of pentecostal subgroups in the traditional Christian denominations. Not that anything approaching a majority of these denominations are becoming charismatic or pentecostal, or that such a majority will appear in the future. But enough have emerged not only to elicit concern and censure from denominational authorities but to merit sociological interest. Although the numerical strength of those practicing this neopentecostalism is not overwhelming, estimates have been as high as five hundred thousand persons spread throughout the major denominations in the United States in 1972 and in 1976 the Gallup poll reported an estimated three million persons involved in some way with the charismatic movement.[36]But Margaret Poloma and others note a significant decline in interest and numbers in the past dozen years or so. She states quite summarily: "The charismatic movement, which was ablaze in the 1970s, has dimmed in the 1980s."[37]

Although the neopentecostal (now commonly called "charismatic") movement can trace its genesis back to isolated cases in the 1950s, it first gained public attention in 1960 when Dennis Bennett, an Episcopalian minister in Van Nuys, California, resigned his office in an effort to stem incipient divisiveness over pentecostal practices by himself and some members of his congregation. Apparently publicity of this episode served as a catalyst to bring to the surface other instances of charismatic activity in nonpentecostal churches. In 1961 support was added from the academic community when nineteen students and one faculty member at Yale University reported receiving the baptism of the Holy Spirit. Similar reports came out of Dartmouth and Princeton soon after. A decade later the movement had been established in all mainline Protestant denominations and among Roman Catholics and Eastern Orthodox as well.

In most cases, regardless of denominational affiliation, charismatics emphasize that they do not wish to separate from their parent churches, but simply want to aid in revitalizing their congregations, their denominations, and Christianity itself by testifying to the extraordinary work of God brought into their lives through the power of the Holy Spirit. Not that such experiences are for everyone, they feel; but they are to be seen as a viable option for those who are touched.

Watson E. Miller sees a possible source of this new emphasis in traditional Christian churches in the fact that "glossolalia (the ability to speak words and phrases of a language unlearned and unknown to the speaker) may . . . be a loud protest against the cold impersonality that sometimes characterizes institutionalized worship."[38] If we add to Miller's suggestion the observation that, except for the occasional conventions of charismatics that attract hundreds and even thousands of people (such as the annual meeting of Catholic charismatics at the University of Notre Dame), charismatics tend to meet in small groups where one observes interpersonal warmth, openness, trust, and emotional support, sometimes even without "speaking in tongues," we may be explaining some of the attractiveness of the movement. Amid rapid social change, the uprooting of many tradi-

---

[36]*St. Louis Post Dispatch*, October 29, 1972; and reported in Constant H. Jacquet, Jr., ed. *Yearbook of American and Canadian Churches, 1980* (Nashville, TN: Abingdon Press, 1980), p. 257.

[37]Margaret Poloma, *The Assemblies of God at the Crossroads* (Knoxville: University of Tennessee Press, 1989), p. 243.

[38]Watson E. Miller, "Glossolalia: Christianity's 'Counterculture' Amidst a Silent Majority," *Christian Century*, September 27, 1972, p. 951.

tional institutional moorings, the breaking of contact with families and friends through job mobility, and other concomitants of contemporary American life, many people are especially receptive to opportunities for open, trusting, intimate contact with others. In very simple sociological terms, they are seeking primary groups and relationships to replace those they have lost.

With respect to Catholic charismatics, Bord and Faulkner identify several factors that seem to coincide by way of background for those Catholics who become charismatics.[39] The researchers speak of a series of social strains that Catholics have experienced at differing levels of intensity and perceptiveness. They have faced first the strain of a changing church as initiated by Pope John XXIII and the Second Vatican Council, which attempted to confront and address the modern world as it challenges the church's authority in areas of personal and community life; second, Catholics, along with others, were caught up in the mass media's contention that "reality consisted primarily of the war in Southeast Asia, various manifestations of institutional racism, and the persistence of poverty in the most affluent country that ever existed;"[40] third, there were the more or less standard tensions that seem to accompany modernization and industrialization—feelings of meaninglessness, unpredictable relationships, difficulties with personal identity—that accumulated for Catholics as well as members of other religious groups.

Further, those Catholics who were caught up in the neopentecostal movement tended to come from higher levels of educational background (only 7.1 percent with less than a high school education).[41] They were decidedly more female than male;[42] their age distribution was bimodal—39.9 percent aged 19–25, 21.3 percent aged 36–50.[43] And they were disproportionally liberal with respect to political views.[44] They were likely to be active Catholics who had participated in church-sanctioned groups and movements such as the Christian Family Movement, Marriage Encounter, and Cursillo, a renewal movement that began in Majorca in 1949 and was introduced to Spanish-speaking Catholics in the American Southwest around 1958.[45]

---

[39]Richard J. Bord and Joseph E. Faulkner, *The Catholic Charismatics* (University Park, PA: The Pennsylvania State University Press, 1983), pp. 43–58.

[40]Ibid., p. 44.

[41]Ibid., p. 9.

[42]Ibid., and Michael I. Harrison, "Sources of Recruitment to Catholic Pentecostalism," *Journal for the Scientific Study of Religion* 13, no. 1 (March, 1974), 53.

[43]Ibid., pp. 9–10.

[44]Ibid., p. 53.

[45]Meredith B. McGuire, *Religion: The Social Context* (Belmont, CA: Wadsworth Publishing Co., 1981), p. 137, and, Bord and Faulkner, *The Catholic Charismatics*, pp. 59–61.

Actually, as Bord and Faulkner observe, there is a high congruence of major themes in Vatican II that later became major emphases in the Catholic Pentecostal Movement (be aware of the sequence: Vatican II in 1963, the beginning of Catholic pentecostalism at Duquesne University in 1967). For example, the opening message of Vatican II emphasized self-renewal with guidance of the Holy Spirit. Pope John XXIII prayed that the Council might be a "new Pentecost." Participation and response on the part of lay-persons were stressed. And there was an expressed openness with respect to charismatic gifts as well as a clear message that the traditional rituals of the Church are not the sole sources of God's grace.[46]

It is significant that whereas denominations at first attempted to discourage the movement by censuring congregations and particularly clergy who participated, much of that opposition has been modified. Thus the movement today, though not necessarily encouraged, is increasingly tolerated. In a sense, this growing tolerance undermines one source of growth for charismatic groups, according to Gerlach and Hine. These researchers found that among important growth factors for the groups they studied was the "psychology of persecution." Ridicule, nonacceptance, and rejection by traditional denominational churches served to stimulate growth, whereas in those instances where local denominational officials did not oppose the movement, recruitment was more difficult.[47]

From the perspective of the host institution (churches) within which the charismatic movement is occurring, such activity would normally and naturally be resisted because it is by definition beyond the control of the host organization. Charismatic activity and authority are a challenge to traditional, organizationally legitimated authority. Who knows what such open-ended authority from outside the organization (the Holy Spirit moving as and where it wills) will produce? The only apparent explanation for the relative tolerance of the movement on the part of the denominations is that most within the movement insist that they are not out to destroy the organization or even to withdraw themselves from it, but want to offer an internal, optional form of religious experience and worship; they desire simply to enrich what institutional religion already has to offer.

The Cult Movement

While the charismatic or neopentecostal movement in American religion is new by virtue of its development within standard denominational

---

[46]Bord and Faulkner, *The Catholic Charismatics*, pp. 67–69.

[47]Luther P. Gerlach and Virginia H. Hine, "Five Factors Crucial to the Growth and Spread of a Modern Religious Movement," *Journal for the Scientific Study of Religion* 7, no. 1 (1968), 36.

religion, pentecostalism is nonetheless an old tradition in Christianity that has attained a considerable measure of legitimacy in its own denominational forms. Another recent development in American religion, however, does not fit within standard denominational forms and is in fact an alternative, if not a challenge, to such standard forms. We are referring to the proliferation of cults[48] in American religion.

New Religious Movements (NRMs) in general are not at all new to American religion. They abounded in the nineteenth century, when they were represented by such religious utopian communities as the Shakers, the Oneida Perfectionists, and the Amana society, as well as by such groups as Christian Science, the Theosophical Society, and Divine Science. The first half of the twentieth century also witnessed the emergence of many NRMs—the Church of Truth Universal–AUM, Psychiana, and the Fellowship of Divine Truth, to name just three.

What seems new in NRM development in the second half of this century are two features: (1) a change in the origin or base of the belief and practices system, and (2) a probable increase in the number of followers, though numbers are impossible to substantiate with assurance. Before we offer some tentative evidence in support of these observations, we must admit to the difficulty of making generalizations of any kind in the area of NRMs in the United States. In the first place, they exhibit a great diversity in focus and message. Thus comprehensive generalizations regarding all NRMs must of necessity be very broad. Second, consistent with our emphasis on the informal structure of NRMs as discussed in Chapter 5, they are likely not to have much in the way of printed material or creeds for an observer to analyze. They have fluid memberships and usually no firm membership statistics—or at least none that they are willing to publish or otherwise report publicly. Further, they are often localized and virtually unknown beyond a given locality or region.

Having acknowledged these methodological difficulties and the consequent tentativeness of our observations, we will return to the two general features mentioned above. First, there is evidence of a strong Far Eastern religious influence in many American NRMs today, although not all of them by any means. Hinduism and Buddhism particularly serve as points of origin and orientation for many of them: Zen, Subud, Vajrayana Buddhism, Sufism, Meher Baba, I Ching, and scores of others. In most cases, these groups and their messages offer something dramatically different from most of Western religion (with the possible exception of some of the Catholic and Eastern Orthodox contemplative and eremitic monastic orders). NRMs that arose during the last century and during most of this

---

[48]Although "cult" is a familiar term and widely used, we shall follow the lead of James Beckford and in subsequent discussion use the less pejorative term New Religious Movements (NRMs). Cf. James A. Beckford, *Cult Controversies: The Societal Response to New Religious Movements* (London: Tavistock Publications, 1985).

century were built strongly on either Western philosophy and Christianity or, at the farthest extreme, on Near Eastern religions such as Egyptian Rosicrucianism—but to very little extent on religions from the Far East. The exceptions to this were the New Thought and Theosophical groups that emerged seventy-five to one hundred years ago. Many modern (within the last thirty-five years) American NRMs share with them quite distinct strains of Hinduism and Buddhism—themes of meditation and getting right in your mind and body with the cosmic forces and fluids of the universe. It seems that Far Eastern Hindu and Buddhist influence in American NRM religion is more conscious and explicit than before.

The second point we want to make about modern NRMs—regarding the numbers of their members—is, as already indicated, impossible to document. We are on even less solid ground when talking about the past. Our impression is, however, that there are more people attracted to NRMs in the United States today than there were in the past.

Estimates from the Gallup Poll mentioned earlier suggest higher numbers later in the 1970s. Gallup reports 6 million people involved in Transcendental Meditation, 3 million in mysticism, and 2 million in Eastern religion.[49] While there is likely much overlap in these figures (that is, many who get counted in more than one category), and while some may have had only the most passing and superficial of contact, the numbers are substantial and so cannot be dismissed casually.

Another observation about contemporary NRMs that we might expect to make, given the new age in which we live and the apparently greater Far Eastern influence on NRMs—namely, that the content of the NRM message or gospel is different today—should not be made at all. Certainly the Power, or Force, or Spirit, or Method, or God is different from one group to another. But the central idea inherent in NRMs both past and present is strikingly similar—that is, they all emphasize a technique of "getting your mind together," of putting mind and body in closer harmony by getting in tune with the energizing or central power or force in the universe. It is truly striking, after listening to members of various contemporary groups and reading their publications, to realize that what each group defines as the problem to be overcome and what each offers as the method for resolving that problem resemble so fundamentally every other group's definitions as to be essentially identical. The problem to be solved is typically a highly integrated pair of issues: (1) Who am I and where do I fit into the world? (identity), and (2) How can I find peace and unity of mind and body, of the spiritual and the material within me? The solution is typically a technique involving, on the one hand, meditation (perhaps using yoga or related postures and exercises, or perhaps by repeating key words and phrases such as one's personal mantra), and on the other hand, small-group encourage-

---

[49]Reported in Jacquet, *Yearbook of American Churches, 1980*, p. 257.

ment, support, and reinforcement. It appears to be crucial for this purpose that the group be small and that members be capable of close contact on a one-to-one basis or with at most a handful of others. In this sense NRMs resemble, and perform functions similar to, the charismatic groups within traditional denominations discussed in the previous section.

If we look at the constituency of NRMs and ask who joins them, we learn several things. From a Gallup Poll conducted in 1977, members of established religious groups were less likely than the unchurched to have been involved in NRM activities with such groups and movements as Transcendental Meditation (TM), Eastern religions, mysticism, and yoga.[50] Further, of those who were members of churches, the more liberal the church the more likely the members were to experiment with NRMs.[51] That is, people with an Episcopalian background were more likely to have contact with NRMs than were Baptists. Such findings support Stark and Bainbridge's observation that individuals with a firm religious affiliation are not particularly likely to embrace new religions. Further, the less secularized the denomination the less likely members are to join an NRM.[52]

Stark and Bainbridge also worked with data from six separate studies of NRMs and found that there were significant differences by denominational background. Those most likely to affiliate with an NRM were Jews. They were followed by people with religious backgrounds other than Protestant, Catholic, or Jewish. Roman Catholics were next; Protestants were least likely of all to be successfully recruited to NRMs. Those with no religious affiliation at all alternated with Jews from one study to the next as most likely/next most likely to join an NRM.[53] The authors point out that few if any of the Jewish NRM participants were from the Orthodox branch of Judaism. Further, Jews of Reform or Conservative backgrounds are on the whole more secularized than Christians in the sense of lower frequency of attendance at worship services or even having formal membership in a local synagogue.[54]

A third part of the answer to the question, "Who joins NRMs?" is the level of education attained by participants. Several studies clearly observe that the higher the level of education, the more likely people were to have had NRM attachments and experiences.[55]

In terms of numbers there are between 500 and 600 known NRMs operating in the United States.[56] Many of these of course have branches just as denominations have local congregations spread throughout the land. So

---

[50]Rodney Stark and William S. Bainbridge, *The Future of Religion* (Berkeley, CA: University of California Press, 1985), p. 397.

[51]Ibid.

[52]Ibid., pp. 398–399.

[53]Ibid., pp. 400–401.

[54]Ibid., p. 402.

[55]Ibid., pp. 406–409.

[56]Ibid., pp. 191–192.

there are many hundreds of local groups. NRMs are most common in California with 167 separate groups represented, but the highest per capita distribution is in Nevada, followed by New Mexico, with California third. Southern states tend to have few NRMs.[57] This would be expected inasmuch as higher concentrations of religiously conservative citizens are to be found in the South.

We have made passing references to the presence of NRMs worldwide. It is important for theoretical and explanatory purposes to note that the phenomenon of NRMs does indeed span the globe—in South America and the islands of the Caribbean, Japan, Korea, and elsewhere in Asia, Africa, Europe, and the Islamic countries in the Near East. The major significance of that observation of the worldwide distribution of NRMs is that such new religious groups have emerged and are emerging within a wide variety of religious contexts. That might suggest that NRMs are less a religious phenomenon and more a response to the societal context within which people find themselves. That is, possibly the social dislocations and normative confusion associated with rapid social change, whether in preindustrial, industrial, or postindustrial society create many candidates for NRMs.

Or perhaps there is an even simpler explanation. Could it be that NRMs are nothing more than what their title suggests, namely, a new religious attempt to deal with the problems and changes that people experience—challenges and adjustments that are universal and timeless so far as humanity is concerned? At this point we might also observe that most (probably all) of the world's religions and many of the individual denominations that constitute those religions were themselves at one time an NRM.

We can suggest both by way of concluding our discussion of NRMs and as an ending for this text that the appearance and "success" of so many NRMs alongside the middle-aged vitality of many standard religious organizations, indicates clearly that religion, whether as an institution or as an absorbing quest for truth, is certainly not dead, nor about to die soon. People continue to ponder not only who and what they are but from whence they come and whither they are going. Is there any meaning and purpose in the world around them and, above all, is there any meaning and purpose for them as tiny, individual specks in the universe? Religion attempts to deal with such questions. As such, religion has a future. In fact, it has a future to the extent that humanity has a future, because religion is an expression of the confrontation of people with their environment, both physical and social, and with each other. It is a reflection both of the precariousness of human existence and of the imperfections with which people relate to people. As such, religion in some form—or rather, in a variety of forms—not only is a part of society but will remain so.

[57] Ibid., pp. 192–193.

Index